Family Counseling

Joseph F. Perez, Ph.D.
Westfield State College

VNR VAN NOSTRAND REINHOLD COMPANY
NEW YORK   CINCINNATI   ATLANTA   DALLAS   SAN FRANCISCO
LONDON   TORONTO   MELBOURNE

Van Nostrand Reinhold Company Regional Offices:
New York   Cincinnati   Atlanta   Dallas   San Francisco

Van Nostrand Reinhold Company International Offices:
London   Toronto   Melbourne

Published by Van Nostrand Reinhold Company
135 West 50th Street, New York, N.Y. 10020

Published simultaneously in Canada by Van Nostrand Reinhold Ltd.

15 14 13 12 11 10 9 8 7 6 5 4 3 2 1

Library of Congress Cataloging in Publication Data
Perez, Joseph Francis.
   Family counseling.
   Includes index.
   1. Family psychotherapy.   2. Family psychotherapy—
Cases, clinical reports, statistics.   I. Title.
[DNLM: 1. Counseling.   2. Family therapy.   WM430.5.F2
P438f]
RC488.5.P45   618.8'915   78-17693
ISBN 0-442-26536-0

This book is dedicated to two families. To my family of origin which gave me my fundamental values and dispositions
and
To my own family which ever provides me with the opportunity to prove the validity of those values and dispositions.

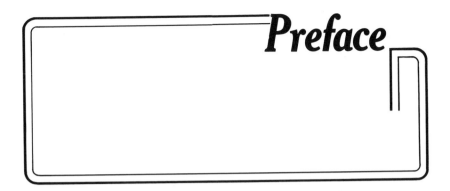

Preface

FAMILY THERAPY: THEORY AND PRACTICE is directed at students in schools of social work, psychology majors, undergraduate and graduate students in both education and the social sciences, practitioners (Ph.D., M.D., M.S.W.), and nonprofessional readers who seek to learn about themselves in relation to their families.

The book developed out of my work with adolescents adjudged delinquent by the courts. The adolescents were referred to me for individual and group psychotherapy. Even as I took the referrals, however, I recognized that those people who had provided and/or been part of the emotional climate in which these adolescents had been reared, also needed a therapist's attention. My clinical education and experience had led me to believe that a person termed delinquent more often than not is one who has been spawned by a delinquent family, that is, a family which has developed neurotic patterns of interaction. My view has been reinforced by subsequent experience: that if I were going to be effective as a therapist with these adolescents, I would need to deal with the families of the delinquents as well as with the delinquents themselves. I made it a cardinal rule that I would not treat adolescents if I could not also meet with their parents. Later I extended this rule to include siblings and even grandparents if they lived at home.

Doing therapy with these families was a remarkably rewarding experience, both in professional learning as a clinical psychologist and my personal growth as a human being. Indeed, my experiences with one family were so clinically rich and emotionally poignant that I felt a need to share them. I wrote up my notes and edited the tapes of the many sessions I spent with this family. This effort makes up the "Practice" part of the book. Each chapter in this part is preceded by the "Focus Guides" and followed by "Discussion Questions." These study aids were designed to help the student glean the maximum amount of information from each chapter and also to develop insight into the complex interpersonal dynamics presented.

The "Theory" part of the book is comprised of those items that I thought were essential to the development of a competent frame of reference for the prospective therapist. At the same time, the theoretical material is different from that found in most other texts in that it includes the personal views of a half dozen practitioners and the pre- and post-therapeutic views of persons who have undergone family therapy. This material enhances the pure theory by providing a measure of relevance and pragmatic experience not usually found in standard texts. The serious student, the one who truly wants to understand family therapy and learn how to do it, should profit much.

The theoretical approach taken is basically the systems approach to family therapy, modified in some measure by my own clinical views about the dynamics of personality. Finally, much research, discussion with colleagues, and innumerable hours spent doing therapy preceded this effort to explain and describe the nature of family therapy.

J.F.P.

Acknowledgments

This text is the product of my two decades of education, training, and experience as a clinical psychologist and psychotherapist. In a real sense, therefore, this text is the product of the synthesized thoughts, theories, and convictions of the many people who taught and supervised me, and whom I treated. Simply stated, I owe much to many, to some whom I never met, to many whom I did. Most notably among the former, stands Harry Stack Sullivan, still my theorist hero, and among the latter, Carl Rogers, who embodies his own compassionate humanist theories and writing.

There are six family therapists to whom I owe even more. These people were kind enough to take time from their hectic schedules to contribute their views about the family therapist. Their thoughts are found in chapter six. Among them are three psychologists.: Alvin Cohen, Ph.D.; Joan Corell, Ph.D. and Stanley Mueller, Ph.D.; two psychiatrists: Sanford Bloomberg, M.D. and Harold Wise, M.D.; and a social worker: David Sprague, M.S.W.

I would like to thank the following people for their insights and detailed comments on the manuscript: Dr. William R. McPeak, Associate Professor and Director, Family Therapy Training Project, Syracuse University School of Social Work; Professor

Charlotte Kahn, College for Human Development, Department of Child and Family Studies, Syracuse University; Professor Robert L. Woolfolk, Department of Psychology, University College, Rutgers University.

I owe a great deal to my son Joseph, as he not only typed the original manuscript and its revision, but also made innumerable minor corrections, both syntaxical and scholarly.

And finally, I want to acknowledge my gratitude to my wife Geraldine, my prime enhancing critic who developed a real talent in insulating me from minor familial obligations when I wanted to write.

Contents

Part One

The Theory

Chapter 1
An Historical Overview

With the end of World War II a general socio-cultural metamorphosis began to occur in American society. The effects of this metamorphosis upon society in general and upon the family in particular, were to be lasting.

Servicemen returned home by the millions. For many, if not most, of the returning men there were two immediate goals, to go to college on the G.I. Bill and to marry. These two events usually occurred at the same time and effected a third subsequent phenomenon, the baby boom. Thus mass education, mass marriage and a skyrocketting birth rate (this last continued unabated until well into the fifties) set the social metamorphosis into motion. American society would never be the same again.

A whole new terminology emerged to describe and explain the changing nature of the society: corporate life, efficiency expert, role image, sexual identity, social mobility, mega-ton and "the persistent threat of 'world-wide holocaust'." Yes, America had changed and the individual person suddenly found himself beset by a bewildering array of pressures both from within and without his family. Indeed, when the individual tried to retreat from the pressures and anxieties outside the family—work, bosses, mortgages and competitive neighbors—and into the "warm and nurturant" bosom of family life, he found the highly touted family warmth wanting, and ironically, sometimes even more anxiety provoking.

The family had always been a favorite unit for exploration by social scientists. Now veritable phalanxes of these scientists began to invade the newly constructed suburbias to explore, define and analyze the changes occuring. Their studies and messages without exception reported what many already knew; yes, America had changed. Yes, America was changing.

The academic studies by the social scientists were frequently popularized in the Sunday supplements and in women's journals. The family, it was reported, was at the heart of much of the change. Families were smaller. They were interacting more intensively. The paternalistic, unilaterally-run family was out. Spouses were now partners. Children, and there was positive status in having at least two, were considered important. Children's opinions, formerly ignored, were now considered important or, at the least, worth listening to.

The changes were occurring at a dizzying rate, and one in particular would have a tremendous long term effect for society and the family: *Parents were pressured not to parent the way they had been parented.* The immediate effect was that families were living in a style with which they were unfamiliar. For too many, too much was new, too much unfamiliar. The pressures upon these "new" families during the decade following the war were considerable and the anxieties they experienced incalcuable.

Now, although there were some primitive models being developed to help small groups and parts of families (explained further on), there really was not too much effective help for whole families during the first half of the century. The prevailing view of mental illness or emotional discomfort was that it was the individual's problem, not the effect of a group or family or the environment.

FREUDIAN THEORY—BRIEF OVERVIEW

The prevailing and prestigious psychology of the day was Freudian. In the colleges the general psychology and "adjustment" texts took a psycho-dynamic view of the individual. Freudian terminology became increasingly popular. Such terms as libido, unconscious conflicts, ego, and id were much in vogue.

A brief summary of certain selected Freudian concepts will help the reader to see better why the individual was the focus and not the new environment in which he was steeped. Indeed, in a real sense Freud's theory put the modern person under even more pressure because of its strong implication that the individual, with all of his intra-psychic equipment, is obligated to adapt. If he does not it is because he is inadequate or sick, a kind of "constitutional defective." This brief overview will help the reader to see how very far psychology has progressed.

The majority of psychoanalysts consider Freud's most important contribution to have been his discovery of the unconscious. Freud believed that the unconscious was by far the most important part of any individual's personality. Indeed, for Freud the unconscious part of an individual's person was what set him apart from any other individual.

According to Freud the unconscious occupies the most important and the largest segment of an individual's general awareness. The material of the unconscious can not be put into thought or even into words. It is arranged in an associative way. The unconscious in most individuals can be described as a seething caldron of needs, emotion and instincts. Ideas are not found in it. Before a person could understand himself or others or *adapt* to his environment he had to have a full appreciation of his unconscious.

The unconscious is thus dynamic and is involved in much activity. Impulses in it are constantly seeking to surface to the upper levels of consciousness. Most of these impulses are inappropriate, as they are associated with the "id" (explained below) and/or are a product of repressions of experiences the ego found threatening, demeaning or traumatic. Repressions are the elements of the unconscious which constantly disturb the individual and cause him the greatest anxiety. The Freudian believes that experiences, particularly negative ones, which the individual undergoes, are forever a part of him. The fact that the individual can't remember a given incident can be unhealthy (again, this is especially true if the experience is a threatening one). A repression then, is a forgotten experience. Further, it is an experience to which is attached emotion, emotion which can be triggered off in an individual's later life by a comparable experience or even a smell, mannerism, sound, or some other reminder. The recurrent emotion generally is accompanied by much anxiety. In Freudian therapy the individual is helped to recall the incident and to understand its meaning. Ventilation of the emotion attached to the memory of the incident usually accompanies the recall and is conducive to the development of insight and better health.

A most important notion in Freud's theory is that the individual is in constant conflict. The conflict stems from the interaction of three entities, id, ego and superego.

The id is a prime source of all motivation. The strength of a person's emotion, desire and instinct are to be found in his id. How slowly or how fast one eats, moves, how much one wants to succeed (in whatever) is determined in considerable measure by the force of the id *and* by the nature and degree of control manifested over the id by the other two aspects of the personality, the ego and superego. The function of the id is not only to propel the individual to activity but to obtain pleasure and to avoid pain of any kind (physical or psychological). Freud taught that the id is amoral, describing it as the primitive nature of man.

In the healthy, mature person it is the ego which makes decisions. Now, the ego has access to the id and is aware of the latter's strivings. In the newborn there is no ego, only the capacity for it. The ego grows, not only because of physical maturation but more importantly, through a phenomenon known as *identification*. This is the process, mostly unconscious, whereby the individual incorporates the mannerisms, values, ideas, and ideals of another person. In the Freudian scheme identification is the principle process by which we become people—good, bad, healthy, or unhealthy.

The superego is conscience. Like the ego the superego is in constant touch with the most hidden strivings of the id. Since the superego is that aspect of personality which represents one's conscience, it is vitally concerned with the primitive, amoral strivings of the id. Indeed, it is perpetually intent upon getting the ego to repress the id's strivings. The principal function of the superego then is criticism of id motives. The individual feels guilty when the superego is overly scrupulous and makes up too large a portion of his or her personality or when the superego is unable to restrain a particular id striving or motive. The superego also tries to dominate the ego. When it succeeds we encounter the individual whom the Freudians term "guilt laden."

The Freudian view then is that man is a walking bundle of endless conflicts, some of which are quasi-resolved, most of which are not. Thus, the ego is in constant mediation between the id and the superego; constantly beset by the need to make decisions, i.e. to permit id strivings to be released or repressed; whether or not to submit to the constant "thou shalt not" of the superego or whether to "live it up."

In this system of thought the individual alone seeks treatment because he's the one who has the problem. He is the one who is sick. He needs a "doctor." At no point in the psychoanalytic tradition did the theory attempt to deal with the alleviation or amelioration of environmental pressure. At no point did this theory address itself to the possible deleterious effects of particular environmental forces on a given individual. He who could not adapt was sick and had to be made well. This method or philosophy of treatment follows what we call the medical model. Focusing on the individual alone, it prevailed into the nineteen fifties. Groups or families were of concern to few therapists.

Even today the traditional psychoanalytic school follows what might be termed the medical model. The analyst is ordinarily an M.D. (sometimes now a Ph.D.) who diagnoses the patient's ills, interprets "free associations" and delivers his view of the cause of the patient's problems to the patient. This process is designed to help the patient achieve insight.

On the road to achievement of insight most patients pass through certain conflict crises, the most notable being the transference phenomenon. Simply defined, transference has to do with the patient's unconscious need to attach repressed attitudes and feelings to the analyst. The transference may be negative (hostile feelings attached to the analyst) or positive (the patient falls in love with the therapist). In any case, its resolution is an indispensable prerequisite to the patient's achievement of insight. In the psychoanalytic view the individual achieves insight when he develops an unconscious as well as an intellectual appreciation of the causes of his repressions and consequent anxieties.

It is important to note that the problems and the conflicts are always seen as lying *within* the individual. If change is to be effected, it has to be effected there, within the individual, not in the environment.

As noted above, it was Freud's view of man which was paramount throughout most of the first half of the century, with psychoanalytic therapy the prestigious and the prime mode of psychotherapy. It was in the early forties however that another view emerged, one which effectively challenged not only Freud's personality theory but the treatment modality as well.

ROGERIAN THEORY—BRIEF OVERVIEW

If psychoanalysis follows the medical model then Rogerian therapy may be said to follow a humanistic one. In the Rogerian scheme of things the one who comes for counseling is not so much sick as he is seeking help. He does not need an authoritarian "doctor" as much as an unconditionally accepting counselor. It was Rogers who popularized the idea of a non-medical, non-doctoral counselor therapist. Rogers is going well beyond the idea that experience is the best teacher. He believes that nobody can really know another individual completely because that individual's experience is very personal, very private. Even more, no one can really understand the meaning of another person's behavior except that person. A man is in the center of an environment which is in constant change, in constant flux. What he feels, what touches him is very private indeed and you can at best only speculate as to what he is feeling and experiencing.

At the same time he believes that the individual is constantly reacting and experiencing in his environment. And this reaction and experience help develop in him a very personal and very subjective view of the world and the people in it. His behavior will reflect this subjective view.

Rogers notes, too, that a man is constantly seeking to better himself, to enhance his grasp of both himself and his environment. Rogers also believes that the individual seeks self-fulfillment. Man, he believes, has many needs, but all of them are secondary to the one main need for self-fulfillment. How well one attains this goal is dependent on how accurately one perceives one's environment and how effectively one adapts to it. Note again that the focus here as in psychoanalytic theory is upon the individual and not upon the environmental pressures which impinge upon the individual, although these may indeed make him ill.

Rogers notes that man is also an emotional being. An individual's emotions vary with the experience he undergoes and with the meaning he derives from the experience. In part because of this emotionality, the individual becomes invested in his environment. He identifies with the physical environment. Perhaps this is why the individual invariably has to go through an adjustment period when he moves from one region to another. The individual invests part of himself in others, too, and when he has to leave them, for whatever reason, he feels unhappy.

A man's investment and identification with his environment and with other people invariably results in the formation of a "self" which is unique, yet consistent in its perception and in its mode of interaction with others and with the physical environment. This self, which is the core of the individual, is in large measure, again, a product of experience. It is the blend of personal, direct experience with the environment which results in the very private "self."

The self behaves and experiences in terms of how it comes to perceive its "self." A person ordinarily does want to change or move for the better, for self-fulfillment. He is afraid to because he has to change his "self," which is the hard core of his personality, since the self involves his perception and his behavior with others.

In the Rogerian view people become tense and have problems when they deny to their own self an experience and the feelings attached to it. For example, when an individual attempts to deny his attraction to or irritation with another person, his behavior with that person often becomes stilted because he feels uneasy with him or her. Conversely, if he were able to accept and verbalize to that "certain person" how he felt then in all likelihood he would be more at ease with that person and more importantly, with himself.

When the individual has an opportunity to discuss and examine experiences which have affected him adversely he usually finds that he can accept them better and in this way help his self to grow. This person learns to accept himself and his behavior and thereby learns to get along better with others.

As the individual comes to accept more and more of his experiences he finds that he develops more confidence in his judgements about others and about his environment generally. Moreover, the values and opinions of others and even of tradition do not become as necessary to him as they once were. Put very simply, the individual who has come to accept himself will believe in himself and his judgements and will act upon them before he will act upon those of others.

The Rogerian philosophy takes a more humane and optimistic view of the individual than does the Freudian view. Nevertheless, this philosophy continues to see the person's problems as inner centered, in the person's mental and emotional psyche. The reason for this is probably the fact that since Freud's was the first psychology and the first psychotherapy, his influence could not be negated completely, even by Rogers.

The reader should already know that the therapist who was educated and trained in the late forties and especially in the fifties and early sixties was invariably exposed to both Freudian and Rogerian theory. Not uncommonly for such a therapist, the Freudian focus upon intrapsychic dynamics was melded with important Rogerian notions, i.e. the client's subjective perceptions of self and the environment. A summary of the principles under which this dynamically oriented therapist operated and, in many cases, continues to operate with families today is in order.

1. Case work reports on the symptomatic and other family members are considered valuable. The belief here is that the more information there is, the more effectively the counselor can function.

2. The *now* problems of a family are viewed as symptoms, products of longstanding neurosis.

3. The focus of the dynamic counselor is the inner state of each of the family members not their external behavior.

4. The needs and defenses (defenses are of kernel concern to the Feudian but not to the Rogerian) of each member are important because the dynamic counselor believes that each member contributes to the sickness and health of the entire family.

5. How each member perceives and what each one expects from the other family members is considered, interpreted and treated by the therapist.

6. Emotions are of paramount importance to the dynamicist. The dynamicist observes closely how love, anger, joy and sadness are expressed or withheld by each member toward each other member. Confrontations, interpretations and ventilation of feelings are encouraged. These methods are an integral part of the dynamicist's approach.

7. The dynamicist views as a prime goal to make each person in the family consciously aware not only of his own motives and dynamics but also of those of the other family members.

8. The dynamically oriented therapist ordinarily follows a well defined procedure, plan or method.

The reader should note that the focus of the dynamicist is always, "to get into the client's head;" that is the focus of the therapy. The individual is seen in the therapist's office in a warm, tolerant, unconditionally accepting climate. In retrospect, the author finds it a little remarkable that few therapists during the latter part of the forties, fifties and sixties pointed out that such a setting, such a climate was at the very best synthetic and essentially unreal and in no way dealt with the individual in his environment. There were those practitioners, however, who did observe that a client improved quickly in the therapeutic environment (during the session, or in the custodial hospital setting). However, as soon as the client returned to his natural habitat he became quite distraught, often very quickly so. Quite apparently, the stresses of the environment made the individual sick. And when he became sick he returned to his therapist, his clinic, his hospital. It didn't seem to occur to most that perhaps there were critical factors—persons, situations, and events which precipitated and then maintained the individual's problems. Few considered the idea of dealing with some of the salient pressures in the individual's environment—for example, treating the people with whom the patient frequently came into contact or restructuring the environment so the person would not have to deal with unimportant but anxiety provoking situations.

At the same time it should be noted that there were those who felt the traditional and prevailing view of man was a bit constricting. For example, Burgess in 1926 wrote a paper in which he observed, " . . . that the family as a reality exists in the interaction of its members." Family members do indeed interact, do indeed affect each other. Unfortunately Burgess's view had little impact on his time or on contemporary treatment modalities.

Then Harry Stack Sullivan came onto the scene. His detached, intellectualized lectures and publication provided an alternative to the psychoanalytic view of what makes a person in modern society tick. His ideas, expounded from the late twenties until his death in 1949, were to have a profound influence on the development of modern psychotherapy.

Sullivan was himself a physician and trained in the psychoanalytic school. However, he departed from the conservative theories touted by Freud and focused on two new ideas—1) that human beings become emotionally ill because they are unable to communicate with others, usually because of anxiety; and 2) that an individual can best be understood if examined not separately but in relation to another person or persons.

These two principles and the philosophy which they spawned, provided both the rationale and the impetus for examination of the individual in his interpersonal setting. Stated another way, Sullivan's theory provided a kind of bridge between the social sciences and a heretofore impersonal, uninvolved psychiatry. In short, Sullivan made the study of the person via the social sciences respectable, even desirable. His interpersonal theory of psychiatry is premised not upon medical knowledge or understandings, but upon social psychological ideas. He was among the first to intensively examine interactional effects upon the individual. It was Sullivan who pointed out that we learn our perception of the world via interaction, that our interactions are based upon our perceptions, and that the meanings which we derive from our interactions in turn further feed our perceptions. His hypotheses and theories were such that they provided rich and fruitful ground for clinical exploration by sociologists and by social and clinical psychologists.

Sullivan's thoughts on interpersonal psychiatry supported and probably fueled the work of Moreno who began to experiment with the idea of treating individuals in conjunction with other individuals. Moreno was among the first to apply the Sullivanian notion that people learn, modify and change their behavior because of the nature and quality of their interpersonal communication with others. As early as 1940 then, the importance of interaction within the group situation was understood to have important effects upon the individual.

To a considerable extent it was this understanding which formed the rationale for the development and growth of the child guidance clinic, especially in the urban east. Here, children were understood to be emotionally disturbed because of the negative quality of their initial interactions within their respective families. A child became emotionally disturbed, Sullivan explained, because its need for tenderness not only had not been met, but had indeed been violated by maternal anxiety. This "bad mother" effected a "malevolent transformation" in the child. Strongly implied in his explanation is the idea that for the child to be effectively treated, mother and child had to be treated conjointly.

Sullivan's interpersonal theory of psychiatry fanned the development of the child guidance clinic. It is interesting to note that his interpersonal theory also abetted the development of group therapy, conducted with adolescent peer groups in the same child guidance clinics. What should also be mentioned is that although marriage counseling was being done in the late twenties, thirties and forties and had been done for countless decades, it was practiced not by psychiatric clinicians, but by the clergy. This was a natural outgrowth of certain religious understandings which people had traditionally held, namely that marriage is a sacrament, that God blesses the marital union, and so on. Understandably then, couples frequently turned to their priest, rabbi, or minister for help with their marital problems.

All of this is mentioned here merely to point out that there were indeed models in operation for family treatment before the advent of World War II, i.e. group therapy, child guidance clinics where frequently mother and child (occasionally father was included) were treated together, and marital counseling via religious personnel.

During and immediately following World War II there was little expansion or development of Sullivan's theories regarding individual communication, anxiety and interpersonal relationships. It was not until the middle fifties that significant research and theory began to emerge which expanded upon his work. As noted, Sullivan saw garbled communication between people as a function of anxiety and as the prime culprit for emotional dysfunction.

Bateson et. al. observed that communication between the person labeled schizophrenic (and members of his family too) apparently had developed interactive and communicative patterns which were conducive to developing a distorted perception of the environment. Thus the individual diagnosed as schizophrenic manifested behavioral symptoms which were directly related to the behaviors exhibited by those in his family. The most salient of the behaviors seemed to be connected with deviant speech patterns and warped ways of talking and listening to each other. The hospitalized patient and his family related verbally via "double messages." That is, the words usually spoken by a family member did not gibe with, indeed were often diametrically opposed to, the behavior effected by the same member. This double message invariably seemed to make the patient more tense, more anxious and frequently precipitated crazy behavior in him. In short, Bateson and his fellow researchers observed that there seemed to be a direct relationship between a schizophrenic's craziness and the family's behavior toward him. An illustration here might be helpful.

The author used to be on the psychology staff of a psychiatric hospital and met regularly with the wife of a patient who was suicidal. He observed that the evening before her scheduled weekly visits and for at least a day and a half after them, the patient appeared to be either more agitated or more depressed. What follows is a simulated transcript of one of their meetings. It is based on the author's observation of a dozen or so meetings between the two of them.

WIFE: Oh darling, I am so glad to see you! (She gives him rather firm slaps on the back.)
PATIENT: Hmph.
W: Poor darling. I can tell you're still sick. Is there anything I can get you! Darling you know how much I love you! Oh I know you won't get upset that I forgot to bring your electric razor. But that's all right you can continue using a safety. Your face isn't broken out *that* bad!
P: Hmph.
W: Can't you at least look at me when I talk to you!

P: (Wearily) Jan, what do you want from me? I'm a sick man.

W: Darling, please let's not fight. It's just that I miss you a lot. Do you have any idea when you're coming home? Don't you miss me, a little bit?

P: (Sighing) Yeah I guess so.

W: You guess so! Don't you realize what I'm going through! Don't you? Will you please look at me. You hate me don't you? You do. I can tell. You won't even look at me. Sick you're not sick. You just want to escape your responsibilities.

(Pause)

W: I'm sorry, I know I'm upsetting you, I don't mean to. You know that.

P: Yeah.

W: Please look at me when I talk. No, if you must know you don't look sick. You just sit here in this hospital, collect your pension from the government (the hospital is a Veterans Administration Hospital and the patient's illness was assessed as service connected) and live it up. You don't have to work, you don't have to be a father or a husband, you don't even have to be a man! Sick! I wish I could afford such a luxury. Who do you think you're kidding! Maybe you get all these phoney baloney shrinks fooled, but I'm not fooled!

The patient's shoulders had dropped with each passing moment. At this point he was just staring straight ahead, not looking at her at all.

W: Will you at least look at me! (She's looking out the window.) You're my husband. For richer or poorer in sickness and in health. You know how much I love you! Can't you look at me!

After watching and listening to the above scene the author knew much better why the patient was depressed generally and more importantly, why he became agitated and/or acutely depressed by his wife's visits. The wife's inveterate diatribes permeated with double messages only reinforced the patient's distorted perceptions of himself, his wife and of the world in general.

The author began to meet with the wife on her visits to the hospital. He taped some of her visits with her husband and played them back for her. She seemed genuinely surprised and not a little embarrassed by the double messages (she called them inconsistencies) in her talk. She appeared especially embarrassed by the vitriolic-like attacks she delivered against him. Indeed, initially she seemed patently unaware that their relationship and particularly her behavior in that relationship had contributed to his depression.

This particular case was one of the author's first. He then began meeting with both of them, while the patient was hospitalized and then on an outpatient basis. It all turned out fairly successfully. At least the patient has not committed suicide and has been gainfully employed for over fifteen years.

To continue with the historical narration, Bateson's work was complemented by that of Murray Bowen. The latter hospitalized not just the patient diagnosed and labeled ill but his whole family. The respective findings of both men gibed. Changes could be effected even in schizophrenic behavior. But change to be real, to be lasting, necessitated focusing not upon the individual, but rather upon the emotional environment in which he was steeped. For example, clinicians began to see that the problem with the autistic child lay with the child's mother and father. Sometimes it lay in the hostility, tension and anxiety which the parents generated in each other, in the household and finally in the child. Again, the emotional problem with the academically apathetic adolescent was not so much a function of intrapsychic dysfunction as it was of his severe case of acne and his peers' reaction to it.

These new views of the cause and onset of emotional dysfunction led to a redefined view of psychotherapy. Theorists began to search for solid theory and if possible, respectability. Sullivan, never forgotten, now came into new prominence. The reader will recall that his views centered on two principal ideas: 1) that people become sick because they feel that they can't communicate with others and 2) the best way to understand people is to examine them in relation to others.

Meanwhile the older, experienced practicing therapists of the fifties were beginning to give attention to the nuclear family. However, rather than exploring the interactive disposition and effects of the nuclear family, they continued to adhere to the study of the individual and his intrapsychic conpetency to adjust to familial dynamics.

It was the younger therapists, the trainees and the interns and those not yet settled into theory and rigid techniques who sought an explanation for what they continued to observe. Sullivan's basic ideas merely whetted their intellectual appetites. His thoughts provided only a quasi frame of reference for their daily observations and judgements about human behavior. Essentially these younger therapists found that Sullivanian theory, while provocative, was still wanting. They continued to search for a theory which more fully explained what they observed. And they found it in Jackson's explanation of homeostasis. This concept is explained in detail in the next chapter. Jackson's ideas regarding homeostasis were founded on work done by Walter Cannon, a Harvard physiologist who published a theory regarding physiological homeostasis (it was he who coined the term) in 1932. It is upon the concept of homeostasis that the so-called systems theory of family therapy (perhaps the most espoused approach utilized today) finds its source.

During the fifties and sixties the view of the role and function of the family began to change. Indeed, the very definition of family moved from the nuclear to include extended kin. Moreover, the concept of homeostasis, with its integral notion that a person serves a very important function in the emotional equilibrium of the total family (later, of any group), began to take hold.

Sullivan's notions regarding the importance and effect of communication among people were rediscovered and then researched. And the research was considerable both in quality and in quantity. Work was reported on the importance of body language, by Woodworth and Schlossberg (1954), Ekman, Sorenson and Friesen (1969), Izzard (1970) and Kendon (1972). Charny (1966), Scheflen (1964) and Machotka (1965) also reported work on the effects of communication on interpersonalization. The critical importance of effective communication for the development of emotional health rapidly became transparent.

The research on interpersonal communication has generated a myriad of approaches and techniques in the practice of group and family therapy. At the same time the more traditional approaches were retained. Thus, analytic therapy is for some therapists today not only a viable alternative but a preferential mode of treatment (Wolfe et. al. 1970). The Rogerian encounter group continues to flourish, as does transactional analysis (Goulding 1972), communication therapy through touch (Mintz 1969), and behavior therapy (Fensterheim 1972). Nathan Ackerman believes that family therapy can take at least ten legitimate forms:

"1. Marriage counselling.

2. Family counselling.

3. Therapy which focusses on one or two strategically important family members, in order to achieve 'detriangulation' and family change.

4. Modification of communication patterns.

5. Therapy which focuses on the emotional interchange among family members.

6. Experiential therapy; encounter and marathon therapy.

7. The crisis approach to family treatment.

8. An authoritarian, manipulative approach to the power alignments in family relationships.

9. Therapy for multiple families.

10. The ego-psychiatric approach and network therapy."

The approach in this text will be primarily the second one in Dr. Ackerman's list. It is the one with which the author is most familiar and most comfortable. The specific theory will involve a systems approach and as will be seen, will borrow also from communications theory. As will be seen too, the author has incorporated into his system of therapy a little of the dynamicist approach, i.e. in the second half of the text the case study is preceded by a social worker's report and the therapy sessions are analyzed in some measure dynamically.

A Summary

Following World War II American society changed. The individual both within and without his family was beset by a myriad of new social and familial pressures. The prevailing and most prestigious psychology of the time was Freudian and focussed precisely upon the individual and not the environment. The emergence of Rogerian psychology upon the scene did little to mitigate the view that it was incumbent upon the individual to adapt. Nothing in either philosophy proposed, recommended or even implied that forces outside the individual should or could be examined to alleviate the emotional discomfort of the contemporary individual. It was Sullivan more than any other who provided the rationale for examination and treatment of the individual in relation to others. He bridged the gap between the social sciences and psychiatry. Unfortunately, however, it took several decades for his ideas to take hold. This was due in no small measure to Freud's view of man and to the fact that mental health people became seduced by Rogers' theories and techniques of treatment. Therapists had only so much energy. Finally, researchers in the fifties began to observe, research and publish papers explaining that mental illness is a function of interpersonal behavior. Their findings indicated clearly that to be lasting any changes effected in a patient needed to focus not only upon the patient, but upon the emotional environment in which he was steeped. Jackson's theory about the importance of homeostatic balance within the family construct was published at about this time (1957). This led to a rediscovery of Sullivan's notions about the importance of communication, anxiety and interpersonal relations and this rediscovery in turn precipitated a veritable Niagara of research in communication theory.

Today there are many forms and approaches to family therapy. The one explained and illustrated in this text with a few modifications is the systems approach to family counseling.

CITATIONS

1. Ackerman, N., "The Growing Edge of Family Therapy." In *Progress in Group and Family Therapy*, ed. Sager, C. and Kaplan, H. New York: Brunner—Mazel Publishers, 1972, p. 442.

2. Bateson, G., Jackson, D. D., Haley, J. and Weakland, J. H., "Toward a Theory of Schizophrenia," *Behavioral Science*, Vol. 1, October 1956, pp. 251–264.

3. Bowen, M., "A Family concept of Schizophrenia." In *Ethiology of Schizophrenia*, ed. Jackson, D. New York: Basic Books, 1960.

4. Burgess, E. W., "The Family as a Unity of Interacting Personalities." In *Family Therapy, An Introduction to Theory and Technique*, ed. Euchson, G. D. and Hogan, T. P. Monterey, Cal.: Brooks/Cole, 1972.

5. Cannon, W., *The Wisdom of the Body*. New York: W. W. Norton, 1932.

6. Charny, E., "Psychosomatic Manifestations of Rapport." *Psychosomatic Medicine*, Vol. 28, 1966, pp. 305–315.

7. Ekman, P., Sorenson, E., and Friesen, W., "Pancultural Elements in Facial Displays of Emotion." *Science*, Vol. 164, 1969, pp. 86–88.

8. Fensterheim, H., "Behavior Therapy: Assertive Training in Groups." In *Progress in Group and Family Therapy*, ed. Sager, C. and Kaplan, H. New York: Brunner—Mazel Publishers, 1972.

9. Freud, S., *The Collected Papers*, ed. Strachey, J. New York: Basic Books, 1959.

10. Goulding, R., "New Directions in Transactional Analysis: Creating an Environment For Redecision and Change." In *Progress in Group and Family Therapy*, ed. Sager, C. and Kaplan, H. New York: Brunner/Mazel Publishers, 1972.

11. Izzard, C., *The Face of Emotion*. New York: Appleton-Century-Crofts, 1971.

12. Kendon, A., "Some Relationships Between Body Motion and Speech: An Analysis of an Example." In *Studies in Dyadic Interaction: A Research Conference*, eds. Siegman, A. and Pope, B. New York: Pergammon Press, 1972.

13. Machotka, P., "Body Movement as Communication Dialogues: Behavioral Science Research. Boulder, Colorado Western Interstate Commission for Higher Education, 1965.

14. Mintz, E., "On the Rationale of Touch in Psychotherapy." In *Progress in Group and Family Therapy*, ed. Sager, C. and Kaplan, H. New York: Brunner—Mazel Publishers, 1972.

15. Rogers, C. R., *On Becoming A Person*. Boston: Houghton-Mifflin Co., 1961, p. 23.

16. Scheflen, A., "The Significance of Posture in Communication." *Psychiatry*, Vol. 27, 1964, pp. 316–321.

17. Sullivan, H. S., *The Interpersonal Theory of Psychiatry*. New York: W. W. Norton, 1953.

18. Wolf, A., Schwartz, E., McCarty, G. and Goldberg, I., "Psychoanalysis in Groups: Contrasts With Other Group Therapies." In *Progress in Group and Family Therapy*, ed. Sager, C. and Kaplan, H. New York: Brunner—Mazel Publishers, 1972.

19. Woodworth, R. and Schlosberg, H. *Experimental Psychology*. New York: Holt, 1954.

Chapter 2
The Approach and A Definition

The contemporary approach to family therapy holds that as a therapist acquires more and more experience with families he will move away from the "ideology and practice of individual therapy" and the principles underlying it (Haley, 1971). As his experience with families increases such a therapist begins to embrace new premises about how human problems are both effected and resolved within the family. These new premises invariably lead to what is generally referred to today as the "systems approach."

Haley notes too that some therapists do not change their views but continue to adhere to the principles and ideas learned early in their education and training. These therapists continue to follow the traditional approaches derived from the Freudian and Rogerian philosophies (outlined in Chapter 1).

It is the systems approach to family therapy which is very much in vogue. This approach focuses on the family's current problems (the now is the issue). How family members interact is closely observed by the systems therapist. Neurosis, even psychosis in a member of the family, is viewed as a function of the interaction between and among the various family members. The belief is that an individual's ill health is the result of his adaptation to the sick environment created by the family. Any emotional problems within a family are not those of the family in toto.

The systems approach is very much concerned with the family structure and particularly with the "dyads" and the "triads" within that structure. The term dyad refers to two persons who are viewed and treated as one unit. In systems therapy the reference is frequently made to the "parental dyad," a common source of familial dysfunction. The therapist's approach is not to focus for instance, on the long suffering wife per se but on both spouses and the behavior effected between the two. The therapist sees his function as helping each person to treat the other differently. His goal is to effect changes in behavioral patterns between the two.

19

The triad is a three person unit. Again, the focus is not one individual but three people and the sequence of behavior between and among the three. The systems therapist views the triad as a rich area for exploration because frequently it involves numerous coalitions and alliances, i.e. a mother allies with her daughter against her son, a father allies with his daughter against his wife, and so forth. The behavior of one individual invariably affects the behavior of the other two in the triad. The child, for example, does not react to just her father or to just her mother but to both *and* to the perceived relationship between the two. Sudden emotional, somatic or behavioral symptoms in the child may well be a function of negative parental interchange and distancing, i.e. the brilliant child's academic collapse just when his parents separate.

An important concern of this approach is to change the sequence of behavior between and among the family members. At a given session the systems therapist will side with one member, encourage members to deal differently with one another, promote a certain alliance (to mitigate special ills) and discourage another. The focus of the systems therapist is upon outcomes and change rather than method. Indeed, the conviction of the systems therapist is that if change is not taking place within the family construct then the therapy is not productive.

To the systems therapist then, a lone family member, even several family members, are not the especial concern. Rather the concern is the *relationship* among all the family members.

The family is viewed as a functioanl unit and is so treated. Family members with more salient problems are viewed as symptomatic of the family's illness. Symptoms by certain family members serve important functions, sometimes even that of keeping a family together. In any case, treatment by the systems counselor does not focus on the symptomatic member alone but on the climate created by the relationships between and among the members.

The more important principles of the system's approach include the following. (These thoughts and any short quotes are derived from Haley's work [Haley 1971].)

1. The systems person views therapy not so much as a method as "a new orientation to the arena of human problems."

2. In the systems approach family members are given "equal weight." No member is more important than any other member. The systems therapist views individual dynamics as a product of intrafamilial relationships.

3. The systems therapist views "the present situation as the major causal factor and the process which must be changed."

4. The time spent in diagnosing family problems is time wasted. The view here is that a diagnosis per se does not help the family.

5. During the therapy hour the therapist is an important part of the family's dynamics. The therapist includes himself in the "context of treatment."

6. Confrontations, interpretations and encouragement of ventilation of feelings are not an integral part of the systems oriented therapist's method. On the contrary, the systems view on hostility is, "to resolve the difficulties in the relationships which are causing the hostility."

7. Flexibility in procedure or technique is a keynote of systems therapy. Indeed, to the systems oriented therapist "any set procedure is a handicap."

8. The systems therapist encourages all the members to tell, to interact with each other and to become intra-familially involved.

9. The systems view is that permanent alliances in therapy result in poor outcomes. When the therapist allies with a family member he makes it clear to all that the alliance is temporary.

10. The systems person believes in live supervision. The trainee is observed participating in the therapy.

11. The systems person's focus is on outcomes and the therapist changes and alters procedure and technique if there isn't positive change in the family.

At the initial contact the systems therapist explores the current problems and their effect on each member. As noted, the systems person is very much concerned with the interaction between members, especially with the observable alliances and the intra-familial conflicts. Unlike Haley, the author believes that one member's dynamics can be the focus of one or several familial sessions. In such instances exploration may focus on *how* a member's behavior affects others in the family. Or again, the focus might be on a parent's mis-learnings while growing up, i.e. what did the father, the mother, learn about the parental role, the child's role growing up in his/her home? Families, the author has learned, pass on elements of ill health from one generation to another. What is ironic and unfortunate is that family members appear to be totally oblivious of both the process and the effects upon each other. The process, they come to learn in therapy, is a function of the interpersonal patterns developed between the members, usually the parents.

In sum, the approach here is concerned with the family in concert. Individual perceptions and expectations are investigated and dealt with when they afflict current intrafamilial relations. Relationships, alliances and interpersonal conflicts are explored and worked through. The view here is that each family member contributes to the family dynamics, to the family personality. Each member of the family can affect or be affected by the needs and aspirations, by the ill health and good health, by the conscience or lack of it, of the other family members. In short, a family's capacity to afflict or heal is dependent upon the interactive patterns developed within the family construct. These are the views of systems theory. They are the views which make the most sense to the author. They are the views with which he is most comfortable. This is why they are presented here.

DEFINITION: A FRAME OF REFERENCE

Mental illness in the family is an interpersonal phenomenon. The emotional health of each member of the family directly affects the health of every other member. When one member feels discomfort or develops symptoms, other members are affected. For example, a man becomes short-tempered because he lost his job. He displaces his irritability upon his wife, who in turn ventilates her own anxiety upon her children. It is people who make people sick. This is especially true within the family. (Bowen 1960; Jackson 1957; Sullivan 1938).

Almost two decades ago, Don Jackson introduced the idea that each family unit seeks to maintain an emotional equilibrium, a "homeostatic balance," as he called it (Jackson 1957). This homeostasis is achieved via the family's own indigenous habits, behaviors and expectations. Each member has a function in maintaining the family's emotional equilibrium. Some of the functions are subtle (the teen-ager who serves as the family clown in time of high anxiety), some blatant (the spouse who too readily serves as the scapegoat for her husband's office anxieties). Simply stated, each person has a role in his family. And each has an emotional investment in this role. Each member of the family then strives in his own way, consciously or unconsciously, to maintain the familial homeostasis. Sometimes, however, a member is unable or unwilling to fill his familial role and thereby precipitates change within the family. And when change occurs intra-familially (i.e. the usually healthy member becomes sick or the member who is constantly sick becomes well), the other family members react to restore the emotional status. Change within the family effects change.

Parents may be viewed as the architects of this homeostasis, of this structure (Satir, 1967). Each structure is in considerable measure a manifestation of the parental personalities. A firm, solid foundation reflects the emotional health of the architects. A shaky one their ill health, or at least their inability to gibe in habits, behavior and expectations.

Parents themselves acquired complex emotional understandings in their own childhood. They learned a myriad of values, attitudes and behaviors which they pass on to their children. This is usually done unconsciously, often imperceptibly. But it is done truly (Bowen, 1960).

Children then, are not only the biological but the emotional products of their parents. Family therapists are pretty much in accord that the child learns to perceive the world through the eyes of his parents. Via interaction with mother and father the three year old has already learned whether or not it is a hostile, threatening world in which he lives or whether it is a loving, receptive one, or it is somewhere in between. Already he's integrated some fundamental attitudes about the emotions and their expression. Yelling is appropriate under certain circumstances. Hugging and kissing are desirable. Crying is O.K., but not always, especially not at the dinner table.

A family can be understood to be coming for therapy because it is paying too high a price for its homeostatic balance. Not uncommonly, a member of the family develops symptoms which have become intolerable in the view of one or more of the other members. Most family therapy encounters are precipitated by this symptomatic member. The family therapist terms this person the "Identified Patient" (Satir 1967). The "I.P." is the member of the family who has been labeled "sick." (The labeling more often than not has been done by someone outside the family, i.e. school, social worker, psychologist, teacher, family physician, etc.) The I.P., it should be noted, may have exhibited his symptoms for a long time and have gone unnoticed by the rest of the family precisely because these symptoms served the family needs. In other words, the identified patient is not necessarily the one who is suffering the most. Indeed, he may even find some secondary rewards in his sick behavior because it may serve important functions within the family.

To illustrate. Alice is an eight year old girl who although intelligent (I.Q. 127) was a poor student and chronically absent from school. Her absenteeism was finally brought to the attention of the school social worker who visited the home. The initial interview revealed that Alice's mother encouraged her daughter's absenteeism. The youngest and only female among four siblings, Alice was a menopause baby. The mother felt acutely lonely and in the interview freely admitted that Alice was: "1) fine company, 2) a darling child who didn't like school anyway and 3) the only one of her four children whom she felt close to and who had ever given her any pleasure."

Alice's chronic absenteeism and even her poor performance in school served important functions in the family. Alice as a truant relieved the mother's loneliness. Alice in school aggravated it. Prior to the initial family session Alice was the identified patient, so labeled by the social worker. It wasn't until subsequent family therapy sessions that the mother began to appreciate that she herself might be the major factor in Alice's dislike for school and her concomitant poor performance there. Indeed, ultimately, the mother came to appreciate the fact that while she was victimizing Alice, Alice was victimizing her in return. Alice learned to serve as her mother's emotional crutch for loneliness and thereby kept her mother from developing more mature interpersonal relationships outside the family.

This case serves to illustrate as well that family therapy is not concerned with the identified patient's dynamics apart from those of his family (Howells 1971). The family therapist does not aim to help the I.P. alone or even help him more than any other family member. Stated succinctly, one individual is never viewed as the lone site of a family's pathology (Minuchin 1974). The family in toto is involved in pathology manifested by the identified patient.

It is legitimate for the therapist to explain this involvement to both the I.P. and the family. To illustrate, Margaret P., her husband and their three children entered into therapy. Margaret was the identified patient. She had voluntarily admitted herself to the state psychiatric hospital twice in the past eleven months for "nervous exhaustion" (her term). Each admission lasted four days.

THERAPIST: O.K., why are we all here?

HUSBAND: Search me. I don't know.

MARGARET: I guess I'm the reason.

THERAPIST: You are? Why?

MARGARET: Well, I'm the one who keeps getting sick. I'm the one who's always ending up in the hospital. I'm the one. I'm the reason.

THERAPIST: Why do you end up in the hospital?

MARGARET: I'm tired. I'm very, very tired.

THERAPIST: Did you ever consider that the demands and pressures you're under at home might . . .

HUSBAND: Pressures! What pressures? For Christ's sakes, all she's gotta do is take care of her house and her family.

THERAPIST: Is that pressure, Margaret?

MARGARET: That's pressure.

THERAPIST: So maybe, Margaret, you're not the reason alone that we're all here. Maybe, just maybe, the reasons are not just you but the whole family together. Perhaps the obligations you feel that they impose upon you, what they all expect from you, maybe those are reasons too.

MARGARET: I never thought about it like that, just like that.

What is illustrated above is a family therapist's view that a family should hear that the so-called identified patient's problems are a product of intra-familial expectations and experience. What is illustrated also is the family therapist's perspective of the nature of family therapy—*familial dynamics* are the focus of his attention *not* those of the *individual* alone (Howells 1962, 1963). It is not Margaret alone who is ill; it is Margaret in conjunction with her husband and Margaret in conjunction with her children. Do the other family members subtly or blatantly "gang up" on her?

Margaret may have been made sick by her husband's demeaning perception of her and/or her role in the family. At the same time her hospital admission may well be the method she's developed to communicate her dissatisfaction with him, perhaps also to ventilate her hostility i.e. *he's* got to take care of the home. By getting sick then, Margaret abets and/or compounds familial problems.

From the therapist's viewpoint then, the identified patient is the product and perhaps the contributor to the indigenous interpersonal ills of any given family. These ills are found in the inherited familial values and attitudes. They are also interwoven with emotions. And emotions and their modes of expression are at the nub of the familial personality. They are its very psychological life blood. How love, anger and joy are communicated or not communicated is a central determinant for how a family will get along or if indeed it will get along at all.

A DEFINITION

We may define family therapy as follows: Family therapy is an interactive process which seeks to aid the family in regaining a homeostatic balance with which all the members are comfortable. In pursuing this objective the family therapist operates under certain basic assumptions. The following list of these assumptions will help the student to gain a better understanding of the systems approach to family therapy.

1. A family member's manifest illness comes not from him alone, but from his interactions with one or more other members of his family.
2. One or more of the family members may function overtly well precisely because another member of the family displays maladaptive

symptoms. A corollary of this is that the identified patient is not the lone member with problems.

3. The family demonstrates motivation for a more fruitful emotional homeostasis by its continued presence in therapy.

4. The parental relationship influences the relations between and among all the family members.

CITATIONS

1. Bowen, M., "A Family Concept of Schizophrenia." In *Etiology of Schizophrenia*, ed. Jackson, D. New York: Basic Books, 1960.

2. Haley, J., "Approaches to Family Therapy." In *Changing Families, A Family Therapy Reader*, ed. Haley, J. New York: Grune and Stratton, 1971.

3. Howells, J. G., "The Nuclear Family as the Functional Unit." *Psychiatry Journal of Mental Science*, Vol. 108, 1962, p. 675.

4. Howells, J. G., *Family Psychiatry*. Edinburgh: Oliver and Boyd, 1963.

5. Howells, J. G., *Theory and Practice of Family Psychiatry*. New York: Brunner/Mazel Publishers, 1971.

6. Jackson, D., "The Question of Family Homeostasis." *The Psychiatric Quarterly Supplement*, Vol. 31, Part 1, 1957, pp. 79–90.

7. Minuchin, S., *Families and Family Therapy*. Cambridge, Mass.: Harvard Univ. Press, 1974.

8. Satir, V., *Conjoint Family Therapy*. Palo Alto, Cal.: Science and Behavior Books Inc., 1967.

9. Sullivan, H. S., "Introduction to the Study of Interpersonal Relations." *Psychiatry*, Vol. 1, 1938, pp. 121–134.

Chapter 3
Theoretical Issues

GOALS

Goals are an important issue in family therapy. Indeed they continue to be the topic and the object for fruitful comment, essay and research (Laqueuer, H. P. et. al. 1964, Grosser, G. H. et. al. 1964 and Rabiner, E. L. et. al. 1962). Minuchin (1974) believes that the development of goals is basic to the therapeutic process. Thus he notes that, "the therapist must assess the family and develop therapeutic goals based on that assessment." Moreover Minuchin's view is that the process of intervention and transformation of the family-patterned method of response is always with respect to "the direction of those goals." And Haley (1972), too, believes they are, or should be, a critical concern of the experienced therapist. Thus he notes that, ". . . the more experienced therapist emphasizes what therapeutic results are happening in terms of quite specific goals . . ." "Outcome", he states, "is a constant focus . . ."

In this author's view, the goals of family therapy are the natural outgrowth of the definition of family therapy provided in chapter 2 and of the natural assumptions attendant to that definition. The general goals of family therapy then, may be stated as follows:

1. To help family members learn and emotionally appreciate that familial dynamics are intermeshed among all the family's members.

2. To help family members become aware of the fact that if a family member has problems, they may well be the effect of one or more other member's perceptions, expectations, and interactions.

3. To persevere in the therapy until a homeostatic balance has been reached which provides growth and enhancement for each of the members.

4. To develop full familial appreciation of the impact which the parental relationship has upon all the family's members.

The more specific goals are derived from those above. They are:

1. To promote each member's tolerance for the idiosyncratic ways of each member of the family.
2. To increase each member's tolerance for frustration when loss, conflict and disappointment are encountered both within and without the family.
3. To increase the motivation of each member to support, encourage and enhance each other member.
4. The achievement of a parental self-perception which is realistic and congruent with the perception of other family members.

THE STAGES OF TREATMENT

Treatment proceeds in stages. These stages are as follows:

1. Development of *rapport* between the therapist and the family and among the family members.
2. The development of an emotional appreciation of intra-familial relationships, dynamics and problems.
3. The development of *alternative modes of behavior* which are rewarding or at least, not threatening to family members.
4. The *application* of alternative modes *via practice* either in therapy or at home.

Stage I. Rapport—Definition and Prefatory Remarks

There are certain words, certain concepts which rapport calls to mind. These include: 1) warmth; 2) trust; 3) confidence; and 4) mutuality. These four concepts are the basic ingredients of rapport.

The qualities which make for an effective therapist are precisely those which are conducive to the establishment of rapport. These qualities are treated in detail in Chapter 6. It will suffice here to note that the therapist must be an *authentic* person who has self-credence and is himself warm and trusting. His confidence in himself is realistic and interpersonally appropriate. He finds family therapy personally rewarding because of the opportunities which it affords him to enhance others.

Obstacles to the Establishment of Rapport

Before launching into an explanation on how to establish rapport it might be well to explain some of the obstacles to its establishment. These include: 1) the emotional health of the therapist; 2) conflict of values; 3) the therapist's focusing too much on technique; 4) lack of familial motivation. We shall discuss these below.

1) The therapist does not have to be a paragon of emotional stability. His personal life, however, has to be of a quality which permits him to do his work sans ideational intrusions during the therapy hour. His emotional strength, his ego, should be healthy and strong enough to permit him to compartmentalize his personal life from his role as a therapist. If the therapist is unable to separate his personal life from his work, if he finds that one intrudes upon the other, to the extent that he is unable to give his full attention to his client family, then he will not be effective.

2) The therapist has his own personal value system. This, too, he needs to keep compartmentalized. If his values interphere with his ability to accept certain familial perceptions or behaviors because they do not gibe with his own values, then he will not be able to conduct family therapy. And, quite apparently, there are today acutely controversial issues which were formerly not issues at all, simply because they were not addressed, i.e. abortion, incest, euthanasia. If the therapist's conviction is that his values are superior and cannot and should not be changed, he will surely encounter difficulty in relating effectively, and thereby in maintaining rapport. Boy and Pine (1976) found this to be true in a recent study. These researchers concluded that the therapist's "tightly guarded value system will often make the counselor insensitive to clients whose values are quite different from his/her own."

3) There are therapists who obsess about the theory and technique of family therapy to the detriment of the family which they treat. Whitaker (1976) observed that, "Dedication to theory in family therapy work is essentially a cop-out, a disguise that will eventually conceal even the process of therapy." And Haley (1972) has also noted that hidebound methodologists who do family therapy are usually "beginners." (Haley includes in this term those therapists who do not change with experience.) ". . . being uncertain (they) would like to have a set of procedures to follow each time." He notes too that, "The more experienced family therapist tends to feel that any set procedure is a handicap." The vital concern of these "beginners" is "to do it right," which when translated means according to a method or theory which they acquired early in their training,

usually before the advent of exploration of the family as a treatment unit. The concentration upon technique is so intense with these people that they lose sight of the family. Rapport for such therapists is at best difficult.

4) Sometimes the family in therapy is not motivated "to redefine the problem" (Freeman 1976) in order to change or get better. This is not unusual, especially when the family has been mandated into therapy via a court order. Families such as these come to therapy with one or more members resentful, suspicious and hostile. Establishment of rapport is usually difficult. It requires a therapist with much appreciation of the familial dynamics and more than the usual amounts of patience. Sometimes too, a family comes self-referred, but with only *one* of the parents wanting to enter therapy. Not uncommonly in these cases the referring parent wants a therapist's support for his or her own diagnosis of the family's ills. Such a case demands the most exquisite diplomacy and mediation by the therapist.

The establishment of rapport between the therapist and the family and its establishment among the family members are very much related. This is especially true if the therapist views himself not so much as a disinterested observer of patient family ills as one who *joins* the family in order to participate in a *therapeutic way* in family interactions. He is for all practical purposes a member of the family during the therapy hour. Minuchin (1974) makes this point very effectively. He employs the analogy of the anthropologist who joins the culture he is studying in order to fully understand the essentials and nuances of the culture. And he notes, "Like the anthropologist, the family therapist joins the culture with which he is dealing." Haley (1972) too sees the importance of this. Thus he notes that, "The more experienced therapist includes himself in the description of the family," and again he observes that the competent family therapist is one who, "does not think of the family as separate from the context of treatment and he includes himself in that context."

The effective therapist, therefore, joins the family for practical purposes. At the same time he retains his professional purposes. Thus he needs to be a member *practically* in order to experience the emotional subtleties and blatant pressures with which the family members live. He needs to learn about the latent as well as the more obvious modes by which family members communicate. Most importantly, he needs to come to understand how the family members' perceptions of each other and outsiders are similar and how they are different. Once he begins to appreciate the perceptional differences intra-familially he can begin to interact with the members genuinely. His rapport with the family as a therapist will develop, establish and firm up in direct proportion to his ability to join the family practically, to be emotionally accepted by the family.

At the same time, the practical role of family member serves the central purpose of the therapy experience, namely *to help the therapist to function in his role of therapist.* In short, the effective therapist is both the coach and the team player, the director and the actor, the foreman and worker.

The therapist then operates within two frames of reference: 1) his emotional and cognitive understandings as a member of the family in therapy and 2) his professional knowledge and skills. It is within these two frames of reference that he proceeds in his work to re-establish rapport among the family members and to promote a more healthful, and more fruitful homeostasis for the family.

A final note about the establishment of rapport. It is not enough for the counselor to work to establish it between himself and the family intra-familially. Rapport is not something which once established can be forgotten. On the contrary, the therapist, consciously and unconsciously, is constantly striving to *maintain* rapport during each moment of each session. He knows when rapport is strong or weak. He knows this by the warmth, trust and confidence which he feels comfortable exuding and/or accepting, and he observes the same among the family members.

Stage II. Emotional Appreciation

Bednar and Melnich (1974) found that once rapport has been established the members are going to find it more comfortable to interact with each other and with the therapist. In any case, the therapist is now in a position to lead the family toward the second stage, the development of an emotional appreciation of intra-familial relationships, dynamics and problems. The therapist does this via a variety of techniques. Those which this author has found to be most valuable are graphically detailed in Chapter 7. Among those described two which are especially effective in helping a family to reach and pass through this second stage are *sculpting* and *role playing.* Both techniques serve to emotionally enlighten family members. Their effectiveness is derived from the dramatic impact which they have on the perceptual stance of each of the members (see Chapter 7).

It has been the author's experience that once a family attains Stage II it encounters little difficulty in passing through Stages III and IV. The reasons for this are that with emotional appreciation of intra-familial problems and dynamics comes an abatement of anxiety and a consequent better cognitive understanding and view of alternative views. Concommitant with the abatement of anxiety too there invariably appears a remarkable increase in the family's motivation not only to confront problems but to *solve* them.

Stage III. Alternative Modes of Behavior

Once the family members have developed an emotional appreciation of the familial problems and their role in the development and maintenance of those problems, they begin to develop and suggest alternative modes of behavior both for themselves and for the other members. To illustrate: the controlling interphering husband finally begins to see that his entry into the kitchen just before supper to give orders and suggestions on how to cook only increases his wife's anxiety and irritation. His son suggests that the father play ping-pong with him before supper and "let Ma call us to supper." The father not only assents but promises to do so. He finds the promise easy to keep because what he discovers about himself is that if he has something to do before supper he feels no need to direct or interfere in his wife's cooking. In addition, he and the whole family find supper more pleasant. And again, the young wife too prone to tears when she can not get what she wants begins to see that her regressive, dependent behavior is increasing her husband's ire and anxiety and alienating him. Her emotional appreciation of the problem leads her to point out to him that he is in considerable measure responsible, since he gives in to her whenever she cries. He sees the validity of what she ways, responds negatively to her tears, and in a short time regressive behavior is lessened considerably.

The author has found that families can be and are remarkably creative in coming up with the most idiosyncratic alternatives. During the past year the author had three families which suffered from a common problem; they were quite anxious and their anxiety was manisfested in being very stiff and formal with each other. Without exception, they felt the need to be more relaxed individually and with each other. What did they do? The first family joined a yoga class, the second a transcendental meditation class, and the third joined a group which organized itself to learn karate!

Stage IV. Application Via Practice

Ordinarily the therapy session provides at most only one or two hours per week to translate the emotional appreciations into alternative behaviors, and to practice them. Since there are at least several dozen more working hours available to the members to do things together over the course of the week, this therapist has found that certain families can profit from home assignments. As with the development of alternative modes, the feasibility and success of application via practice lies within the unique structure of the indigenous family.

Some points to note about home assignments are listed below:

1) The therapist asks the members about the feasibility, the practicality, of carrying out assignments at home. If the members are searching for joint activities to carry out the therapist may make a tactful *recommendation*. Not only is no family ever ordered into an assignment, but no family member should feel even the slightest twinge of guilt for not endorsing a proposal. Accordingly:

2) The therapist often prefaces the initial discussion of home assignments with a few remarks about how home assignments are not appropriate for all families. For example, living space might not be suitable, i.e. for these people to plan to cook a meal together in an efficiency type kitchen may precipitate more anxiety than it will abate! And again, family schedules vary remarkably. Today many spouses work evenings. Assignments which require such a person to abbreviate his schedule are usually unrealistic and may intensify rather than abate familial anxiety, especially if the person has to be concerned about the financial cost.

3) The therapist usually allows time during the session, usually toward the close, to discuss the assignment, specifically the what, how, where, and so forth.

4) The therapist is exquisitely sensitive to the hesitant or wary reaction to a home assignment by any member, especially a parent. Sometimes a member, out of a sense of love or guilt, foolishly commits himself to an assignment which he is neither able nor ready to fulfill. The therapist knows this and, if appropriate, steps in to question the wary reaction. The therapist does this because he knows well that if there is not a 100% commitment by each of the members the assignment will not be therapeutic or enhancing.

THE SETTING

Research has been done to show that the physical environment affects individual and even group perception (Mintz 1956; Maslow and Mintz 1956). These studies showed that the esthetic quality of the setting influenced the degree of optimism or pessimism with which the subjects perceived the faces of others. It is reasonable to deduce from studies such as these that perception by the family members of the therapist and of each other will be influenced by the setting where the therapy occurs. The view here is that perception is the critical determinant for the general quality of interaction in any interpersonal setting. Therapy is no exception.

Chaiken et. al. (1976) showed that how the client perceives the setting influences strongly how he relates to the therapist. Thus, the "intimacy of his self-disclosure was significantly higher in a warm intimate room . . . than in a cold non-intimate room."

The author has discovered that a room furnished like a comfortable, well used living room seems to provide a very appropriate setting. The furniture should be esthetically attractive yet appropriately functional. It should be of a type that can be moved about with little effort. Also, for the therapist who finds it useful, audio and video-taping equipment should be installed. (Its presence in the room, however, should be unobtrusive.) Also, it is the prudent therapist who makes some provisions for children. "A box of simple toys is about all that is needed" (Bloch, 1976).

A final point might be that there should be ample space for any and all activities attendant to the therapy. Haase and DiMattia (1976) found that the ". . . variable of room size was found to be the most significant variable . . . Smaller rooms tended to inhibit." It is important that family members not have to be restricted with respect to where or how they want to seat themselves. Where and how the members sit in relation to each other is important. On this point Minuchin noted that, "the way in which they position themselves can provide clues to alliances and coalitions, centrality and isolation." Quite apparently, the therapist's competencies and his ability to help a family should not have to be constrained because of a lack of physical space.

FAMILY STRUCTURE

Early in the therapy, the therapist observes and examines the structure of the family. The basic question which he has to explore is how the members relate to each other. Another question might be to explore the nature of the parental dyad. And a third might be who is allied with whom and against whom.

The demands which family members place upon each other determine the ways in which they interact. Minuchin states it thus: "Family structure is the invisible set of functional demands that organizes the ways in which family members interact." He goes on to explain that the structure evolves from the patterns of interactions developed by the members as they relate intra-familialy.

The following edited excerpt taken from an initial interview illustrates the complexity of family structure. Alan, Mary, Mike and Nancy make up the family.

THERAPIST: Alan, you were saying that your wife Mary doesn't want to prepare meals because. . .

ALAN: Because she's too lazy. She's not a wife anymore.

MARY: It's not that I'm lazy. I'm just too tired after working eight hours. I'm just too tired, too tired. Nobody wants to do anything, anymore. Nobody . . .

ALAN: Nobody wants to do anything anymore because you don't want to do anything anymore. Damn it, all you want to do is to nag and fight.

MARY: You just don't, you just won't understand will you? Nancy here never does anything I tell her or even ask her to do. She won't make a bed, help me fix supper or wash a dish.

NANCY: Oh mother! Dad's right you're just a nag. I just don't see why I should have to make my bed every day. I sleep in it. You nag me about that.

ALAN: Yeah. What do you nag her about that for? Christ, Mary you don't even make our own bed!

MARY: Oh you won't understand will you? All I want is some help. There isn't any in this family.

MIKE: What about me? I . . .

MARY: You! We don't even see you. You eat at home but never with us. You sleep at home but that's all. It's like you're our "Star Boarder," not a son.

Mike and Nancy too at this point had put on sullen, resentful expressions. Neither spoke again until questioned by the therapist.

MARY continues: Nobody helps me. Nobody listens to me. It's like I'm not a mother anymore. I don't know what I'm doing . . .

ALAN: That's it. That's it. You said it. You're not a mother anymore. You haven't been acting like a mother for a long, long time. You never make a bed, iron a hankie, cook a meal. I'm so damned tired of frozen dinners!

This family is coming for help because the emotional price which they are paying for their homeostasis has become intolerable. The mother finds it hard to continue in the role of the I.P., if indeed she is that.

The family interacts with anger and resentment. The parental dyad seems to be the underlying cause for much of the family's ills. Mary appears no longer to be able or willing to meet the demands which her husband places upon her, those of cook, housewife, and so on. Mike or at least Nancy, surely, seems to be allied with their father against their mother.

In such a case the therapist can readily understand that this is a family which needs restructuring. The demands and functions which each member places upon the other (especially within the parental dyad) need to be explored, examined and ultimately changed or at least modified, if the family is going to achieve a more healthful homeostatic balance.

THE MUTUAL UNDERSTANDINGS

Before the therapist can begin his work with the family he and the family have to arrive at some mutual understandings. Among these are:

1.   that changes in family interaction patterns do indeed need to be effected.

2.   that the family is composed of individuals with individual needs, and that these needs influence one another within the family; that one member's needs may be precipitating and maintaining the problems of the symptomatic member.

3.   that sometimes the therapist may want to schedule the parental dyad only for reasons of privacy. Sometimes too, the needs of only one member (I.P. for example) "will need special attention" (Minuchin 1974).

4.   that while ". . . the whole group does not have to be present at one time . . ." (Beels and Ferber 1972) committment and allegiance to the therapy must be total by the therapist and by all members of the family.

What we have here of course is a therapeutic contract. It is a contract which all of the members must understand and agree to. Anything less than total committment by all cannot result in effective *family* therapy.

A THERAPIST'S RISKS AND PROBLEMS

A point noted above bears reiteration. The therapist needs to function both as a member of the family and as the professional therapist. He cannot permit his necessary emotional involvement as a member of the family to intrude upon and/or hamper his function as therapist. What the effective therapist has to do, of course, is to be exquisitely sensitive to the fact that he is constantly operating at two levels—the cognitive and the emotional. The first level permits him to function in his role as a therapist, the second in his role of family member. As the therapist he observes objectively, he analyzes, he interprets to himself and when appropriate, to the family. As the family member he necessarily becomes immersed in the family's dynamics and thereby runs a constant danger, namely that of becoming seduced by the neurotic intra-familial dynamics. For example, if he allies himself for too long with the passive-dependent but manipulative husband against the aggressive and demeaning wife he runs the risk of blending with the husband in the wife's perception. His effectiveness with the wife as a therapeutic manipulator, as an idea source for tasks to try will be curtailed at least for a time.

The therapist is constantly beset by two objectives. To protect and strengthen the personal integrity of each family member and secondly (and necessarily in this order) to promote general familial solidarity. On first glance these two objectives would seem to complement each other. Frequently they do. Thus, the individual who feels good about himself can usually contribute more warmth toward other family members, can be more enhancing generally. At the same, as was noted in the preceding paragraph, the individual who feels that he/she is being "ganged up on" is going to feel alienated and his/her suspicions or paranoid notions will be reinforced. Under such circumstances the therapist must be cognizant of the fact that he is *not* promoting personal integrity nor familial esprit de corps.

In short, the family therapist in his dual role of player—director necessarily walks an emotional and cognitive tight-rope. What this author has learned is that the best therapeutic method is to reward and support any and all enhancing remarks, any and all responsible behavior by one member toward another. As Hale (1976) observed, ". . . responsible actions are in fact therapeutic actions." This is true not only for the therapist but for the family members as well. Conversely, behavior by a member or members which demeans another is discouraged tactfully. To illustrate, if both parents harangue about their adolescent son's sullen refusal to participate in family activities as if he were not present, then it behooves the therapist to protect the adolescent by interrupting the harangue and asking him if there are reasons for his non-participation. Or again, if the therapist or any other person present were to ask one member of the group a question and be answered by a third member the therapist should involve himself. An effective technique is simply to re-address the question to the original member and to express more firmly your interest in *that member's* response.

To illustrate:

THERAPIST: Betty, your mother says you're a bear in the morning. Are you?

MOTHER: Is she ever! She stomps around the house, slams doors. She acts as if she were living alone. I'm sick of it. If she just . . .

THERAPIST: (Looking at Betty) What do you have to say about it all Betty? I'd really like to hear what *you* have to say about it.

The adaptation capacity of the effective therapist must be considerable. At times he may well feel like a therapeutic gymnast. A major reason for this is that families include children as well as adults, and adolescents too. The language used by the nine year old is obviously different from that of the seventeen year old. The therapist has to communicate cognitively and emotionally at all three levels. And he needs to do this without seeming to be stilted, affected or condescending. This can be and usually is emotionally draining. Quite probably, it is the most demanding aspect of the therapist's role.

TERMINATION

Last Session

Freeman (1976) believes that "how naturally the terminating phase is experienced" is dependent on how successful the therapist was in the initial phase in helping the family to redefine its problem. According to Freeman termination without anxiety is a sign of successful therapy, of an effective therapist.

Termination sometimes occurs because of negative reactions to the therapist by a parental member, usually the father (Shapiro and Budman 1973). Sometimes, too, termination occurs because a parent member finds that the intra-familial changes being effected are making him uncomfortable, if not downright anxious, i.e. his passive-dependent wife is becoming very assertive. And so the family does not return.

Generally, however, the therapist and the family mutually agree upon termination. More often than not it is the natural outcome of a family no longer in need.

A Given Session

The family must learn that sessions have a time limit. Some family members refuse to respond to the more obvious cues that a session is at an end. It is a prudent therapist who provides for such circumstances. He can alert a secretary or whoever to knock by a given time. A therapist does this in order to teach certain members that therapy time is precious. To let them ramble on indicates to them that the therapist's time is not very valuable. Also therapists have discovered that some individuals have a positive talent for long ruminations after the time is up. It may be but one aspect of a larger syndrome to obtain and/or exert power within the family, i.e. by dominating the talk at the close one can manipulate and control both the family and the therapist. As noted, to let the person go on is to reward basically unacceptable behavior. The therapist may want to confront such a member about this behavior at a subsequent family session.

CITATIONS

1. Bednar, R. L., and Melnich, J., "Risk, Responsibility and Structure: A Conceptual Framework for Initiating Group Counseling and Psychotherapy." *Journal of Counseling Psychology*, Vol. 21, No. 1, 1974, pp. 31–37.

2. Beels, C., and Ferber, A., "What Family Therapists Do." In *The Book of Family Therapy*, eds. Ferber, A., Mendesohn, M., and Napier, A. Boston: Houghton Mifflin Co., 1972.

3. Bloch, D. A., "Including the Children in Family Therapy." In *Family Therapy Theory and Practice*, ed. Guerin, P. New York: Gardner Press, 1976, p. 176.

4. Boy, A. V., and Pine, G. J., "Equalizing the Counseling Relationship." *Psychotherapy: Theory, Research and Practice*, Vol. 13, No. 1, Spring 1976, pp. 20–25.

5. Chaikin, A. L., Derlega, V. J., and Miller, S. J., "Effects of Room Environment On Self-Disclosure in a Counseling Analogue." *Journal of Counseling Psychology*, Vol. 23, no. 5, 1976, pp. 479–481.

6. Freeman, D. S., "Phases of Family Treatment." *The Family Coordinator*, Vol. 25, July, 1976.

7. Grosser, G. H. and Paul, N. L., "Ethical Issues in Family Group Therapy." *American Journal of Orthopsychiatry*, Vol. 34, 1964, pp. 875–885.

8. Haase, R. F., DiMattia, D. J., "Spatial Environments and Verbal Conditioning in a Quasi-Counseling Interview." *Journal of Counseling Psychology*, Vol. 23, No. 5, 1976, pp. 414–421.

9. Hale, W. D., "Responsibility and Psychotherapy." *Psychotherapy: Theory, Research and Practice*, Vol. 13, No. 4, Winter, 1976, pp. 298–302.

10. Haley, J., "Beginning and Experienced Family Therapists." In *The Book of Family Therapy*, eds. Ferber, A., Mendelsohn, M., and Napier, A., Boston: Houghton Mifflin Co., 1972, p. 161.

11. Haley, J., "Beginning and Experienced Family Therapists." In *The Book of Family Therapy*, eds. Ferber, A., et. al. Boston: Houghton Mifflin Co., 1972, p. 166.

12. Haley, J., "Beginning and Experienced Family Therapists." In *The Book of Family Therapy*, eds. Ferber, A., et. al. Boston: Houghton Mifflin Co., 1972, pp. 155–167.

13. Laqueuer, H. P., LaBurt, H. A., and Morong, E., "Multiple Family Therapy: Further Developments." *The International Journal of Social Psychology*, Congress Issue, 1964, pp. 70–80.

14. Maslow, A. H., and Mintz, N., "Effects of Esthetic Surroundings: Initial Short-term Effects of Three Esthetic Conditions Upon Perceiving 'Energy' and Well-Being in Faces." *Journal of Psychology*, Vol. 41, 1956, pp. 247–254.

15. Mintz, W. L., "Effects of Esthetic Surroundings: Prolonged and Repeated Experience in a 'Beautiful' and Ugly Room." *Journal of Psychology*, Vol. 41, 1956, pp. 459–466.

16. Minuchin, S., *Families and Family Therapy*, Cambridge: Harvard Univ. Press, 1974, p. 111.

17. Minuchin, S., *Families and Family Therapy*, Cambridge: Harvard Univ. Press, 1974, p. 51.

18. Minuchin, S., *Families and Family Therapy*. Cambridge: Harvard Univ. Press, 1974, p. 124.

19. Minuchin, S., *Families and Family Therapy*. Cambridge: Harvard Univ. Press, 1974, p. 143.

20. Minuchin, S., *Families and Family Therapy*. Cambridge: Harvard Univ. Press, 1974, p. 129

21. Rabiner, E. L., Molinski, H., and Gralnick, A., "Conjoint Family Therapy in the Inpatient Setting." *American Journal of Psychotherapy*, Vol. 16, 1962, pp. 618–631.

22. Shapiro, R. J., and Budman, S. H., "Defection, Termination and Continuation in Family and Individual Therapy." *Family Process*, Vol. 12, March 1973, No. 1, pp. 53–67.

23. Whitaker, C. W., "The Hindrance of Theory in Clinical Work." *Family Therapy, Theory and Practice*, ed. Guerin, P. New York: Gardner Press, 1976, p. 162.

Chapter 4
Communication

As the author has noted in a previous publication, "communication is *a* if not *the* central issue in psychotherapy" (Perez 1968) regardless of the nature of the therapy, individual, group or family. The view here is that effective communication is an indispensable requirement for effective therapy. Indeed, quite simply, if the communication between members is poor, the therapy will be stymied; if there is no communication, there can be no therapy. It is perhaps for this reason that Schauble and Hill (1976) believe that the essence of therapy is teaching communication skills.

Satir (1975) would seem to concur, as she has observed that, ". . . for me, the communication approach is the main tool," in family therapy. She believes that there are five prime ways which people utilize to communicate. These include: "placating, blaming, super-reasonable, irrelevant and congruent."

Placating involves outwardly agreeing with another person even when your feelings are directly contrary. Such a discrepancy between feelings and show can only structure problems both for now and later.

Blaming is the method used by a person who desperately needs to demonstrate that he has power. The blamer may be hypercritical, dictatorial, generally ornery, etc. He has a very important need to be obeyed, again, to prove to himself that he is a powerful person.

Super-reasonable is a method employed by those who are not able or are afraid to show feelings.

Irrelevant is the method in which the words spoken have little or no relation to what is happening in the individual's immediate environment.

Congruent is a method in which the feelings gibe perfectly with the behavior effected. It is the healthiest form of behavior.

Satir explains how each of the above methods of communication influences the body. Like so many others in the field she believes that, "We speak with our whole bodies." In a forceful way she points out that words affect facial expression, body motion, muscles, skin, and so on. Speech, she feels, is an all-body phenomenon.

DeRivera (1977) apparently agrees with Satir. Thus, he has noted that, "Emotions are always embodied . . . They both influence the body . . . and reflect the condition of the body." Much of our internal conflict is vented upon our body. Perspiration, headaches, ulcers, and skin rashes are all manifestations of our unresolved conflicts. According to Szasz (1961), complaints of bodily symptoms are nothing more than "cries for help and their pictorial representations." The person with the ulcer pains may be telling himself that he's steeped in too much anxiety. The woman with a bad eczema may well be telling people generally, or more usually those close to her, "Help me—I am in trouble and I do not understand why."

It was Haley who observed that the communication systems of the family are different from those of other groups or units. The familial unit is unique. He cites research to support the following assumptions regarding the nature of intra-familial communication:

> There are several basic assumptions to family study: (a) family members deal differently with each other than they do with other people; (b) the millions of responses which family members meet over time within a family fall into patterns; (c) these patterns persist within a family for many years and will influence a child's expectations of, and behavior with, other people when he leaves the family; and (d) the child is not a passive recipient of what his parents do with him but an active co-creator of family patterns.

Communication occurs on more than just a verbal level. As Haley (1968) notes, "communication between people is extraordinarily complex; they communicate verbally, with vocal inflections, with body movement, and with reference to unique, past familiar incidents." Confounding the problem even more is the fact that emotions and behaviors more often than not are interwoven with the words to confound the message conveyed and the meaning received, i.e. "I am *not* angry that you forgot" she said to her husband icily. A minute later she knocks over the glass of chianti on his light blue trousers.

The whole topic of human communication is extremely complex yet fascinating. The messages between people are seldom emitted or received on one level. This is especially true intra-familially and in a family therapy session. Communication between people can be said to occur on two levels, the conscious and the unconscious. With respect to the latter, Freud cogently explained the dramatic and practical intentions which people have when they express their unconscious feelings and attitudes via word slips, memory losses, accidents, etc. These behaviors are emitted from the unconscious and they are most meaningful. In Freud's view, "the slip itself makes sense." He described the unconscious message, "as a valid mental process following out its own purpose."

An unconscious message takes various forms and guises. Each message reflects the indigenous ways which a person employs to make contact with another. The complexity and the confusion, both in the messages emitted and those received, reflects the acute need which the human being has to communicate, to maintain contact with others. At some level, we all know that we have to be in contact with our environment. Our emotional health demands it. We are human. We have needs and these usually can be met only by other people.

It was Abrahan Maslow (1954) who taught us that an individual's emotional health is a function of the extent to which his basic psychological needs have been and continue to be met. These needs include security, love and self-esteem.

In this context *security* is defined as the need for emotional safety, to avoid threatening or painful situations, to obtain a sense of contentment derived from being steeped in a familial environment which centers upon routine and familiarity. Security is derived also from the ability to predict with a high degree of accuracy the emotional reaction of other family members.

Love is defined as a need to enhance and to be enhanced. It has to do with giving and receiving support and acceptance. Here it has to do with the need which one has to feel that he belongs to a given family, no matter what.

Self-esteem. In considerable measure the extent to which this need is met is determined by the extent to which the security and love needs are met. Self-esteem has to do with a person's sense of worth, with the sense that one can do well in this life if one thinks one is worthy. Competence, independence and a sense of freedom are elements of self-esteem.

The important family function continues to be to meet these needs in each of its members because as we have noted again and again the family's emotional homeostasis is in considerable measure a product of the individual good health of each of its members.

It is precisely when the individual feels that these needs are not being met by his family that his emotional health suffers, that the quality of the family's homeostatic balance necessarily declines. The basic psychological needs are best met when communication is unfettered. They are met poorly or not at all when communication is emotionally garbled by embarrassment, fears, or latent hostility.

A term used to explain garbled communication is "double message." An example was supplied above, i.e. the wife whose icy tone belied her words about not being angry. Her anger was of such an intensity that she *accidentally* spilled wine on her husband's lap. Quite apparently she was determined that her message would "get through," albeit it did not gibe with her words! Examples of the double message are many and varied, i.e. the rejecting mother who continues to help dress for school the child who complained of a sore throat. All the while she asks, "Are you sure you feel well enough to go, dear?" Or again, the workaholic father and husband who complains several times about having to return to work after supper and then leaves a half hour earlier than usual. And finally, the young husband who finds his new wife's meal distasteful but responds to her queries about its tastiness with praise. Then he leaves most of it, feigning a lack of appetite.

The double message invariably has deleterious effects upon the family. And the family conditioned to relating via double messages more often than not develops coping problems. The members are confused, bewildered because they are quite unable to interpret the messages they are getting. And the inability to interpret messages ultimately results in the inability to comment, often even to perceive discrepancies. This phenomenon has been termed "the double bind." It was first researched by Bateson et. al. and reported in a paper in October 1956. It has received considerable attention since then (Clausen and Kohn 1960; Rioch 1961; Watzlawick 1963).

The children in such families are particularly vulnerable. To illustrate, the child comes in from school and finds mother in obvious pain. "What's the matter, Ma?" "It's nothing dear. A simple headache. Nothing at all." A little later when the child is playing too rambunctiously the mother screams "Didn't I tell you I had a headache, a vicious headache. How selfish can you get!" The child reared in such a system of double messages and binds becomes emotionally unhealthy because she is being reared in a neurotic system of communication, with a whole new language. (Bateson, 1966) Quite apparently, security, love and self-esteem cannot be promoted under these circumstances.

This then, becomes an essential function of the therapist in the session, namely, to promote communication between and among family members so that they can more effectively meet each other's psychological needs.

At the same time, it was Satir who observed that the therapist's concern and focus regarding communication should not be only with whom he treats. He should be vitally concerned with his own pattern of communication. All too often, "the therapist is not aware of his own double-level messages. He is not aware of how much what he is trying to keep inside affects what shows on the outside, and what the actual message is the other person receives."

The therapist is fully cognizant of the fact that communication between and among individuals can be effected in other ways too. There are, for example, certain personal and particular behaviors which tell much. These include *appearance, space utilization habits* and *body motion*. These three are communicative modes to which the experienced therapist is alert.

The facial expressions which family members wear, how they dress, comb their hair, and the use, if any, which they make of cosmetics are all manifestations of personal and familial self-image. Personal and familial appearance frequently reflects the values to which the family adheres. When mother, father and daughter come into the room impeccably well groomed while Johnny enters looking like both he and his clothes need to be washed the message is unmistakable. Whether or not the therapist wants to deal with the message will be dependent on a variety of factors. The point here is that by taking notice of such a discrepancy in grooming intra-familially, he will be aware of Johnny's alienation from the family.

Where families sit in relation to the therapist can be important for how the therapy will proceed. Knight (1976) for example, found that how close the therapist sits to the clients can effect client comfort. Similarly, Stone and Morden (1976) found that, "subjects talked longer about personal topics at an intermediate distance than they did when seated close to or far away from the interviewer."

Equally important, how family members arrange themselves in relation to each other reflects considerably on how they feel about each other. How the members stand, sit and lounge when they are together can tell the therapist something about the quality and the nature of their communication. The adolescent who chooses to sit on the distant edge of the group is letting the therapist know something about his emotional detachment from the rest of the family. Or again, the wife who chooses to sit in the chair opposite her husband even though invited by him to sit on the couch next to him is also letting the therapist know something about her feelings of separateness from her spouse. Concommitant non-verbal behavior is critical in communication (Ekman and Friesen 1969; Kendon 1972). Body motion communicates so very much. With some exceptions people who are tense sit that way and those who are relaxed generally sit that way. Body motion includes facial expression, gesticulations, hair stroking, crossing and swinging one's legs, etc. How people move their bodies reflects the quality and intensity of their current emotional state. Body movement is thus an invaluable source of data to the observant therapist and offers rich topics for exploration.

THE AVENUES OF COMMUNICATION

Prefatory Note

In the course of one's daily life the typical individual may use one, some or all of the following five avenues of communication: 1) Consonance, 2) Condemnation, 3) Submission, 4) Intellectualization, and 5) Indifference.

A given avenue may be a temporary or periodic way of interacting or it may well be a deeply rooted method in one's personality. Which avenue or avenues one uses is determined by prior learning and the intensity of the threat which one perceives and the consequent anxiety which one feels. An individual may well have a penchant for one avenue of communication, but few people, if any, relate purely and all the time via one avenue only. Nevertheless, for purposes of clarity and explanation the avenues are treated separately here. However, the author recognizes fully that for most people each is *not* an ingrained, characteristic way of communicating. Typically, people straddle the various avenues.

Consonance.   The healthy avenue of communication is termed consonance. Consonance refers to communications where the emotion and the behavior gibe perfectly with the message given. The person who has learned to communicate in a consonant way is one who is secure enough to say what's on his mind. At the same time this person is secure enough not to have to be rude or tactless. To be consonant does not mean to be a boor. To be consonant does mean to be honest because consonant communications are the communications of an individual who is basically authentic.

Consonance then refers not so much to candor as it does to emotional integrity. The consonant person's spoken words gibe with the emotions he feels. His behavior, also, fits perfectly with his words and feelings. The consonant person's cognitive and emotional judgement promote, enhance and meet the basic needs of other family members.

More often than not, consonance is its own reward. Why? Because the consonant person finds reward in his enhancing communication. He gets good feelings about himself when he relates in a loving way. Quite simply, consonance is what the family in therapy strives for and what the therapist promotes. It is the vehicle by which the family can establish its most effective homeostatic balance.

Condemnation.   A common reaction by the individual who feels constantly threatened is to condemn those around him/her. The condemnation can take various forms, i.e. nagging, hypercriticism or being generally ornery. The condemner type is one who frequently suffers from a low self-esteem. He attempts to raise it by belittling those closest to him. His unfortunate emotional conviction appears to be "I get bigger if I make them smaller." The ever present need to put others down feeds his nagging intolerance of others. Unfortunately for him and those around him, the more he is threatened the more intolerant he becomes. Achievement by another person in an area where the condemner has not been especially successful usually results in minimizing or depreciating the other's success.

The condemner is often an authoritarian person. People, issues and situations are black or white. His position on any topic is absolute. His arguments are based not upon reason so much as emotion. The issue to the condemner is not so much not to lose as it is not to *appear* to lose, for his fragile self-esteem is inextricably interwoven with whatever position he takes. To lose for this person is to lose face, to lose stature. And stature, of course, is what he desperately seeks. It is precisely this search which frequently leads him to display a Napoleonic complex; to rule, to demean, to be in control. What should be noted is that when a family member utilizes condemnation as his prime mode of communication he may well be utilizing this avenue in order to meet another's needs in the family, i.e. submission (or again, a member may be submissive to meet the condemner's needs!). In any case, although the condemning individual is a very difficult person to live with, his penchant for controlling and ruling may be in response to the dependent needs of another or other family members.

Submission.   The submissive person is often a guilt-ridden individual who blames himself for the ills which befall him or his family. When a person chooses the submissive avenue of communication, he is in some measure surrendering to the environment.

Not uncommonly, family members learn to relate via condemnation to the person in the family who has a penchant for submissiveness. To illustrate, a husband comes home early on a given day and complains loudly, "Why do I have to wait two hours for supper?" Submissive wife: "We're having baked pork chops and they take a while."

HUSBAND: "But you know I often get home early on Monday! Christ, why didn't you plan something else? And why did you have to bake the chops? Why couldn't you just fry them?
WIFE: "Don't be angry, I'm sorry. Perhaps you're right. I probably planned badly. I should have known" . . . etc . . . etc . . . etc.

A more appropriate and consonant rebuttal to the condemning husband would have been something like, "Supper isn't ready dear, because
you didn't tell me you were coming home early."

The wife in the illustration was unable to make such a response
because she has acute feelings of self-doubt. She feels unworthy. Self-
doubt and feelings of unworthiness create an insatiable need for manifest
reassurance, if not affection. The irony is that this need to be liked blocks
the submissive family member's and other members' ability to meet the
self-esteem need. Why? Because the submissive avenue does not permit
taking a strong stand on an issue, does not permit adherence to strong
conviction whenever that conviction is going to anger another person.

The submissive person is motivated to avoid anger in himself (he's
not justified, he has no right to be angry) and especially in the other person
because of his constant need to be liked. The sum effect of these dynamics
is to make the submissive person feel even more inadequate.

The submissive method then, is to give in, to agree, to conciliate. As
noted, however, the motive is not so much to enhance others, to meet the
needs of others, as it is to get others' approval. Manifestly, the submissive
person is a giver. In truth, he's a taker. He's a taker because he's a leaner,
he's a dependent person. And he leans and depends because he doesn't
believe that he has much to give others.

To sum up then, the submissive person, like the condemner, is
difficult to live with. His feelings of ineptness and inadequacy put family
members under constant pressure to support, to guide, to direct, to lead
him. And again, when the dependency pressure becomes too demanding
the family members may well respond via condemnation. And ironically,
as was noted above under condemnation, this person's mode of communication may be partly in response to another family member's need to
condemn.

Intellectualization.   This avenue of communication focuses exclusively upon the rational, mental and intellectual faculties. The intellectualizer par excellence is the one who behaves and interacts as if he has no
emotions. Sometimes he even believes it! When confronted by a problem
he reviews it, takes notes, lists the possible results of one course of action
versus another. This person may or may not make a decision quickly. He
may or may not be efficient about implementing the decision. What
matters most to this individual is the *process* of reflection, review and
generally mulling over of a problem in a detached, unemotional way.

The constant problem for the intellectualizer is that his feelings,
recognized or not, do not always gibe with his actions. Stated another way,
sometimes the intellectualizer finds himself conflicted between rationality

and emotionality. He may not feel attracted to a boss, a worker, or a neighbor, but concludes that it is politic, profitable or important deliberately to prolong interaction with these people and to give the appearance of enjoying it. Some intellectualizers have even programmed themselves to be "professionally nice."

The most unfortunate aspect of intellectualization as an avenue of communication, especially within the family, is that it usually keeps people emotionally apart, emotionally distant. Typically, intellectualizers love to verbalize, love to talk, discuss, analyze and review. At the same time they have real difficulty relating emotionally. Intellectualization as a prime mode of communication within the family is unfortunate because it does very little to bring the family members closer together. Stated another way, it is not rationality which draws family members close to each other, it is positive emotions. Intellectualizers within the family are cool, calm, detached and aloof. Obviously they are not people whom one can easily snuggle up to.

At the same time let it be noted that intellectualization as a communicative mode can indeed meet basic needs. Intellectualizers usually shy away from emotions. And precisely for this reason intellectualizers are frequently attracted to intellectualizers. They marry and frequently meet each other's basic needs, especially security and love (in the sense of acceptance and somebody to belong to). It should be noted too, that in times of trial and turmoil the family member who can maintain a detached stance is often the one who can best help to maintain the family's emotional equilibrium.

It is when the intellectualizer and the non-intellectualizer (indeed a vivacious gregarious type) marry that problems in the reciprocal meeting of needs can arise. Again, sometimes a parent member *cultivates* the intellectualization avenue over time and thereby increases the tensions and raises familial anxiety. A not uncommon example is the young married couple in which one member works to support the other through college. Shortly after graduation they separate. The reasons once given to this author were: "I outgrew her." "He's so cold to me. he's no fun. he's so intellectual." "She's positively mindless." Enough said!

Indifference.   If there is any avenue which can be termed unhealthy it is this one. As an avenue of communication it can never enhance, but only threaten and demean. Indifference is founded upon fear, anger and /or a need to manipulate. When practiced, indifference violates basic psychological needs, both of the one who practices it and of the one who is the object of it. The author has learned that there are various behaviors practiced intra-familially which are designed to communicate indifference.

A common indifferent behavior is *silence*. One or some members do not talk to another member. This may last a short time (a few minutes) or a long time (days or weeks) depending upon the issue and the familial dynamics. The short lived silence is not uncommon in many families. A family may wish to shy away from vented anger for fear it may precipitate even more intense ire; they may have a penchant for intellectualization or, again, they may feel energetic enough at the moment to fight. It is for these reasons (there may well be others) that some families practice indifference as the lesser of two evils. Their emotional conviction apparently is: better silence than ranting, raging or behavioral violence.

Sometimes a situation arises which might be termed *quasi-indifference*. An example of this is the angry, non-talking wife who prepares a meal for her spouse, serves it to him but won't sit down and eat it with him. Such a person is conflicted about communicating or she wants to interact, but not too much!

Occasionally families become involved in *ignoring* behaviors. People talk, but icily or at least without their usual verve. At these times they avoid looking at each other. Their talk is only about what must be discussed (get bread and milk on the way home), and all conversation scrupulously avoids discussion even hinting at personal and/or important issues. It is during these times, too, that family members become involved in irrelevant tasks. The whole idea is to keep moving around. Don't sit still because if one were to sit still, he might have to deal with the real issues, namely with each other, our needs and how can we satisfy them.

A person who has studied communication within the family for a long time is Don Jackson. He believes that families can be categorized in terms of how they communicate. Families develop patterns of interaction which are unique to them. In the Jackson scheme the category into which a family fits is determined by how it defines its relationship via its communicative patterns. Jackson has outlined four categories: 1) a stable, satisfactory relationship; 2) an unstable, satisfactory relationship; 3) an unstable, unsatisfactory relationship; and 4) a stable unsatisfactory relationship.

The stable satisfactory relationship is one where consonance is the prime mode of communication. In such a relationship all parties are both cognizant and agree as to who is in control of the relationship. Jackson notes that, "a person defined as being in control of the relationship is the one who initiates action, decides what action will be initiated or establishes what areas within the relationship shall be controlled by the other person." Obviously people living in such a relationship as this have achieved an optimal homeostatic balance and do not ordinarily seek family therapy.

In the unstable satisfactory relationship there are longer periods of instability than in the preceding relationship, but there are rewarding periods of stability also. The instability is usually precipitated by external or internal forces. Jackson offers as an illustration a girl who is experiencing the onset of puberty. She seeks to relate in a more adult, womanly way both to her friends and to her mother. The mother, however, seeks to keep her daughter's behavior child-like because she does not want to be criticized by her friends or is afraid of feminine competition at home, and so on. The problem here, observes Jackson, is again one of definition and control, i.e. the girl wants to define the relationship with her mother along the lines of two women of equal status, the mother along the lines of mother-child. The unstable satisfactory relationship then is one which is affected by new events and changes. The instability will continue in the new relationship until all of the parties have mutually arrived at and accepted the definition of the relationship. Examples of this include: partners working together in a new business and a retired grandparent coming to live with a nuclear family. This type of relationship or situation is the one which is most receptive to and benefits most from family therapy.

In the unstable unsatisfactory relationship there is constant instability because there is no agreement as to who is in control of the relationship and because the family members feel compelled to redefine the relationship as soon as a modicum of stability is achieved. Communication between and among the members may be characterized by psychosomatic illnesses and complaints. This occurs, Jackson notes, because such messages "can be denied as messages," and can serve as irrelevant topics of conversation, i.e. "Oh, my head hurts so," complains the wife. "You poor thing," commiserates her husband, "How long have you had it?" etc. A common form of communication in this relationship is submission characterized by a synthetic unconcerned deference. The problem is that this avenue is travelled by the principal parties at the same time. Condemnation is utilized, but again, at the same time. The effect of their communicative maneuvers is to keep the relationship undefined and in a constant state of flux. This family is resistant to therapy and especially to achieving a more fruitful homeostatic balance. Their equilibrium seems to be premised upon one member of the family being sick—all the time. His recovery invariably poses a considerable threat to one or more of those viewed as well. That there be a sick member in the family (he can even be hospitalized) is crucially important to the familial dynamics.

In the stable unsatisfactory relationship people have agreed never to confront one another about who is in charge or even about their respective behavior. The effect of this is a relationship in which no one has invested very much emotionally. The mode of communication in this family is indifference characterized by silence and much ignoring behavior. The relationship is termed stable precisely because all the members ignore potential areas of dissatisfaction with the relationship. The manifest stability then is plastic, or better, cosmetic. Real, honest feelings, concerns and unhappinesses are not discussed, are not even emitted. To outsiders the relationship may seem ideal, to insiders it is at best indifferent. Jackson notes that within this kind of relationship there is much rigidity and compulsivity. External authorities, law and order, and organized ritual are held in the highest esteem by the principal parties. Why? Because these externals provide them with the opportunity not to focus upon the intrafamilial relationships. Families in this category are very difficult to deal with in therapy because the members have conditioned themselves to their own or another member's behavior. Quite apparently, unless such resistance is broken down, therapy can not successfully proceed.

CITATIONS

1. Bateson, G., Jackson, D. D., Haley, J., and Weakland, J. H., "Toward a Theory of Schizophrenia."*Behavioral science,* Vol. 1, October, 1956, pp. 251–264.

2. Bateson, G., "Slippery Theories." *International Journal of Psychiatry,* Vol 2, 1966, pp. 415–417

3. Clausen, J., and Kohn, M. L., "Social Relations and Schizophrenia: A Research Report and a Perspective." In *Etiology of Schizophrenia,* ed. Jackson, D. D. New York: Basic Books, 1960.

4. DeRivera, J., "A Structural Theory of the Emotions." *Psychological Issues,* Vol. 10, No. 4, 1977, p. 34.

5. Ekman, P., and Friesen, W. V., "Non-verbal Leakage and Clues to Deception." *Psychiatry,* Vol. 32, 1969, pp. 88–105.

6. Freud, S., *A General Introduction to Psychoanalysis,* New York: Perma Grants, 1949, pp. 25–71.

7. Haley, J., "Family Experiments: A New Type of Experimentation." In *Communication in Family and Marriage,* ed. Jackson, D. D. Palo Alto, Cal.: Science and Behavior Books, Inc. 1968, pp. 262–263.

8. Jackson, D. D., "Family Interaction, Family Homeostasis and Some

Implications for Conjoint Family Psychotherapy." *Therapy Communication and Change*, Vol. 2, Palo Alto, Cal.: Science and Behavior Books, Inc., 1968, p. 193

9. Kendon, A., "How People Interact." In *The Book of Family Therapy*, eds. Ferber, A., Mendelsohn, M., and Napier, A., 1972.

10. Knight, P. H., and Blair, C. K., "Degree of Client Comfort as a Function of Dyadic Interaction Distance." *Journal of Counseling Psychology*, Vol. 23, No. 1, 1976, pp 13–16.

11. Maslow, A., *Motivation and Personality*, 2nd edition. New York: Harper and Row, 1970.

12. Perez, J. F., *The Initial Counseling Contract, Guidance Mono.* Series, Series II. Boston: Houghton Mifflin, 1968, pp 14–19.

13. Rioch, D., "The Sense and the Noise." *Psychiatry*, Vol. 24, 1961, pp. 7–18.

14. Satir, V., "You As a Change Agent in Helping Families to Change." In *Helping Families to Change*, eds. Satir, V., Stachowiak, J., and Taskman, H. New York: Jason Aronson, Inc., 1975, pp. 41–49.

15. Satir, V., "You As a Change Agent in Helping Families to Change." In *Helping Families to Change*, eds. Satir, V., Stachowiak, J., and Taskman, H. New York: Jason Aronson, Inc., 1975, p. 41.

16. Schauble, P. G., and Hill, C. G., "A Laboratory Approach to Treatment in Marriage Counseling: Training in Communication Skills." *The Family Coordinator*, Vol. 25, July 1976, No. 3.

17. Stone, G., and Morden, C.,"Effect of Distance on Verbal Productivity." *Journal of Counseling Psychology*, Vol. 23, No. 5, pp. 486–488.

18. Szasz, T. S., *The Myth of Mental Illness*. New York: Harper and Row, 1961, p. 302.

19. Watzlawick, P., "A Review of Double Bind Theory." *Family Process 2*, No. 1, March 1963, pp. 132–153.

Chapter 5
The Family in Therapy

The family which enters therapy is one which has been termed dysfunctional. The equilibrium which this family has achieved is at best acutely painful. What is ironic but not surprising about the dysfunctional family is that it often does not know how it got to the point of needing help. Most of the family members recognize that something is drastically wrong, especially if there is an identified patient. Most too, however, are at a loss to explain convincingly, or at times even rationally, how or why the acute problems arose. And when there are opinions (more frequently there are), those of one member of a dysfunctional family almost never gibe with those of another. If they do gibe, all too often it is only so that the majority in the family can displace their frustrations upon the hapless I.P. The effect of all this is to compound bewilderment in the family and even worse, to confound communication among its members.

What is also true about these families is that they vary sharply in their respective states. Brown and Manela (1977) found that the needs of the families treated were considerably different because the marriages were in varying states of dissolution. What these two researchers found, then, was that families differ considerably in what they seek from the therapist, i.e. while some might seek to obtain an optimal equilibrium, others sought only to obtain a functional one and still others sought support to divorce.

The reasons which lead to an insupportable homeostasis, of course, vary. The I.P., if there is one, may no longer be able or willing to fulfill his role of the manifest familial symptom. Or it may be that one of the parents does not want to function in a leadership role. Or again, communication between and among family members has broken down. Reasons such as these lead a family into therapy.

Perhaps the most comprehensive research on the dysfunctional family was accomplished by Stachowiak (1975). In a ten-year longitudinal study he found that dysfunctional families exhibited these kinds of symptoms:

1. an inability to plan and carry out tasks and resolve problems together (low productivity).
2. an inability to develop effective leadership patterns, i.e. whoever was leading the family was not generally supported by other family members.
3. expression of conflict was extreme, i.e. there was either too much or too little.
4. a generalized inability to communicate clearly.

A family's entry into therapy for the first time has to be a novel experience. The therapist knows that there are certain unique factors operating at the initial session. Most apparent is the fact that the therapist and the family are unknowns to each other. They are strangers. Add to this the fact that the family does not know what to expect, and one can see the stage has been set for the development and perhaps display of high anxiety.

The therapist is very much aware that family members vary in their emotional reactions to the initial session. To one of the members (often the father) being present may be an admission of failure, impotence and/or incompetence; to another, it might be a relief; to a third, a threat. A veritable kaleidoscope of feelings may well be present then, at the initial session. Guilt, indifference, anger, resentment, suspicion and fear are all common feelings among members when they enter into therapy for the first time.

Finally, this bewildering climate may be made even more complex by a not uncommon belief among new clients in family therapy. This is the belief that the therapist is some kind of doctor (more accurately, witch doctor) with magic potions or better, a magic wand, which he need only wave to effect a miraculous cure. In short, the expectancy systems and the perceptual climate in the initial session are a veritable emotional melange.

Following are reports written by six individuals who were in family therapy. The first two individuals were patients of the author, the others were not. All the individuals were asked to respond to the following questions:

1. Describe conditions within the family before therapy.
2. Describe conditions within the family after therapy.
3. What, if anything did you find out about yourself in relation to the family?

There were no restrictions or mandates imposed regarding the length of the reports. The six individuals were asked only to answer the questions to the best of their recollections and as completely as they could. The respondents were told that their identities would be kept secret.

CASE I

Father—sports editor, small newspaper,
33 years old, 1 child 9 years old, boy

Before Therapy

Before therapy all my wife and I did was fight. What we fought about was my work. According to her I worked too much and too often. I felt I had to. She felt I wanted to. What I saw was that she resented my working mostly because she felt I enjoyed it. And I did enjoy it. I enjoyed playing the current season sport one night a week and I enjoyed watching sports on T.V. on week-ends.

What I realize now was that it wasn't my work or sports that we fought about. It was that I neglected her and I neglected our son. Looking back on that time I wonder at my own insensitivity! I simply had no idea of the negative effect which my behavior had on my wife.

When we weren't fighting, we weren't talking either. The pattern was simple prolonged physical absence from home, bitter fights (when we *both* raged), icy silence (mostly my wife), and a short-lived reconciliation which I would bring about by phone calls from the office and flowers and goodies which I had delivered to the house.

Except for the short-term reconciliations life at home was hardly what a person would call comfortable, pleasant or emotionally elevating. It was to put it simply, depressing. It was depressing for me, for my wife and it had to be hell for our nine year old. The kid never saw me and when he did I was fighting with his mother. It was depressing and it was scary too.

I think we would have continued like that (depressingly) if our boy had not started wetting and soiling the bed. After seeing two general practitioners we were referred to Perez.

After Therapy

Our problems were not as bad as we had imagined them. All we needed were five sessions. Things are much better because we agreed on a schedule that I'm able to keep about 85% of the time. The three of us have breakfast and dinner together.

I spend only one evening away from home for me. I couldn't give up my membership in the town leagues. That's the only night I'm out alone. It's good exercise which I need, and I keep tabs on what's going on athletically in town. My wife and son come watch me play.

We talk a lot now. I'd forgotten how pleasant it can be to talk regularly with my wife without fighting. Our son doesn't soil the bed anymore and wets very infrequently (only once in the past three weeks).

Things are better because I gave and my wife gave. She never cottoned to sports much and before, like she said, they took me away from the family. Now I've arranged to spend meals and hours with both of them every day. She gave too. She brings our boy to watch me play and she signed him up for Little League!

About Me:

What I learned about me was that I had abdicated my role in the family not only as a father but as a family member who can enhance the others. That's what therapy showed me about me. I was scared about being needed, about being the family "caretaker." I discovered I can give to my family.

People need people, especially in the family. My wife and my son need me. Once I got to appreciate that and that I can do it it was all easy, even cutting down on my outside committments. What I learned is that my basic committment is to my family.

Like my wife asked me in therapy, "What's all the glory and money worth if we make each other sick?" Our son was the "identified patient." He was because my wife and I made each other sick. We "sickees" made him even sicker than us.

Thank God, it all worked out O.K. finally. I've learned something else about me. I like being needed.

CASE II
*Mother I—Secretary, 37 years old, 3
children 2 girls, 1 boy*

Before Therapy:

Before family therapy we were a group of people being maintained, directed and controlled by a loving man but a man who was none the less a despot. I, being the only other adult member of this group, became the buffer, interpreter and fighter for the children, myself and for the leader. I seemed to spend endless time explaining to this one about that one. Who did what and why and how and when. Constant interpretation all around. I felt caught in a gigantic maelstorm, being pulled under, and I did sink——into alcoholism, the most frightening period of mine and my family's life. That's what brought us into family therapy—alcoholism and its consequent pain.

After Therapy:

Since family therapy there is much more openness. Each member is more verbal with each other member. (We were never a silent family, but now I encourage all members to tell it "like it is" to whomever needs to hear it). I find myself saying less and less during a discussion (and when I do it's direct and to the point.) There seems to be a tremendous storm, words fly this way and that, then a *very perceptible* feeling of relief; the air literally is clear and good. All of us exclaim things like: "Wow, that was something!" "Hey, Dad, I love you." "Ma, you're the greatest!" "You kids are really great!" "What would I do without you?" "You're worth it!" Unimportant traditions have been discarded; significant family values have become more meaningful because each member has fought for and/or shared in the process of accepting or rejecting that tradition or value.

We are now, in fact, like many pieces of iron. We are put through fire, melted, shaped, fused, soldered and we cool to a solid mass. We have "fought the good fight" and it has made us strong.

About Me:

Family therapy; I should really toss out the word 'therapy' and I will. The family, my family, our family, *this* family has made me feel so secure, loved, protected, admired, respected and wanted that I am very confident, honest and competent most of the time in whatever I do. This family makes me realize that love is a pain in the neck and I really could do without it sometimes, but there really isn't another thing in this life so worthy of my commitment.

CASE III
*Girl—13 years old, mother, father, and
one sister—fraternal twin*

Before Therapy:

Before therapy I was always sick. Betty who is my twin sister was always healthy. She is also smarter in school and she is much prettier than I am. I'm the one who everyone picked on—my father, my mother and my sister always picked on me. Sometimes I had the feeling my parents, especially my mother really, hated me. All the stories which she told about me and Betty when we were babies always described me as the jerk, the cry baby, the sick one, the spoiled one, the bad one.

Before therapy I always seemed to be falling, spilling, dropping, tripping. A regular clumsy ox, that was me. And when I did fall, spill, drop or trip I'd hear from Mom, Dad or Betty, sometimes from all three about what an ass I was. At supper I didn't dare carry anything from the kitchen to the dining room because I was scared I'd spill it.

About three years ago Mom stopped dressing us like we were identicals because obviously we weren't. Anyway, Betty and I started combing and doing our own hair our own way. Betty usually got compliments. I usually got yelled at. One line I'll never forget was "Why do you do that to yourself? What are you, the original ugly duckling?" Sometimes she called me that in anger, sometimes would you believe it, lovingly?

My problems really started about a year ago when I started gaining a lot of weight. I got to the point where I weighed 35 pounds more than my sister who's the same height as me. Mom and Dad and Betty nagged me all the time about being fat. My father told me I looked like a walrus, my mother a blimp (whatever that is) and my sister just a regular fat-ass. See, I live in a real skinny family with a gorgeous mother and sister and a father who runs two miles every day and brags he still fits into his old army uniform. It was funny, the more they nagged, teased and yelled the hungrier I got. I think it was Ma who got us into therapy.

After Therapy:

Things are better now. We went for seven sessions. I think Dr. Perez wanted us to go longer. Daddy was getting a little sick of the time it took. (I think he was getting sicker about the money it was costing.) But things are better. I think it was the second session that did it. Dr. Perez asked me and Betty to role play each other. Mom started to cry, even Daddy did. I have to admit I got a lot of satisfaction from doing that. Betty was great as me, just great! Especially when she said, "You and Ma just like to gang up on me because you're ashamed of me. Sometimes I think you want me dead cause I don't act as beautiful or as phony as the two of you." Mom almost passed out.

Ever since that session Mom and me and Betty have been closer, especially me and Betty. Betty and Mom never tease me or nag me about eating. Dad still does a little, but only a little. But what are fathers for? P.S. I only weigh 12 pounds more than Betty now.

About Me:

What I learned is that I can be me and be O.K. Dr. Perez asked me at one point, "Is your worth tied up to how you think you compare to Betty?" I thought about that for weeks. The answer is no. I'm me and I don't have to be an ox or an ugly duckling either. I have a bachelor uncle (my mother's brother) who embarrasses everybody (especially my father and mother), but whom I love. He's so natural and honest. When he heard we'd been in family therapy because of my problems (which I got from others I know now) he exploded at my mother. I'll never forget his words, "For Christ's sakes Margaret, she looks just like you did at her age. Just like you, spitting image. Why would you want to bug her? Didn't you like yourself? Or are you afraid of competition?" I learned a lot from my uncle's words, almost as much as I did from the therapy. Aside from the fact that there's a good future as far as how I'm gonna look someday. I don't know how important that is. What's more important is how I'm going to look at myself. How I'm going to like *myself*. See his comment and his question, "Didn't you like yourself?" reminded me about the surprising things which Mom said in therapy about being an ugly duckling. "Think beautiful swan inside, the outside will take care of itself." Dr. Perez wrote that on my birthday card. I'm working at it.

CASE IV
Father—47 years old, 2 children in college
one 9 year old, wife runs dress shop, minor
executive in chemical plant.

Before Therapy:

We've been married for 23 years now. For the last three years my wife has been managing a dress shop. I used to think that our troubles started when she went out to work. I realize now they started long before that.

For 20 years we never had an important fight. We never even talked loud. Everyone did as I expected. By everybody, I mean my wife Joyce and the two older kids. Our house was not child-centered. It was not mother-centered either. It was me-centered. I led and everybody followed.

Then Joyce went to work, at my urging. She needed to work because we had two kids in expensive colleges. After she went to work everything changed. She'd come home tired and began to complain about having to take care of the house. I didn't think too much about it at the time. I figured these were the usual problems associated with the working mother. Joyce told me I should help. I did. And a funny thing happened. I began to do more and more and she, less and less. She began to work evenings, then she was promoted to manager. I saw her less and less, sometimes only two or three evenings per week. The one who suffered the most was the baby, now nine years old.

We weren't a family anymore. The older kids were gone off to college. My wife was gone off to work. I felt like I was going off—the edge. I was scared. I was alone every night with just the baby. It was lonely, very lonely. I began to drink and too much. Then Joyce asked me for a divorce. I refused and she went to our lawyer, a friend of over twenty years. He recommended we see a counselor. We did.

After Therapy:

I've changed. Therapy changed me. But I was ready for the change. What I realize now is that I went into therapy wanting to change. Joyce started to change before therapy.

What I learned in therapy is that for twenty years Joyce leaned on me. She got her self-esteem from my achievements. I directed and controlled her life. As I listened to her say things like this in the sessions, I knew it was all true. One of the more poignant moments of all the sessions for me was when she described how utterly lonely she'd been for so many years, how unloved she felt and how incredibly bored she'd been for twenty years as a housekeeper, mother and wife. I believe it. I'd spent only three years alone and I'd nearly cracked up.

It's different now. It's different mostly because now we share everything from babysitting to housework to sex. Sometimes now I lean. Sometimes she leans. She directs, I follow. I direct, she follows. Now we support each other. It's different and it's good.

About Me:

As I wrote above I'm a changed person. The biggest change I think is in my give and take. I used to think that I was giving when I directed, when

I controlled. No. It's not like that. I was taking.What I've learned is that a father, and husband, gives to his family when he lets, no when he encourages them to make their own decisions for their personal lives. What I learned about me is that I can do that and be happy, no, be happier.

What came as a pleasant surprise for me is that Joyce and the two older kids and the youngest, they are all or at least they seem to be, better people. At least they seem to be more content with the changed me. I know I am.

As I've become more tolerant about them, I've become more tolerant about me. I don't constantly have to prove to them or to me that I'm competent, in control and good. I guess the best indication of that is that I don't feel the need to win every argument, that I'm the boss when we all get together at holidays, that everything I touch is just so, perfect.

I'm just another person with some uniquely fine points and many foibles. I love and am loved by my family. I've got at least three good friends. Recently I learned that I'm known generally as a guy who tries real hard at whatever I do.

"He tried real hard at whatever he did." I'd be content with that as my epitaph.

CASE V
Mother—Nurse, 41 years old, 3 children, all girls

Before Therapy:

If we had not gone into therapy I'm sure we'd be divorced now and I just don't know where the children would be, with him or me, maybe split up, I don't know. My life was very, very lonely before therapy. My husband came home late at night. He always "worked" late. I thought he might be "fooling around." I since learned he wasn't, but thinking that he did had the same effect as if he was. I literally began wasting away, inside and outside.

At first I'd wait up till eleven o'clock and even later for him just to talk to him, but we never seemed to be able to talk. He'd be too tired and simply go to bed. I'd get more depressed and more frustrated. Like the books say, there was no communication. There were no fights, no recriminations. There was simply nothing. After a while, I just gave up and went to bed early, before he came home. Our bedroom, incidently, was a sleeping room, period.

There was no communication between us parents. My daughters

spoke to me in put-down tones, except the youngest who's always been affectionate. I felt hapless, helpless and just plain hopeless, as a woman, as a mother and as a human being.

Our life as a family was drab, dreary and dull. It was also terribly depressing. What brought things to a head was when my youngest daughter was sent home from school drunk. That scared us more than anything. We went to see the guidance counselor. One thing led to another and we all went into therapy.

After Therapy:

We communicate now or at least we're all not so secretive. I learned that I was as bad as the others in not talking. "Mom, all you ever did was just look so mournful! You never asked me or any of us for help. And you didn't do anything about anything." I was like that! That's really the difference between before and after.

I, *we all* do things. My daughters help—cook, clean and wash, where formerly I did everything—very late. This help, this pitching makes me feel like I'm part of a family.

The best part is my husband and me. He's home for supper every night and goes out to the work he so loves only two evenings a week and he's home by 10 P.M. Now, we use the bedroom for more than just sleeping. I mention that for a reason. I learned in therapy that a person's sex life often reflects her general life. Life for me anyway has become exciting. A man and a woman have a wonderful capacity to make each other's lives exciting.

About Me:

The most important thing I discovered about myself in therapy is that I really can make my children and my husband happier. It's such a basic thing. How come I didn't know it before? I don't know. I discovered it late in life, but like they say better late than never! And I learned something else just as important, that I have a capacity to make their lives miserable. How awful, but how true! It's so much more fun making others happy. I'm grateful I get my kicks that way and not the other!

I've discovered something else too. When you work toward another person's happiness you get an awful lot of respect. My daughters, my husband respect me. I see it in their eyes, their tones. I enjoy it!

CASE VI
Boy—16 years old, single parent (mother) and one sister

Before Therapy:

Before we went into therapy I was never home. I was never home because I didn't want to be. Our house was a mess. It was messy cause it looked like a pig sty (and I'm not exactly the Mr. Kleen type), but mostly it was a mess because of Ma and how she acted.

After Dad died a year ago, Ma fell apart. She fell apart completely. It's kind of scary when a mother falls apart. She didn't clean up anymore, she didn't cook our meals, she never did a wash. She never did anything. The house was a mess. A rotten mess.

Ma was a mess. She started drinking. Jean and I couldn't figure out when she started doing it. Doesn't matter. Drink had two, no three effects on Ma. She'd scream like fury at me or Jeanie; or she'd cry her eyes out moaning about how she got screwed in this life; or three, she'd go to sleep. Jeanie and I were always praying for number three.

So that's why I was never home. Jeanie went to the alcoholic clinic in town to get help for Ma and the three of us ended up going into therapy.

The only good that came out of the time before therapy was that Jeanie and I stopped fighting like we'd done all the time before Dad died. We even got sort of close. We used to eat lunch together in school and we'd stay up evenings once in a while commiserating. There's nothing like an alcoholic parent to bring kids together and to make them mature.

After Therapy:

Ma stopped drinking. It's like a new world. Order has returned to our house and to our three lives. She cooks, cleans and washes, but she alone doesn't do these things. The three of us do them. Sometimes we do do them alone, sometimes we do them together. (I got so I like getting supper.)

Ma went back to work as a secretary. I know that helped her even though she comes in around five bitching sometimes. Her bitching is different now though, there's a kind of humor in it. Last night she described her boss as an old fart. Jeanie asked her why is he an old fart. Ma just looked at her and said, "He makes a stink wherever he goes!" Anyway, Ma's better so we're all better.

Jeanie and I learned that we had to help her rather than condemn. We were always condemning her, putting her down. My father used to do that to her. I picked that up from him strong. Jeanie picked it up only a little. Anyways we didn't help Ma much after his death. We hurt her an awful lot. The hurt we gave her and the fact that she never thought she was too much is the combo which led her to find solution in Seagram's 7.

So now all three of us understand better. We talk and we're all much closer. Although I think Jeanie's the one who's closer to Ma. I don't mind that. I'm just so real glad when I see the two of them especially Ma laughing over something. It makes me feel real good.

About Me:

This past year has changed me. The therapy we went through helped the change (I think for the better). The therapy helped me appreciate and understand the hell my mother was living in. Therapy helped me see things better. I got so I think I got to see a little bit like Ma and Jeanie saw things, especially people, especially me.

What I learned is that my mother and Jeanie are really important to me and I'm important to them. I used to be embarrassed about kissing Ma and especially Jeanie. I'm not even a little bit embarrassed about it now, inside or outside. I guess I'm not embarrassed about it because I know they both like it. That's one of the things I learned from therapy, that there's no embarrassment when you know that something you do for somebody makes them happy.

So what I've learned, maybe I'm only starting to learn, cause I'm only sixteen, is that I can love and I can help others. What's true too is that there are times that I also need to be loved and helped.

As was pointed out at the beginning of the chapter there are certain common denominators in the behavior and life style of the dysfunctional family. These common denominators seem to be confirmed when we examine the self reports. A careful scrutiny of the six responses to the first question indicates in a pretty clear fashion that before therapy the families described themselves as:

1. incompetent intra-familially. They were quite unable to solve mutual problems. Their interactions were characterized by marked insensitivity or inability to meet each other's basic psychological needs.

2. non-supportive of each other. This was especially true of those in parental roles. Trust apparently was a rare commodity intra-familially.

3. intensely conflicted. The reactions to the conflict oscillated from one end of the emotional continuum to the other, from vitriolic anger to indifference.

4. uncommunicative. Verbal interaction was characterized by negative responsiveness or unresponsiveness. Little or no concern was shown to relate to each other in any meaningful emotional way.

   These first four findings gibe perfectly with Stachowiak's research with dysfunctional families discussed above. There are more observations however, which can be made about these one-time emotionally imbalanced families.

5. The emotional climate seemed generally gloomy. A general sense of despair seemed to be the constant companion of the respondents. This despair was complemented by feelings of boredom and loneliness.

6. The members seemed oblivious to the impact which their behavior had on one another. Members seemed to be emotionally isolated from one another.

7. Often family members lived with a sense of fear and/or constraint.

The descriptions of family life after therapy also contain elements of uniformity. These include:

1. A sense of increased personal and familial competence.

2. Mutual support and trust seem to have improved.

3. Interactions seem to have become more rewarding with the abatement of conflict and the consequent removal of stress.

4. Verbal, behavioral and emotional communication seemed characterized by consonance.

5. The emotional climate seemed happier, more optimistic.

6. An increased awareness of one's place in the family and the effect which one has on the others.

7. A sense of vibrancy and increased motivation for intra-familial participation.

8. Freedom from fear and constraint.

9. Optimism permeates the view of the family and life in general.

The responses to the third question (p.56) also contain two common elements. Thus, all six individuals indicated that they had grown personally in two significant areas:

1. self-esteem
    and
2. the ability to give of self.

In short, family therapy was a positive enhancing experience for the respondents. It was such because the respondents felt the family became more sensitive to and responsive to their basic psychological needs. In addition, their own respective awareness of the needs of others was broadened and confidence in their ability to meet the needs of other family members was increased.

THE FAMILY RUSSO—TRIAD, DYAD AND THE I.P.

The case which follows is about a three member family which the author had in therapy for approximately six months. It is included here because it exemplifies well how acutely dynamics can be interwoven and needs confounded within the familial triad and the parental dyad within that triad. The case is included also because it shows how a hapless third party (the I.P. in this case) can also be the one who precipitates acute turmoil by acting out and thereby ironically helps to effect a more healthful familial homeostasis.

The family is composed of the father, Michael, age 44; mother, Ann, 42 and their daughter Nancy, 14. Michael and Ann have been married for twenty years. He is a self-taught auto mechanic and the owner of a service station. His wife is a school teacher who returned to work about five years ago.

Their respective descriptive histories of family life before therapy follow. The question I asked each to respond to was this:

"Explain what life was like among the three of you before therapy. Include the events of early years if you think they are relevant."

Michael's was drawn from a cassette tape and edited, but only for syntax. The others were written. The therapy session is in part an edited tape interview and in part reconstructed from the author's memory.

Before Therapy: Michael

We went in to see Perez because things were really bad at home. They'd been bad for a long, long time. My wife Ann was the one who called him. She wanted to for a long time. I didn't 'cause even though I'd heard about going for family help to a "shrink," I'd never done it before and nobody I know ever did either. I was born, raised and lived all my life right here in the South End. It's what people call "Little Italy." We never go for help. Anyways, Ann called.

Things had become real bad because Ann and me had become what you call, "distant." We either didn't talk or we yelled. Mostly Ann yelled. She yelled at our kid Nancy, but mostly she yelled at me. Sometimes I thought she was cracking up.

We started becoming really distant about five years ago. Ann went to work or rather she went back to work as a teacher. I didn't like the idea 'cause Nancy was only nine years old, but Ann made such a stink over it I went along with it. Well, once she started working things went from bad to worse. Although to tell the truth they were never that good between us.

We got married twenty years ago. Ann wanted a baby right away. Well, we didn't have one right away. Months and years went by and she didn't get pregnant. For a while I was really starting to worry about it. We got so we fought about it. Then she went to the doctor and found out it was her fault. She had a "tipped uterus." I never knew exactly what it meant. All I knew was that I didn't have it. It's a helluva thing to say but I was glad it was her and not me. I'm sure she would've drove me crazy if I couldn't have made a kid for her. Anyways, she had an operation and got pregnant within a couple of months.

That pregnancy was something else. She had morning sickness, afternoon sickness and night sickness. I mean she milked it for all it was worth. She drove me crazy. I mean, having a baby is no big deal in our family. My grandmother had eleven kids, my mother had seven. Every one of my five sisters had at least three, one had six, Hey! Kids is what life's all about. When I found out Ann was pregnant I was really happy, 'cause I wanted a kid too. But I swear to God by the time four months had gone by I almost wished she wasn't pregnant. That's how bad it got! She stopped working after she was only three months gone. She said she didn't feel good. She crawled into bed and never got out of it as far as I could see. She never worked or cleaned. My mother had to come and do that. I couldn't sleep with her for the rest of the pregnancy. She just lay there like a big blob and got real fat. She gained about 35 pounds.

After the baby came it was worse. All the attention went to the baby. I didn't mind it at first, but it started to become a drag. She just refused to have me in bed until we had a real blow-out and I belted her. She straightened out after that, kept the house clean and we slept together.

Things sort of lingered along for about nine years and then she called up and got a job as a substitute teacher. I didn't mind that too much, 'cause she seemed better with me and Nancy. Then she took a job full-time. That's when things started to go real bad. She started to treat me like she did after Nancy was born, like I was in the way. If I went near her, just to talk even, all she said was, "Leave me alone." She treated Nancy bad too. Poor kid didn't know which way to go. It's a good thing she had a lot of aunts and cousins to play with. At least that's what I thought.

To be honest about it what bothered me most about Ann was that I know everybody in the family (my sisters mostly) talked about her and felt sorry for me. Ann never got along with my sisters or my mother. See, Ann's real pretty but she's not Italian. I think that combination has caused a lot of problems, for her and for me. All the women in the family are jealous of her because she's the prettiest and everybody puts her down for not being Italian. But it's not all the family's fault either.

She never tried to understand me or my family. A lot of times I swear to God I was ready to divorce her, but nobody ever got divorced in our family and Ann's too much of a Catholic. I don't know what else to tell you except it wasn't much of a marriage or much of a family life before we went into therapy

Perez's note. What is most curious about this taped account, made after the therapy, is that Michael never mentions what precipitated the family's entry into therapy.

Before Therapy: Ann

Many times for the past twenty years I wondered why I married Michael. What I've finally learned is that I married him because he was handsome (still is I think) and because I was supposed to get married. During the past couple of years I've realized that I never should have married. I'm more suited to being alone. Please understand, I'm not so unhappy now about it all. It's just that I've grown up enough to realize that I could have gone another route and probably been a lot happier at least for the past twenty years.

How were things before therapy? They were awful, almost intolerable. Ours was not a marriage, it was more like an alliance and a distant alliance at that.

The cards were stacked against us, mostly me, right from the start. We never should have gone to live in the South End. I'm auburn haired, blue eyed, and those physical traits are enough to make you look very different from anybody else around here, especially in this family. From the beginning I stood out, and I was never used to nor did I like standing out. In fact, I was considered and consider myself shy. I still do, for that matter.

I was the only child from a quiet, unemotional family. Both my parents died in an auto accident when I was still in college. My name was Kelly, but we didn't consider ourselves "Irish." At least my father wasn't one of those professional American Irishman that crawl out of the woodwork every year on St. Patrick's Day. We were quiet, American, but very much Roman Catholic. And then I met and married Michael whose family is so Italian, no, Sicilian, that at times I became sickened by it. I remember once when my father-in-law introduced me to some strangers (at Nancy's christening yet) as, "a pretty Irish lady who becoma' Siciliana by injectionia." A few moments later I withdrew to the bathroom and threw up.

It isn't just that they're so uncouth and gruff. It's that they are so damned *loud*. They cry loud, laugh loud, talk loud. They even sleep loud! (We went to the beach once with some of Michael's relatives for a week. I didn't sleep the whole week between the snores and the farts!)

There was so much to adjust to in Michael. I thought I was marrying into a Catholic family but discovered after the fact that I'd married into a family of pagans. They seldom went to church, gave only pennies to the collection basket and ridiculed the priest (who was Irish). All of this was pretty much of a shock for me because I'd been brought up a strict Catholic (almost like a Methodist I've learned). I went to only Catholic schools, including college.

College was also a problem between us. Michael had never gone. I think he's come to resent that. When we first met and right after we were married he used to brag about the fact that I was a college graduate to his friends. Then he stopped and he hasn't done it since.

We used to fight so much. I think we did at first because I unconsciously felt my identity was being eroded. I rebelled against being placed into a mold—cook, cleaner and chief bottle washer, or as they put it in Italian, "chiesa, cocina e 'childreni" (church, kitchen and children). Those were the woman's functions. I rebelled.

I wanted a baby desperately when I was first married. I realize now I did not so much for myself or the baby but just to prove to myself and to the whole family of Russos that I, too, was a woman.

When we were first married sex sickened me. (It doesn't now.) I guess it scared me more than anything else. Anyway I didn't like it. But I really tried to get pregnant and when I didn't I became very tense. It became a vicious circle. At first the problem was diagnosed as a "tipped uterus," then just simple anxiety. I didn't have Nancy until we'd been married over five years. Believe me, Michael's family let me know that.

We went into therapy because of Nancy, no I've learned better. We went into therapy because Michael and I were, or at least acted, incompatibly. Nancy was our scapegoat, at least she was for me. After she was born I found I couldn't work anymore. I'd never realized how much I enjoyed teaching until I couldn't do it anymore. I can still remember rinsing off a diaper in the toilet and thinking, 'Dear God four years of college for this!' I stayed home for eleven years and damned near lost my sanity.

My life improved dramatically when I returned to work. I threw myself into it body and soul. I've always had a real fear of failing (although I never have failed), so I really did work eighty hours a week. (Many teachers claim that but very few do it.) The result was that the house went to pot. Laundry, cleaning, cooking, went undone. Michael began to blow-up. I ignored it. Then he began to make himself scarce. I was happy about that. He wasn't around to bother me. He'd always worked too many hours at the garage, but now he never came home, not even for supper. That was unusual. In our worst days he'd always insisted on eating supper with me. I could have cared less. But there was Nancy. She cared. She started taking her meals at her grandmother's then at her aunt's houses. That bothered me at first. I forced myself not to think about Nancy being supervised by my in-laws, who I know gossiped about my inadequacy as a mother. I decided I was not going to let Michael's sisters ruin my teaching career. I needed my time to prepare my classes. And when Nancy wasn't home I could do it better. So I didn't check on her always when she didn't show up for supper.

It was four months ago that we found out that she was pregnant.

We went into therapy.

Before Therapy: Nancy

My life was awful before we went to see Dr. Perez. It was awful mostly because my mother was a bitch all the time to me. I was a bitch to her and my father was never home. Before we went into therapy I really and sincerely believed I hated my mother. It was for a lot of reasons but mostly I guess it was because of the phoney way she used to act. She never told it like it was. I was almost ten before I found out that she usually meant the opposite of what she said. I never knew what mother really wanted. Like she'd say, 'Be home by three o'clock.' What she really meant was I could get home by five o'clock on Tuesday, Wednesday and Thursday because she had to prepare lesson plans. If I got home a minute after three on Monday and Friday she went crazy. I always felt like I was walking on pins and needles with her because I was nervous and I hated her for that. She always put everybody down, my grandparents, my aunts, me and especially my father. I hated her because there was no love in her, or so I thought. She never used to say anything nice to me or to daddy. She was so unhappy. I guess I hated her for that too.

What a difference between my house and all the others in the family. When I walked into my gloomy house from school the very best I ever got from her was a bitchy hello (honest, Ma could say hello in a bitchy way). When I walked into my grandparents house it was so different! It was like the walls were oozing sunshine. All I got was hugs and kisses and goodies to eat. From eighth grade on I avoided going home. Ma would tell me to bring my friends over but if I did, all she'd do was nag me in front of them and embarrass me too. Sometimes she'd even embarrass them. Like once she said to a friend of mine last year, "My word, Mary, are you wearing make-up?" She made Mary feel like a hooker. I didn't come home that night, a school night, until 10 o'clock, which was late even for me. Lucky for me my father wasn't home. He would have killed me. As it was my mother got more hell than I did. She told Dad when he came home at 11:30 and I made out like I was sleeping. He really blasted her out. She blasted him out too, though. Bad scene. That's how my house was though, either a very bad scene or no scene at all. Mostly it was no scene at all.

Then I discovered that boys liked me. They thought I was pretty. I started hanging around school later just to watch them practice football, basketball, soccer. It didn't matter. I never had a "steady." I liked so many of them! I went with a different boy every week, well, well every month. I could never bring any of them home, so I'd meet them in the evening at the corner and we'd walk around and on Friday and Saturday nights we'd go to parties. I told ma I was at Mary's house. It didn't matter 'cause she didn't care. Dad cared I think, but he was out working so it was like he didn't care either. He wasn't home.

I had my first experience with sex when I was thirteen and a half. It happened during winter vacation. I'm not sure but I think it happened because I had no place to go, I was just plain bored at home. My grandparents were real sweet but they're grandparents. I'd stopped going to my aunts cause I knew Ma didn't like it. She thought that they gossiped with each other about how Ma didn't take care of me. (Even though I hated her I wanted to protect her. Weird, huh?) Anyway I went over to Mary's. Her parents worked. Mary went into her bedroom with her boyfriend. Me and another boy used her parents bedroom. A lot of girls are scared about sex I wasn't scared so much as I was curious. What I found out was that it wasn't all that much. That was my first experience. I had my second the next day. I got to like it more and more until I found out I was pregnant. Then I got scared, really scared. When I found out I started throwing up and feeling real queer. When I missed my period the second month I knew, 'cause I'd had it regular since I was in the middle of the seventh grade. I didn't dare tell my father. So I told the old bitch. I don't know why, but I wasn't scared telling her. I remember feeling very adult, even a little proud, sort of. She was at the kitchen table bent over, cutting out some paper dolls for her kindergarten class. And I told her.

I really half-expected her to scream and call me names. Mostly I expected her to scream. She didn't. She just turned white as a sheet and sat down. Then she put her head in her arms and began to cry soft. That's when I started to cry. As I was crying I thought the weirdest thing. 'God, it's the first time since I can remember that me and Ma did something together. How sad! It had to be crying!'

Ann Russo made the initial appointment for family therapy. She did it on the recommendation of a social worker connected with a medical center located nearby. (I was to learn this later.) At the first session I had no background on the nature of the problem.

The Russo family triad appeared for their first appointment on a Monday night. They entered the room. Michael was grimfaced yet appeared to be a trifle embarrassed; Ann had red, tear-rimmed eyes and Nancy seemed almost bright eyed.

"Well, come in, come in. I'm Joe Perez." Michael shook my hand indifferently. Ann gave me some limp, moist fingers. Nancy just smiled and said, 'Hi,' a trifle too loud.

Quite apparently and understandably, they were all very anxious. Michael sat in a large easy chair, Ann on the couch alone, and Nancy took a high-backed small chair, one that younger children (5–10 years) usually took. They all had positioned themselves apart, I observed, one from the other.

"Well," I asked, "What brings the Russos here on such an awful night?" (It was raining and quite cold.)
Silence.
Then Michael opened up with, "Look, I'm not so sure this is a good idea. I mean this was my wife's idea."

I looked at Ann. "You're the one who felt the Russo family should come to me?"

"Yeah," she murmured.

"Why?" I asked.

She looked at her husband. She was either very scared or very embarrassed.

Michael fired impatiently, "Well Christ, tell him. We're paying enough for this."

"Well, the social worker at the Hill Medical Center referred you to me. She said you could probably help out. We need help." she finished tremulously.

"Why did that social worker, I mean what were you doing there? Were you in treatment for . . .

"I had an abortion three days ago." Nancy said softly.

I was looking at Michael when Nancy said it. He winced at her words. I could feel Ann's eyes on me. I don't think I showed any reaction.

When I'm at a momentary loss I often hide behind a simple recitation, a reflection.

"You had an abortion."

"Yeah."

Silence.

Again it was Michael who broke the silence. "Anyways that's why we're here."

Some clarification was needed for all of us. I addressed my words to all three. "You're here because you want to know what's happening in your family. Why you got pregnant, Nancy, what led you to get so far away from your parents. You're all here because you're not getting along . . . "

Ann interrupted me with a nervous laugh. "No we're not getting along, not even a little bit. He's never home and she's never home."

"Oh Ma, you're always home all right, but you don't talk except to nag, me and Dad."

Michael spoke testily, "Don't talk like that to your mother."

"Oh God, Dad, she usually only talks to nag both of us you know that and if she's not nagging she's criticizing nanna or nannu* or one of my aunts."

"Well even so, she's your mother and mothers aren't supposed to be talked to like that. I was brought up to respect my mother."

"Mothers are respected if they deserve to be respected," Nancy said, a little sullenly.

Pause.

Ann sighed, then spoke. "There's truth to that Michael, a mother should be respected for what she is, not just because she's a mother."

"You don't think it's the role, but the person who fills it that counts," I said.

"Exactly." she said.

Pause, then a silence.

I remembered thinking I should have kept my mouth shut. My

---

*Grandmother or grandfather.

remark, with the word "role," had probably put a lull in the triologue. I needed to listen better.

Ann sighed, "I really haven't done that much to be respected, have I Nancy?"

Michael blared out, "For Christ's sake Ann, she's your daughter, not your mother. You don't ask . . . "

Nancy interrupted him, "No, you haven't been Mom."

"Where have I been. What have I done or not . . . "

"Hey, Ann (Michael was interrupting), I don't think you ought to ask your . . . "

"Michael, for heaven's sake will you shut up!"

Michael fell back as if he had been struck. Even Nancy looked a little shocked. Quite apparently Ann had never spoken like that to her husband, at least in front of a stranger. At this point I was very much a stranger.

Ann herself seemed surprised by her own outburst. She looked at me, at her daughter and then burst into tears, but she didn't move from her chair. She dabbed her eyes and continued talking, all the while looking at Michael.

"Nancy did it. Nancy got pregnant I didn't."

"But why? Why? Why? Because we've failed as parents, that's why."

"You failed, I didn't. I did every thing I was supposed to as a father and as a husband. Besides that, she's a girl. Mothers are supposed to raise girls not fathers. Fathers . . . "

Ann interrupted him. "And where does a girl learn about boys? From her father that's where."

They were both going at it pretty well. They seemed to be fairly evenly matched in terms of ability to express and make points. I didn't feel the need to support one or the other. Nancy and I watched.

"Yeah and where does she learn to be a lady?"

"Oh Michael you're right I haven't given her as much as I could, I haven't been as close to you, Nancy, as a mother should." She was still crying, dabbing at her eyes occasionally with a hankie.

"Yeah ma, but Dad, you haven't been close either."

"You're trying to tell me that you got pregnant because I wasn't close to you? Who you kiddin'."

Nancy looked at me. I cleared my throat. "Uh you don't feel, Mike, that the problems we all have here are connected?"

"Well, whatdaya' mean?"

"Aren't you all a family?"

"Sure."

"Well then, don't you think that the problems might be family related?"

"Of course they're family related," said Ann. "If Nancy's got problems we contributed to them."

Michael was getting angry. "You did, I didn't. My job is to work. And I work and I work damn hard."

"You work so hard Daddy that I think you use that as an excuse not to be home, 'cause I don't think you want to be home."

Michael looked at her and very condescendingly said, "Ah, what do you know about it?"

Nancy glared at him. "That's what I hate. That's what I hate when you treat me like a baby. Like I don't know anything."

"Well, you *are* a baby. You're only fourteen," he yelled at her.

Nancy screamed back the words that explained the manifest reason for their entry into therapy, "I am *not* a baby. I am a woman. I *had* a baby."

Michael turned a trifle pale.

It was Ann who spoke. "Is that why you got pregnant to prove to us, to me especially, that you're not a child anymore, that you're a woman?"

I wondered if Ann has just thought that or if she had perhaps heard that as an explanation for the "why" of the pregnancy from someone at the clinic. I was never to know.

"I don't know. The shrink at the clinic said that it happens a lot because girls are very hostile to their parents, usually their mothers."

"There, what did I tell ya'," chirped in Michael with apparent satisfaction.

"Oh, Michael, if she had said that the doctor told her it was because the father wasn't a good father you would have said it was bullshit."

Michael looked irritated by the answer.

"No, I wasn't going to say that," he said.

We were coming to the end of the hour. I felt I should make a stronger impact than I had up to now.

"Mike, where do you think each of you fits into the family?"

"Whaddya' mean where do we fit? We're a family. We each of us got our jobs. My responsibility is to work, to bring home the bacon . . ."

"Good grief, Michael, is that all you're responsible for? Just work?"

"Lemme finish will ya'? I was gonna say that my job is to take care of the family."

"Well, Daddy, I don't guess you've been all that terrific, have you?," said Nancy in an almost saccharine-like tone.

"Don't get fresh," he said to her.

"Michael," I said, "I would imagine that taking care of the family would include being loving, and . . . "

"I do that. Don't I do that, Nancy?"

How interesting I thought. He called Nancy, not Ann.

"Yeah Daddy kisses and hugs me once in a while."

"I'm lax there," admitted Ann. "I never kiss or hug."

"But I never seen the two of you hug or kiss," said Nancy.

"That's your mother's fault. You go to nannu's or my sisters' house you see it. Right?"

"Yeah," she said.

Nancy seemed sorry that her comment had led to a condemning remark, a put-down of her mother. Yet this probably had been the pattern over the years. An observation by Nancy of an inadequacy in one parent probably led to the other parent's condemning remark.

"I'm not Italian," said Ann. She said it in an indifferent tone.

"Well gee ma, just because you weren't born Italian it doesn't mean that you were born frozen either."

I thought Michael would split his gut by the guffaws he let out. More importantly still, Ann laughed too. That made me feel good. And when she reached over and playfully squeezed her daughter's arm, I felt even better. I remember thinking, there might be sickness in this family, but there's also a lot of health.

We ended this initial session only moments later and made another appointment. I was left with the following impressions of the Russo's.

Michael didn't like airing family problems in therapy. He also was very role conscious, and while he saw himself as the family's provider and caretaker he shied away from any idea that he was in some measure responsible for Nancy's pregnancy. During the first session he had clung desperately to the idea that if Ann had just done her maternal duties everything would have been O.K. He seemed very resistant to change.

If Michael seemed to be a reluctant attendant of therapy, and unreceptive to change, Ann was neither. On the contrary, she seemed most receptive, most eager to effect changes which would be conducive to a more healthful familial homeostasis. She freely admitted her faults and seemed positively eager to get closer to her daughter.

Nancy seemed receptive to getting closer to her mother too. There was little doubt in my mind that Nancy's acting out was a reaction to the coldness and distancing emitted by the parents, to each other and to her.

I had almost two dozen more sessions with the Russos. My initial impressions proved to be fairly accurate. Michael has changed only a little; he continues to work long hours, but now devotes his weekends to Ann and Nancy. The evening supper has again become a family ritual, and is apparently far more pleasant.

I had several sessions with Ann and Michael alone. These were enlightening for all of us. I learned that there never was any important sexual dysfunction. Nevertheless Michael's increased attentiveness and Ann's apparent vocational fulfillment have improved their sexual relations even more.

The most important changes have been made by Ann, however. She and Nancy have become very close. They spend their evenings together. The two have joined a family swim team at the local Y.W.C.A., and if they're not seen there, they're in the local Malls shopping. Michael approves of all this. Now he can fill his role of hardworking head of the family without feeling guilty about the hours he puts in at work or anxious about Nancy's whereabouts.

I had two sessions alone with Nancy. My initial impression was correct. Her problems stemmed from the feelings of indifference and the sense of isolation she derived from the parental dyad. Today she is another teenager, no sicker, no healthier than the average.

Finally, I never cease to marvel at the ironies effected by human dynamics within the familial constellation. Thus, although Nancy's delinquent acting out did indeed get her illegitimately pregnant, this same acting out ultimately worked to bring about a more healthful emotional equilibrium for the family triad.

CITATIONS

1. Brown, P., and Manela, R., "Client Satisfaction with Marital and Divorce Counseling." *The Family Coordinator*, Vol. 26, July 1977, No.3
2. Stachowiak, J., "Functional and Dysfunctional Families." In *Helping Families to Change*, Satir, V., Stachowiak, J., and Taskman, H. New York: Jason Aronson, Inc., 1975.

Chapter 6
The Therapist

There is research which shows that experience per se is not the most important factor for effectiveness as a therapist. Two researchers discovered that a mere hundred hours of therapy may be enough for some individuals to function with competence and skill (Carkhuff and Truax, 1965). There is also research which demonstrates clearly that the theoretical orientations, i.e. psychoanalytic, non-directive, and so on, is not a factor for therapist effectiveness (Wrenn, 1960). And a study by Strupp (1957) showed that the techniques utilized were not the critical factor for therapist effectiveness. For example, in his comparison of Rogers (non-directivist) and Wolberg (psychoanalytic) Strupp found that both were "warm, accepting and non-critical; both encouraged the patient's expression of feelings; and . . . greater self-acceptance in their patients." What these research findings show is that experience, theoretical orientation and technique utilized are not the critical determinants for effectiveness as a therapist. The implication is strong in these studies that it is the counselor's personal qualities, not his education and training, which are a more promising criteria for evaluation of his effectiveness.

PERSONAL QUALITIES

What kind of person is the family therapist? Does he incorporate qualities which are especially unique? In Satir's opinion, "he is not omnipotent" but is a "resourceful person." At the same time she feels apparently that the therapist must be in excellent contact with reality, for she observes that the therapist should be, "a model of communication," "and should not fall into the trap . . . of suiting reality to himself." (Satir 1967)

Haley believes that flexibility is a critical factor in the therapist's make up. The "therapist is a flexible person subject to and willing to change his view of how and why people become sick" (Haley 1971).

One researcher discovered that the therapist is one who has a need to be nurturant (Munson 1961). Three others found that the need for nurturance is not as strong as the need to be "intuitive and psychologically penetrating" (Mills, Chestnut and Hartzell 1966).

A very comprehensive study about what therapists believe to be the most important qualities in the experienced professional therapist was conducted by Menne (1975). This researcher asked seventy-five experienced therapists to contribute statements of what qualities make for an effective therapist. These statements were then edited and organized into a set of one hundred and thirty-two proposed competencies. Three hundred and seventy-six experienced therapists responded to this set of competencies. The qualities which were deemed most important out of the set of one hundred and thirty-two were as follows:

1. Professional ethics—how the therapist conducts himself in therapy and in relation to his clients was given number one priority by the respondents. (It would seem that the therapist is a person of exquisite conscience.)

2. A sense of self-awareness, particularly as it relates to such items as competency and incompetency, values, attitudes and biases, ranked second.

3. Personal characteristics including respect for others, maturity, intuitiveness and flexibility were rated third.

4. The ability to listen and communicate was also given high priority and ranked fourth (Menne 1975).

Findings such as these indicated clearly that the therapist is a person who finds reward in giving, in helping others. Interestingly, at least one study shows that the act of helping invariably benefits the helper as well as the one helped (Rakos and Schroeder 1976). Could one reason why family therapists do their work be that they themselves are psychologically enhanced by the process?

The therapist knows that how his clients perceive him is critical for the conduct of the therapy (Wile 1976). And it is precisely the therapist's personal qualities which strongly affect how he is perceived by the people whom he treats. Indeed, his general behavior influences how his family clients perceive his warmth and competence, the general therapeutic climate, his general appeal and client satisfaction (Scheid 1976).

Now research data is of critical value because it is objective, detached and authoritative. At the same time research data by its very nature lacks for warmth and "human interest." Moreover, the nature of the topic, the qualities of the therapist, would seem to suggest the need for the personally human and subjective view. Accordingly, the author asked selected colleagues to present their personal views on the subject of therapist personality. Six practicing family therapists were asked to respond to the following question:

What qualities make for an effective family therapist? Their responses follow.

Therapist I

*Female Ph.D. Psychologist. College teacher. Also in
private practice.*

Until more research is done on the topic, the answer to the question, for me, is speculative. I am convinced, however, that the family therapist needs to have the same qualities that are basic to good client-centered therapy, namely, the ability to feel and show unconditional positive regard toward the clients and to create an atmosphere of warmth and acceptance and safety.

Further, however, I suspect such a therapist would, as is true of many people, come from a family of origin which had its own problems in communication. I believe that the therapist who comes from such a family would more easily develop empathy with troubled families.

The effective family therapist, I should think, rushes to the latest movie thriller, never goes to bed without a detective novel on his/her bed table, dreams of someday being asked to serve at Scotland Yard or in the FBI. In other words, the therapist has a strong need to do detective work and to experience high adventure; for indeed, the unraveling of the family's interactions is both.

A family therapist, furthermore, must have a sense of drama. The therapist must be able to pick up from the family very quickly some words or actions that are theatrical, point them out, and play them for all they are worth. For example, if all the other family members turn their backs as the father comes into the room while at the same time saying how much they all love him, that is dramatic! The therapist must have a skill similar to that of Chekov who had a superb ear for the quietly dramatic. In *The Sea Gull*, for example, two lines right smack at the beginning seize the audience's attention and promise to sustain it:

MEDVEDENKO.   Why do you always wear black?
MASHA.   I am in mourning for my life.

The family therapist must also be relatively uninhibited, wildly creative, willing to make up on the spot ways with which the family can come to understand itself, while at the same time being supportive and non-judgemental in good client-centered fashion. These qualities are exemplified by Virginia Satir. I once observed her growing frustration with a family who denied there was anything wrong with their interactions. She took a washline and held on to one end. The other end she handed to the strongest denier, directing him to hold on to the rope as he interacted with his family members while they all walked around in front of Satir. Very shortly some members were literally tied in knots. They got the point. Peggy Papp's use of the family sculpting technique in which family members have a turn at placing themselves in spatial relationship to the others and rearranging the tableau to each member's satisfaction is certainly creative also. This technique allows each member to make dramatic suggestions for improved family relations without having to use words (which are usually laden with defense mechanisms).

Finally, the family therapist must be able to learn to think of systems in need of repair, rather than individuals who are at fault. In family therapy, that is, there comes to be no identified patient; only an ineffectual system of communication.

Therapist II

*Male Ph.D. Psychologist. College teacher. Also in
private practice.*

An effective family therapist is a person who is willing to risk becoming professionally immersed in family dynamics, where the anxiety level is high, pitfalls abundant, and amount of data tremendous. Whereas the therapist treating an individual can remain aloof and relatively detached, the family therapist has to be prepared to "get his hands dirty." He is a player on the field who becomes a part of the game which means that he has to pour large quantities of energy into continually sensing his position relative to the other "players." The ability to keep a correct distance, shift alliances, and intervene at appropriate times is crucial to the functioning of an effective family therapist. What I'm saying is that the therapist must be flexible. Basically, however, a family therapist will most likely function best if he or she enjoys families i.e. their love for each other, their fears, concerns, hopes and goals. This is high human drama witnessed at very close range.

Therapist III
Male M.D. Psychiatrist, Director of state funded
public health clinic. Also in private practice.

The first personal quality that I would mention would be the quality essential for any therapist, individual, family or any other kind. That is, there has to be an interest in *helping other people*. That interest often originates in one's own personal life experiences of a psychologically uncomfortable if not traumatic nature. There are, of course, many other environmental circumstances other than intrapsychic problems which also make one sensitive to the needs of others and allow one to sublimate the need to be understood and the need to understand others and to help them.

The second important personal quality is that one has to be *comfortable with powerful feelings*, both one's own and those of other people. This also makes, incidentally, for one of the essential qualities for any kind of therapist, but it is especially important for the *family therapist*. Often in individual therapy, one can hide behind the pose of the neutral therapist and not allow any feelings to be exposed. I feel personally that this is a handicap even in individual therapy. Certainly in family therapy where quite often one of the goals of therapy is to improve communication among family members and the expression of powerful feelings, the therapist himself or herself has to be comfortable with powerful feelings, again one's own as well as those which will be expressed within the family therapy process.

A third important personal quality, and I do not mean to mention these in order of priority or importance, is that the therapist has to have *a reasonably intact personal psychological life*. If not a reasonably intact personal family experience, then intensive psychotherapy to correct whatever distortions and problem areas are left over from one's earlier family experience. One of the errors made in family therapy which I have learned from my experience in the supervision of family therapy as well as through my own self-awareness, is that too often family therapists impose their own value systems, their own concept of the way that families should be, onto the family with which they are working, and very often this demonstrates a lack of an awareness of just what a normal family should be like or what is normal and what is abnormal. Often therapists try to impose an idealized version of family life onto the family group, one stemming from their own unmet earlier needs for an ideal family in their personal life. Again, intensive psychotherapy increases one's self-awareness and corrects distortions and biases which are brought into the family therapy process. I am not saying that intensive psychotherapy is essential for every therapist, but certainly if the therapist's personal psychological life is not relatively intact, he will bring the residual distortions and problem areas into the family process and either cause harm or retard the progress in family therapy.

Another important personal quality is the intellectual capacity for abstract thinking, for psychological insights, and for handling on an intellectual level the incredibly complex interactions which are potentially present in any family. It has been said that in a family of two parents, two children and a therapist, there are something like thirty-two possible family systems and/or alliances, and the therapist has to be intellectually capable of grasping as many of these systems rapidly and being aware of them simultaneously while measuring and judging his own response and interaction within the family therapy process. Also, the family therapist has to have enough freedom from his own anxiety and depression and other feelings to be able to prevent these feelings from influencing his responses. Again, this depends upon a relatively intact personal life and-/or intensive psychotherapy to correct the distortions, but another important quality in being able to use intuitive judgements and responses within the family process is the need for a good self-image on the part of the family therapist. The therapist has to accept himself before he can accept the frailties and fragilities in family members with whom he is working. Again, getting back to the personal quality of having a relatively intact personal life, this also becomes important in terms of remaining objective, keeping one's countertransference reactions, feelings, thoughts, impulses, and biases out of the family therapeutic process. I am thus including self-awareness and control over one's countertransference reactions as another personal quality necessary for an effective family therapist.

Therapist IV
Male Ph.D. Psychologist.
College teacher. Also in private practice.

In many respects I do not think that the personal qualities of a family therapist are particularly different from those of other types of therapists, indeed from thousands of interpersonal relations in general. I see the need for openness to others and to one's self. By this I mean an awareness of and sensitivity to the feelings of others and to what is going on in yourself as you relate to others. I see the need for *warmth*. By this is meant a caring concern yet non-controlling reaching out to others. *Genuineness* is another meaningful characteristic. By this I mean the therapist does not mask or hide him or herself. *Clarity in communication* is also a valuable characteristic. The therapist's communications should leave little, if any, doubt in the family as to what he is thinking, feeling, observing or intending to do. I also see the need for the therapist to be perceptive in terms of the *non-verbal aspects of communication* that others send. Much information is connected through body postures, gestures, etc. Thus the therapist must be comfortable looking at other people and seeing their bodies. I see a need for the therapist *to be in touch with his own values* so that these may be stated, if need be, but not imposed. I think it is also important that the therapist have a *healthy respect and liking for himself*. Without this quality the therapist may be afraid to act, to do something because he might be wrong. He must be able in a sense to say to himself, 'Sure I might be wrong but basically I trust me so here goes.' This leads to an additional characteristic and that is I see a need for the therapist to be willing *'to risk his own neck'* by a willingness to confront the family with the issues as he sees them. In other words the therapist must be willing to respond to the family, to do something or to intervene in such a way that hopefully he will act as a catalyst for change. This is probably riskier in family therapy than in individual therapy because the family may then in a sense 'gang up' on the therapist to protect themselves and their customary ways of doing business, of living together. Since the therapist is human this can hurt, yet the risk must be taken if change is to occur. *Humor* is another quality that is helpful to a therapist. The ability to laugh at what we do with and to each other can sometimes help put events in perspective.

I am sure that there are other characteristics that could be listed. My intent is to avoid being 'textbookish' in style. I am trying to describe those characteristics that seem to be at work for me. The order of presentation in no way reflects an order of importance, but instead is a reflection of the characteristics as they spontaneously occurred to me. In fact, as I now review them, they scare me, in a way, because I seriously doubt if I am fully able to practice what I preach.

Therapist V
Male M.D. Psychiatrist, Professor, Medical school.
Also in private practice.

You ask some questions about family therapy that go to the core.

About the personal qualities. I believe that the effective family therapist is one who has been in the role of identified patient in his or her own family. Or the role of the Lamed Vovnik—the saint and central connecting person—of the extended family system sacrificing his or her own center for the purpose of being the center of the family where the members as a whole do not share the responsibility of making the family work. Being this central connecting figure of the family is of course not enough, but the therapist should have been able to work his or her way out of this role and position—out of the family emotional mass or cytoplasm to the point where the responsibility for making the family work is shifted to the family as a whole.

Therapist VI

Male. MSW. Social worker in a public health clinic.
Also in private practice.

Above all else I believe a family therapist needs to have a clear sense of personal identity in relation to his/her spouse and family of origin. Working with couples and families has such potential for stirring up one's own unresolved or troublesome interpersonal issues that a family therapist needs to feel confident he/she can extract him/herself from the emotional system of the family when necessary. I don't believe every one *must* go back and work on their own family of origin, but it certainly helps to have at least an awareness of trouble spots that may arise.

I believe an effective therapist needs to be comfortable shifting back and forth between an active and passive role, with perhaps a greater facility for assertive behavior. Some people see this as "charismatic," but that is not the sense I mean. Whether being active or passive a therapist needs to be able to convey a sense of warmth, respect and empathy for the family and the struggles of its members.

An effective therapist needs to have a degree of emotional and cognitive flexibility, in particular the ability to think of several alternative strategies and interventions at any given point and to be able to shift gears emotionally as the family moves along. A fine attribute in this respect is to have a sense of humor in the midst of emotional seas.

ANALYSIS OF THE RESPONSES

A close scrutiny of the six responses reveals certain common qualities. The most salient appears to be the therapist's need to help, the need to give (a point remarked earlier and observed also in Menne's findings). All six respondents feel that a therapist should be one who has a need to invest in other people and who ordinarily derives emotional dividends from such investments.

Another quality thought to be important and noted by more than one respondent, was the therapist's willingness to take risks, to stick one's neck out, "in order to effect healthful changes." The strong implication here is that the therapist to be effective must be emotionally secure or as one respondent put it, "have a reasonably intact personal psychological life."

It is interesting to find that at least three respondents felt that the therapist's family of origin was an important factor in shaping his emotional maturity to do therapy. The family of origin, they suggest, should have provided the individual with a sense of identity and the emotional wherewithal to function more empathetically with the families he treats.

Flexibility, as was true in Menne's study, was also mentioned here as an important quality in the emotional repertoire of the effective therapist. The therapist must be someone who can "shift gears emotionally."

In the course of writing this chapter the author remembered in a vague sort of way some lines he had once read, lines which he thought just might be appropriate in describing an effective therapist. He found the lines in Tolstoi's *War and Peace*. Spoken by Prince Andrew about General Kutusov, they are an apt description of the behavior which the effective therapist seeks to incorporate into his therapy hour:

> He will not devise or undertake . . . but he will hear everything, remember everything and put everything in its place. He will not hinder anything useful nor allow anything harmful . . . (he) can refrain from meddling."

Beyond Effectiveness
The Competent Therapist

The level beyond effectiveness is competence. It is the level which the professional, dedicated family therapist seeks to achieve. The family therapist who strives for competence is one who incorporates certain characteristics. These are:

1. Intellectual ability
2. Healthy self-esteem

3. Congruence
4. Motivation
5. The capacity to derive meaning from each therapy session.

They are discussed below.

1. The competent therapist is one who is intellectually able. His intelligence is such that it never hampers, but only facilitates the therapeutic process. His general knowledge, his level of cognitive and emotional comprehension, reasoning and verbal fluency are such that they abet sessions with the client family.

2. The competent therapist feels good about himself both as a person and as a therapist. His sense of worth as a therapist is a function of the apparent ability which he displays in his work. In no way is his sense of worth tied to the lack of performance, inadequacy or ineptness which he might see in those whom he treats. The competent therapist is not one to grow bigger in his own view because of his need to see others as smaller.

    His healthy self-esteem permits a resilient-like quality to emerge in his personality. Thus, when he errs in therapy, as he will on occasion, he is perfectly able to "bounce back" and try again. This resiliency is infectious and by it he teaches the family members to accept their own foibles. What the members come to learn, of course, is that in such acceptance lies a healthier self-esteem. The therapist's healthy self-view enhances not only his own performance and behavior but also that of the family members. Extended research by Fitts (1972) led him to conclude that there is indeed a strong relationship between one's behavior and how one views one's self. "The more optimal the self-concept; the more optimal the behavior will be."

3. The competent therapist is emotionally in tune with himself and with his client family. His competence as a therapist is in large measure a function of this congruence. His emotional congruence leads him to serve and enhance others. The irony is that he derives his own personal enhancement from his service to the families which he treats. In other words, emotional congruence is its own reward, and happily, the competent therapist finds reward in giving.

    Emotional congruence permits the therapist to be open with the families he or she treats. He does not have to hide anything, either emotionally or cognitively. The importance of this was noted by Fisch et.al. (1972) when they observed that the family therapist, "should always say what he believes . . . his communications should be . . . guileless." (An emotionally open stance has the added merit of helping to abate the paranoid feelings with which many families are beset.)

Precisely because the therapist is in tune with his or her own feelings he is able to deal with the strong emotions ventilated often in therapy by others and occasionally by himself. Finally, it is also emotional congruence which permits the therapist to take the risks discussed above by some of the six therapist respondents.

4. The therapist is highly motivated to perform optimally in his work. His motivation is high because, as noted, his self-esteem is healthy and he is emotionally attuned to both himself and his clients.

    The competent therapist is motivated to alter his style, to introduce new methods not only to effect change in the family but to explore his own capacities and complexities. This therapist is committed to a disinterested search to discover his own best potential and to become that potential. To paraphrase Maslow (1954), "What a competent family therapist can be, he must be." What all this means is that the competent therapist is not only receptive to change in his methods and conduct of therapy, but more, he is willing to risk change in himself.

5. There are therapists who have conducted the same session one hundred times. Then there are therapists who have conducted one hundred sessions, each one, once. The latter is the competent therapist. Each session is a growth experience for him. In each he learns. From each he derives an important meaning which he utilizes at a subsequent session.

Now, not every session is enhancing. There are those which are threatening, even for the therapist who scores high on each of these five criteria. There are sessions which are emotionally debilitating, even demeaning. No matter. The therapist who continues to derive significant meaning from his experience with the family is one who will grow, is the one whose penchant for competence will be realized.

TRAINING

If the therapist's personal qualities are of critical importance for his effectiveness as a family therapist, his education and training are of no less importance. The literature, however, while it abounds with case studies, readings and general research, contains but few articles which deal with training programs for family therapists. For example, Simmons (1971) compared and contrasted clinical training programs of the sixties and did not even allude to family therapy. Again Rotter (1973) discussed the various and new psychotherapeutic approaches of the future, but did not mention family therapy as one of those approaches. The author finds this at the very least puzzling, since he is aware of at least two dozen training programs being conducted in the northeast alone, both in universities and in hospitals. It is curious that these programs have not received professional attention in the literature.

By and large the programs being conducted are designed to provide training at various levels of competency, from simple orientation, to paraprofessional to the professional levels. The view today is that family therapy can be accomplished by psychiatrists, psychologists, social workers, nurses and even those with no special professional affiliation or status. Training programs, especially those in hospitals, admit people at all levels of skill and education. Haley (1971) appears to have expressed the contemporary position succinctly, "A therapist is now often judged on his merit—the success of his therapy—not upon his professional background." Delegates to a recent national conference dealing specifically with the training of psychologists at different levels also supported this contemporary view. However, while they stressed the importance of multi-level training they also felt that there was a "need for portability of credit for completed work" (Korman 1974). Presumably this idea was included in order to help those who so desired to develop better credentials. And credentials, it would seem, have some importance in the client-therapist relationship, at least initially. For example, the results of a study by Spiegel (1976) were that, "Findings support the importance of counselor credentials in determining clients' initial impressions of counselors." Whatever might be one's position regarding the importance of credentials there is little disagreement about the importance of training programs.

The common denominator in the programs examined by the author was that without exception they contained a variety of experiences in *both* theory and practice. That a training program contain both was considered important by at least one professional association as early as 1958 (APA, 1958).

Mendelsohn and Ferber (1972) have described their program conducted in New York City. There are four levels to the program. Level I involves an introduction and orientation to family therapy. At level II the trainee becomes immersed in the treatment of the family. The intent is that the graduate of Level III be a full-fledged practitioner. These first three levels take approximately one year to complete. Level IV is designed to produce the teacher of family therapy. This is a continuing education level, the intent of which is to keep the therapist's mind "open and growing." At the first three levels the trainees are required to meet with a given number of families for whom "they have some clinical responsibility." In addition, they are required to undergo an hour's weekly supervision and to attend one two-hour seminar per week.

What Mendelsohn and Ferber present here is a theoretical, flexible, open-minded program. Quite apparently, their flexibility and open-mindedness is a response to the varying needs of the trainees and to the fact that their trainee candidates are at considerably different levels of professional skill. Their program seeks to meld relevant theory with profitable practical experience. The most noteworthy aspects of the program are the importance it puts upon 1) a trainee's first-hand contact with families, 2) trainee-supervisor participation in interviews, 3) utilization of audiovisual aids, and 4) the fact that training be accomplished in small groups.

Constantine has also described an impressive program, one conducted at Boston State Hospital. Applicants to the program are from a host of different professions and levels of skill, from psychiatrists to mental health aides. This is a two year program. The first year is divided into two semesters and each semester is divided into four functional units. The curriculum of each sequential unit is designed to "gradually" prepare the trainee for his first live family experience. The belief held by the directors of the program is, "that only a minority of students benefit from the 'sink or swim' approach." The first live interview situation does not occur until near the end of the first year. The first year is well structured and quite apparently "goal directed." The trainee is given more freedom in the second year with gradual emphasis placed on the trainee to be responsible for what he learns. During this second year "trainees see a minimum of six families, three in on-going treatment, three for evaluation."

The most salient aspects of this program are:

1. integration of multiple learning approaches, both deductive and experiential.
2. well structured, especially the first year.
3. goal directed throughout.
4. the non-pathological family is a major focus.

5. "The theoretical base is . . . a unifying theoretical framework into which many theories at all levels may be cast."

Haley (1976) has expressed the view that a prospective trainee should seek a training program which incorporates the following methods and philosophy.

1. The therapists are observed while working via a one-way mirror.
2. The trainees are observed and "guided" while working.
3. The trainees are video-taped. The trainee will have time to review the tapes at leisure, alone and/or with a supervisor.
4. The center teaches the trainee a variety of techniques and thereby helps the trainee to develop a flexible professional repertoire.
5. "The presenting problem is emphasized and taken seriously."
6. "Outcome is emphasized." Haley believes that the "destination of therapy" should be the focus, not the *process*.

AN INITIAL COMPENSATORY PROGRAM

It is the author's conviction that applicants for a family therapy program should be screened to determine their levels of sophistication in theory and skills already acquired. If the conclusion of the screening is that an applicant does not possess enough background to profit from the regular program, then an initial compensatory program might be offered as a preparation for the regular program.

Compensatory Program

I. Didactic Content

A. Readings and discussion in the following areas:
    1) Personality—individual and group
    2) Abnormal psychology
    3) The family today
    4) Human development, child to senior adult.

II   Experiential Content

A.   The object here is to help the prospective trainee to get in touch with himself and his feelings.
1)   Role playing, as family members, parents, adolescents and children.
2)   Sculpting in order to explore the trainee's relationship with his family of origin.

THE TRAINING OF SIX THERAPISTS
Personal Thoughts

The six therapists who responded above on the subject of personal qualities were asked also to respond to this question:
Describe the courses, subjects, practical experiences which were most valuable to you for both your preparation and continuing work as a therapist.
Their responses follow:

Therapist I
Female Ph.D. Psychologist. College teacher.
Also in private practice.

I have had the privilege of working as a co-therapist with a colleague who is expert in family therapy. He is training me; through his criticisms and through our analyses of the tapes of the families we see together, I learn a great deal.

I have learned a lot also, attending workshops sponsored by the Ackerman Family Institute and other sponsors of workshops on family therapy. Reading the literature in this field has been helpful too; it is creative and very stimulating. I especially like the works of Satir and Minuchin . . . Indeed, I'm hard pressed to find a book or article on the subject from which I learned nothing.

I must give most credit for my preparation, however, to my training for the Ph.D. in counseling psychology. There I learned to admire the philosophy and practice of client-centered therapy. Although family therapy focuses on systems rather than people, I personally like to treat the system with the same care that I treat the sole client. In fact, my training in group counseling at Carl Rogers' Center for the Study of the Person in La Jolla, California, directly applied client-centered therapy to group interaction. There lie the true roots of my preparation.

Therapist II

Male Ph.D. Psychologist. College teacher.
Also in private practice.

My work as a family therapist was helped immeasurably by a two year internship in family therapy at Bristol Hospital in Bristol, Connecticut. On a once-a-week basis we would meet with two families, following which other family therapists and staff persons would review our videotapes and give extensive feedback. My confidence and skills grew tremendously after this experience, and I never again felt that panic and helplessness of my first family therapy session. At present, I keep up with the field of family therapy through workshops, current journals and books, and by always using a female co-therapist, which is very useful in critiquing our sessions and growing as therapists.

Therapist III

Male M.D. Psychiatrist.
Director of state funded public health clinic
Also in private practice.

I have read in journals and in resource textbooks a good deal about family therapy. I have attended family therapy workshops. But probably most important have been my own individual experiences with family therapy supplemented by my attendance at workshops and reading which allowed me to develop a certain style in family therapy. My training and education in individual psychotherapy has been of enormous importance to me in doing family therapy and, as such, has colored my family therapeutic approach. My personal approach in family therapy remains a combination of individual, diagnostic and therapeutic approaches combined with family systems, family alliances and the interactional-interpersonal approach. I will always be influenced by my training in individual and analytically oriented intensive psychotherapy, but this has been significantly modified by my less formal training in family systems and alliances within the family therapy field. In addition, I have done a good deal of supervision of family therapy with my staff here in our in-patient psychiatric unit and in our out-patient department and in my supervision of school counselors and therapists who are working with families, and I have learned a great deal from supervising others who are working with families, as well. Also, many of the people with whom I have worked as supervisor have attended family therapy workshops of their own and have brought back for my edification things that they have learned from their attendance at these family therapy workshops.

Therapist IV
Male Ph.D. Psychologist. College teacher.
Also in private practice.

My training at this point in time in family therapy is minimal. Therefore, I will answer it from the point of view of what I think I draw heavily from now and what I think would be beneficial in the way of training.

In terms of formalized courses the following areas are extremely useful:

1. Personality theories.
2. Abnormal psychology.
3. Group dynamics.
4. Marriage and the family.
5. Counseling techniques.
6. Social psychology particularly in terms of role dynamics.
7. Developmental psychology such as child, adolescent, aging.

I also think that an internship of a minimum of one year's experience with adequate supervision is a must. In this year the individual should see a variety of families ranging from 'average' to highly disorganized. Ideally the sessions should be video-taped for supervision/learning purposes. At the least they should be tape-recorded.

I have also profited from seminars and workshops in such areas as transactional analysis, Gestalt therapy and communication skills. These have provided me with tools that I can conceptualize with as well as techniques to intervene with. In addition I have been able to train clients to use these tools in order to alter their own lives. Reading has been an important source of learning too!

Naturally, just working with a wide variety of clients is a valuable experience. In other words experience counts; it can make up for a lot of theoretical weakness. Through experience a therapist learns to trust her-/himself. The theory or words to describe what one is doing can be built up later on. Ideally the two should go hand in hand.

I have also found that having a colleague(s) to discuss families with is a tremendous asset. There is so much going on in any one session that it is easy to get lost. After all, you are dealing with a complex set of interactions in a group that has already established its norms, its ways of interacting that it is implicitly out to defend. No wonder as a therapist you could end up with your head spinning. Along with a colleague to talk with I think it is valuable to have a co-therapist to help keep track of all the action, to discuss different perspectives and to act as another model for the family.

I think that the following kinds of experiences would be of value in continuing to work with families:

1. Course(s) in systems theory in general.
2. Course(s) in family therapy.
3. Supervised experience with families.
4. Research into family dynamics.
5. Cross-cultural courses on family styles of interacting.

Therapist V

Male M.D. Psychiatrist. Professor, Medical School.
Also in private practice.

As far as what has prepared me to do the work:

1. Fifteen years of working with families in family practice. And especially in those family situations which brought me to the home.
2. Teaching a seminar on the family where students presented to me their three generation family stories.
3. Personal therapy and contact and co-therapy with Carl Whitaker. A blessed visit to R.D. Laing.
4. The viewing for hundreds of hours of my own family's reunion (videotape).

5. The observation of videotapes of critical sessions of family therapy of other therapists.

6. The study of the anthropology of the family, particularly of the tribal medicine practiced by the African Bushman.

Therapist VI

Male MSW. Social Worker in a public health clinic.
Also in private practice.

There is no question in my mind that the best way to become an effective family therapist is to have a direct supervision via one way mirror or video-tape of actual therapy. These experiences have been the most valuable to me, with listening to audio tapes preferred over verbal reports. One such experience I have already mentioned above is an example. Working with an experienced co-therapist has also been valuable to me, although I never really felt like an "equal" co-therapist as a beginner.

From an intellectual point of view I owe a great deal to my master's degree program at the New School of Social Research in New York. This was a program based on the History of Ideas and I specialized in the history of sociology and psychology. It was here that I learned to understand and appreciate the historical development of ideas and evolving nature of conceptual systems. My biggest lesson was that there was no final, complete or best view of reality.

This intellectual basis has been the mainstay of my involvement, since the theories behind family therapy took into account this changing view of reality and the notion that there are several "levels" that can be understood.

Consequently, any course or workshop that furthers my understanding of this view of reality I find stimulating. Two examples may help to illustrate: 1) The recent conference in New York on the "Double Bind" where I had an opportunity to talk with Gregory Bateson, as well as hear and see in action such people as Jay Haley, Murray Bowen and others. 2) I have recently become involved in working with deaf clients and hope to eventually do family therapy with the deaf and those with impaired hearing. The fact that the deaf grow up with a world view based on a different type of language and primarily manual communication is quite a fascinating and challenging problem in therapy and requires the therapist to "think" and "speak" in ways quite foreign to the hearing world.

ANALYSIS OF THE RESPONSES

The content of the responses is remarkably similar. For example, more than half of the respondents are of the opinion that use of the video tape machine is a valuable asset in the development and maintenance of their own skills as therapists. Note that this idea gibes with those who develop training programs. At least four of the therapists felt that continuous reading in the field was important and beneficial. Indeed, one observed that, "I'm hard pressed to find a book or article on the subject from which I learned nothing." Workshop attendance was considered a valuable aspect of training by more than half the respondents. Supervision, undergone or given, was also mentioned by a majority as an important factor in the therapist's training. Of more than passing interest, too, was the fact that three of the therapists indicated that opportunities to discuss their work with renowned people in the field (Rogers, Bateson and Whitaker) was of especial benefit. Finally, a majority of the therapists indicated that their theoretical training (not in family therapy per se) was important in their development as family therapists. Presumably, they feel that they have been able to adapt their earlier dynamic learnings to the systems approach.

CITATIONS

1. Carkhuff, R. R., and Truax, C. B., "Training in Counseling and Psychotherapy: An Evaluation of an Integrated Didactic and Experiential Approach." *Journal of Consulting Psychology*, Vol. 29, 1965, pp. 333-336.

2. Constantine, L. L., "Designed Experience: A Multiple, Goal Directed Training Program in Family Therapy." *Family Process*, Vol. 15, December, 1976, No. 4, pp. 373-387.

3. Education and Training Board, "Criteria for evaluating training programs in clinical or in counseling psychology." *The American Psychologist*, Vol. 13, No 2, 1958, pp. 59-60.

4. Fisch, R., Watzlawick, P., Weakland, J., and Bodin, A., "On Unbecoming Family Therapists," In *The Book of Family Therapy*, Ferber, A., Mendelsohn, M., and Napier, A., eds., 1972.

5. Fitts, W. H., "The Self-Concept and Performance." Nashville, Tenn: Dede Wallace Center, Monograph V, April, 1972.

6. Haley, J., "Approaches to Family Therapy." In *Changing Families: A Family Therapy Reader*. New York: Grune and Stratton, 1971, pp. 227–236.

7. Haley, J., "Family therapy: A Radical Change." In *Changing Families: A Family Therapy Reader*. New York: Grune and Stratton 1971, p. 284.

8. Haley, J., *Problem Solving Therapy*, San Francisco: Jossey-Bass Publishers, 1976, pp. 190–191.

9. Korman, M., "National Conference on Levels and Patterns of Professional Training in Psychology. The Major Themes. (A Report)." *American Psychologist*, Vol. 29, No. 6, June 1974.

10. Maslow, A., *Motivation and Personality*. New York: Harper and Bros 1954, p. 91.

11. Mendelsohn, M., and Ferber, A., "A Training Program" In *The Book of Family Therapy*, Ferber, A., Mendelsohn, M., and Napier, A., eds. New York: Houghton Mifflin Co., 1972, pp. 239–271.

12. Menne, J. M., "A Comprehensive Set of Counselor Competencies." *Journal of Counseling Psychology*, Vol. 22, No. 6, 1975, pp. 547–553.

13. Mills, D. H., Chestnut, W. H., and Hartzell, J. P., "The Needs of Counselors: A Component Analysis." *Journal of Counseling Psychology*, Vol. 13, 1966, pp. 82–84.

14. Munson, J., "Patterns of Client Resistiveness and Counselor Response." *Dissertation Abstracts*, Vol. 21, 1961, pp. 2368–2369.

15. Rakos, R. F., and Schroeder, H. E., "Fear Reduction in Help-Givers as a Function of Helping." *Journal of Counseling Psychology*, Vol. 23, No. 5, 1976, pp. 428–435.

16. Rotter, J. B., "The Future of Clinical Psychology." *Journal of Consulting and Clinical Psychology*, Vol. 40, 1973, pp. 313–321.

17. Satir, V., *Conjoint Family Therapy*. Palo Alto, California: Science and Behavior Books, 1967, p. 97.

18. Scheid, A. B., "Clients Perception of the Counselor: The Influence of Counselor Introduction and Behavior." *Journal of Counseling Psychology*, Vol. 23, No. 6, 1976, pp. 503–508.

19. Simmons, W. L., "Clinical Training Programs 1964-1965 and 1968-1969: A Characterization and Comparison." *American Psychology*, Vol. 26, 1971, pp. 717–721.

20. Spiegel, S. B., "Expertness, Similarity and Perceived Counselor Competence." *Journal of Counseling Psychology*, Vol. 23, No. 5, 1976, pp. 436–441.

21. Strupp, H. H., "A Multi-dimensional Comparsion of Therapist Activity in Analytic and Client-Centered Therapy." *Journal of Consulting Psychology*, Vol. 21, 1957, p. 307.

22. Tolstoi, L., *War and Peace*. London: Oxford University Press, 1931. trans. by Maude, Lousie, and Aylmer, Vol. II Book X, p. 447.

23. Wile, D. B., "Personality Styles and Therapy Styles." *Psychotherapy: Theory, Research and Practice*, Vol. 13, No. 4, Winter, 1976, pp. 303–307.

24. Wrenn, R. L., "Counselor Orientation: Theoretical or Situational." *Journal of Counseling Psychology*, Vol. 7, 1960, pp. 40–45.

Chapter 7
Techniques

How effective the therapist is in the development of the treatment process will be dependent in considerable measure on the methods and the techniques which he employs.

The author has found that there are certain techniques which facilitate the treatment procedure outlined in Chapter 3.

The techniques which the author has found to be most helpful include the following:

1. Sculpting.
2. Role playing.
3. The effective handling of silences.
4. Confrontation.
5. Teaching via questioning.
6. Listening.
7. Recapitulating.
8. Recapitulation via summarizing.
9. Clarification and reflection of affect.
10. Video-taping.

SCULPTING

Sculpting is a technique which permits the family member to reveal to others in the family and not infrequently, to himself, his perceptions of the various intra-familial relationships. Sculpting permits him to do this without the anxiety usually precipitated by verbalizing his perceptions and feelings. As Duhl (1973) noted, therapists "use sculpting to take the conflict out of the verbal mode." What sculpting does is to permit an individual member of the family to put his feelings into action. He does this by arranging the other family members into what might be termed "the family relationship tableau." This tableau of the family which he puts together is all-important. It shows how he perceives the rest of the family to be in relation to him and in relation to each other. It is the reality which he perceives, the one to which he relates.

The beauty of this technique is that each member of the family is given an opportunity to look through each other member's eyes at the whole family. And of course, the therapist gets the same opportunity.

The therapist starts by asking for a volunteer to be a sculptor, who will arrange each of the others in the room as he sees them to be in relation to himself and to each other. What the author has learned is that an occasional individual is unwilling, perhaps even surly about trying the technique, but that most people are at least willing to participate. Invariably, too, at least one member of the family, usually the one who made the appointment, is positively eager to try it.

As the volunteer sculptor gets involved in his tasks of positioning the others in relation to himself, the others usually begin to get involved too. Their involvement, unfortunately, is not always supportive, but may be negative and critical. For example, 14 year old Mary, shy and inhibited, positions her mother with her back to Mary and three feet away and then places her father with his back to Mary and three feet away and then places her father with his back to both of them and five feet away. Mary is telling both of them in a most eloquent way how she perceives their relationships to be both in relation to her and to each other. Under such circumstances the mother and/or father may well object, and vitriolically. If and when this happens, it is the therapist's function to support and protect the relationship tableau. A useful technique, too, is to ask, "Isn't each of us entitled to his own perception of the family?" The therapist also stresses that whoever chooses to do so will be given an opportunity to sculpt his or her own perception of the family.

As the sculpting proceeds the members learn that the space between members is not the only significant aspect of the intrafamilial relationships. The sculptor's perception of the *how* and *why* of the members' positions in relation to each other is as important as *where* they are placed. Thus, the therapist should observe, and if he is puzzled, should question the sculptor. For example, a teen-ager places his mother between the other children and the father. Is she an obstacle to communication with Dad or a protector of the children? When mother and father are placed opposite but close to each other, is their position viewed by the sculptor as adversarial or closely communicative? Questions such as these help clarify the thinking not only of the therapist and the rest of the family, but frequently of the sculptor too.

Finally, what this author has learned is that those who are least powerful in the family (children, passive adults) seem to enjoy and benefit most from this technique. Heretofore, they have seldom been asked their opinion, or if asked they have been blocked from expressing it fully. As sculptors they are provided with a choice opportunity to be heard fully and without the anxiety of having to verbalize.

ROLE PLAYING

Another technique which the author has found to have merit is role playing. Please note that there is only one requirement for role playing—the role player must try to act and feel the way he thinks the person does who fills the role which he plays.

Role playing provides each member of the family with the opportunity to try on another role. The truth is that most people feel hamstrung, limited, often threatened and occasionally, even bored by their roles. Too often, they feel quite unable to break out of them. Not uncommonly too, many people behave as if they have been condemned to *one way behavior.* Role playing releases them from these feelings of condemnation, i.e. a daughter via role playing can become an instant mother.

Complementing all of this is the fact that when the individual changes roles he invariably changes also the avenues of communication which he naturally traveled. Thus a daughter can not only become an instant mother, but a *submissive* daughter can become a *condemning* mother.

This author has learned that role playing facilitates change in family therapy because a family member is given an opportunity to perceive the world through the eyes of any other member including those of the identified patient. What more effective way to come to understand and emotionally appreciate the problems of another than to try to experience them? When the condemning mother and the submissive daughter reverse roles and experience the grimace, laugh, posture and the talk of the other, both parties necessarily communicate much to themselves, to each other and to others in the family.

Mother, especially, gets a new, unattractive view of herself. Other members too get a different view of her because her behavior is being displayed by another person. And a totally new perspective of the mousey little daughter (who herself has a lot to learn about the maternal feelings) is presented to everyone.

Therapists who have employed this technique have discovered that families are almost always emotionally rocked by role playing each others' perceived roles. When role players interact their communications are unmistakable—I perceive the world which you perceive. I derive the meaning which you derive.

THE EFFECTIVE HANDLING OF SILENCES

Some families have a definite penchant for silence. They are successful in relating to each other with few words, emotions or behaviors. The members, for whatever reasons, prefer quiet and silence, and these families function successfully.

Silence in the family which comes for therapy, however, is a different issue. When a family coming for therapy is silent, their silence is frequently a product of the following emotions: shyness, fear, hostility, or a generalized anxiety.

Shyness and fear are understandable. After all, at the initial contact especially, the therapist is a stranger. Who can easily discuss without some qualms one's personal problems with a stranger, even if he is a "professional?" Add to this the presence of people who have contributed, if not created, one's emotional ills and the reader can begin to appreciate a few of the reasons for the shyness, fear and consequent silence of some of the families.

Hostility is sometimes the reason why certain family members are silent in therapy. They resent being brought into therapy. They have it rationalized as a lot of "crap." Not uncommonly, the adolescents in the family (usually males) and the husbands and fathers play the silent game during the first couple of sessions.

Another reason may be a generalized familial anxiety. Most of the members are "up tight" and their "up tightness" inhibits communication, especially talk. Conflicts and frustration have led to increased familial tensions. This type of family learned a long time ago that the best thing to do with conflicts and frustrations is to keep them bottled up, simply to keep silent about them. The therapist understands and appreciates some of these dynamics and has developed techniques to help family members open up. These techniques include the "wait out."

Patience and the "wait out."

The therapist simply sits, takes the family's cue and is silent. He should be aware that this may well be a traditional family stance, a silence filled with much anxiety, and the only stance which the family knows. By sitting quietly with them he may help to develop in them a sense of trust for him. Ironically then, silence might be the vehicle by which he gains acceptance into the family.

At the same time the therapist is aware that this silence which he endures with the family may well be both the cause and the symptom of the family's too painful homeostatic balance. Accordingly, if the therapist begins to feel that the emotional climate is too tense, too anxious for one or some of the members and/or for himself (he's a legitimate barometer too), he may wish to opt for the next technique.

CONFRONTATION

Confrontation is an art which when practiced effectively facilitates the whole therapeutic process. At the initial session the therapist often finds that it is appropriate to confront a family constrained by shyness or embarrassment. The appropriate confronting comments in such a situation might include the following:

"You're all very quiet, huh?"

"Are you always like this, quiet I mean?"

"Who's usually the most talkative?" (The author has discovered that it's a good idea to look at the one who made the initial contact when asking such a question.)

Confrontation is a technique which involves candor. Commonly, confrontation by the therapist emanates from an honest and sincere emotion and a finely tuned cognitive awareness of what is happening in the session. The therapist confronts when he feels or sees that the talk or behavior to which he and the other family members are exposed is blocking the therapeutic process.

The artistry in confrontation comes in:

1. the ability to pick the proper emotional climate.
2. the ability to discern that this is indeed an appropriate technique for both the individual and the family in question.
3. the consonance of the therapist's affect with the words.
4. the ability to choose words which are suitable, which will not alienate

the individual or his family but will, indeed, increase positive familial interaction.

The author has learned that confrontation of an offending family member is often best accomplished by asking another member (usually, but not always, the offended one) a question like, "What do you think of that" or "What is your response to that?" There are two reasons for such an approach. First, it promotes interaction intra-familially. Second, it obviates the possibility of the therapist being seen as some kind of hostile villain who attacks one or more members. The frequent result of such a perception is the development of alliances between and among members, thereby solidifying family members against the therapist and/or each other. Such occurrences, of course, only compound the problems and issues with which the therapist must deal.

It should be noted, too, that confrontation might not be an appropriate technique for every therapist, as it requires a strong assertive quality, a quality which might not gibe with the personality of every therapist. And so, as is true of other techniques, the effectiveness of confrontation will be premised upon the therapist's cognitive belief in the validity of its rationale and on how comfortable he is with it personally.

TEACHING VIA QUESTIONING

At least one other therapist believes with this author that teaching is a legitimate function of the therapist (Satir 1975). The reader should bear in mind that teaching therapy can result in learning and subsequent positive changes only if the family is exposed, not pressured, to its respective understandings and appreciations. A point to bear in mind is that the needs to be met are those of the *family*, not those of the *therapist*. The therapist should find out the style which is most consonant with his own personality. The author has found that the question and answer method works well for him.

Illustrative Transcript

The therapist is meeting for the second time with a three member family. Mother, Marie; Father, Al; and son, Billy. The son is the identified patient.

THERAPIST: Well now, how are things going?
AL: Well O.K. I guess. But I don't know that these meetings are all that good, I don't know if they're doing that much good.

THERAPIST: You don't see that much profit in these meetings?

AL: No offense, but I don't.

THERAPIST: Tell us, what do you remember about last week? Why don't you review what happened?

AL: What happened?

THERAPIST: Yeah, what happened? What did we talk about?

AL: Well, we told you we're here 'cause of Billy here. He got into trouble with the school . . . dealing you know. I don't have to go into . . .

THERAPIST: Not if you don't want to. But what did we point out about relationships, about how families . . .

AL: Yeah, yeah. I know what you said. But that's your opinion. That's just a lot of psychology.

(Short Pause)

I'm not sure I buy it.

THERAPIST: (Gently) you don't buy what?

AL: That all our problems are related.

MOTHER: Oh, Al. Of course they are.

AL: Christ, Marie! Isn't Billy responsible for what he done? I mean are we responsible for his selling marijuana in the school yard?

THERAPIST: Question is, why'd Billy do it? What can you tell us, Billy?

BILLY: I don't know. I guess I got problems.

AL: That's the trouble with you kids today. You got problems. Christ, I got problems too. I work. I work sixteen hours a day to put bread on the table. Work boy! I work for you here and for your mother.

THERAPIST: You work for Billy and Marie? That's a problem?

AL: Of course it's a problem.

THERAPIST: And you've got this problem called work mostly because of Billy and Marie? Is that right?

AL: Mostly. Yeah.

THERAPIST: (Pause, with a chuckle and gently) You see any connection here between your problems and . . .

AL: Yeah! Yeah. I see your point—all our problems are related.

MARIE: We're a family.

The above example is a trifle simplistic perhaps, but it serves to illustrate that questioning gently and with a specific objective in mind can be a useful technique in family therapy. It is doubtful after such a short exchange that Al does indeed buy completely the notion that all family problems are in some measure related, especially when his son was caught selling marijuana. Al would prefer to shed any culpability, and so he talked about personal responsibility. It was when he talked about his own "problem" related to working hard for Marie and Billy (we can discount some of his *why* of working hard) that he was able to see the networklike relationship of family causes and effects, motives and behavior. His view at this point is at best only cognitive. Continuing therapy should help to make the view more deeply appreciated. The point of all this is that it was the teaching-questioning technique which brought Al to see it at all and more importantly, to discuss it openly.

Teaching via questioning then, can be desirable. However, it would be inappropriate to use it exclusively, to rely upon it too heavily. The reality is that therapy is not an academic endeavor, but rather a search to ameliorate emotional ills. In sum, questioning, while helpful, is only one technique in the repertoire which the therapist continues to develop. In conjunction with sculpting and role playing and the other techniques considered below it can be useful.

LISTENING

A major reason that families enter therapy is that the members are unable and/or unwilling to listen to each other. These individuals are unable to function successfully because they "tune out" their environment, the people in it and even themselves. Their anxiety is such that they permit themselves to perceive so very selectively that after a while they are at best only marginally in contact with the rest of the world. We term these people emotionally ill. These are the emotionally blind who have unconsciously opted not to see. These are the cripples who, unfortunately, have become so perceptually diminished that they can not get through a day without such emotional crutches as amphetamines, tranquillizers and alcohol.

Listening as defined here involves more than just aural functions. Listening in family therapy has to do with being *sensorially attuned* to the whole family. The success of the family therapist will be a function of the extent to which he is sensorially attuned to the family which he treats.

Patterson (1959) believes that listening is, "the basic, most universal, most important technique in counseling and psychotherapy." Listening is "the basic and most important technique" because it helps the therapist to steep himself within the family's emotional milieu. The therapist who listens facilitates the process which Minuchin terms, "joining the family," and thereby, more quickly and more easily involves himself in the emotionally intimate moments of the therapy.

The therapist who is able to communicate that he listens both cognitively and emotionally expands and magnifies communication (Patterson 1962). "It is the first and basic activity of the counselor," because it is the foundation upon which rapport is built. As noted, a major reason for the family's emotional dysfunction is that no one has been listening to anyone. When the therapist listens then, he meets lonely, starved needs. Listening can only promote security, a sense of belongingness, and enhance self-esteem. Simply stated, when the therapist listens he's saying something. He's saying, "You are important."

Effective listening is not easy. Even the experienced therapists and those knowledgeable about its crucial importance can go astray. It is so easy in an emotionally laden session (at least for this therapist) to interrupt a family member with a question or even with what is meant to be a supportive remark. The effect invariably is to transfer the focus from the family member to the therapist. The author has learned to mitigate this problem somewhat by bearing in mind this notion, this question: "Whose needs am I trying to meet, mine or theirs?" The therapist who interrupts to give advice or a long discourse only serves to let the family members know that he is not especially interested in them.

Listening is concerned with being sensitive to all sounds, not just to words. It involves being attuned to non-vocal sounds such as clapping of hands, foot-stomping or finger snapping. Sounds such as these were termed *strepitus* by Westcott (1966, 1967). The sensitive therapist is one who observes, listens and learns about a family, i.e. the parent father who snaps his fingers to obtain silence from other family members can well communicate the patroon-like perception he has of his role and place in the family. Westcott also coined the term *phasis* to refer to voice tones, so important in reflecting the degree and quality of affect in one's voice. Phasis refers also to sighs, emotional cries and gasps. The sensorially receptive therapist "picks up" such non-language signals and is in a far better position to respond appropriately and more effectively make contact with the family members. In addition, therapists are aware that certain words are emotionally charged in general, i.e. sex, love, bed wetting, suck, lover, etc. And certain words are emotionally charged for particular families. Recently the author had in therapy a middle class white family, parents and a fourteen year old boy, all three of whom became incensed whenever any terms relating to race relations were introduced into the discussion, i.e. black, prejudice, affirmative action, etc. Only a little questioning elicited the fact that two black families had moved into their previously all-white neighborhood.

The reader might find the following list of practical techniques conducive to more effective listening.

1) **Posture.** The therapist should sit in a way which permits him to relate comparably to all the family. He should, if he chooses, be able to have eye contact with each member. His posture should be neither too

relaxed (I don't care) nor too tense (man, am I nervous!). His posture should say something like, "I am indeed interested."

2) **Privacy.** The therapy hour should be free from outside interruptions and distractions. Phone calls, outside messages as much as possible should await the end of the session. The therapist who permits outside interruptions is meeting *his* needs not those of the family. Moreover, he debilitates his ability to listen and thereby communicates such messages as "I'm a very busy man" and worse, "You people are not very important," or at least, "You are not as important as this business which I have to take care of."

3) **Behavioral Response.** The listener-therapist is fully cognizant about the messages, both latent and blatant, associated with body motions. He fully appreciates the fact that body motion is a function of emotion, sometimes covert, sometimes manifest. When the emotional climate warrants it, the therapist responds appropriately.

4) **Intrusions, internal.** No therapist can function optimally if he permits himself to be distracted by his own ideational intrusions. This author has had to learn to resist and suppress thinking about his own concerns during the therapy hour. Compartmentalization of one's own problems, however, is not always easy; at times it is downright difficult. The process of conscious suppression and resistance becomes a little more facile if the therapist bears in mind that the focus of the hour is the family, not the therapist.

RECAPITULATING

Frequently at counseling sessions certain family members go into long, ruminating and unfocused discourses. The reasons for these discourses are as many and varied as the people and the families whom the therapist will encounter. Some people are seeking much needed attention. Others are afraid and/or insecure. The long verbal smokescreen sometimes serves an important purpose, namely, to keep others at a distance. Then there are those people who are acutely anxious. These people learned a long time ago that long disjointed monologues burn up some of their excess anxiety. Or again, this same anxiety may well be interphering with their ability to organize their thoughts and communicate their feelings, hence the long unfocused verbal stream.

Whatever the reasons for the rambling discourse, the point is that the family therapist has to deal with it. Not uncommonly, certain family members belittle the member who has a penchant for long monologues. When this happens the therapist should step in, not to confront the belittler, but to recapitulate. When the therapist recapitulates he *verbally edits* the family member's ruminating soliloquy. He ties and connects together the disjointed phrases and poorly arranged verbalizations to try to preserve the important sense. In short, when he recapitulates the therapist interprets the talk of one member to the other. Auerswal (1974) found that such an effort, "enhanced an important goal of counseling, to talk about one's feelings."

The therapist recapitulates for several reasons. Long verbal discourses usually contain much latent meaning about the verbalizer and the family, more especially about the nature of their relationship. Secondly, when he recapitulates he helps the verbalizer focus, sharpen and delineate his thinking. The verbalizer, who may well have been free associating, usually is not aware of everything he has said. Thirdly, by recapitulating the therapist teaches the other family members how to better treat one of themselves. In sum, by recapitulating the therapist can meet and enhance both an individual and the family.

The sample which follows illustrates the recapitulating technique. This is a two member family. Mother (Marilyn) and daughter (Beverly), age 24, come in for therapy. It was Beverly who called for the appointment. Marilyn is the identified patient. Marilyn has been quite depressed since the death of her husband, four months ago.

THERAPIST: Well, now you were saying last time, Marilyn, that you spend an awful lot of time crying.
MARILYN: Yes, I do. I spend an awful lot of time crying.
BEVERLY: Lord, that's all she ever does, cry, cry, cry. She's too much.
MARILYN: You're so cruel. You're so heartless. I can't help it. Beverly, I don't know why I put up with you. I don't. I cry a lot because I have a lot to cry about. The only man in my life, your father, passed away. You don't seem yet to understand that. You're so heartless. (softly weeping) I cry a lot but you didn't cry at all even when he died, either at the wake or at the funeral. I guess I'm crying for both of us. You just don't seem to understand. Sometimes we all need to be taken care of. I'm crying because my anchor, my strength, my supporter died. Your father took care of me. God, I feel so lonely. God forgive you Beverly, you're no company. Maybe it's because you don't understand.
BEVERLY: No, I don't understand. Heavens sakes. Act your age! You go on so-o-o-o long about the same things. Dad's been dead for almost five months now. You drove *him* crazy, too.

MARILYN: Oh, you are a mean one. (Her eyes are tear rimmed.) You're so strong. So hard! Nothing phases you too much even your own father's death. You just took that in your stride. And he was such a good father! Such a good father! Well I can't take it in my stride. He meant too much to me. (Turning facing the therapist) He was so good to me always. He took care of things. A place for everything. And everything in its place. He used to say that all the time. He was a meticulous man, neat as the proverbial pin. I never had to pick up after him. In fact he used to make my breakfast every Sunday morning and every morning during the working week he used to bring me my coffee. He was a reliable man who was in control. (She sighs in a quiet, helpless, almost vulnerable way.) No one understands now. Beverly's right. I do go on so. You're probably confused.

THERAPIST: (chuckles) I'm perennially a little bit. But I feel you told me and Beverly a lot. Your husband took care of you not only as a husband but sometimes even in a sort of fatherly way. He's gone now and you feel like a lost child. (pause) Especially since Beverly refuses to uh . . .

MARILYN: To be a mother to me?

BEVERLY: Oh, Mother. Don't you see? That's why we're always fighting so much! That's why I didn't cry when Daddy died.

MARILYN: Oh! My. (pause) Is it possible?

The excerpt illustrates how a therapist listens attentively and then takes the most meaningful points of a member's discourse and recapitulates them. The effect is to communicate to both family members important aspects of the essential problem.

RECAPITULATING VIA SUMMARY

A corollary to the recapitulation technique explained above is the summary. In family therapy sessions there are lengthy periods when most or all of the members have made many comments, exchanged innumerable pleasantries and/or hostilities. In situations such as these the therapist may find it valuable to tie all the comments together, to sum them up as it were. When she sums up she is explaining what the varied comments mean to her and thereby, perhaps, to others. The author has found that recapitulating via summary can be a pretty good teaching device in therapy (if the family is emotionally receptive). An appropriate time to recapitulate is at the end of a session (See Chapter 11), but it can be profitable at any point in a session.

CLARIFICATION AND REFLECTION OF AFFECT

Family therapy is characterized by a continual oscillation of feelings. Feelings are at the core, at the very nub of the therapy process. The dysfunction of feelings, the disconsonance between feelings and behavior are a major reason why families come into therapy. Often one or more of the members, commonly, though not always the identified patient, is beset by what might be termed "feeling confusion." This member is not sure what his feelings are. More particularly, he's not sure what he feels about the other members of his family. He's not too sure if he likes or dislikes them. Worse still, he's very unsure what their feelings are toward him. His feelings of anger, especially when with the family, once a periodic thing, are with him regularly now. Then again he may be disturbed by his inability to express the anger which he feels. All of this troubles him. What may trouble him even more is that too frequently his behavior does not gibe with his feelings. In short, this person does not always seem to be able to *manage* his feelings appropriately.

At the outset the therapist must communicate that he respects and equally important, responds to feelings. The therapist never shies away from feelings. If anything he moves toward them and communicates an exquisite sensitivity concerning them. This does not mean that he is under some kind of mandate to always accept them as valid and just, i.e. hate especially. Rather he lets any and each member know that he, the therapist recognizes and does not condemn their existence. He simply wants to know about them and is willing, even eager, to *listen* to what the individual believes to be the "why" of them.

The therapist who can communicate his positive view and receptivity to feelings is an odds on favorite to succeed. He who can not do this or worse, who tends to shy away from feelings, has the deck stacked against him. The reality, both emotional and cognitive, in the therapy setting is that the therapist who can not react appropriately to the feelings emitted by any member is one who is perceived as quasi-rejecting by one or more members of the family. The rationale which continually operates with each family member is, "my feelings are me." The therapist who recognizes this simple dictum is more likely to be successful. He who does not is doomed to failure. The "why" of this is simple. First, the feelings oriented therapist can relate better to each member of the family and secondly, feelings are the rationale, the *emotional rationale*, for words spoken, for behavior exhibited. In sum, the communications even to the most confused of family members by the unfeeling therapist may be difficult to understand, but they are positively clarion emotionally and they are these:

"You do not know how to deal with my feelings. You reject them. You reject me."

This therapist has learned that there are two techniques which can facilitate emotional communication and acceptance between the therapist and the family. These are clarification and reflection.

Clarification

Concerns the content of the words spoken.

Clarification deals with the conscious, mental, intellectual aspects of the individual's delivery. When he clarifies, the therapist directs his attention to the cognitive *meaning* of the verbalization. The therapist explains what he understands that the individual's discourse means for him (and thereby for others). The intent here is to help member(s) to understand feelings via the words spoken.

A young couple make up the two member family in the following excerpt. John is a graduate student, Jenny, a full time registered nurse. Their marital problems center around John's apparent need to dictate, control and program their lives. It was Jenny who called for an appointment.

JENNY: At first I didn't mind it. I didn't mind his compulsive ways. Lately it's been bothering me and a lot.

JOHN: We fight all the time. And I'm getting sick of it. She just won't listen to me.

JENNY: And why not? Why not, won't I listen? For two years now we've been married and *all* I do, all I've ever done is listen. I'm simply not a computer. You can't program me like you program a computer. Don't you see? I'm a person. I got a perfect right to make decisions. Marriage doesn't mean you run my life. Where's the partnership? You point me and I go? I can't live my life completely according to what you want.

THERAPIST: What you're saying Jenny is that you feel that you're being molded into a kind of robot-like extension of John.

JENNY: Precisely. Exactly, I have to clean the house when he wants.

THERAPIST: Speak to *him* Jenny, not me.

JENNY: Anyway I have to clean the house when you want. Cook what you want, when you want. I don't even mind cooking and cleaning but can't it at least be on my terms since I'm going to do it? And as far as that goes I'm not sure I should *always* do it *all the time*. I'm working 48 hours a week too. Everything is when you want, what you want, how you want. (Jenny's normally high pitched voice was getting very loud.) John, I'm really getting . . .

JOHN: Can't you talk softly?

JENNY: (Turning to the therapist. Very loudly) See, I can't even talk the way I want!

THERAPIST: Correct me if I'm wrong folks, but the problem here seems to be that Jenny, you feel put upon by excessive demands, and by having your life computerized according to what, you, John, want. You don't feel your needs are being met in this marriage, only his.

JENNY: Yes, that's well put. Don't you see, John, your needs seem to be paramount to mine. Isn't that what I complain about, John?

JOHN: (sighing) Yeah, I suppose.

What the reader should observe are Jenny's responses to the therapist's clarification. Both responses are positive, indicating that she accepts the clarifications put forth. Readily accepted clarifications are also signs that the therapy group is on the same cognitive and emotional wavelength.

Reflection

When he reflects, the therapist focuses upon the emotions being ventilated by one or more members. His concern here is of feelings underlying the words spoken by a given family member and the behaviors effected. Reflection of feeling, like confrontation (discussed above under silence), is an artistic endeavor. Accurate, effective, perceptive reflection is a function of keenly sharpened listening skills and being emotionally attuned to the family dynamics generally and to the particular member speaking. Reflection is an art because it is founded upon the sensitivity of the therapist's emotional antennae. The focus of reflection is not upon the expressed but upon the unexpressed, upon the affective meaning implied. How does the therapist do all this? This author is very much aware of the irony of trying to teach about reflection of feelings via the printed word. Quite apparently, it needs to be observed, heard and ultimately done to be learned. Nevertheless, it should be noted that a therapist can facilitate reflection if he responds with words, inflections, voice lilts and tones which complement and are consonant with the lines spoken by the family member(s).

Reflection of feeling is illustrated with the same two family members.

JENNY: Anyway what was I saying? Oh yeah, I have to be my own person, I just can't . . .

JOHN: Oh, Jenny, all you ever concern yourself with is you. All we've been talking about at these sessions, which we can't afford by the way, but that you wanted, is you.

THERAPIST: Sounds like you're feeling resentful, maybe hostile, John. Jenny's spending good money for what seems to you a lot of silliness.

JOHN: Yeah, right on!

JENNY: O.K. maybe it is true. Maybe I want sessions for me, just for me. Then what's that say for you?

JOHN: (Apparently bewildered) What? I don't get you. What are you talking about?

Pause.

THERAPIST: What I think she's saying is that she needs to have these sessions here because she doesn't feel her needs are being met at home.

JENNY: Exactly. I'm just not going to be shaped and molded, into something or somebody that I'm not or don't want to be. I have my own needs.

JOHN: Needs. Schmeeds. That's a lot of crap. Look, in case you forgot we're married. It's the marriage which has needs. Right now I have to study for my degree. I can't use valuable time screwing around cooking and cleaning houses and worrying about the unimportant things. The way I see it if I don't get my degree this marriage is not going to get off the ground, not now, not ever.

THERAPIST: What you're really saying here is that you feel Jenny's needs are not as important as yours because it's you who is under the pressure, it's you who has to get the degree which is going to give the family status and probably a lot of money to boot.

JOHN: You got it. You said it better than I did.

The therapist takes the expressed communication and expands upon its even more powerful underlying intent. The validity of the therapist's work is seen in the argument and the assents with which the members receive the reflections. Again, the reader should be aware that the tones and inflections he uses emotionally gibe with and complement the verbalizations of the family member.

VIDEO-TAPING

Carl Rogers (1961) once observed that, ". . . the only learning which significantly influences behavior is self-discovered, self-appropriated learning." The video-tape playback provides a tool to "discover and appropriate" for one's self about one's self. This is true not only for family members but also for the therapist, whether he be a beginner or one of much experience.

More often than not, a family therapy hour is a time of high drama, filled with emotion, telltale behaviors and verbalizations permeated with "double entendres." No therapist (even with an assistant monitor) can catch all of this human drama. Properly utilized, the video-tape can not only do so, but can then play back the hour for examination, discussion and reflection.

Most people who view a tape for the first time focus upon themselves. Alger (1969) has shown that if self "image impact" is strong then the individual can benefit. However, if the "image impact" is weak then the usefulness of the video-tape is diminished.

The typical individual begins to examine his place and impact upon the family very quickly after his first "image impact." Thus, the controlling husband, the demeaning wife, the surly adolescent all have an opportunity to get a different perspective of themselves, of their affect upon others and of the reaction which others have to them. For example, the controlling husband viewing himself for the first time begins to appreciate better the extent of his control and the impact which it has upon the family. He watches and sees how his wife, son and daughter check his expression before and after they speak. He notices for the first time the angry grimaces which his wife makes to his daughter when he "corrects" his son. Similarly, the well intentioned but anxious wife after a particularly emotionally intense session is asked by her husband at the beginning of the replay to count the number of times she put him down. She is surprised to count eleven times in the space of twenty-five minutes.

The value of the tape becomes even more readily apparent in the replay because interpersonally negative kinds of behavior are generally denied when occurring live. During the replay both the behavior and the denial are viewed. To illustrate, fifteen-year-old Alice is talking to her sixteen-year-old brother, "You know how I don't care about your *ugly* acne. No, I don't mind it at all. It's all in your head." On replay she sees herself looking away as she says those words and her brother also points out to her forcibly that she didn't look at him even once during the session. An especial value of the video-tape technique then, is that it *records* the double message. It gives both the sender and the intended recipient evidence that there were indeed two messages. The recipient comes to understand better that his interpretation was accurate and thereby perhaps, reinforces the validity of ' is hurt, anger, embarrassment, etc. The replay proves to him and to othei that he wasn't "crazy." The sender too, is given an opportunity to understand better the why of the recipient's response.

In sum, a video-tape is a valuable tool and one which can facilitate both learning and positive change in the family treated. Despite its considerable value, however, use of the video-tape machine like most tools can be abused i.e., if one were to tape a fifty minute session and then replay it, the replay for such an amount of time "may be too taxing unless each viewer has a specific and active task." Bodin (1972) suggests such tasks as making observations, taking notes or expressing the current emotion felt. In any case the therapist should use discretion and his best judgement on the amount of time spent viewing a replay.

Finally, most families are receptive to the video when told that its use can indeed ease learning and enhance the treatment. Initially, the video seems to inhibit certain families from participation, especially those families where there is much suspicion about intra-familial motives. In such cases especially, the therapist would be wise to elicit arguments from all of the participants that the video-tape be used.

CITATIONS

1. Alger, I., "Therapeutic Use of Video-tape Playback." *Journal of Nervous Mental Disorders*, Vol. 148, 1969, pp. 430-436.

2. Auerswal, M. C., "Differential Reinforcing Power of Restatement and Interpretation on Client Production of Affect." *Journal of Counseling Psychology*, Vol. 21, 1974, No. 1, pp. 9-14.

3. Bodin, A., "The Use of Video Tapes." In *The Book of Family Therapy*, eds. Ferber, A., Mendelsohn, M., and Napier, A., New York: Houghton Mifflin, 1972, pp. 318-337.

4. Duhl, F. J., Kantor, D., and Duhl, B. S., "Learning, Space and Action in Family Therapy: A Primer of Sculpture." In *Techniques of Family Psychotherapy, A Primer*, ed. Blich, D. A., New York: Grune and Stratton, 1973, p. 60.

5. Minuchin, F., *Families and Family Therapy*. Cambridge: Harvard Univ. Press, 1974, p. 89.

6. Patterson, C. H., *Counseling and Psychotherapy: Theory and Practice*. New York: Harper and Row, 1959, p. 168.

7. Patterson, C.H., *Counseling and Guidance in Schools*. New York: Harper and Row, 1962, p. 117.

8. Rogers, C. R., *On Becoming A Person.* Boston: Houghton Mifflin Co. 1961, p. 276.

9. Satir, V., "Problems and Pitfalls in Working With Families." In *Helping Families to Change,* Satir, V., Stachowiak, J., and Taschman, H. New York: Jason Aronson, Inc., 1975, p. 135.

10. Westcott, R., "Introducing Coenetics." *American Scholar,* Vol. 35, 1966, pp. 342-356.

11. Westcott, R., "Strepital Communication." *The Bulletin,* Vol. 12, 1967, pp. 30-34.

Part Two

The Practice

Chapter 8
Some Clinical Data

REPORT OF SOCIAL WORKER

John Whiting lives about three miles from the center of town. The house is situated on an acre and is approximately twenty years old and of a colonial-type architecture. It is big, rambling and was built by Mr. Whiting himself. He is a self-employed carpenter. There is a long, gravel driveway leading up to it; trees, flowers, and shrubbery abound. The place is not too well maintained, however.

Mrs. Whiting is a pretty auburn-haired woman who looks much younger than her 40 years. Mr. Whiting is only a few years older than she but looks to be in his middle fifties at least. Both appear to be unhappy, even desolate. I should note here that it was Mrs. Whiting who provided virtually all of the information. Mr. Whiting responded to my questions in one or two word answers. He was polite but non-communicative. He was not unfriendly, however.

They are very concerned about their son John. Mrs. Whiting reported that to the best of her knowledge the trouble started only recently. It seems that in the past month they have had to see school authorities about John, who was involved in selling marijuana at school. I checked on this with the assistant principal, a Mr. Sortino, and found that it was indeed true. Mr. Sortino had caught him at it. Also in the past week, Mrs. Whiting has had to go down to the police station to pick up John. He had been involved in a fight in front of the South End Dairy Bar and was drunk according to Sgt. Perkins who was on duty that night. Officers Mazzola and Acito, who stopped the fight, reported that John was choking the other person (also a teenager) and might well have killed the fellow if they had not intervened.

Mrs. Whiting reports that she and her husband have been married for twenty years. They have two older boys, Thomas and Francis III, neither of whom is living at home any longer. They are rooming together on Green Street here in town. Both boys, he indicated, were also problems growing up but not to the extent that John is presently. Neither had ever been involved in any law-breaking. There is also a younger sibling, Alice, who is twelve years old.

If nothing else, Mrs. Whiting is genuinely and sincerely concerned about all this turmoil with John. Mr. Whiting gave me this same impression. She feels that, "Everything is closing in on me." Three months ago she was admitted to the State Psychiatric Hospital. She states that it was for nervous exhaustion and depression. I was unable to obtain the hospital records to confirm this diagnosis. At any rate, she was in the hospital for approximately three weeks. She states that she enjoyed her stay, as it got her away from (her words) "family pressures and demands." These pressures have now all returned via John's delinquencies. Several times during the interview she murmured, "We're in trouble in this family," or "We're a family in trouble," or words to that effect. At this point I was inclined to agree.

Later on in the conversation she indicated that her depression and consequent stay in the hospital was a function of an unwanted pregnancy. She miscarried while in the hospital. She explained this miscarriage to herself then and does now as "God's will." She believes this because it is the only miscarriage which she has ever experienced. Another baby, she honestly believes, especially at this time would have, (her words) "sent me over the edge."

I asked her what the 'family pressures and demands' were which had brought on her 'nervous exhaustion and depression.' Her response was vague. "Mostly it was the pregnancy, the worry of it." One more time I inquired about the 'family pressures' to which she had first alluded. "I don't know honestly. It's probably all tied up with being bored, with being a bored housewife." I believed her, that is, I believed that she didn't know, that it might well be tied up with being bored. I believe in retrospect that Mrs. Whiting did not want to use her husband as a scapegoat, but that she very much had him on her mind when she talked about being bored. There is little question that Mr. Whiting is a very quiet man. I could understand a woman feeling bored when with him.

My best judgement on the basis of this interview is that Mr. Whiting is a detached introverted man who does not involve himself very much in the family. According to Mrs. Whiting, and he did not object, it was she who brought up the children, she who disciplined and she who rewarded them. It seems to be a lone parent family with two parents. What seems to compound the problem further is the fact that Mrs. Whiting is very much an emotionally dependent person yet her husband, does not seem to be one upon whom she can lean. He has too many problems of his own. I do not know what these problems are specifically, but they do indeed inter- phere with his ability to be a nurturant, demonstratively loving husband. Mrs. Whiting's present desolate condition is a dramatic testimony to this. Also, Mr. Whiting's obviously unhappy state may well be an indirect function of his feelings of ineptitude as a husband.

According to Mrs. Whiting her pregnancy with John was perfectly normal. She did not gain a disproportionate amount of weight (22 lbs.), she suffered no morning sickness or any difficulty of any kind. She delivered John as a full term baby. He weighed 8 lbs. 3 ounces.

As a child John followed almost a stereotyped developmental pro- gression. He crept at nine months and walked at just under a year. He was able to feed himself before he was two. He was fully trained before he was three and a half.

According to Mrs. Whiting, John was a very easy child to rear. He was a passive, introverted child who accepted maternal requests easily and gracefully. Virtually no paternal demands were ever made.

An interesting aspect of John's childhood was his uncommon and abiding interest in religion, specifically the Roman Catholic Faith, its doctrines and teachings. According to Mrs. Whiting, John took to his C.C.D. (Confraternity of Christian Doctrine) classes in a positively zealous fashion. He led his First Communion class in knowledge of prayers and doctrine. He was rewarded for his efforts and at the first Communion class served the Mass. The pastor of the church, a Father Carrig, reports that John Whiting learned the mass prayers and routine faster than any boy he'd ever known. Father Carrig is now 62.

John's devotion to religion did not end with his first Communion (age 7) nor with his Confirmation (age 12). In between those years he served Mass as an Acolyte of the church (alter boy) on an average of four times per week. And if John did not serve the Mass, he attended it at 7 AM, virtually every day.

Mrs. Whiting was heartened by this behavior. She is a Catholic. Mr. Whiting, who is a non-church-going Protestant, apparently was indif- ferent; at least he admittedly never took notice of John's zealous invol- vement in religious life. Mrs. Whiting was heartened by John's spirituality. She often observed him kneeling by his bed saying his rosary. The latter were a gift from his maternal grandmother on the occasion of his first Communion. John hung them on his bedpost and according to his mother fingered them to sleep every night. She reports that until he was fourteen or so, he often spoke to her about becoming a priest.

John's inordinate interest in the church, it's teaching and it's practices, continued unabated into the ninth grade, his last year of Junior High School. Sometime during that year his daily attendance at Mass began to wane. It has never perked up again. Presently he does not attend church at all.

Until the age of fourteen John's life was fairly typical. He had a good number of friends, was a better-than-average student in school, played in Little League and even in the Babe Ruth League. In the winter he sledded and ice skated. His teachers (3d, 5th, and one 7th grade) remember him as a quiet, serious boy who laughed uproariously when another boy did or said something even marginally funny. They report that while he was not a leader he was well liked by his peers.

Perhaps the most significant fact about John's life for the past couple of years is that he has been heavily involved with a girl, Diane Henessey. He calls her "Dee." They have been going together since the middle of tenth grade. His mother says that he spends virtually all of his free time with her. They are, according to her, "inseparable." Mrs. Whiting does not know Mrs. Henessey but has the distinct impression, on the basis of a short phone conversation, that John is *persona non grata* in the Henessey home. She herself likes "Dee" and sees her frequently, as John brings her home four or five times per week. This pleases her, but it worries her a little too. Perhaps they are spending too much time together. I asked pointedly if it concerned sex. She blushed a little (Mr. Whiting did too), but admitted she'd not brought it up to John. She did not know how. If this family enters therapy there is much to be explored.

Ethel Johnson, MSW
Consulting Case Worker

Personal Views by the Family Members to: Describe Conditions within the Family before Therapy

Before Therapy: Francis

This the first time I ever dictated into a tape recorder. Off the top of my head? How was it before therapy? I was inhibited. I couldn't make it sexually and I was just a big blob socially.

My wife thought I didn't care about anything about sex, about how I was with people. I cared. I didn't know how to show it. I was unemotional, still am for that matter, but now I can show how I feel, at least I can in the family.

How was it before therapy? It was tough at home. I was quiet, probably too quiet. My wife yelled a lot, probably to make up for my quiet. I knew she was frustated. I think I knew that before she did, I just didn't know what to do about it, or how to do. Mostly I suppose, what to do.

I was quiet and when my wife wasn't yelling the whole house was quiet. Like a morgue, a morgue filled with people that were dead as far as spirit, or talk or love. We all lived in an eight room tomb, and it was like I was head zombie. (chuckle) I never thought about it like that until just now. That sort of sums it all up.

I didn't do much 'cause I guess looking back now I just didn't know what or how to do. But I guess I'm repeatin' myself.

Before Therapy: Kathleen

What I remember most clearly before our sessions with Dr. Perez was that I was very, very bored and that I raged and nagged a lot, at the children and at my husband. I went through periods where I felt so bored I cried. I walked from room to room crying. I used to cry out loud, "We're in trouble. We're in trouble." I thought then I meant "we" as a family. I realize now I meant mostly "me" as a person. I was bored but I couldn't keep up with simple housework or meal planning or cooking or whatever. I was bored and at the same time I had no interest at all in doing anything. In fact the only way I knew I was even alive was that I yelled—loud and often. Thinking about it now, that's why I did it, to confirm that I was alive. I got kind of perverted joy when I was in the process of screaming. Afterwards I'd feel very guilty. Then I'd hate myself for doing it. Then in a little while I felt tired and very, very bored again. That's what it was like for me before therapy—boredom, seething anger, screaming, guilt, self-hate. Vicious circle after vicious circle.

My husband was like a mute. He paid no attention to me, in or out of bed, which didn't help anything especially my feelings of self-hate. We had no relationship. Looking back I guess we hadn't had one for a long time.

So what I did to compound mine and the family problems was to isolate myself for hours at a time. I'd spend most of the day in my bedroom crying, dozing and just being depressed. I withdrew into my bedroom and let the house ship sink. The kids got the brunt of it, especially Alice. Laundry was never done. The house was a mess. Supper was never ready. And I didn't care except to yell at Alice to get supper or help out.

I didn't care. Nobody seemed to care about anything. Those times were unspeakably dreadful.

Before Therapy: Alice

Before we went for our counseling mom was always sick, or too tired to do anything. She didn't seem to have too much interest in doing anything for the family. She used to make me do most of the work that she was supposed to do, like getting supper and picking up the house. She wasn't really sick, sick like with a fever. But she had an awful lot of headaches. I think she started to get them every afternoon when me or John, mostly John, came in from school.

Daddy never talked. I guess that's one thing that stands out a lot. Daddy was like "deaf and dumb," he never said anything about anything. But to be fair about it, nobody talked, like to each other. It was like a church at home and just about as quiet as that too. Everybody avoided everybody. And looking back on those awful days I learned that avoiding (avoidance) is like an infectious disease. It really gets to you.

Mom screamed a lot too. Mom and Dad used to fight a lot. Mostly mom screamed and dad listened. I remember one fight that was real bad. Daddy had said something like, "Oh Kathleen, don't make a big deal out of nothing" and then she screamed real loud even for her "Jesus Christ Almighty all that ever comes out of your mouth is, 'Don't make a big deal out of nothing' Nothing, nothing, nothing. Oh, Francis. You are the nothing. Don't you see that!"

In a way she was right. Daddy seemed to care about nothing. He went to work. He worked hard but he wasn't like in the family. He was more like a ghost who hung around. He never bothered anybody, either me or John anyway. But he was there. Always there. But he was like unimportant or invisible.

But the worst thing about everything was supper every night. Very tense, very up-tight. I got so I hated supper. Mom had this whole thing (I think dad did too) that we had to eat together every night. Well every night was fight night or worse. No one and I mean no one said a word. Not mom, not dad, not John and I was too scared that if I opened my mouth we'd have a battle royal so I didn't talk either. I remember those supper times with horror.

Before the therapy John and I were very distant or anyway we weren't what you'd call close. We never talked. I guess we acted like mom and dad.

The only other thing I can say about that awful time before the therapy is that mom was mad. Like all the time she was in a rotten mood. Sometimes she was so mad or she was in such a rotten mood she acted crazy, I mean really crazy. Like I remember I was at a Junior High School dance and she came to pick me up earlier than she was supposed to. She saw me dancing with this kid and she thought we were dancing too close. Well she came up to me and right in front of the whole gym she started yelling at me. That was the worst moment I can remember. Those times were like just—ugh!

Before Therapy: John

We all went into therapy because I got caught selling weed in school and 'cause I got caught ripping-off a tape deck. The judge made us go into therapy. Best thing that ever happened to us.

Before we started meeting with Perez the house was either very quiet like an abandoned house or noisy like lunch time in a school cafeteria. When it was quiet it was like quiet. My father's a quiet guy. Real quiet. He didn't even walk loud. In fact you might say he was like a ghost. Haunted the house. It got so dad made me real uncomfortable, gave me the creeps. He just sort of looked at me. Just looked at me. Stared at me. Then he'd shake his head and walk away. Weird! That was the quiet part—dad. Then there was the noisy part—ma. Ma was as noisy, as loud as dad was quiet. If dad never talked, ma never shut up. If me or Alice spilled something at supper dad never said anything, maybe he didn't even notice, I don't know. But Ma, she ranted and went bananas. When ma wasn't feeling good which was like most of the time supper time was disaster time.

Our house was cold. It wasn't warm. No affection. Except for ma once in a long while hugging or kissing Alice there was no affection shown. My father was like an iceberg toward everybody. And, I don't remember my mother ever holding me or kissing me before our therapy sessions. Maybe it happened when I was real small but I don't remember it.

*   *   *   *   *

Each of the chapters which follows is preceded by Focus Guides and followed by Discussion Questions. Both the Focus Guides and the Discussion Questions were designed with the reader in mind; to help him glean the maximum amount of information from each chapter and to help him develop insight into the complex interpersonal dynamics presented.

Chapter 9
The Initial Interview

FOCUS GUIDES

1. As you read this chapter consider the nature of the parental dyad. How do Kathleen and Francis Whiting view each other? Is there respect for one another?

2. Consider how each of the four Whitings views himself.

3. Which avenues of communication does Kathleen utilize with each member of her family? Which avenues does each of the others utilize with her, with each other?

4. How would you rank-order the Whiting family in terms of motivation for family therapy? What reasons would you give for the position of each on your list?

5. Do you think that there might be a latent triad within the Whiting family? If so, what is its composition?

The four members of the Whiting family arrived for the first session on a Monday evening. I greeted them at the door of the family counseling center, which is decorated like a comfortable but non-descript family living room; three easy chairs, two couches, a coffee table, and so forth.

"Please sit," I said, "Make yourselves at home."

Kathleen walked over to the larger couch. Alice followed and sat next to her. Her husband hesitated a moment, then sat two chairs over from his wife, in a worn easy chair. John sat further away, in the chair most distant from his family. I always take note of how members position themselves because I've learned that how the family positions itself in the room is often symbolic of the intrafamilial relationships. My initial impressions from the positions they took then, was that John and his father were loners within the family, but that probably some kind of relationship existed between Kathleen and Alice. We would see.

I offered them coffee, coke and brownies. Kathleen accepted only coffee. Alice took a coke and a brownie.

We exchanged amenities for a few moments and I made a banal comment about the weather. It was to that, that Francis nodded pleasantly. "Yeah, I haven't lost any days for the past two weeks."

"You're a carpenter, aren't you!"

"Yeah, self-employed."

"Are you working outdoors, right now?"

"Yeah, he's shingling a house over in Riverdale, "Kathleen interjected.

"Oh, do you come home for lunch Francis?"

"Not if I pack him one," she responded for him. "He prefers to come home."

"And what do you prefer?"

"Well, it's six of one and half a dozen of another. If I make it and he takes it, then I don't have to worry about lunch the next day, but the problem is that I have to remember to make it and I don't always. And if I don't, then I have to stop whatever I'm doing and make his lunch 'cause he's coming home, either way it's a bother."

"You resent making it."

"I guess I do, a little anyway."

"I see."

"Has it been a source of trouble between the two of you, Mr. Whiting, uh, Francis?"

"I don't . . ."

"Oh, it has sometimes," Kathleen interrupted.

"I see."

"How's work going, Francis? Has it been pretty good so far this year?"

"He never earns enough. He works so hard but it's never enough." Again Kathleen had answered for him.

"What do *you* think, Francis? I'm interested in what *you* think."

"It's been O.K., I mean like I haven't missed many days at all this year."

"You enjoy your work."

"Yeah, I do."

"I take it you're good at your work and you . . ."

"Well, he may enjoy it, but he always comes home so tired. He . . ."

"Mrs. Whiting, right now anyway I'm interested in what Mr. Whiting has to say."

Several times now Mrs. Whiting had interrupted her husband or had answered a question directed at him. I wondered how many times over the course of their marriage he had been subtly, even embarrassingly, put down in private conversations and in front of others.

"You come home tired sometimes."

"Yeah, sometimes."

"Often," Kathleen contradicted. "He's just not interested in doing much of anything, or participating in anything at home. Comes in, eats and then goes into the dining room where he closes the door and watches the "boob tube" that his sister Phyllis gave him two years ago. He doesn't want to do anything. And you have to admit Francis, that you go to bed real early."

Francis just sat there looking at me, not responding.

Francis, how would you respond to Kathleen?"

"You can't respond to Kathleen. She's got her mind all made up. You can't talk 'cause she does all the talking, all the time. Every time I try to say something she talks louder and faster. I can't keep up with her."

"Don't tell me, Francis, tell her," I said.

"What do you mean, you can't talk to me. That's all I ever wanted, you to talk to me. All I get from you are shrugs and mostly silences." Kathleen's voice had risen several decibles.

Francis shrugged, looked at me and said, "See?"

"Tell her, Francis, tell her how you feel, or is it true that you're silent and you just shrug at her?"

At this point Kathleen had edged forward on the couch and was about to speak. I raised my hand and signaled her to hush up.

"Yeah. I guess there's some truth to the fact that I've always been a quiet guy."

Alice now interjected with, "Yeah, daddy, you've always been . . ." It was Kathleen who elbowed her to be quiet.

Francis saw Kathleen's movement.

"Yeah, like I was saying, I've probably always been too quiet. I guess I take after my father. Runs in the family."

I nodded, "I see."

"Yes, he was a quiet man, Mr. Whiting. But he was a strong man too. People treated him with a lot of respect. A lot."

"That's true," said Francis.

The obvious implication in Kathleen's comment was that Francis was not strong, was not treated with respect by people. And, of course, his response, "That's true," rewarded her demeaning remark. I began to understand, then, that if Francis was weak, was the passive one in this marital relationship, it was because his emotional make-up permitted it and unconsciously he reinforced it.

There was a moment when no one spoke. I looked at them."Well, now, what's the real reason we're here?" There was a momentary pause and, predictably, it was Kathleen who answered.

"Judge O'Brien," she murmured, "He said we all had to come for family therapy. It was one of the conditions of John's probation. But you know that, Dr. Perez."

"Yes, I do. And, uh, call me Joe. I'm more comfortable in this kind of situation to be on a first name basis."

"Well, if you must know, I'm not. I've never, ever called a doctor by his first name. I know it's kind of the fashion today, but I'm not comfortable with it."

"O.K., suit yourself. Maybe as we get into our sessions you'll become more comfortable with it. Up to you. And you're right, I did know about O'Brien and the fact that he made family therapy a condition for John's probation. My point in asking was to learn if you believe that that's the real problem in your family?"

"Why, what do you mean?" Kathleen asked with apparent sincerity.

"Well, only that I believe that adolescent delinquency is very much family related."

Kathleen nodded. "Judge O'Brien said something like that."

"Do you believe it?" I asked.

"I, I don't know. I guess my problem is I don't see it, I don't understand it," she said.

I glanced at John. He'd not uttered a word since arriving. There was a noncommittal expression on his face. But there was interest too.

"John, what do you think?"

" 'Bout what?"

" 'Bout your family. You think your family had something to do with your getting into trouble?"

"I dunno."

"What do you think the problems are in the family. I mean, what do you think the basic problem in the family is?"

"Nobody cares about nothin'."

"Do you care?"

He shrugged. "I care about as much as any of them do."

"Which isn't much, I gather."

"Yeah," he said tonelessly.

"Alice, what do you think?" I asked.

She nodded and smiled in a pleased way. "I never thought you'd ask me," she replied. Even as she glanced at her mother for approval, she seemed determined to talk. Her exuberance and motivation were a refreshing balance from John's inhibited, scarce comments.

"I don't agree with John about nobody caring. I think my mother cares and I know I do. My mother yells a lot at him and at me too. If she didn't care she wouldn't do that. It's John who doesn't care."

"How about you, Francis, do you care, about what happens and what's going on?"

Francis looked at me forlornly as if to speak, but again he was interrupted, this time by his twelve year old.

"Oh, daddy cares too, but he just doesn't know how to show it. He's a little bit, blah."

I looked at Francis, ignoring her comment. Quiet apparently, Alice had acquired her mother's perceptual and interpersonal stance within the family. She took a condescending view of her father and was not at all inhibited about expressing it.

"What do you have to say to Alice about that, Francis?"

"Ah, she . . ."

"Tell her, not me, Francis."

He rivetted his gaze on her. "Alice, you're still very much a little girl. You don't know, you . . ."

"Oh, Francis," Kathleen cried out. "Francis, Francis. If we don't do anything else here, let's be honest with each other. Alice is just telling Dr. Perez what she really believes. Don't put her down. The poor child is being as honest as she can."

"The poor child" beamed at her mother. A little satisfied grin played around her mouth.

"I wasn't going to put her down, Kath, I was just gonna' say that it's true that I'm quiet like you're so happy about telling everybody. She's learning to do that from you. That's all."

"What do you mean that I'm so happy about telling everybody," she queried, obviously embarrassed.

"Well, you do. I swear I've heard you say that I'm too quiet, I don't care. You even said something like that in front of Dalton.* Oh, Kath, you want to be honest. Why, why don't you just admit it?"

Kathleen was obviously upset by these words. "I never said you didn't care. I never said that. I just said you couldn't help it. You couldn't, you've never been able to show how you really feel about things. So let's be honest, Francis, does it really matter if you do care, if you can't show it?"

"I think it does," he said, but without too much conviction.

It was Kathleen now who shrugged and who looked away. From the few exchanges so far it seemed clear that Kathleen was very much in control. Her self-assurance, her convictions, delivered so unequivocally, indicated pretty clearly that she dominated, if not the whole family scene, certainly the marital relationship.

I turned to John. "John, tell us all what you think about all this, uh, that your father cares but doesn't know how to show it, that he's, uh, blah?"

"Yeah, about what Alice was saying. Dad's like that. He's . . ."

"Tell your father, John, tell him, not me."

With obvious discomfort, he did turn to look at his father."Yeah, dad, you're like that. I guess I always knew it but I . . ."

"Oh, for heavens sake," Kathleen began to impose something, but again, I signaled her to refrain.

John looked at her obviously much annoyed. "For Christ's sake, ma, I was gonna say that," now looking at her instead of his father, "if he had a chance to talk when he wanted to, maybe then . . ."

"But, John, that's all I've ever wanted him to . . ."

"Bullshit."

The expletive silenced the room. Kathleen blushed. Alice put her hand to her mouth in a sympathetic gesture for her mother. Francis just stared fixedly at his knees.

I tried to lighten the mood. Chuckling, I murmured, "I guess I've heard the word before, but, uh, I was wondering. What did you mean by it. Uh, what did you want to say?"

"Ma just runs things. She . . ."

"Tell her, John. Tell *her*." (In the initial session it's difficult getting members of the family to address their comments to each other.)

"O.K., ma, maybe you want him to talk and to run things but you sure

---

* The high school principal.

don't show it. Everytime he opens his mouth you jump in, shut him up or contradict him."

"Oh, John, how can you . . ."

"That's not true, John, mom is always telling him to take a stand with you, even with me."

"Yeah, but if he does ma hollers. She . . ."

"Do you hate me so much, John, do you?" asked Kathleen.

"Oh, what's the use?" He shrugged and was silent.

Kathleen turned to me. "How can I make you understand?"

I smiled. "Kathleen, it's important for me to understand, but what's really important is that the five of us understand what's happening."

She looked at me quizzically. "So what's happening?"

"Well, the impression I get is that all of us, all five of us are not relating to each other very effectively. Communication between and among us . . ."

"What's all that double talk mean?" She asked. "I mean, be specific." Francis, John and Alice looked to be just as perplexed as Kathleen.

"Well, for example, Kathleen several times you interrupted Francis. I signaled you not to do it but you tried again. Alice and you seem to have made an alliance to prevent him from becoming involved in family matters."

"An alliance, an alliance. You make it sound like we're all of us in a war or something."

"Well, that might not be such a bad way to explain what's happening. There's a war of sorts going on. Alice is on your side, I think. Part of the trouble in this war is that Francis won't fight. Maybe he doesn't want to, maybe it's because you won't let him. I don't know."

"Where's John fit in?" she asked.

"Where do you fit in John?" I asked.

"I don't fit," he replied without hesitation.

"Tell us what you mean, explain that for us," I said.

"Well, I'm like my father. I'm not fighting with anybody. I . . ."

"What do you mean, you're not fighting with anybody?" asked his mother. "We're all here because of you. I'm not here for myself. If it wasn't for you, John Whiting, we would none of us be here. And that's the plain truth."

Condemnation seemed to be a prime method of communication in this family.

"So you feel, Kathleen, that the reason you're here is because of John's offense?" I asked.

Without hesitation she responded, "Yes."

It was Francis now who volunteered. "Oh Kath, let's be fair. How many times have I heard you say we're in trouble as a family?"

"Yes, that's true," she murmured.

"We probably all got problems, if we're in trouble as a family. Kath, you probably do yell too much and, and I buy that bit about an alliance between you and Alice." He looked at Alice then, and said, "You know you and your mother have been taking sides against me." This was a quiet man but not a hapless one, I thought.

Alice turned a little pink. She said nothing.

John looked around as if he wanted to say something.

"Yes, John," I prompted.

"Eh, we're screwed-up. And I'm not the only one," he said with a kind of latent excitement in his tone. John seemed to be taking an interest. Maybe it was the fact that he was not turning out to be the scapegoat, the fall guy. Or maybe it was because his father had quasi-defended him.

There was a moment of silence. Our time was almost up. But I wasn't about to call a halt, even though this session had been more diagnostic than anything else. I wanted more from John. "John, a while ago I think you said something like, 'Nobody cares about nothin' . . .'"

"Yeah, I did."

"O.K. Tell me, *who*, specifically, who cares the least in the family? Take a moment and then tell that person, not me."

He sat there, I thought a little self-consciously, looked up and said, "I dunno and I'm not crappin' around, I dunno" He turned to his sister. "You're probably right, ma yells a lot and probably it's because she cares. But I think dad cares and he can't help a lot about how he is. And I don't believe that crap about if he don't show it then it doesn't matter. I think it matters. For all we know he's eatin' his guts out. And I don't know if that's true, but if it is, that's gotta' mean somethin'. I mean, geez, he's here."

I've heard other teen-agers make comparably insightful statements but I never cease to marvel at the insightfulness some adolescents possess. It confirms what I've long believed, that insight is not so much a function of age or intellect as it is of emotional sensitivity, responsiveness.

"Alice, what do you think of all that?" I queried.

"I got to admit that he's probably right."

"You got to. You mean you got to but don't want to?" I said in a teasing tone.

She turned a little pink and chuckled, "I want to. But you know what's one of the first problems in this family?"

"Tell me."

"First problem is we never do nothing together."

I've never been a prime exponent of the idea that the family which plays together stays together. Some family outings involve activities which have little or no appeal to one or more members. The result often is not so much pleasant interactions as harsh clashes. At this point, however, I was not about to discourage any proposal by anyone in this troubled family.

"What did you have in mind, Alice?" I asked.

"Oh, I don't know. It just would be so nice to do something as a family. It'd be different."

"Sure be different," agreed John.

"Why don't you discuss it among yourselves." I got up and walked to the back of the room and poured myself a cup of coffee. I heard them discussing a picnic, a beach outing, finally a movie. They settled on a movie. Kathleen, I observed, did most of the talking. Alice seemed unhappy with the decision.

"A movie. Oh, mother. A movie we can't even talk to each other."

"Daddy, what . . ."

"I think a movie's O.K., Alice," he observed.

I agreed with him. As a starting point it was probably the least threatening of any social evening. Togetherness. I thought the decision pretty good.

"What do you think, John?" I asked.

"I'll go along with it."

At this point we couldn't realistically ask for much more.

DISCUSSION QUESTIONS

1. Do you believe Kathleen and Francis can continue in a fruitful marriage? Why or why not?

2. Rank-order the self-esteem of each of the Whitings. Defend the position of each one.

3. A line in this chapter was, "Condemnation seemed to be a prime method of communication in this family." Who condemns most after Kathleen?

4. The author has a tentative hypothesis that, "John's behaviors were the unconscious actions of a concerned adolescent seeking in his own way to help his parents come closer together?" Do you agree or disagree? Why or why not?

5. What clues do you have that Alice is not totally identified with her mother?

Physical Descriptions and Minor Observations—Kathleen, Francis, Alice

Kathleen is an auburn-haired, hazel-eyed woman who is about 5′4″ and carries her sexually attractive figure in a graceful way. Her small, pert nose and the upper part of her face are liberally sprinkled with freckles. The freckles make her look younger than her forty years, almost girlish. Despite her assertive, aggressive, at times domineering way intrafamilially, she gave me the general impression of a warm, vibrant person, articulate and very fluent. I suspect strongly that most people outside the family, both men and women, are attracted to her.

Francis is a sparse haired, tall man (I'd judge about 6′2″). He's broad shouldered and has a paunch developing. His lined face and stooped walk make him look about ten years older than his 42 years. Francis presents himself as a kind of quiet loner. I'd bet that he has experienced many social situations where he felt he had left a poor, at best indifferent, impression. The expression of emotion seems to make him anxious. It's for this reason perhaps, that he projects the image of a man constantly beset with personal feelings of ineptness.

Alice might be described as a budding Kathleen. She's now almost as tall as her mother but will probably grow a few more inches. She has the same pert nose and freckles, with the latter, I swear, almost in the same places as her mother. Her interpersonal stance was very comparable to the maternal one. At the same time I got the feeling several times that Alice is seeking to break away from her mother, to be more assertive, perhaps more aggressive, again, like her mother.

Notes and Analysis

An adolescent's acting out is frequently a response to unmet needs within the environment, usually within the family. Thus, even before I met with the Whitings I had the notion in the back of my mind that John Whiting's difficulty with the law might possibly be a reaction to internal familial dynamics. After our first meeting I thought that this notion might just have some validity. I still wasn't sure. So far I had few answers, a lot of questions. Some of these last included:

1. Were John's delinquent acts a reaction to the parental dyad?
2. Was he acting out because he was rebelling against his mother's apparent dominance of the dyad, her put-downs of Francis?

3. Was John's acting out a response to John's perception of the diminution of Francis as a person and as a man?

4. Or again, were John's behaviors the unconscious actions of a concerned adolescent seeking in his own way to help his parents come closer together?

5. Was he trying to help them realign their dyad and thereby effect a less painful homeostasis for the entire family?

6. And what was the nature of the Kathleen-Alice alliance? How strong was it? Was it a truly close alliance emotionally or was it just an alliance of convenience, i.e. did it exist simply because there was no other person to whom Alice could get close?

What *was* clear from this first meeting was that Kathleen is the dominant force within the family, she is the powerful one, and presents herself as its spokesman, She had to be reminded of her inappropriateness in this regard a couple of times.

Initially, her husband Francis presented himself as the original quiet man. His own words in this regard were ". . . I've always been a quiet guy." He even had it rationalized, "runs in the family," he noted. At the same time it should be observed that he did stand up to Kathleen, pointing out to her that Alice learned to put him down from her. He also showed some verve when he said to Alice, "You and your mother have been taking sides against me."

Kathleen communicates with Francis and with John primarily via condemnation. As noted in the chapter on communication, this avenue generally involves nagging and hypercriticism. She exemplified this well throughout this first interview. "He's (Francis) just not interested in doing much of anything," and "All I get from you are shrugs and mostly silences," and of course there was the devastating comment about her father-in-law in comparison to Francis, "He (father-in-law) was a quiet man . . . but he was a strong man, too. People treated him with respect." Yes, Kathleen is in the habit of relating to her husband in a condemning, demeaning way. Why?

The answer just possibly might lie in a few lines uttered by Kathleen. What do you mean, you can't talk to me. That's all I ever wanted, you to talk to me. All I get from you are shrugs and mostly silences." And in response to these lines Francis shrugged and muttered one word, "See."

The point here is that the response pattern developed by Francis in response to Kathleen's condemnation seems to be one of submission. It was only at my urging that he confronted her. He even needed my urging to confront his daughter. It would seem then, that within the family Francis presents the picture of the quiet, even indifferent, passive-dependent father who has abdicated the husband-paternal role. Even as I write this I feel that I'm right. But at this point it's more a feeling reaction than a definitive, cognitive conclusion.

The reason the Whitings came to see me was because of John's problems with the law, a kind of paternal symbol for many in our society. As I think about my first five questions and as I reflect upon how Kathleen and Francis relate to each other I begin to feel more and more that if the questions were framed as statements they would indeed have at least some validity. John has incorporated some of his father. Thus he said, "Well, I'm like my father. I'm not fighting with anybody . . ." At the same time John asserts himself and in a most aggressive way.' . . . Every time he (Francis) opens his mouth you jump in, shut him up or contradict him," and "For Christ's sake, ma . . ." and "Bullshit." Quite apparently, John is not happy incorporating the total contemporary Francis. His brief but insightful comments toward the end of the session had a mature quality and more importantly, were in defense of his father, somebody quite apparently, whom he has not given up on. Also, his latent excitement and apparent interest in the *idea* of therapy for the family and in a family outing, serve to indicate that John's acting out may well have been a function of his unconscious need to effect a more fruitful homeostatic balance within the family. A few other points should be noted.

1. Alice presents the picture of the healthiest Whiting, touched least by the intra-familial problems. This may be due to the fact that while she's incorporated much of Kathleen's assertiveness, she still doesn't have to fill the role of wife or mother. In other words she has few responsibilities within the family.

2. Kathleen seems to be the most resistant to therapy and where it all may lead. Her own words in this regard were, "I'm not here for myself." As she sees it she's helping out—John and possibly Francis.

Chapter 10

Therapy with John, The Identified Patient

FOCUS GUIDES

1. As you read this chapter consider whether John is the legitimate identified patient within the Whiting family.
2. Is the hate which John feels justified? Reflect upon where it might come from.
3. Consider why Dee became so attractive to John.
4. Consider why John perceives the world and the people in it as he does.
5. As you approach the end of the chapter consider whether there is much or little hope for John's future.

PEREZ: C'mon in, John.

JOHN: Hey, hi.

P: John, I'm glad you came this evening. I felt I needed to talk to you alone, you know, without your parents.

J: Yeah.

P: Well, what did you think about our first session?

J: I dunno. I dunno that it accomplished a lot.

P: Well, I met your family. I found out some things, like your mother's in charge of the family, sort of. Alice is much closer to your mother than you are, that your father's psychologically divorced from the family.

J: Humph. You found all that out, huh?

P: Yeah.

J: Well, I guess maybe it was worth it.

P: Yeah. But today I want to find out all I can about you. How you fit into the family. You know as well as I do that the reason we all came together is 'cause of Judge O'Brien's order.

J: Yeah.

P: All I know is that you were involved in an attempted burglary of a cassette radio.

J: Yeah. That's true.

P: Why? What was it all about?

J: I needed the money.

P: How much did you need?

J: Fifty or sixty dollars.

P: Did you have to steal it?

J: I needed it fast.

P: You did?

J: Yeah. Well I, me, I didn't need it my girl needed it.

P: What for?

J: Kinda personal.

P: John, I'm . . .

P: She needed it. I mean I'm not a real crook, whatever else a lotta' people think about me.

P: I believe you.

J: She needed it for a doctor.

P: A doctor?

J: Yeah.

P: An operation?

J: Yeah.

P: She needed about $110.00 and you had to come up with half, right?

J: Yeah.(Pause) How'd you know?

P: John, you're not the first to come through here with that problem. You won't be the last either, I'm sure.

J: I guess.

P: You still like Dee?

J: Christ, yeah.

P: Why?

J: Why?

P: Yeah, why?

J: I only known her about six, no about eight months I guess. Why? 'Cause I always feel good when I'm with her.

P: How good?

J: Good, like when I was a little kid. Like when I was a little kid I used to be real holy. Confession, communion, Mass, every day. It all made me feel good, inside and outside. I felt like I was somethin', somebody, like I was, blessed. (Pause) You think I'm puttin' you on?

P: No, I don't.

J: Yeah, anyways, Dee makes me feel like that, like when I was a kid, an innocent, pure kid.

P: You don't feel like you're a pure innocent kid anymore?

J: Christ, no

P: Why not?

J: Listen, Doc.

P: Call me Joe.

J: O.K., Joe, I ain't got my mother's hangups. Joe's O.K. with me. Anyways, Joe, I'm not innocent no more.

P: Why not?

J: Hey! I'm flunkin' in school. I been suspended, Sortino's* on my ass the moment I walk in. I even deal in school.

P: Sell pot?

J: Yeah.

P: You been caught at it?

J: Yeah.

J: So now you feel because you've established the reputation you have you're sort of all done. You're not innocent anymore.

J: Well, I don't know if I'm sort of all done, but I sure ain't innocent anymore.

P: You're more sophisticated. You're grown up.

J: Yeah, but my head's not on straight. Let's tell it like it is.

P: O.K. Let's. How's your head not on straight?

J: (Pause) Well, I want money but I don't wanna' work. I'm bored up to my ass in school. Teachers turn me off. They're all such phonies. They're all such shits. They screw off more'n the kids do. The only thing I like in school is creative writing. You believe that?

P: Yeah.

J: I had this English teacher in creative writing. She gave us three writing assignments during the whole year. Lazy bitch didn't want to read them. When I turned mine in early she read it in study and came up to me 'cause I was in study with her and she told me she had to give me an "A" but she didn't believe I wrote it. "It was too professional for me." That's what she said. "It was too professional for me."

P: You wrote it, though.

J: Betch' your ass I wrote it.

P: So how'd you make out for the rest of the year?

J: I flunked.

---

* Vice-principal—High School disciplinarian.

P: How come?

J: If I turned in anything else, if I turned in what I really can do, she'd tell me the same thing. Screw her.

P: I see. So you figure that by doing your best all that would happen is that you'd be put down. Nobody would believe that the notorious John Whiting, delinquent, pot seller and general nuisance of the school, should be a talented writer.

J: Something like that, yeah. (Pause) You got a way with words.

P: Thanks.

J: Anyway, Dee's my girl.

P: You known her long?

J: Nah, just since last Christmas.

P: When did she get pregnant?

J: February. I think.

P: How'd you feel when you found out?

J: Scared.

P: Scared?

J: Yeah, I didn't know what to do, where to go about it. I was scared.

P: She was too, I'll bet.

J: Yeah, but I didn't let on to her that I was. Anyway, we got it fixed. That's one of the things I learned out of it. All you need is money.

P: You both felt she should have an abortion?

J: Christ, yeah. What else could we do? How could I marry her? What would I do for a living? Become the number one pot seller of Middletown? Ha! That ain't no way to support a family. I know that much.

P: Who'd ya' learn it from?

J: Probably my old man. It's probably the only thing he believes in, hard work and being respected, I guess.

P: What else do you think of him?

J: He's not too much. I guess maybe that session we all had did accomplish something. I found out something. I found out that he cares in his own way. My mother's always been pretty tough on him.

P: She won't let him assert himself.

J: I don't know that he's ever wanted to but if he does now it's pretty rough on him.

(Pause)

Anyway, Dee's the only thing I got goin' for me.

P: She gives you a feeling of being important.

J: She does, yeah, she does.

P: Where do you spend your time together?

J: My house a lot. Her house a little.

P: Her mother doesn't approve of you?

J: She's a real bitch. She's even worse than my own mother. She just looks at me, her mother does, and I feel like shit.

P: She puts you down a lot.

J: Yeah. And a lot of the time it's not that she says anything, it's the looks. You know what I mean?

P: Yeah, I think so. She sends out real bad vibes.

J: Yeah. At least my mother yells. When ma's mad ya' know. 'Course most of the time she's mad about nothing. And me, she's always mad at me. (Pause) Anyway, Dee's the only one I feel good with.

P: Yeah, you keep goin' back to Dee. You in love with her would you say?

J: She's a real girl.

P: Did you have sex with anybody before Dee?

J: Not really, no. (Pause) Well, we just fooled around a little. But we didn't have . . . uh, like, I mean real sex.

P: You just fooled around a little, before Dee.

J: Yeah. Ya' might say Dee was the very first. And, uh, I'm not interested, I was never interested in anybody but her. Dee's my woman.

P: I take it she feels the same way.

J: I never met anybody like Dee. She's not selfish.

P: You figure most people are?

J: Yeah, most people are out for themselves. They don't care about anybody. Look at my own family.

P: Your family are all selfish?

J: Well, I don't know if that's the fair word, but they're all up-tight about themselves, if ya' know what I mean. They're so up-tight about themselves they got no time for anybody else.

P: Like you, you mean?

J: Yeah. If ma was half as nice to me and dad as she is with strangers, we wouldn't have half the problems we got. Like she'd be yellin' like hell at somebody in the family and the phone would ring and she'd be just as sweet as sugar with her hello and how are you?

P: Yes, I believe that.

J: Yeah, she's good with other people. Yeah and to be fair, sometimes she's O.K. at home. Mostly she's kinda' in bitchy moods, if you know what I mean. Seems she's been like that for an awful long time now.

P: John, We've been talking a little about a lot of things, but we really haven't gotten to what you said a little while ago, you know, when you said, "My head's not on straight."

J: Yeah, and I told you I don't wanna' work and I'm bored. I'm all screwed up.

P: You don't see any purpose in your life, uh, you don't know where you're going.

J: Yeah, and I don't think I can get there either.

P: Where?

J: Anywhere.

P: And that bothers you a lot?

J: 'Course it bothers me a lot.

P: All right, let's do it like this. What is it you know that you *do* want?

J: I'd like to be able to marry Dee, get a place to live alone with her and buy a motorcycle.

P: So you do have goals. You do have objectives.

J: If that's what you mean by goals. Yeah, I guess so.

J: Problem is you don't seem to know how to meet your goals.

J: You could say that and you know a big reason for that is that I got what Sortino calls a "bad rep." I got a bad rep in school, and I got a bad rep outa' school.

P: You mean nobody's willing to give you a chance?

J: Right.

P: The way you see it, even if you tried you couldn't make it.

J: Yeah.

P: But the reality is, John, you're only sixteen. You're very bright. Those are two real plusses if you're sincere in trying.

J: Problem is, oh, Christ, I don't know. . . .

P: What?

J: It's people, people. People give me a pain in the ass.

P: You could do a lot if you didn't have to deal with people.

J: Yeah.

P: You're afraid of people!

J: I dunno. Maybe.

P: Or are you afraid of yourself?

J: What d'ya' mean by that?

P: The way I see it, and I'm not sure yet, the first problem here is, uh, here is you and how you feel about yourself.

J: Whaddya' mean?

P: You figure it like this, if I don't try I don't fail.

J: What?

P: John, you got it figured that there's no way you can be a winner. Somehow, and a lot of it has got to do with your family, you figure you're bound to lose, no matter what.

J: You think that I think I'm a zero?

P: Yeah. I think that you think that.

(Pause)

That's why, not the only reason but a big one, that you keep going back to Dee. Dee's got status for you. I imagine she's pretty, attractive and a lotta' people envy you for having her as a girl.

J: Yeah, that's true.

P: She's the only success you can point to.

J: And I screwed that up too. I got her pregnant.

P: (Chuckle) I suggest that was a mutual thing. I wouldn't beat myself over that.

J: Yeah, you're probably right.

P: You've believed that for a long time.

J: Never thought about it, but I guess that's so. Oh what's the point of talking about it? I'm like dad.

P: You don't figure you can break the mold.

J: What?

P: You figure you have to be like him.

J: Well, I don't have to be like him. But so what? I'm ending up like him. Right? Before you said something like "the reality is," well the reality is I'm like him. Christ, I'm worse! I'm on probation, he never got that far!

P: When I said, "the reality is" though, I didn't finish. I said the reality is you're sixteen, you're not 66!

J: Yeah, well, right now, Doc, I feel like I'm 666.

P: That's 'cause right now you're depressed. You're feeling real bad. You're on probation. You look back on a history of trouble, you feel like you're a zero and whatever good hopes you have, you don't know how to make them come true.

J: Yeah, I suppose.

P: One of the problems, big one, is you don't have anybody you feel you can look up to, anybody you feel you want to be like.

J: So?

P: So, maybe if you knew or saw people you wanted to be like, then maybe you'd know better what you yourself wanted to be.

J: I don't get what you mean.

P: I think a lot of your problem is like you say, you think, not think, you're convinced you come from a long line of zeros.

J: Yeah, my father and my brothers.

P: O.K. And you think you're just like them, even that you think you gotta' be just like them.

J: Yeah.

P: Why do you?

J: What?

P: Why do you have to be just like them?

J: I dunno'. I dunno, Doc you got me all screwed up right now.

P: O.K., maybe I've moved too fast. Maybe we both have. Uh, today's Tuesday. When can you see me again?

J: Uh. Right now I'm all fuc-uh, screwed up.

P: How's Thursday? Give you a couple of days to think.

J: Yeah, O.K., Thursday.

P: Good. 'Cause Friday we're all gonna meet together. O.K., see you Thursday.

Thursday

P: Hey, hi.

J: 'Lo.

P: Been thinkin'?

J: Yeah.

P: What you been thinkin'?

J: A lot. You're right 'bout some stuff. But you don't got it all figured out. I mean, you make it all sound so neat and simple like it's all neat and simple. (Pause) And I don't think it is.

P: O. K. I'll buy that. Maybe I did make it, make you out to be . . .

J: Look, lemme talk. I don't want to forget nothin' that I wanted to say.

P: O.K.

J: See, there's a lot you don't know about. I don't feel like I gotta' be like my old man and my brothers. I do sometimes, I do sometimes but sometimes I don't. It's true I think they're zeros. A lot of it has got to do with my mother. She's always puttin' my father down. I hate her for that. She used to put Tom down an awful lot. I remember that, Frank too. Then when they left the house she started on me, like, "Your're just like your father," and Christ, do I ever know what she thinks of my father! (Pause) And you know what's real weird about all of this is that all of us guys in the family all came to believe it.

P: Believe what?

J: That we're all zeros. I mean we used to say it to each other and about each other. Like I remember Tom used to say it all the time about Dad, and about Frank too. And then I used to say it about Tom and Frank and about Dad too. Only we didn't use the word zero so much we used another word, "nothin'." Like, "Dad's a nothin'." Imagine that! Dad's a nothin', we'd say that all the time. Ma said it, Tom said it, Frank said it, so I said it. And now Alice says it. Only she don't say it like that. She's got her own word, "blah." But no matter how you add it all up it still comes out to zero.

One question would both clarify and recapitulate both monologues.

P: Are you saying that it's all your mother's fault?

J: Well sort of. It's really both their faults. If my mother puts my father down, then a lot of it's got to be his fault. That's why I hate him. He lets her dump on him.

P: Why do you think that?

J: Why? I dunno' except one thing my father said when we all met the last time. It stuck in my mind. He was talkin' about bein' too quiet and what he said was, "I guess I take after my father. Runs in the family."

P: Are you saying that your father lets himself be put down because it's sort of a Whiting family trait among the men to be quiet, uh, to meekly accept being put down?

J: Yeah.

P: But, John, you're hardly meek.

J: Yeah, but I'm pretty quiet.

P: Do you let yourself be put down by many people?

J: No. I guess not. (Pause) Well, what do you think?

P: I think you've done a lot of thinking in the past couple of days. That's good.

J: Yeah.

P: I think there's a lot of truth to the fact that probably your mother has been putting your father down over the years and you all learned to put him and each other down. The psychology of this is very . . .

For no apparent reason it was at this point that John exploded.

J: Down, down, down! I'm sick of all this psychology crap.

P: What?

J: You really wanta' know how I feel? I hate them all. Why do I hate them? Because I'm the one who's the family shit. Not Tom. Not Frank. They're not even home anymore—and now I know why. They wanted to escape my crazy family. They wanted to escape being shit on.

P: You're the one everybody shits on.

J: You want the truth, the pure truth? There's so much hate in my house it comes outa' the woodwork. My mother hates my father. My father hates my mother. Alice hates my father and they all of them, hate me. That's how it is.

P: And you hate them all back.

J: Yeah. (Pause)

P: And do you want to?

J: Who wants to hate?

(Pause)

You're right, I been doing a lot of thinkin'. About that, you're right. My mother and my father, they're screwed up. I know I am, but they're just bad, maybe worse.

(Pause)

P: I can understand how you'd feel this way from everything you've said and from what your family said last time we met. I'm glad we had these couple of sessions alone. I figure that there might be some things that you felt you needed to say to me alone first and the stuff about Dee. I figured maybe you're not ready to discuss that with your family yet. But you know, John, your feelings about your parents and Alice, those you ought to share with them if things are gonna' get better for you and for them.

J: Yeah. You been sayin' that. I know that. We all oughta' talk to each other. I know that.

P: That's why we're gonna' meet as a family again.

DISCUSSION QUESTIONS

1.   Now, where do you think that John fits in his family?

2.   Would you characterize John as a mature person? If so, why? If not, why not?

3.   What do you see as the principal cause of John's unhappiness?

4.   The author feels that John has a conscience because of how he responded to Dee's need for money. Is there a relationship between conscience and love? If so, how would you explain it? If not, why not?

5.   Are you optimistic about John's prognosis?

Physical Description and Minor Observations—John

When John presented himself for the interview he appeared in blue denim jeans and a long-sleeved red plaid shirt. Both articles needed laundering. The red bandana handkerchief which he wore around his brow contrasted sharply with his long, dark-blond hair. The only expensive item of attire were his shoes, thick soled, kid-skin half boots. Altogether then, John's studied intent was to present the rather formidable picture of the "cool," uninterested, mildly bored adolescent. Ironically, the altogether "effect" was of a ridiculous scarecrow: straw-colored hair and passé style of clothes, hanging too loosely on too slender a frame.

After my two meetings with John I had reached these understandings about him:

1.   Intellectually, John functions well above average, probably in the bright-normal to superior range. This estimate is based upon his very adequate vocabulary and the intuitive, keen insightfulness he expresses in conversation.

2. John is a scared, bewildered kid who doesn't know where he is or where he is going.

3. He's unhappy and he's not at all sure about the why of it.

4. At sixteen he feels like the family scapegoat, an emotional whipping boy.

5. He feels that he has been emotionally short-changed. A response to this is his search for love, met in some measure at this time by Dee.

6. The boy harbors a remarkable amount of hostility and it is principally directed toward those who engendered it in him, his mother and father. He is aware at some level that for years he's been the object of their displaced hostility.

7. At this time I see him as the manifest symptom of the frustration which over the years his parents have developed toward each other. The questions then, which I framed at the end of the first therapy session with the family may have some validity. These centered around the idea that John acted out in response to the parental dyad.

There are those who would say "Nonsense! The boy got caught stealing a cassette because he needed a lot of money fast to help pay for an abortion for his girlfriend." All that is true, but I see the stealing of the cassette simply as a symptomatic act, a symptom of the real issue at hand which is the intense attraction to Dee. Some of his comments in this regard were: "She's a real girl . . . I was never interested in anybody but her. Dee's my woman." I'm convinced that, for John, Dee provides both symbolically and actually, that which his family does not provide, namely: love and self-esteem. Consider just a few of his comments, "Dees's the only thing I got goin' for me" and "Perez: She gives you a feeling of being important? John: She does, yeah, she does." And, I never met anybody like Dee. She's not selfish."

The clear implication, of course, is that he finds her to be a very loving person. In addition, she's a kind of status symbol for him, one which his self-esteem hungers for.

For whatever reasons, Francis and Kathleen Whiting are and have been unable to communicate love to him. Even worse, both seem to relate to him via condemnation. and he feels both the inability to love and the condemnation acutely, interpreting it as selfishness and even hatred. "There's so much hatred in my house it comes outa' the woodwork. My mother hates my father. My father hates my mother. Alice hates my father and they all of them, hate me. That's how it is." It is precisely these feelings toward his family which made Dee so terribly attractive to him. And if she meets his needs and meets them well, his family meets them not at all. And there is an added bonus to his relationship with Dee. She makes him feel like a man. He notes along this line, "She's my woman." She makes him feel like a man in a world which treats him like an inadequate boy.

Among his problems, a principal one is his current perception of the world. He perceives a world filled with phony, selfish people who are out for themselves. As noted already, his view is that his family is filled with hate. Teachers engender in him little more than indifference, probably a lot of hostility. His own words are, "Teachers turn me off." Indeed when talking about people in general he observes, "Most people are out for themselves. They don't care about anybody." On reflection then, we can better understand one of his earliest comments "People give me a pain in the ass."

Despite all of these problems and conflicts John indeed possesses strengths. He is of above average intelligence. Physically, he will be an attractive man (right now he's too skinny)–blond, blue-eyed and tall. Already, despite the problems with his self-esteem, he is able to carry on a meaningful relationship (with Dee). What this means, of course, is that he has a high capacity and need to love and that he can accept love too. Note that despite his little tantrum about hate, when pressed by my question his response was, "Who wants to hate?" His response to Dee's need for love was immediate, albeit inappropriate, suggesting that in his own in-adequate way he possesses a conscience, another strength. His greatest strengths however, lie in his remarkable candor; in his refusal to deny, to lie to himself about himself or about his relationships with others. Thus it was John who made such comments as, "My head's not on straight, I'm all screwed up." Therapists have long noted that the first step in the amelioration of problems is an admission of them. And despite his somewhat less than optimistic self-perception and perception of the world in which he lives, John is very much in contact. Reflect on this exchange:

PEREZ: You both felt she should have an abortion.
JOHN: Christ yeah. What else could we do? How could I marry her? What would I do for a living? Become the number one pot seller of Middletown? Ha! That ain't no way to support a family. I know that much.

These are the hard, pragmatic observations of a young man very much attuned to the world in which he lives. My thoughts at this point in the case are that John seeks to be a man, and more importantly, to understand what that means. In this search (and hopefully discovery) lies the potential for a healthy individual.

Chapter 11
Excerpts of
Three Interviews

This chapter includes excerpts from three subsequent meetings with the Whitings. The tapes of these meetings were edited, abbreviated and synthesized for readability.

FOCUS GUIDES

1. As you read the chapter, observe how Kathleen manipulates or attempts to manipulate her family.

2. Consider how Francis begins to alter his intrafamilial stance. What might have brought this about?

3. As you read on, reflect on John's notion that there's a lot of hate in the family, on Kathleen's notion that there's a lot of love. Is one right, the other wrong, or is there a perennial love-hate conflict within the Whiting family?

4. Consider. Is John really getting closer to the family? Why or why not?

5. Reflect on the sketches by Francis and Kathleen about their respective families while growing up. Are they worthwhile areas to focus upon in family therapy?

6. Reread the chapter to be sure that you understand what emotions and dynamics were ventilated to make Kathleen leave the session crying.

The next evening the four Whitings arrived promptly at 7:30 and at the second meeting took the same seats they had had at the first session, a typical familial procedure.

After the usual exchange of banalities I looked at Alice and asked, "How was the movie?"

She shrugged, "Nothin' much."

"You didn't enjoy it?"

"It was O.K. A movie's no way to get to talk. I think I said something like that. I mean . . . "

"Oh Alice, stop being a wet blanket," piped in Kathleen.

"But mother, we didn't even go out for a snack after. All we did was go to a movie and go home. I mean, geez, who talked to who?"

"There was no talking, no interchange?" I asked.

"No. Nothing. It was, uh . . . It was, how can I put it, tense. Yeah, tense. Embarrassing. Isn't that awful, we're all tense with each other."

There was a lull, an uncomfortable one. I cleared my throat. "Oh, look. There's a technique which might just be appropriate at this point."

"What do you mean?" asked Kathleen.

"Well, it's called sculpting."

"Called what?" asked Alice with apparent curiosity.

"Sculpting. The idea is to sculpture out a scene. A tableau, a picture of the family."

"What do you use?" she asked.

"The family," I answered.

"You mean I use mom and dad and John to make a picture?"

"Right."

"A picture of what?"

"Of how you see each person and you in relation to each other."

I looked around. "Are we willing to try it?" Kathleen and Francis were receptive. Alice appeared interested, even eager. John looked bored.

Alice volunteered. She jumped up. "Let's try it. May I go first?"

I smiled, "Sure." I cleared the center of the room of a footstool and a small, backed chair, waved my arm and in my best director's voice boomed, "Lights, camera, action and go get 'em!"

Alice led her father to the right edge of the cleared center. Then she led John to the left edge, approximately ten feet away from him. She took her mother and placed her in the middle between them, about five feet from each. Then she sat down.

"What about *you*, Alice?" I asked.

"Oh me! Oh wait, first." She went to her father and turned him around facing the wall, away from Kathleen. Then she changed her mind and turned him, but just a little, so his left side was facing Kathleen. She went over and moved John, so his right side was facing Kathleen. Then she stepped to within two feet of Kathleen on John's side and positioned herself sideways to Kathleen. She sighed and said, "Yes, that's how it is."

I surveyed the scene. John and Francis were on the fringes of the family. Kathleen was in the center but close to neither. Her daughter was closer by far than the other two, but in some ways almost as close to John as she was to Kathleen.

Predictably it was Kathleen who broke the silence and the tableau.

"Oh, Alice, it's just not like this. Not at all. You're dead wrong."

Alice looked at her mother and with some verve replied, "It's just like that, mother, and you know it."

I said, "Oh, each of you can draw a tableau too. It's true of course that we all see things differently and we're all entitled to . . . "

Kathleen interrupted me walking to her chair, "I didn't come here to play childish games." The others sat down. There was a lull. I was determined to wait it out.

Again, it was Kathleen who spoke, "I was going to say before we started making tableaus that Alice, that was a terrible thing to say–that we're tense with each other and you used the word embarrassing, that you were embarrassed by your parents."

"For Christ's sakes, ma, she didn't say that she was embarrassed by you," John shot in.

"Oh, mother, how could I ever be embarrassed by you or because I'm with you. Everybody keeps telling me I look just like you. Everybody says I even act like you."

"How do you feel about that?" I asked.

Alice glanced, and not a little fearfully, at her mother.

"Why don't you look at me," I suggested. "Tell me. How do you feel about people thinking that you look and act like your mother?"

"I don't know," she said in a soft, sincere tone.

"You don't know?"

"No."

Kathleen was looking at her a little too intently. I looked at her and asked, "What are you thinking, Kathleen?"

"I'm thinking that that's a very embarrassing question to ask a twelve year old."

"Why?"

"Well, what twelve year old wants to be seen as her mother. After all, I'm forty . . . "

"Yeah, but you don't look it Kath," Francis volunteered.

I continued to focus upon Alice. "Alice, you must have some feelings about this."

"Yeah, Mom is young looking."

"She's pretty," her father added.

Kathleen's intent look had softened. A little smile tugged at the right corner of her mouth.

"Oh, Alice, do tell us," she urged.

I was a mite irked. No, I was damned angry. I knew Alice would tell us now. Her mother had given her permission. This was one of the problems

I had already learned. Feelings and statements tended to come out only if Kathleen permitted it. I had hoped that Alice would have expressed herself sans the usual maternal O.K.

"Well, I like looking like you, mother. I guess that's true.

"But," said Kathleen. Had her tone hardened?

"Kathleen, I'd appreciate it a lot if you'd let Alice tell it her own way," I interjected briskly. Alice, I noticed, had edged over, more than a little bit over, to the other corner of the couch. Afraid of what she wanted to say? I thought so. She probably felt she needed support. I was determined to provide it.

"Well, you *are* pretty, mother, but I'm not you and you're not me." She was looking at her mother with what looked to be a little of Kathleen's own type of defiance.

"I know that you're not me darling," Kathleen responded just a little too sweetly.

"Mother, you're too protective. I want you as my mother, not my protector. You're too protective."

"Protective?" Kathleen looked genuinely puzzled.

"You still pick me up at school."

"Only when it's raining."

"Christ, ma, she won't melt," John quipped.

Alice shot her brother a thankful look.

"Lots of times I want to be with my friends," added Alice.

"Well, why didn't you tell me. You've never told me that. You never tell me anything. I'm the only one in this family who ever does any talking."

"I tried a couple of times but you're always mad. I get scared when you're mad. I don't want a mother who's mad always."

"I'm not mad always."

"You are too when you pick me up at school. You come pick me up and you do it like you don't want to. Why do you bother? I don't want to be a bother to my mother. I just want a regular mother. Why do you bother to pick me up?"

"If what Alice says is true, why do you Kathleen?" It was Francis who asked the question. There was only simple curiosity in his tone.

Kathleen seemed puzzled herself. "I don't know. I don't know."

"I think it's all got to do with this, 'look like and be a baby bit'. I think it's that you're just over-protective. I think it's all got to do with that. Really mother, I think I'm perfectly able to decide what to wear to school. Kids still just don't wear dresses to school that much. They just don't."

"I think jeans are all right once in a while and you know perfectly well that . . ."

"Well, if they're all right once in a while, why aren't they all right whenever I want to . . . "

"It's just more sophisticated to vary your wardrobe. My God, Alice, you have a closet full of dresses . . . "

"And you bought them all," Alice replied with feeling.

"And she just said that none of the kids wear dresses. So what the hell good are the dresses that *you* bought." John said almost sneeringly.

"You don't have to swear to make a point, John," she responded sarcastically.

Alice added, "Oh, mother, don't be such a hypocrite. Look like a lady. Be a lady, blah, blah, blah. And you swear more than anybody in the family."

Kathleen was acutely embarrassed. She looked at Francis, almost beseechingly. And happily, he rose to the occasion. "Alice, it's none of your business if mother swears. It's not for you to tell her how to talk. Try hard to remember that you're only twelve and she's your mother."

Kathleen looked grateful. She said nothing. I looked at them. The four of them were all talking to each other. It was hardly love flowing back and forth. But there certainly was a lot of pent-up emotion being ventilated. Francis had shut Alice off. She edged even further away from her mother and curled up at the corner of the couch like a pretty little kitten, I thought.

There was a momentary lull. I was determined not to lose the emotional and verbal interchange. A question would be very appropriate, I thought. I looked at the youngest Whiting. "Were you surprised by your father's comment?"

Alice looked at me and nodded.

"Why were you surprised?"

"He doesn't usually do that."

"What?"

"Defend mother."

"If you think he should do that, why don't you tell him."

Alice looked at her father with a little embarrassment, "Daddy, I . . . "

Francis seemed upset. "Alice, I don't want compliments from my twelve year old daughter. I know what I'm supposed to and not supposed to do."

Quiet.

"Well, daddy," she asked gently, quietly, almost whisperedly, "why, why don't you?"

The question was a hard one, maybe a cruel one, but I'm sure it came from whatever affection Alice had for her father.

He looked at her with embarrassment, anger, confusion? I couldn't tell. He started slowly, looking down at the floor.

"You know, you kids, are kids. You're kids who just don't know about me and your mother. You don't know what it was like for us. And why should you? We never told you much about what it was like growing up for us. I'm tired. I'm very tired. I'm goddamned tired (his voice had risen, cracked a little) of being told I'm quiet. That's how I am. I am what I am. Why can't I be respected for that? My father was quiet. Nobody criticized him for it. We all respected him for it. Everybody tells me I'm unemotional. My father and mother, they never showed me much emotion, love, whatever you want to call it." As I sat there listening to Francis I concluded that this supposedly quiet man was also very much a thinking person.

"Fran (I'd not heard Kathleen call him Fran until now), Fran," she repeated softly, "It worked for them, it doesn't for us."

"Damn it, Kathleen. My mother went along with him on it, on not being all emotional. She supported him. You don't. You're always yelling. So much you show me up. You yell. I don't, and the kids compare us and put me down 'cause I don't. I'm not mad at you, but let's let up on it."

"But Fran . . . "

"Let me finish, Kath. There's some truth to what Alice says." Francis was not looking at his knees anymore. He was looking directly at Kathleen. "You do swear more than all of us and you're always telling her to be a lady. It's not right for you to do that, but I don't think it's her place to tell you about it either."

"Whose place is it, Francis?" I asked.

"It's mine. It's mine," he said wearily.

There was a momentary lull. And it was I who broke it. "And if you don't, Francis, then what happens is that John or Alice take over and do tell her, and fights, resentment and a lot of hostility result."

"That's for sure. There's a lot of hate in this family," John said, aping his father's weary tone.

"But there is love too," said Kathleen.

"Ha! Christ, you gotta' be kidding', ma."

There was a look of real shock on Kathleen's face as she cried out, "Oh, I am so tired of all this! I am, am just sick of this so-called therapy. Is this, all this, supposed to be good for us? To have our children, a twelve year old and a sixteen year old, feel perfectly free to speak so critically, so rudely. Is this supposed to be good for us?"

The questions were addressed to me, but I didn't respond. I took them to be rhetorical. And I was right. She continued.

"I mean, ever since I came in here tonight all I've heard is how inadequate I am as a mother and this from a twelve year old! Now this sixteen year old who's still wet behind the ears tells me there's no love in me. I mean for heavens sakes!" She was looking at me now. I saw no need to respond. Kathleen was just beginning. That was obvious to all of us.

"A little while ago, Francis, you said something meaningful, very meaningful and very true, and I don't think anybody but me here heard it. You said, 'I am what I am and why can't I be respected for that?' You said that and goddamn it all (she looked directly at her daughter as she cursed), that's really the point of everything. You are what you are and I am what I am and these two children can't seem to understand it. My father swore like a trooper. We accepted it. Just because he did that didn't mean that we had the right to do the same. I didn't dare swear, nor did anybody else in my family. And you, you Miss Alice goody-little-two-shoes who doesn't like to be told what to wear, you have no conception what it is to be dictated to about clothes styles. My father told me what to wear every day of my life. And I accepted it." She stopped and sighed. There was a pause. A long pause.

I felt that some clarification of her feelings was in order. I spoke, "If I read you correctly what you're saying here Kathleen, is that you should be respected for who you are and what you are, nothing more, nothing less. Alice and John here have very little appreciation of what your life is like now and none at all for what it was like when you were their ages. Your father literally dictated you life. He was a man and he picked your clothes. You're a woman and all you want to do is guide Alice, give her the benefit of your experience. Yeah and just because you swear that doesn't give Alice and John the same right. You are an adult and the parent and with rank goes its privileges."

"Exactly. Exactly." She said, looking at me gratefully.

Francis spoke, "Kathleen, when I was saying about 'I am what I am' it was you who pointed out something. And I been thinkin' for the past five minutes, you were right. It was you who pointed out, 'It worked for them,' it worked for our parents but it doesn't for us."

There was a pause.

"Maybe, Kath, maybe a little of it is because we're not the complete bastards they were."

"Why, what do you mean?" asked Kathleen.

She had been stopped in the middle of what we all thought was going to be a very long diatribe. She looked at him with curiosity, puzzlement and was it, respect? We waited for his reply.

"You told me and I knew about your house. I remember you told me how you never had any privacy as a kid. We give them that, maybe even too much. Your father was cruel, he beat your mother. Our kids never saw anything like that."

"So why are we here, then?" I asked.

"Search me," Francis sighed. "All I know is I spent half my life trying to understand my father. I always thought that was my responsibility. Now I find myself spending the other half trying to understand my kids. Christ!" Francis was a reflective man, no doubt about it.

"Dad." We all turned to John. He'd moved over, to the chair right next to his father. "Dad, what kind of a guy was he, your father, I mean?"

Francis seemed a little what? Disconcerted? by John's move. He responded, though looking down again at his knees.

"He was a tough guy."

"Tough?"

"Tough guy to know. Cold. Like I told you before, very quiet."

"Did you like him?"

No response.

Again John asked, "Did you like him?"

"I liked him better than I liked my mother. 'Course I didn't like her at all, so that's not much of a comparison."

"So you didn't like him too much."

"I'll be honest with you, Johnny, I never talked to him much. He wasn't , uh, approachable. Like to talk to him you sorta' talked to him on a dare, if you know what I mean."

John was looking at him intently. "I think I understand," he said with sympathy.

"Oh Johnny," his father looked up at him and not unkindly said, "No you don't, you can't. You just couldn't know what my house was like."

I didn't want John or anybody else for that matter shut off. Some reflection of what Francis had said might help them all to continue on this vein. I asked, "You said your father wasn't approachable, he was, uh, self-righteous, sanctimonious, arrogant, uh, what?"

"Exactly, most accurate way to put it is that he was very sure of himself. I swear to God I never met a guy like him. He never doubted himself or at least he never showed us kids that he thought he might be wrong. If he thought something was right, it was right, and if he thought it was wrong, it was wrong. That's what I meant, Johnny, when I said you couldn't know. How could you know? It was like livin' with God."

"But it wasn't exactly heaven," Kathleen interjected.

"No, it wasn't heaven. It was hell."

"Why was it hell?" aked Alice, seemingly confused.

"It was hell because I was never right. I always seemed to want or to do the wrong thing. Christ! When I was in high school I wanted to get out of that house."

"See, you kids with all your silly, piddly complaints, you don't know what hard parents are really like," Kathleen chimed in.

There was another pause. I looked at John. "What do you think, John?"

"Maybe she's right. I think my father's right, I . . . "

"Don't tell me. Tell him." I nodded toward Kathleen and Francis.

"What I was gonna say," he was looking at Kathleen, "was no, Mom, you're not like what you describe your parents were. Me and Alice have a lotta' privacy. But I don't think it's because you respect us, our privacy. I think it's 'cause you guys just don't care. And Dad certainly isn't like his father, he sure don't act like God, but for a long time now I got the same ideas he used to have about wanting to get outa' the house. So maybe you guys are better parents than your parents were, but from where I sit you gotta' change even more. I don't know, we feel turned off by you like you guys felt turned off by them. Maybe it's like Dad says, it runs in the family."

I looked at Kathleen, whose legs were crossed and whose arms were folded across her bosom. She had positioned herself like an impregnable emotional fortress. It was I who asked, "Do you think it runs in the family, Kathleen?"

"I'm not sure what it is you're asking me about," she replied with not a little defiance.

"What do you think runs in the family, John?"

"Kids gettin' turned off by their parents," he responded.

"Oh, every family's like that," she quipped. "Haven't you heard about the generation gap?"

"Yeah, but in our family it's not a gap. It's the Grand Canyon," he shot back.

"Oh Mother, why can't you just admit some things," Alice blurted out.

"What things?" She asked frostily.

"Oh Mother, supper every night is such an up-tight time. I'm always either a nervous wreck or embarrassed 'cause you're either nagging daddy, or complaining about John or me or if it's not one of us three, then it's about yourself and one of your headaches that you're always complaining about. And speaking of headaches, you get one every time there's a little work to be done."

"Oh Alice, how unfair. How utterly unfair. That's just not true."

"You do, mother. You do too. You always seem to get a headache after supper or you run upstairs crying so I have to end up doing the dishes. That's how you get me or John to do things, by always pretending to be sick so you can be waited on. Do you want to know what John and I call you behind your back? You know what?" Alice didn't wait for a reply. "We call you 'Your Majesty' 'cause you always want to be waited on, like a queen."

"Yeah Ma, you rule the house like a real tough person," said John bitterly.

Kathleen's anger was transparent, but she did not speak. It was Francis who broke the tension. With positive wonderment, he said, "Listening to the kids reminded me I used to call my mother Queen Victoria."

"Christ," John reiterated, "it does run in the family."

"Oh, I am so sick of all this. Is all this supposed to be a therapy session or is it a pick-on-mother time?" Kathleen looked at me. Her legs were uncrossed, her arms hung limply at her sides, the impregnable fortress had crumbled. She was no longer angry. She looked at me, "Please tell me what's going on."

She was asking for clarification of the very intense feelings she felt herself and which were being expressed. I replied, "What's going on is simply that the rest of the family, John and Francis, see parallels between this family and the ones you and he were reared in. His house was dominated by a Queen Victoria type and Alice and John feel that you function like a, a "tough queen," I think John called you."

"Well, my own house certainly wasn't run like that! My father ran my house like a despot."

"What was your mother like?" I asked.

"She was a nothing. She was beaten down to a nothing by my father."

"Nothing. You just called your mother a nothing," John said tonelessly.

"Well, she was. So what?"

John turned embarrassedly toward his father, "No offense, dad, but that's what I got used to calling you."

"So what?" Kathleen repeated.

"Well geez, ma, I'm just trying to show you that what we're talking about, about problems running in families, there's a lot of truth to that."

"But I called my *mother* a nothing. You call your father a nothing. There's a little difference there." She looked at me for corroboration. Some recapitulation and reflection was in order.

"I was just thinking about some of the things you've said here today.

You didn't admire your mother at all. Apparently you didn't want to be like her. But your father, I guess, was the strong person in the family and he swore a lot in the family and he put your mother down. I think you said, 'he beat her down to nothing.' Now what . . . "

"And that's what you do to daddy," Alice cried out. "Honest mother, sometimes you act like a, a, ogre."

"Oh, my God. Are you saying that I act like my father in this family?"

"Well, I wanted . . . "

"Oh, I'm leaving. I've had enough of this, this psychological garbage." Kathleen got up and headed toward the door. Francis and Alice rose to follow her. Neither John nor I got up.

"Mother," Alice called plaintively, please come, sit down."

Francis called to her, "Please Kath, come back."

Kathleen turned. She was crying and was searching frantically but unsuccessfully for a handkerchief or a tissue. She stood near the door. Her husband handed her his handkerchief and in the process of taking it from him she dropped her pocketbook and what looked like a basketful of feminine ware spilled all over the floor. Kathleen sank to her knees and bawled like a young child. "Oh damn, damn, damn, she cried. Francis and Alice got down beside her and picked up and refilled the purse. Francis helped her up and led her over to a couch where they sat together. His arm was on her shoulder. She leaned toward him with her head down and dabbed at her eyes with the hankie. Alice sat next to me.

There was what seemed like a long pause while we all regained our composures. For a moment I felt that I might have let things go too far, too fast. I wondered if I shouldn't have been more protective of Kathleen, more supportive. But if I'd done that I might have shut off a lot of feelings. An awful lot had been said. I wasn't sure *I* could digest it. I doubted that the others could.

The Whitings were emotionally drained. The session was over. However, a recapitulation and perhaps some teaching by me was in order.

"I want to share some of my feelings and thoughts." They all looked at me expectantly except for Kathleen.

"I think what this session showed us if nothing else is that you get to know a family best when you see each member *in relation to* each other member. When we started out Kathleen showed a strong need to control everybody. How'd she do that John?"

"She interrupted." He said.

"Yeah," I replied. "She interrupted and she looked at each of you in ways that told a lot. A couple of times she gave Alice permission to talk by how she looked at her. But her dominance of the session declined fast as the rest of you asserted yourselves. Alice usually you're an ally but you withdrew your support and, in fact Alice, you attacked her. I had the feeling that you want to be treated like more than just a girl. Remember what you said?"

"Something about I wanted her to be a regular mother," she answered.

"Yeah. 'I want you as my mother, not my protector . . . I want a regular mother.' You said that too. One thing that came through loud and clear is that you, Francis, and you, Kathleen, want to get closer. When John and Alice jumped on you Kathleen, Francis really supported you. I got the feeling again and again that all four of you are very receptive to a new kind of parental relationship."

"You think so?" Francis asked.

"Yeah, I do. John you said something like that, that your parents had to change even more to be better parents. Most families feel that how parents go so goes the whole family. John and Alice, when you two allied together against your mother, what happened?"

"Daddy got close to Mom," said Alice.

"Right."

"But there was an awful lot of hate flying around here," observed Francis.

"Yes there was, Francis," I answered. "But there was much love and compassion shown too. You and you too, Alice, got up and just now helped Kathleen. Right now your arm is on her shoulder. Maybe you can't always show it, but you're showing it now, Francis. But you must feel some of this. I remember you saying a little while ago, 'We're not the complete bastards they were.' I took this to mean that, unlike your own parents you and Kathleen do love your kids. Despite the hostility there's a lot of goodwill in this family. We have to work our way through the hostility before we can be understanding of each other. We all need time to reflect on the past hour. We have to reflect on it each of us and digest it if we can. I'm going to try. Let's end it for tonight. We'll meet next Tuesday same time and station."

A Short Excerpt From the Subsequent Session

When they arrived at the next session, four days later, they all appeared a bit quiet, almost silent.

"How would you feel about doing some role playing?"

"What's that?" asked Francis.

"One of you plays the role of the other. Uh, I remember Alice, you saying that people said that you acted like your mother. Well, if you role played Kathleen you'd act like Kathleen, but here's the thing, you're to try to *feel* like Kathleen too. You'd be Kathleen in your own mind, act like her and try to feel like her."

"Oh Mother, let's role play," she cried out with all the honesty and verve that I'd genuinely come to appreciate.

Kathleen was smiling at her daughter. Quite apparently, she too was receptive. "Yes, O.K.," she assented.

"You be me and I'll be you. Uh, let's see," she looked at me. "What do we do?"

"Well, pick a scene. Any one you want, like you coming home from school, or anything you want. It should be a scene that you're both familiar with, one that will let both of you experience what you think the other's feelings are."

"Oh, I know. Me coming home from school late," exclaimed Alice.

Kathleen looked doubtful but only for a moment. "O.K.," she agreed.

I noticed that Kathleen was acting a mite different, different and in a more positive way than in our last couple of sessions. She seemed quieter, more agreeable, less intrusive. I wasn't sure what it all meant. At least, not yet.

The two of them stood up in the center before John, Francis and me, and began.

Alice, hands on her hips, chest thrust forward, with a glaring expression on her face began in an icy, almost bitter tone, "Well, well, well if it isn't our local social butterfly! Getting home after a hard day and a lot of responsibilities met. Home at last. She's going to give us the privilege of her company now."

"I'm sorry mom. I'm sorry," murmured Kathleen. "I couldn't help it. The kids . . . "

"The kids. The kids! (Screaming) It's always the kids, the goddamned kids. I'm sick of it, sick of it, do you hear? You have responsibilities, do you hear? Do you think that life is just one big bowl of cherries? You might just as well learn. It's hard. God knows it's very hard."

"I'm sorry Mom. I really am. Don't get mad please. I won't do it again. I won't. I hate to see you get so upset. Please don't and look, it's only a quarter to four."

"School ended an hour and a half ago! Where the hell have you been? Have you been with, *with a boy?*"

"Oh mother don't, please don't make it sound like, I was doing something wrong, like it's dirty or something."

There was a pause.

The tones, the content, the glances, the body stance which each assumed, captivated the three of us. Quite apparently, both mother and daughter had a remarkable understanding and feeling capacity for the other.

It was Alice, in her maternal role, who broke the short dramatic silence.

"It's you who's bringing up the dirt, not me. All I want to do is have you benefit from my experience. The sooner you learn, the happier you're going to be (Wearily) You'll see."

Kathleen answered, "What *will* I learn? Tell me. What are all these mysterious, awful things. My gosh, Mother. You make it sound as if life is filled with nothing but dangers, disasters and dreadful people. (Starting to cry real tears) I hate to say this to my own Mother but I really think you're kind of sick."

Alice responded. The full impact of her mother's words was obviously not lost on her, for she responded with, "Oh Alice. What a thing to say to your own mother! If I'm sick, I am because my life's been so-o-o hard. There's never been anybody who understood or who even cared to understand. Oh Alice, you're the only one. I always thought maybe, just maybe, there could be you who cared, who could be, who *wanted* to be close to me. I've always felt so alone, so awfully alone."

"Oh Mother, I do know . . . "

"No you don't. If I've been hard on you it's because I didn't want you hurt. I don't want you to make the mistakes I've made. Oh darling, I know it sounds strange, but it's because in my own weird way, I love you!"

It was a very poignant moment and yet a trifle embarrassing. There was something of the soap opera in this and yet there was also a strong element of the pathos. The eyes of both were tear rimmed. Kathleen held our her arms to her daughter and embraced her.

There was a pause. They all looked to me expectantly. "Well, what did we learn? What did we get out of this?" I asked.

Kathleen spoke softly, "I never realized how, how smart you were Alice, how much you understand about me." She turned to me, "You know, this was the very best thing we've done since we started coming here. I got more out of this than I have out of anything."

"Why, Kath? Why did you? What was there about it, that made you feel that way? Why was it so profitable?

"I don't know. It was weird. Kinda' psychic, almost spooky. For a while there I really thought, I felt like I *was* Alice. Anyway I knew exactly what to say."

I was not surprised at her remarks. I'd heard this precise reaction any number of times. It was not psychic, weird or spooky. They lived together. They were very close emotionally. There was a lot of cross identification between the two.

Kathleen continued, "I didn't realize how much I knew about her, about me, about us."

I turned to Alice, "How about you, Alice?"

She turned to her mother, "Mom, I just never dreamed you knew me so good. You were real cool in everything you said. Anybody who can say what you said about being sick just isn't that sick."

Kathleen hugged her again. "Oh baby, we are much closer than we realized."

I looked over at Francis, at John. Both were smiling. No question about it, the role playing had added a sense of warmth and solidarity to the entire Whiting family.

DISCUSSION QUESTIONS

1. Can families transmit interpersonal methods, both healthy and unhealthy from generation to generation? If so, how? If not, why not?

2. Do Francis and Kathleen indeed want to get closer? What evidence is there of this?

3. Alice feels her mother is over-protective. Why would Kathleen want to relate in an over-protective way to her daughter?

4. How much did the learnings acquired growing up in their respective homes influence Kathleen's and Francis's, John's and Alice's present lives?

5. Which do you think is the more effective technique in family therapy, sculpting or role-playing? List the reasons for your choice.

NOTES AND ANALYSIS

Kathleen's needs for dominance and dependence were well exemplified in this session. She controlled the initial moments with her inter-ruptions and via her looks and her words. At one point she deigned to give Alice permission to speak, to emote. Kathleen's dominance, however, dissipated rapidly as the session proceeded and the hostility toward her increased. Indeed, latent dependency needs began to become manifest when she looked to Francis for support. These same needs became blatant with her realization that she had for a long time played a quasi-"paternal" role within the family or at least one which she perceived to be paternal. I believe that this is an important point because I am convinced that it was from this perception by Kathleen that the familial structure of the Whiting family evolved. It was from this perception set a long time ago, before the birth of either John or Alice, that the demands, expectations and roles within the family became patterned. And it was from this perception that modes of interaction developed and became rigidified. In short, the realization that she had played a kind of melded autocrat paternal-ma-ternal role was indeed harsh for Kathleen. This realization has to be an important milestone in the Whiting family therapy. Note that despite the apparent pain she experienced, Kathleen did indeed return to the family group.

I must confess that for a moment when she turned to us and I saw her tears, I wondered if her behavior was not just an emotional ploy, a man-ipulative method, another version of the passive-aggressive histrionics which Alice had described, " . . . speaking of headaches, you get one every time there's a little work to be done." I am convinced now that her reaction and the emotions she emitted were genuine.

One item is now clear. Kathleen structured her life so she wouldn't have to play the role which her own mother played, passive dependent and the constant object of displaced hostility. Kathleen wasn't going to let happen to her what happened to her mother. Her determination in this regard is apparent. The effect was a homeostatic balance for the Whiting family which was seldom enhancing for its members, often acutely painful and at best, only tolerable.

Reflecting on Kathleen's tearful reaction at the close of the session, I wonder could that have been motivated in some measure by the fact that she saw some of her own mother in herself. Momentarily at least, she was the member of the family who was "beaten down to a nothing."

The irony and the tragedy of Kathleen Whiting's emotional life is that she incorporated into her personality the worst qualities of her mother and her father, both. It is for this reason that within her own family Kathleen has become not only her mother, but her father too. Thus, in the session not only did her children try to beat her down like her mother was "beaten down," but she is perceived in the same light as her father—the family "ogre."

Another item is also clear now. Unconsciously and unwittingly Francis fed into and literally reinforced Kathleen's perception of her own and his role and mutual demands which organized the family, which set the patterns for their interaction. Francis utilized two avenues of communication with Kathleen: 1) submission and 2) indifference. Both avenues violated her basic needs and at the same time had the unfortunate effect of reinforcing her notion that she was the only parent in a two-parent family.

Despite all of this what is clear now is that there is affection among the Whitings. Francis and Alice got up to bring Kathleen back from her aborted attempt to leave. They both helped to pick up the contents of the purse. Francis led her back, sat with his arm on her shoulder. I'm convinced that all of these behaviors were a function of love. Apparently John is able to communicate his affection least, perhaps because he has received the least. Or again, perhaps he still harbors too much hostility.

Francis, for all the comments about his quietness spoke up and at times, I thought, insightfully. I thought that one of his more profound comments was, " . . . we're not the complete bastards they were." I took this to mean that, unlike their own parents, he and Kathleen love their children, even if they are both unable to communicate it. Probably it is this mutual inability to communicate which precipitated John's acting out to effect a more enhancing homeostatic balance for the family. But the family learned a lot in these sessions, and the most important learning was that while Kathleen and Francis were never emotionally equipped to communicate love they're going to expend new efforts to do so.

The role playing scene did much to engender feelings of warmth, love and closeness. Thus, it served to reinforce the notion that they were going to try to communicate love and warmth. Also it clearly demonstrated, not only to Alice and to Kathleen, but to all four that they can indeed feel and communicate their feelings. Why? because they *know* what each other's feelings are.

There were other positive outcomes from this session. John and Alice learned that both Kathleen and Francis had problems with their parents, some of which John and Alice have inherited. They learned that their grandparents inflicted pain upon their parents, inculcated "hang-ups." They learned, I believe, that there are emotional radii which transcend the generations.

Chapter 12

Therapy with Francis and Kathleen

FOCUS GUIDES

1. Consider the expectations which Francis and Kathleen had for each other. Were they well thought out? Were they realistic? Were they a source of conflict?

2. As you read along what strikes you as a prime source for the conflicts between Francis and Kathleen?

3. Consider Francis's unwillingness to confront Kathleen about her apparent unwillingness to fill the role of housewife. Was it better not to confront?

4. Reflect on Francis' impotence. Is it consistent with the marital relationship? Does that explain it?

5. Francis feels he met his commitment to the marriage. Did he?

For a number of sessions I'd had a nagging thought, namely that I was not giving Kathleen and Francis and their relationship as much attention as it warranted. My best judgement was that Francis' expectations about a husband did not, perhaps never did, gibe. The demands which they placed upon one another probably had a great deal to do with the relationship they had or, more accurately, didn't have. I'd learned a long time ago that the parental dyad and the relationship it emitted was a critical determinant for the nature of the familial homeostasis. Accordingly, I decided to ask to see them without the children.

My original thought was to have no more than one meeting with Francis and Kathleen alone. The breadth and the depth of the dynamics discovered and covered, however, necessitated three. The tapes of these three sessions were edited, abbreviated and synthesized for readability.

"Come on in, c'mon in, Kathleen, Francis. Uh, I wanted to see both of you alone."

Kathleen and Francis came in, he a little sheepishly, she, I thought, a little embarrassedly. They sat down together on the couch opposite me.

"Like I said, I wanted to see you both alone, for one session."

"Well, what was it you wanted to know?" asked Kathleen.

"Well, we've seen each other a number of times and we've talked enough now, so I think I'm getting to know the Whiting family pretty well. Most of the problems which exist, I think, stem from . . ."

"Me?" asked Kathleen nervously. She was twisting a handkerchief in her hands.

"No, no Kathleen, not you per se. From both of you, uh, more accurately from the kind of relationship you and Francis have created. Let me make this real clear to you. Any problems which exist in your family do not come from you alone. Francis has contributed to the making of them, too. For that matter, the kids have, too. Your interaction with Francis, uh, the expectations you had for him and he had for you and the demands you both put on each other all that . . ." I knew I sounded garbled.

"I don't think I understand."

"O.K. Try to think. What did you expect of Francis when he married you?"

"What do you mean, expect of him?"

"Well, did you expect him to be the provider, and how did he meet your expectations? Did you expect him to be strong, dominant or weak and dependent? What did you expect of him?"

"Well, of course I expected him to be the provider. I was pregnant."

"So you expected him to fill the role of provider."

"Well, of course. Is that wrong?"

"No, no. And you need not be defensive. There's no right or wrong, I'm just trying to show . . ."

"If we both acted like the other one expected us to." Francis completed his first comment. He was obviously interested in this.

"Yes. Exactly."

"Well, Francis has been a provider. He's provided O.K. I mean it could be better, but I don't think that not having enough money is why we're here."

I didn't want to focus all my attention on Kathleen. "What about you, Francis, what expectations did you have for Kathleen?"

"I dunno. I never thought about it. She was pregnant when we got married. She was gonna' be a mother. She's always been a mother and a housewife. I don't guess I expected much else."

"Well, has she been an adequate mother, an adequate housewife? Let's take housewife first."

He looked at her. A little fearfully? I wasn't sure. "Ah, she's O.K."

"No. I'm not. You used to complain that I didn't always make the bed, iron, that supper wasn't ready."

"Yeah, but that was a long time ago. I don't anymore."

"He doesn't anymore 'cause he knows it won't do much good. I hate housework. And the truth is I'm not the best housewife."

"How do you feel about that now, Francis?"

"I dunno." He sounded sincere. "I never think about it."

"Well, think about it now. Your mother, what kind of a housewife was she?"

"Very efficient," Kathleen chimed in.

"How was she, Francis?"

"Yeah, she was very neat."

"Do you resent Kathleen's, uh, admitted inefficiency?"

"Yeah, I s'pose I do. I used to a lot more'n I do now."

"Did you ever speak to her about it?"

"Nah."

"I don't know that we ever fought about it," said Kathleen. "At least he," she turned to Francis, "you didn't ever make an issue out of it, did you, dear?"

"No."

"Did you want to?" I asked. "Let's be honest, Francis."

"Well, I guess there were times I sorta' got mad about it, but I couldn't see makin' a big deal, a big hassle over an unironed shirt or something."

"Are you trying to start another scene here, Doctor?" Kathleen asked this a little heatedly.

"No, Kathleen, I'm not. Let me point something out. A few moments ago you said that Francis never made any issue out of your lack of enthusiasm for housework, that a shirt was unironed, or what-have-you. What I want to point out is that just because, or maybe precisely because he did not make an issue out of something that bothered him about you in the early stages of your marriage, that wasn't necessarily healthy. In fact, it might have been better if he had."

"Why?" she asked.

"Just wait," I said. "How much did it bother you, Kathleen's unwillingness to do housework?" I asked.

"Oh, I dunno."

"Did you care about it a lot, once in a while?"

"Yeah, once in a while it might've bugged me. If I was late gettin' to work and I couldn't find a clean shirt then I . . ."

"Oh, come now," Kathleen cried impatiently, "marriages don't go sour because of a dirty shirt."

For whatever reason Kathleen was feeling more threatened than usual. As gently as I could I said, "Kathleen you interrupted him. Let's hear what Francis has to say."

"Yeah, I was gonna' say I'd get a little mad if I was in a hurry and I couldn't get a shirt."

"Why didn't you tell her?"

"Cause it would start a fight."

"And you preferred to wear a dirty one to asking her to have a clean one ready for you."

"Yeah."

"What's the point of all this, anyway?" asked Kathleen irritably.

"The point is that right here on something as common, maybe even silly as a clean shirt, we can see an important pattern of your marriage being laid down. Francis didn't like something. You, Kathleen, were not meeting his expectations, but because of the kind of person you are, Francis, and apparently still are, you preferred to not say anything than express how you felt. Quite rightly, Kathleen, you concluded it wasn't that important to him. But at home, Kath, when your own father didn't like something your mother knew about it, right?"

"Damned right," she nodded.

"So you learned quickly that Francis wasn't like your father. Maybe even you've thought often that Francis didn't care about too many things 'cause he never complained about anything."

"Yeah," she nodded. "I've thought that."

"But what we're learning now is that Francis just didn't want to start a fight. Or maybe you really didn't care. Which was it, Francis?"

He looked perplexed. "I dunno."

"Kathleen sure can yell. She always could."

"And you weren't used to yelling."

"No, I wasn't. There wasn't any yelling in my house ever."

"And you didn't know how to handle it."

"I guess that's right, yeah."

"The easiest thing was simply to give in and put up with a dirty shirt, or a late supper or whatever."

"Yeah," he affirmed.

"And so, in not confronting Kathleen about how you felt, you gave up a lot of your rights as a husband, as a partner in the marriage. You led her to believe that her way was O.K. with you."

There was a pause. "See Kathleen, that's what I meant when I said that a lot of the problem here was not just you but came out of your interaction with Francis. What about Kathleen as a mother, have you let her know how she's done in your eyes, as a mother?"

"No, I guess not."

"Well, tell us now. How do you feel about it?"

Francis was nonplussed. This confrontation method was diametrically opposite to his own style. In his usual embarrassed way he was looking down at his knees.

"I don't know what to say," he replied desolately.

"Well, I'm sure Francis doesn't think too much of me as a mother or for that matter as anything else."

"Oh Christ, Kath, that't not true, not true."

"What's a mother supposed to be like, Francis?" (Even as I asked this question I wondered about "anything else.")

"She's s'posta' take care of her kids," he mumbled.

"Does Kathleen do that?"

"Oh, she tries," he said too softly.

"Oh, for God's sakes, Francis, will you for once be honest with me and with yourself. You think, no, you're sure, that I'm a lousy mother. I've known that for a long time and you think that I think you're a lousy father. I think I'm beginning to understand something, something, now." She looked directly at me. "You think that most of our problems come from the fact that we don't talk to each other about how we feel about each other. Right?"

With this statement she had effectively clarified pretty much what had transpired in the session up to now.

"Right. And what each of you thinks about how the other's doing in his role as a parent. Like I'm sure that you, Francis, had certain expectations about how a mother and wife is supposed to perform and you never let Kathleen know. Maybe it ate away at you too, I don't know. 'Course this may have fit in with your own needs too, Kath."

"How so?"

"Well, we touched on this at one of our last sessions. It made you upset."

"Yeah," she replied."You think I act like my father . . ."

"Well, you did incorporate some of your father's way into your own personality. We all do take on some of both parents' ways, not just the like-sexed parent. Francis, you have some of your mother's ideas about some things, I'm sure."

He nodded. "Yeah, I guess I admire efficiency in a woman. I was

doing some repairs over at the Watsons'. That Watson lady, lemme tell
you, runs a tight ship as a mother."

Kathleen shot him a dirty look. "And our own ship is sinking, eh?"

"And so you're disappointed, maybe even angry with Kathleen." I
said.

"And you think if Francis is angry he ought to let me know."

"Yeah, especially if it's eating away at you, Francis. I think you should
let Kathleen know. It's better to let each other know what's bugging you
about the other. Otherwise, what happens often is that you become more
distant from each other or you become irritated, angry, upset about trivial
things."

"What do you do if you're just not the angry type?" asked Francis,
with a kind of baleful but terribly honest look.

"He's not talking about being angry, Francis, he's talking about being
honest."

"Yeah, that's right, Kath. I am. But it's not a moral honesty, so much
as an emotional honesty. See, Francis, a basic problem here is that as a
child growing up you got the idea that getting angry was wrong."

"I guess that's so. Both my parents were very controlled people. They
never got mad. If they were mad they controlled it very well. Looking
back, I suppose they overdid it. But I don't think that they were completely
wrong either. I mean, Jesus, supper in our house is more yelling time than
eating time."

"Yeah, but I'll bet that a lot of the reason for that is precisely because
Kathleen feels you never talk to her about how you feel about things,
important things," I suggested. The look on his face indicated that this
thought had never occurred to him, that in a real sense he was the cause for
the yelling he detested so.

Kathleen nodded. "Yeah, but I'm the one who's guilty of the yelling. *I*
do it. Alice mentioned that last time. I've thought about it a lot. She's right.
What's funny about it all is the fact that I remember dinner in my father's
house. It was hell for us kids. I should know better."

"Knowing with your head and knowing with your emotions are two
different things."

"What do you mean by that?"

"Well, just because you know something's wrong doesn't mean you
can stop doing it, even if you know it might hurt you or somebody you
love. You grew up in a house with a strong, domineering and even cruel
father. O.K. And you may well have hated many things about him. Your
mother was, as I understand it, weak, passive and dependent. For whatever
reason, your emotional choice was to be more like him than her. It was
preferable as you saw it to be dominant than passive, to be strong than to
be weak."

"God, I find that hard to accept, that I'd rather be like my father than my mother."

"I appreciate that, Kath. Francis, you fed into the whole thing, just by choosing not to confront Kathleen when she bugged you doing and not doing things that you didn't like. Francis, tell me, you think I'm wrong in how I see it?"

"Sounds pretty right," he said meekly.

"Is it right?" I asked sharply.

"Guess so," he said looking down. There was a pause.

"Francis, how do you see your relationship with . . . No, how do you see your marriage? What do you think of your marriage?"

He looked surprised by the question. So did Kathleen.

"I love my wife," he answered simply.

"Why?" I asked. "Why?" he was really perplexed by the question.

"Yeah, why. She hasn't measured up very well as an efficient housewife or mother."

"Yeah, well maybe I'd just as soon not have, uh, an efficient woman living in my house. I hated my mother."

I was the one a little perplexed now. It was a damned good point and one that frankly had not occurred to me. Quite understandably Francis could well prefer *not* having an efficient woman around. The price of efficiency as he saw it in his mother anyway, was rejection. Efficient women didn't have time for loving. Francis, I concluded, was a very astute guy.

"Uh, good point," I responded. "Yes, perhaps that's true. May well be. So you love Kathleen."

"Yeah, I do."

"But hon, maybe you do, but you never show it. You don't tell me."

"Do you act it?" I asked.

"Act?"

"How do you show it?"

"Guess I don't," was his glum response.

"No, you don't Francis. I mean even in the privacy of . . ." She stopped.

Francis was reddening.

"Of the bedroom," I finished the sentence.

Kathleen nodded.

I didn't know how far we would go or how willing they were to discuss it. I was convinced that Kathleen wanted to. I glanced at Francis. He was stony faced now, but I'm sure he was more than a little rattled.

"Tell me if you want to, Kathleen."

"I won't if Francis doesn't want to." She looked at him.

"Christ, Kath, how can I say no now?"

Francis was, if nothing else, I concluded, a very honest guy. That he was too embarrassed to say no was what he was telling us.

"Well yes, we're having our problems."

"Francis doesn't, uh, want to have relations?" I asked.

"I want to," he said.

"You can't," I responded.

"Yeah," he muttered with a long sigh.

"Well," I sighed back, "I'm not surprised."

"You're not?" Kathleen ask interestedly.

"No. All the indications are . . . but wait, tell me how long's it been like this, that you can't, Francis."

"Uh, I don't know, couple of months maybe."

"And before that how often did you have relations?"

"Not too often. I don't know. What's often?"

"Typical, they tell me, is once, twice a week maybe."

He looked at her. "Well, we never did it that much. Maybe three, four times a month. Kath's a Catholic."

"We practiced rhythm for the longest time," she added.

"I see. Anyway, now it's been two months or so since there's been any sex, right?"

Francis nodded, "Yeah."

"O.K.," I nodded back. "You didn't want to, you couldn't, uh, what?"

"Both," he answered, "both. Christ, don't ask me, I mean, I don't understand it, I don't."

Francis was mortified by the discussion, so much so, I felt myself becoming uncomfortable. However, I felt or saw no alternative but to continue.

With all the sympathy I could inject into my tone I said, "I know you don't understand it, Francis, I'm positive of that but maybe, just maybe if we can even touch on the emotions of it all, you might just find it really helpful."

"Whaddya' mean?"

"Well, as I understand it, you'd like to be able to get together with Kathleen. Is that right?"

"Yeah," he said with a mite of impatience.

"Well, impotence isn't caused ordinarily by your conscious awareness, but it's a product of emotions, feelings, uh, how to . . ."

"You mean I can't with Kath because I don't feel right toward her?"

He'd said it simply, easily, and better than I.

"Yeah," I said a little weakly. "You don't feel right toward her."

Kathleen had been quiet but apparently more than interested. She'd edged forward on the couch and was looking intently back and forth to each of us. For the past few moments she seemed to have focused upon her husband.

"I don't know for sure how you feel, Francis. But one thing I do know is that sex, in marriage especially, is just another way of expressing how spouses feel toward one another. Now as I understand it, you, Kathleen, are willing but you, Francis, are . . ."

"I'm willing," he cried.

"But for whatever reason you, uh, can't."

"Yeah," he replied ashamedly.

"Which brings me to my point. You've got a lot of negative feelings toward Kathleen that you won't or better, can't seem to admit to yourself. And these feelings are preventing you from performing sexually."

"Sounds awful complicated," he said.

"It isn't really. Your body's telling Kathleen more accurately how you feel than what you've been telling us."

"Are you trying to say that I don't love my wife?" He said this in a choked, shaking voice.

"I think the truth is you do and at the same time you've got a lot of hostility toward her, a lot of very negative feelings, almost none of which you've ever let yourself express toward her. And they're coming out now in this way. You're unable to love her sexually."

"You mean Francis hates me?" Kathleen asked this in a kind of shocked way.

"Oh, come now. Few people just plain love their spouses. Most married people have some negative, even a lot of negative feelings, dissatisfactions with their spouse. Thing is, most of them express some of those feelings."

Short pause.

I turned to Francis and asked, "When was the last time you expressed any dissatisfaction with Kathleen?"

He looked at me sheepishly, "I dunno," he replied.

Kathleen looked at him and not unkindly said, "Oh, Francis, you never complain about anything. You know you don't."

"Yeah, I guess I don't."

"And because he doesn't you think that, that's why he can't do anything with me?" Although it was a question, it came out more like a statement.

"Well, there could be a lot of reasons. That's for sure. But I think a big one has to do with a lot of repressed hostility you have toward Kath, Francis."

Francis sat next to his wife, a little woodenly, I noticed but surprisingly composed.

I asked curiously, "Francis, you ever get mad inside?"

"Yeah."

"Well, what do you do about it?"

He looked at me. "I dunno, not much. It goes away, I get over it."

"What about at work?"

"I work alone."

"What about the kids when they were young. They must've got on your nerves. Didn't you ever get after them, you know, spank or yell at them?"

"I raised the kids when they were small," said Kathleen.

"That's true. I always figured it was her job." He paused and almost as an afterthought added, "I worked."

Kathleen corroborated his statement. "Francis was almost never around when they were small. He even worked Sundays, moonlighting. If I complained a lot, and I guess I did, he'd always answer with such honesty that, I didnt know what to say back. How did you put it, Fran, 'I'm committed to my work,' something like that."

"Yeah, that's true," he nodded.

"You still feel that way?" I asked.

"Look, I guess I done a lotta things wrong. One of them was not taking, uh, not helping to take care of the kids. You know what I realize? That Watson woman, she runs a tight ship, but you know, Kath, I was planing down a door upstairs and I heard her and her husband with their kids. You know, they seem to be able to do something we never been able to do."

"What's that?"

"Enjoy the kids. We never enjoyed the kids. Be honest with you," and he looked at me, "and with you, doc. I guess I always found them more a pain than anything else." He said all of this in a kind of choked up way. If one had never heard him speak before he would have concluded that Francis Whiting had a cold. The truth was, however, that Francis Whiting was emoting. I really thought for a moment that he might cry.

Kathleen looked at him. "Fran, I always suspected that. Why didn't you ever tell me?"

"Christ, Kath, how could I? You were always bitching about them. What was the point of both of us doing it?"

"But damn it Fran, I did bitch a lot, an awful lot, but I did it 'cause you never did a damned thing to help. Just like even take them off my hands for a couple of hours on Sunday. I mean, God, Fran there was no help. No help at all." Kathleen's voice had risen sharply on the last couple of sentences.

Francis shrugged, "I know, I see that. I do see that," (pause) "now."

There was a silence for almost a minute. I looked from one to the other. They both were looking down apparently engrossed in thought. It was Francis who broke the silence. "We should never have had any kids. Neither one of us was cut out to be a parent. We don't, we never had the constitution for it."

I was inclined to agree. Neither was emotionally equipped to deal with, to meet the infinite demands and obligations which children, just by their existence, impose upon their parents. Yet, the reality is, I thought, the kids are here. They have to deal with them. But the problem was not only the children. Their lack of relationship with them was an extension, a symptom of their problems with each other and with themselves.

It seemed as if Kathleen had been reading my thoughts or at least we were on the same wavelength, for her next words were, "I think you're right, Fran, we probably should never have been parents. I never wanted any either, if you must know. But what could we do with them, once I was pregnant? In those days you just didn't get an abortion. It was illegal everywhere. And I'm not sure I could have done that anyway. But what I'm starting to see is that our kids aren't the problem, it's not them, it's us."

He nodded.

"We're so different you and I. Yet, we're so much alike," she said to him.

"What do you mean by that?" he asked

"We're both such private people. Maybe you're a little more private than me. You could be perfectly happy living alone, so could I, that's how we're alike, but I have to see people, you don't."

Fran nodded again.

And imply, almost detachedly, Kathleen continued, "Neither one of us seems to be able to give. My excuse, maybe it is and maybe it isn't, is that I've spent twenty years giving to you and the kids. I can't anymore, that's how I feel, that's why I went to the hospital. Lord, Fran, you can't give, and I'm just realizing now you never could. It's not that you're selfish, it's . . ."

Francis jumped up. He was angry. My thought was, 'Christ, finally!'

"That's not true, that I can't give. It's just not true. I'm just different than you. We're two different people. Listening to your goddamned complaining for twenty years, worrying sick every month if I'd make enough money, then every day comin' home dead tired to squallin' kids and a naggin' wife, a wife that put me down in front of everybody. I met my commitments in spite of everything."

Kathleen had started to get angry when Francis had started, but the anger had melted away as he proceeded and was replaced by surprise.

There was quiet again. I broke it. "What do you say to that, Kath?"

"Francis, you always end up with your little speech about

commitment. Life is nothing but one big bloody duty to you. A wife wants more than a dutiful husband. Kids need more than a dutiful father. I mean, what about affection, what about love?"

"Kath," I said, "We each of us love in our own way. If I read you right, Francis, what you're saying is that your love is and was expressed by working, supporting the family and putting up with frustrations that you didn't know how to cope with, is that right?" I wasn't sure that I should have interrupted with this clarification.

"Yeah, that's right," he nodded.

"But what's all this got to do with the fact that Francis can't make love to me?"

"A lot, I think," I replied.

"I wouldn't be surprised if Francis doesn't feel emotionally castrated by you."

"What?" she cried incredulously.

Francis too looked astonished

"You see, Francis understands that love for him is expressed not with words, hugs, or kisses, but with meeting his conscience obligations to his family. I'd bet anything he's done that scrupulously. You, Kathleen, don't and apparently can't understand it. Your understanding of love is the more usual one, with words, a kiss, a pinch, a little present for no special reason, helping with the kids and so on." Even as I said these words I wondered how they would be received.

She nodded in agreement and I felt relieved and real good.

I continued, "Well, Francis feels rejected by you, probably has for a very long time. Not only does he feel rejected, he feels demeaned. He offers love as he sees it and you put him down for it. He says he's been putting up with it for years and years. Now his emotions are rebelling unconsciously and via his body are telling him something like, 'To hell with her, shut her off, you don't need her!' "

"You mean Francis is unconsciously punishing me?"

"Honestly, I'm not sure, but it's a good possibility. There's a lot of anger in Francis toward you, about twenty years of it."

"Twenty years!" Kathleen echoed. "Twenty years, oh, wow!"

"But Christ, you pointed out before yourself that there's more than just anger in me. I think I love Kathleen too, I know I love her."

"And I'm sure you do to," I chuckled. "Kathleen, physically is very easy to love."

"Why would I want to punish her? For Christ's sakes why?" Francis asked this with sincere bewilderment.

"I think that has to do with how well you know her, and with the fact that you've never learned how to express your anger; not to her and not to others for that matter."

"I don't know what you mean. What do you mean by that?"

"Well, what you've probably felt, mind you, is that where you can hurt her the most is in her femininity. Kathleen is very strong here and much aware of her femininity. Depriving her of sex, attacking her in a most precious concern, her feminine self-esteem, you figure that's one way to really get to her."

"Well, if she's so strong, why should it bother her so much? How can I hurt her if she's so strong?"

"Because sex is a most effective way to communicate 'you're really something as a person,' by not doing it and when she wants to, you're saying, 'you're not too much as a person or as a woman.' That would hurt any person, man or woman and a lot, after a while."

"Yeah, I can see that," he assented.

Throughout this exchange between me and Francis, Kathleen had remained quiet. Her interest in what I had to say was transparent. Now she spoke. "I've been listening. A lot of this is like a revelation. And I must admit I have to agree." She chuckled. "And it isn't that I got to, I want to. I suppose what you're saying here is that Francis isn't able to with me because I don't make him feel much like a man."

She had said it easily, accurately and succinctly.

"Yes, I'm saying that. I'm saying exactly that."

"I see." She sat back, crossed her pretty legs demurely and sighed.

We all paused, looked at each other and I said a little hesitantly, "Kath, how can you help Francis to feel more like a man?"

"What?" she asked.

I repeated my question.

"Why I guess generally, not to put him down, not to nag him, not embarrass him in front of the kids, not to . . ."

"Can't you think of anything positive, Kath?" Francis asked.

"What?"

"Everything you said began with, 'not to'."

"I guess this is both your problem, Francis. I think you might be being a little harsh. You'll find it just as difficult, I'm sure. I mean I have to ask you a comparable question, how can you help Kathleen to be a more competent wife and mother, a more effective woman in the house?"

"Show my love more," he answered simply.

"O.K., your answer is easier to come up with. However, I suspect it may pose problems to implement for you."

"Yeah," he nodded, "I'll bet."

I turned to Kathleen. "Any thoughts on how to help Francis?"

She shook her head. "No, you know the problem is like you said a while ago. It's me and him together and how we act toward each other. I feel it sometimes. I feel like I'm in control and you seem to want it like that,

Francis." She had turned to look at him. "What do you think?"

"Yeah. There's truth to that. And I think that's why we, I can't make it with you in bed." He turned to me and said, "Oh, what the hell. Let's get it all out. I started to get turned off about six or eight months ago.

"How so? Why?"

"Why?" echoed Kathleen.

"That's when you started to get, uh, aggressive in bed. Up to that time. I was calling all the shots. That's when I got turned off."

I glanced at Kathleen. She had turned a little pink, her head was down.

"So that, uh, turned you off. You felt that Kath was trying to dominate the bed scene as well as everything else."

"I guess so, yeah. And she wanted to start trying different things, that, uh, that I didn't want to."

"Why not?"

"I just didn't think it was proper for a wife. I mean, geez, it was the kind of stuff I used to hear about when I was in the service." There was a pause. "I guess I never let myself think about it too much, but it was 'cause like you say she was trying to take over in the bed."

"And that's where you drew the line."

"I think that's what happened, yeah."

Kathleen's pink face had turned red. Francis had noticed. He was becoming increasingly embarrassed. He lowered his head.

Kathleen spoke. "You know, maybe this is all proper in therapy but I do think it's awful personal business. I . . . ."

"Oh, Kath," Francis responded with irritation. "It's you who started it, who brought it up. Maybe you're embarrassed. Christ, how do you think it makes me feel? You bringin' up the fact I can't get an erection. What do you think that does for me. Talk about bein' put down. Jesus!"

Kathleen's redness had vanished. "But your talking like that makes me feel like some kind of nymphomaniac or at least a sexual pervert. Heavens sakes, you are my husband. It's not like I was with another man."

I felt Kathleen needed a little support. "Yeah," I nodded, "but more important even, we might ask, why did Kathleen act like this?"

"Why?" Fran looked puzzled.

"Yeah, why was Kathleen being aggressive? You know sexual behavior in the bedroom, like I said before can be symptomatic. How spouses behave in bed is generally consistent with how they behave out of bed. So, if Kathleen was starting to behave aggressively in bed she wanted some behavioral expression of your love, since it was the only way you were showing her any at all. After all, Fran, among other things sexual intercourse can be a way to demonstrate real affection."

Francis was quiet. So was Kathleen. I had the feeling that for a while now she was comparing me to Francis. This made me a little bit, but just a little bit uncomfortable. I had to be very careful not to let Francis feel put down; I had to be even more careful not to let myself be emotionally seduced.

Francis, meanwhile, was becoming increasingly threatened. "I know," he said archly, "that sex is a way to show love. Geez doc, I'm not a kid. But Kathleen here wanted to . . ." He stopped again, too embarrassed.

"So she wanted to stimulate you because by not having sex with her you were, she felt anyway, rejecting her in the last way, in the only way you were still demonstrating some measure of affection for her."

"Yeah, maybe."

"You're unconvinced."

"Yeah."

"My problem at this point is that I don't have all the details. I suspect but I'm not sure of what . . ."

It was Kathleen who said it. "I tried to use my mouth."

"And you were repelled by that, Francis." It was a statement, not a question and I said it without any emotion.

"Yeah, I was."

"Well, symbolically, especially between marrieds, there are those who view the act of fellatio as putting the man in the dominant role. Maybe Kathleen was trying to say to you, 'You're my master and I'll do anything you want. That's how much I love you.'"

"Oh, that's bullshit," Francis's voice crackled with disgust.

I continued, ignoring his expletive. "Maybe you were repelled, Francis, because it was too threatening to have Kathleen in what you felt was a servile position precisely because she's your emotional support and she wants you to be hers."

"I don't know if I got all that," he said honestly.

"Both of you have a need to be dependent upon the other. A little while ago I asked Kathleen how she could help you to be more of a man and you pointed out to her that she was saying all the negative things, you know, she was not gonna' do this and she was not gonna' do that, she wasn't gonna' nag or put you down. Well this approach of oral sex by her, some might see this as an attempt to make you feel that she's not the dominant one in your relationship, that you are."

Francis turned to Kathleen. "Is that right?" he asked curiously.

"I, I don't know," she said again turning a little pink. "I, I don't know why, I guess I just felt like it."

"That's what I think," he replied.

Even though I believed my interpretation was accurate, I didn't press it. Neither, I felt was emotionally ready to accept it. I had learned a long time ago that a person's emotional life can't be re-ordered via intellect only. I had expressed my view. It was their choice to accept and utilize it. Time would tell.

"One thing I got out of this," Kathleen said, "is the point you made about how you act in bed is consistent with how you act out of bed, so I suppose if we're sensitive to each other . . ."

I don't know why she stopped. She seemed to be thinking.

"Yes," I said, "if you're both sensitive to each other's needs outside of bed, bed shouldn't be threatening to either of you. Anything you feel you can do to enhance Francis has got to be good. And anything Francis, that you can do to enhance Kathleen, obviously that's gonna' be good too. Neither one of you needs to list or go over now what to do, how to act with each other."

Francis had been nodding while I had been talking. He'd been looking at his wife.

"I'm convinced you both do have negative feelings toward each other. You have to. Both of you. Both of you feel put down by the other and a lot. In a real sense John's delinquency is a symptom of the delinquent feelings you two have toward each other."

"Are we gonna' go back to that hate that we got . . ."

"No Fran, all he's saying is that we do have hateful feelings but that doesn't have to matter much 'cause we also have positive feelings toward each other."

"Exactly. And if you both talk and express to each other, and constantly, about how you feel, both the negative and the positive feelings, well then . . ."

"Things oughta' get better," said Francis.

"Yes," I said.

"The talking and the expressing is going to be especially hard at first for you, Francis."

"Yeah."

"Although I've heard again and again about how quiet you are. Admittedly there've been moments like that here, but you certainly have not come off like the original quiet man."

"Yeah."

"And Kath, there's a lot you haven't said but you must be aware of where you've put Fran down and . . ."

She nodded as I spoke and raised her hand to hush me up. "I know," she said with a smile.

I turned to Francis. He, too, had a little grin on his face. I grinned back. I'd never seen him smile before. "I got a lot of thinkin' first."

I was tired but pleasantly so. Over the years I'd learned to gauge the effectiveness of a session by how I felt at its close. I felt good about this one. Real good.

DISCUSSION QUESTIONS

1. Why do you think Francis and Kathleen have stayed together all these years?
2. Was Kathleen's resistance to her roles of wife and mother symptomatic of something?
3. What do you see as Kathleen's weakest and strongest assets?
4. What do you see as Francis' weakest and strongest assets?
5. Do you think that Francis and Kathleen can have a fruitful marriage? What reasons can you give that they should stay together?

NOTES AND ANALYSIS

Most therapists are of the opinion that the emotional health of a nuclear family is the function of a parental dyad. This chapter confirmed much that I had suspected about the relationship between Francis and Kathleen. Certainly they have suffered much over the years. They built their marriage on a very shaky foundation. She *expected* him to marry her. She was pregnant. And after what we learned about his sense of duty and commitment it's safe to assume that he felt honor bound to marry her. In short, they both felt that they *had* to marry each other. Apparently personal choice or other viable options were denied them perhaps because of the time frame in which they lived, perhaps because of the values of the cultural milieu in which they were steeped. No matter. From the very beginning they encountered problems. Indeed, it is safe to conclude that the potential problems for their relationship existed in each of them before they ever met. The source for these problems lay in the values and expectations about the parental role which they acquired in their respective families. From both this session and previous ones and from the personalities which they exhibit it is possible to infer much about what both learned growing up at home.

Francis learned that fathers are strong and that they control. He learned too, that emotional displays are crass and inappropriate. "Both my parents were very controlled people. They never got mad."

Mother was "Queen Victoria." This would mean that while men might be controlling and stronger, women can control more than men, especially within the home. Basic aspects of the maternal role, he concluded, include rearing children, being neat and being efficient.

Francis noted in the transcript of the session that he hated his efficient mother. Quite apparently, one ordinarily does not hate a loving mother. What I conclude from this is that Francis learned that mothers are supposed to be efficient, but also emotionally detached and not warm, but cold. It is not especially speculative to infer that he learned that women are difficult to get close to.

Unquestionably, he learned about the "nobility of work." Even today he finds work enhancing, perhaps an escape too. Via work he escaped boredom, loneliness, and having to deal with domestic chores. Moreover, work and being the provider was his basic role in the same way that a woman's basic role involves the rearing of children.

What I conclude from all of this is that Francis entered marriage ill-equipped emotionally to deal with the obligations imposed by the roles of husband and father. Obviously he felt unloved at home. What this means is that he probably never learned to give or receive love with a feeling of reward. In short, the values, ideas and ideals which were held out to him as being important, desirable and rewarding did not include those which were conducive to the creation of a warm, nurturant and loving home.

What about Kathleen? What did she learn and not learn at home? Unquestionably, the learning which was impressed upon her most strongly was that a man in his role of a father is a very strong person. This means he is dominant, aggressive and very controlling. It is reasonable to infer that she came to think that fathers walk all over mothers, perhaps that men walk all over women. Certainly they walk all over children. Via her father too, she learned that a man is vulgar and/or crude. Swearing, for example, she learned is very much a part of the masculine scene.

The mother and woman image presented to her was very different. A woman in her role as a wife and mother is weak, dependent and perhaps passive. What Kathleen apparently concluded in light of her own experience as a child at home is that a woman may well end up as a nothing if she is not assertive.

Kathleen learned too, that a man is the provider for the family. He works and works hard, providing the daily bread, and therein lies his superior status. It is speculative perhaps, but not unrealistic to think that Kathleen perceives the wife's or woman's status as inferior to that of the husband, the man, the provider.

Kathleen came to understand also that the feelings and frustrations which a woman or children have are unimportant to a man. He does not care about them.

As is true with Francis then, we can reasonably assume that Kathleen growing up was not exposed to an emotional climate which would teach her how to be a successful parent. Indeed, two fundamental learnings acquired early and unfortunately retained too long seem to have been, "life can be cruel and love is not obtained at home."

In sum, both Kathleen and Francis came into the marriage cognitively and emotionally ill equipped to function in the roles of spouse and parent. Even more, their expectations about each other conflicted sharply. He expected a cool, efficient woman who found some kind of reward in maternal, wifely chores. She found these threatening and expected a man who was strong, dominant and controlling. In turn, these characteristics were, if not threatening to Francis, at least not inculcated into his personality. Condemnation and ultimately recrimination became common aspects of their relationship. The effect of all of these dynamics upon Francis was impotence. This was the understandable outcome of a relationship long beset by conflict. I do see the impotence, as I noted in the therapy session, as a function of hostility. I do think he misinterpreted Kathleen's attempt at oral sex because he unconsciously wanted to. He deliberately saw her as trying to take over in the bedroom. This provided him with his proverbial "last straw." Some might see his impotence as a cry for help. I see it rather as his method of breaking away from her in order to obviate the feelings of being controlled and dominated. For twenty years he had felt manipulated and publicly demeaned, at times even psychologically castrated. In a very dramatic way impotence was for him a kind of sexual-emotional vendetta. And as is invariably and unfortunately true in these kinds of familial battles it hit where it hurt most. For Kathleen this was in her feminine self-concept. As was noted in the chapter on communication, "we speak with our whole bodies." Francis spoke. The message, while not transparently clear, was nevertheless acutely distressing and not just to Kathleen but to Francis too.

Still I see remarkable strength in this relationship despite all the conflicts and problems, personal and mutual. The most salient has to be their remarkable capacity to endure and bind the awful anxiety which each has felt in the relationship with the other. To put it simply, how much worse can it get? If nothing else they have been through an incredible amount of pain with each other and with their children and they have endured it all and survived. In such endurance and survival has to come strength.

The ability to endure and persevere with each other has to be a product of the conscience and the feelings of tenderness which were displayed at times in the therapy. Their experience in therapy should also be added to these strengths. Their willingness to participate in the therapy and hopefully, the profit derived, should contribute even more toward making this parental dyad stronger.

Chapter 13
Final Session

FOCUS GUIDES

1. Observe what changes have occurred in each of the Whitings.

2. Consider as you read along who among the Whitings has changed the most.

3. Consider the question of privacy. Why do you think it is so important to Kathleen and John?

4. Consider John's comment, "love is a bitch." How would you interpret it?

5. Consider Francis' idea that one's life is not one's own. Is it reasonable or unreasonable? Why?

As was their habit, the Whitings arrived promptly at 7:30 for their last session. Kathleen entered first, followed by Alice, Francis and John, in that order. I heard Kathleen murmur something unintelligible to Francis about where to sit. He nodded to the couch and both sat down, she gracefully, he heavily. Alice took a chair to her father's right and John sat next to her. I sat down facing the four of them.

Kathleen per usual opened the session. "Is this really going to be our last meeting?"

"I think so. I thought we all felt that there's not too much we've got left to cover that we haven't. As we said the last time we'll have a follow-up session in about a month.

"Well, there have been changes in these past couple of months, that's for sure," she nodded with a smile.

"Let's review how you all feel with what's happened, with what's going on in the family."

Alice piped up. "I'll tell you this. Supper time is much better. Sometimes it's even fun."

"Your mother isn't yelling so much."

"Yeah, I mean no, only once in a while," she answered.

"That's one resolution I'm still working hard on," Kathleen volunteered.

"To cut out yelling?" I asked.

"Well, yes. I suppose. But I was thinking more about supper time. I still remember that as a horror in my father's house. There's no reason why we can't at least have a good . . . "

"Man, that's killing you, Ma," John chipped in with a smile.

"If you mean by that that it's not easy, you're right, Johnny," she admitted. She turned to me. "You know, one thing you said back when we started had to do with expressing how we felt, that it was good to do that. I don't believe that it's necessarily good to express how you feel. Sometimes I just feel like yelling at John and Alice, especially for not picking up after themselves. But I don't 'cause it'll just start more haranguing back and forth."

I nodded in agreement. "Yeah, sometimes it's better to overlook or ignore little problems." There was a pause. I glanced at both of the younger Whitings. "What do you guys figure are your mother's rights?"

Alice looked puzzled by the question. "Why, what do you mean?"

"This is one of the things I wanted to bring up tonight," I said, perhaps too slowly, "What are each of our rights in the family? Each of us has them. And the idea is, if each of us respects each other's, things ought to change even more for the better, at least that's the idea."

There was a pause.

"So, what are mother's rights?" I asked again.

Another pause.

Kathleen spoke. "Maybe I could explain what I think they ought to be."

"Sure," I said.

"Privacy," she replied.

"What?" I asked.

"Privacy. My rights," she said thoughtfully, almost dreamily, "center around privacy. There was a time that all I wanted was a hot meal. I used to complain regularly about that."

"Yeah," nodded Francis in agreement. I noted that he still retained some quietness. This was his first utterance. No, Francis would never be outspoken, I thought wryly. "Yeah," he repeated, "when Tom and Frank were still little and John here was born, that's the main thing you complained about, not having a hot meal. I remember you'd get the supper for the family but by the time you sat down to eat it, yours was cold."

Kathleen sighed, "That's all over, thank God. But my need is privacy. I guess it's always been that."

"What do you mean by privacy?" I asked.

"Well, I don't mean to be, be, uh, isolated from the rest of the family. I mean the right to be alone, moments to myself."

"Christ, ma, you got all day to yourself."

"Yeah," chirped in Alice.

Francis said nothing. He was listening. He looked at his wife with curiosity.

"What I mean," she said rather loudly, "is the right to talk on the phone without being interrupted by who's that, Mother, what did they want, etc., etc.; or, I like to sit down and read after supper, sometimes I like to read right up to supper if I'm into a good book and I'm constantly badgered about the supper." She turned to Francis. "You see that, hon?"

He nodded slowly. "Yeah, yeah, I see that. You got a right to have time to your self. I think we all got that. But where does it end?"

"What? What do you mean?" she asked.

"Like, Kath, you got a right to read or be alone after supper, but that's askin'a lot before supper," he said.

"Why?"

" 'Cause sometimes you really get into a book and you don't want to leave it and get the supper so we're all standin' around waitin' and I just don't think that's right. Sure, you got a right to your privacy, but we all got obligations to each other, too. You know what I mean?" He said all of this in his quiet, even-tempered way.

Maybe Francis wasn't exactly outspoken, but he made sense when he talked. His family listened. I observed that John and Alice, too, had what, satisified or were they merely contented looks on their faces? I couldn't be sure. Francis will never be a dominating man, I remembered thinking, but certainly he was making his presence felt. He was a part of the family scene.

Kathleen looked at him. "I know what you mean, Fran, I know perfectly well what you mean," her tone was impatient, "but honestly, I feel put upon when you all nag me about supper not being ready. I just don't think it's fair."

"Geez, ma, what do you expect, what do you expect? You expect Dad to get supper?" John asked testily.

"Well, no, I don't expect that," she answered "but why couldn't I get more help, let's say for getting the dinners on weekends? Or why can't we all go out to dinner as a family once in a while? We've never gone out to eat as a family." She was looking at John when she started but at her husband when she finished.

Francis nodded, "Yeah, I haven't taken the family out to dinner, that's true, but Kath," he added gently, "I do barbecue for the family on week-ends. I do that a lot,"

"Yes, that's so. I guess I was complaining about never eating out."

"Yeah, but to get you back to the point. You think you got the right not to have dinner when we expect it?"

Kathleen smiled. "No, you're right. What I got to learn is not to get involved in a book before dinner."

I was finding the conversation a trifle too specific, perhaps even banal. I said, "I think the point here is the one which Francis made a while ago. We each of us has obligations to each other. We should all reach some kind of an agreement on what those obligations are. I think that's what's really important because we're not going to deal with every specific irritation which each of us may have."

"Yeah, but there are some major ones," said Kathleen.

"A supper not ready when you expect it sets a bad mood for the whole night," added Francis.

"Yeah," chimed in John.

"O.K.," I said, backing off a little lamely.

"I'll work at not reading before supper."

I sighed. Actually it was all going pretty well. They were talking to each other and even more, resolving issues. I was hoping that they could come to grips with principles. There was a pause and I jumped in, "What's the major obligation each of us has toward the other?"

"Not to bug each other," said Alice quickly and simply.

"What do you mean by that?" asked her mother.

"Just not to bug, sort of like your privacy." She looked at me for clarification.

"You mean not to intrude on each other's lives. Like Kath, you want time to yourself after supper, say, and everybody agrees to it, then they should not bug you during that period," I said, explaining what I thought Alice had in mind.

"I agree with that," said Kathleen.

Francis nodded.

It was John who said, "Well, speaking of rights, have kids got rights?"

"Of course you've got rights," said his mother.

"Yeah, but I figure I got the right not to be bugged, not to be hassled. And I think I'm the one in this family who's hassled the most."

"Maybe, John, but that's probably 'cause you're the one who intrudes on our lives the most," said his father.

"Yeah, but if I did that's 'cause like we've been saying here for a long time, that's 'cause you and Ma weren't exactly acting right."

Francis nodded. "I know, Johnny."

"Well, what do you figure your rights are?" I asked.

"Well, I like that privacy bit that Ma came up with."

"Privacy is not secrecy," said Kathleen with perhaps a little pomposity.

"Whaddya' mean? he asked.

Francis surprised all of us by answering for her. "You want your privacy. That's fine and O.K. and you're certainly entitled to it and I understand you don't wanna' be hassled. That's fine and O.K. You're no different than me. I don't wanna' be hassled either. But, Johnny, when you're being private, doing what you like, that don't give you the right to do something or not do something that's going to hurt me or your mother. You understand what I mean?"

"No," he answered. He looked honestly puzzled.

"O.K. You got a right to your privacy. But that don't give you the right to do things secret that are gonna' get you into trouble."

"Why not? Everybody's got a right to make mistakes," he answered with some defiance.

His father nodded. "You're right there. We all gotta' make our own mistakes, but Johnny, if you get into trouble I'm hassled just as much as you are."

"I know, 'cause you're responsible."

"Yeah, that and . . ."

"And what else?"

" 'Cause I'm nervous about you."

"Yeah? Christ, Dad, you never show it."

"I am though." And he said it in his usual awfully quiet tone. None of us doubted the truth of it.

"Why you nervous?"

There was a little pause and in a strained, almost whisper-like tone, Francis said, " 'Cause I love ya', that's why."

Kathleen's hand went to her mouth in surprise. John was too astonished to reply. Francis's response, however, was more dramatic. He turned a deep shade of pink and he looked down at his knees, sort of like Francis had often done at past sessions. But it was Alice, with her child-like candor, who summed up the feelings of all of us. "Geez, dad, that was nice. I never heard you say that. That was sooo nice." She jumped to her feet and kissed her father on the check. Now Francis turned a little more pink, but he smiled.

"That *was* nice," I contributed.

"Yes," Kathleen murmured, "there have been changes." She turned to me. "Have you any idea how hard that must've been?"

I looked at Francis. For a moment I thought about asking Francis to discuss how he felt. But then, I thought, 'What purpose? What purpose would be served?' Kathleen's observation had reinforced the fact that changes, emotional as well as behavioral, had indeed occurred.

I turned to John. He was still looking down. "John, what do you think about what your father said about your right to privacy doesn't give you the right to get involved in activities so that you intrude on his life?"

"Yeah, you're right there," he nodded toward his father.

Alice piped up with, "You're right. What you're really saying is that we're a family and . . ."

"We've got obligations to each other"; her mother finished the sentence for her.

There was a momentary lull. All four seemed to be in deep thought. John broke the lull. "Ya' know I used to complain that there wasn't any love in our family. I guess there is, but ya' know what I'm thinkin' here?"

"What?" I asked.

"I was thinkin', love is a bitch."

Both Kathleen and Francis looked at him, astounded. Francis, however, seemed only curious.

"Whaddyda' mean by that, John?" he asked.

"Just what I said," he replied. "You said I made you nervous. I buy that. And you said I make you nervous 'cause you love me. I buy that, too. I guess if you didn't love me you wouldn't get nervous."

"That's about the size of it," Francis responded, nodding.

"Trouble is," John continued, "trouble is whenever I want to do anything now I'm gonna' feel guilty."

"Only if it's gonna' hurt me, or your mother or Alice. And me and ma and Alice, we got the same pressure on us, if you want to call it pressure."

"That's a pressure," John said.

"I hadn't really thought about it in just this way," I volunteered, "but I suppose the pressure you're talking about, Francis, is the price you pay for family support." I turned to John, "Yeah, I see what you mean, love can be a bitch."

"Maybe, maybe," Kathleen said, "but it's an awful lot better than feeling like nobody cares. I'd rather be pressured to do what I know my family expects than to feel like I can do whatever I want 'cause nobody cares about me."

"Yeah, Ma, that's easy for you to say 'cause you're the mother here," he said a little heatedly.

"What's that mean?" she asked.

"Well, you and Dad, you're over forty. I still gotta' learn a lotta' things. I'm still learnin'. I know I screw up. I want to, uh, experiment. Now what I'm hearin' is I gotta' watch it. I gotta' watch it a lot how I experiment. That's a down. That's a put-down."

Francis nodded sympathetically. "Yeah, I can see that, son. Like you say, love's a bitch. But I bet growing up without it has gotta' be more of a bitch." He paused. "You want to experiment. Sounds good. I guess what you mean is you figure you got the right to make mistakes, right?"

"Yeah, guess so," his son nodded.

"I think we talked about that already and I don't wanna' beat a dead horse son, but I agree you got the right to experiment, make mistakes or whatever you wanna' call it, but you don't got the right to abuse yourself."

"Whaddya' mean, abuse yourself?"

Francis looked a trifle perplexed. "I'm not sure I can explain what I mean," he said honestly.

"Well," Kathleen suggested, "if he abuses himself, he's abusing our love for him, isn't he?"

"Yeah, yeah, that's what I was trying to get at," Francis said with expression.

"See John, if we love you, your mother and me, and you experiment, as you call it, with trouble, then you're abusing what we got in you, our love, our, our faith."

"Well, I don't see that at all. 'Cause I'm a separate person. I got my own life to lead, I got a right to do, to live my own life."

"Well, that's true too," said his father agreeably, "but what's also true, like it or not, is that when you got a family your life isn't your own life completely."

I'd been sitting quietly for a while now very much taken with Francis's exchange with his son. No doubt about it, Francis had changed. He continued to be a generally silent man, I supposed, but where several months ago he projected the image of a hapless, helpless, hopeless man who was silent because he had nothing to offer, now his silence enhanced a man who exuded a quiet confidence. Moreover, I had come to learn at each session and especially at this one, that Francis was a man who used his silent moments to enjoy a very good mind.

"You mean my life's not my own?" asked John incredulously.

"No, not completely, just like mine is not, and your mother's isn't. We all belong a little bit to each other."

"Well, how can we have rights, then, if we belong to each other?"

"We all of us got all the rights in the world," said Francis thoughtfully, "just so long as we don't abuse the love we got for each other and just so long as we don't intrude, that's a nice word, intrude on each other's privacy."

"No offense, Dad, but it sounds like a put-down, well not a put-down, but it sounds, uh, well, stifling."

"How do you figure that?" asked Francis.

"Well, how do I get to know what *I* want, me, if I always gotta' worry about the family?"

"You got me all wrong. It's not all one way. I didn't mean like you just give and worry about the family. I didn't mean that your mother and Alice and me too, that each of us just lives to give to the family. I believe we all got our own lives too."

"Do you mean, Francis, that each person has his own identity?" I asked.

"Exactly, that's what I mean. We each of us got our own identity. We're all different and we all of us got a responsibility to make each other better. There, that's what I mean. And when any one of us screws up we all got a responsibility to help out because all of us are hurt a little bit."

"How do you figure we're all hurt if one of us screws up?" asked John.

" 'Cause we all got a commitment to each other," said Francis simply.

John smiled wryly. "There you go with the commitment bit. I'm startin' to understand better some of the things you been sayin'. It all comes down to this commitment thing."

His father grinned a little and replied,"I been thinkin' a lot about this. A lot. Yeah, it all comes down to this commitment business. I guess that's so. I started out my thinkin' about me and the family there at my commitment and that's right where I ended up, with this idea of commitment. I realize now and maybe it's too late that my responsibilty to you and Alice is to help you understand by my example what a total commitment is. I made it, I think, when I married your mother. But the problem was, nobody knew, not even your mother. Nobody knew it except me. My problem, and it became a problem for all of us, look at your trouble, at *our* trouble, my problem was I never let anybody know. I never said anything to nobody. See, John I screwed up. I did. And a lot of people suffered. You and Ma and Alice and me. For all of that I am heartily sorry."

The three other Whitings sat there quite apparently magnetized by the sincerity and the contrition of Francis's statement. The emotional climate and their expressions told me that he was expressing their contrition too. I couldn't help thinking that now it remained for all of them to translate the talk, the contrition, the sincerity and the commitment into the reality of their lifestyle. At this point there was nothing which I could add. Certainly there was nothing to clarify, explain, or amend. We ended.

DISCUSSION QUESTIONS

1. What are the most salient changes which have occurred in each of the Whitings? Why have these changes occurred?

2. Which factor among the following was the most important in effecting changes among the Whitings?

1) therapy, 2) changes in home life, 3) the personalities of each, 4) the familial motivation for change.

Explain and defend your choice(s).

3. Can you rank-order the Whitings in their capacity to love? Explain your number one choice.

4. Whom do you see as the dominant figure in the family today? Explain your answer.

5. Do you think it's true that the price one pays for family support and love is the pressure and guilt which one feels when he wants to act out? Explain your answer.

NOTES AND ANALYSIS

In this last session we saw that time and therapy have wrought some positive changes among the Whitings. Francis is one who has changed, at least within the family. Formerly, he projected the image of a quiet, self-effacing man with an apparent penchant for dependency. This image seems gone. Francis now presents the picture of a secure, supportive, if still quiet man. More importantly, where formerly his children viewed him as a "nothing" type, he is now held in positive respect. Both John and Alice relate to him this way, if not deferentially. His statements, sometimes quasi-profound, suggest that he may well become the family spokesman, if not its soft-spoken patriarch.

Kathleen, especially in relation to Francis, is much changed. Her hypercriticism, demeaning comments and crass interruptions no longer seem to be part of her repertoire, at least toward her husband. They are not in evidence with her children either. This is not to say that Kathleen has undergone a metamorphosis in personality. She probably will ever be an assertive, if not an aggressive woman. With her family at least, she seems to have the negative aspects of her aggressiveness under control.

John's negative, surly stance in relation to the other three seems to have dissipated considerably. Undoubtedly, this is a response to the improved parental relations and especially to the improved paternal status in the eyes of all three. Put simply, John now has a man to look up to, and both he and the man seem to be the better for it.

Alice too, seems to be more content with the improved parental dyad. Endowed with much of her mother's verve she continues to function as the family's, 'Miss merry sunshine', dropping rays (or kisses) here and there.

Several points especially need to be made about this session. One is that the family apparently will continue to cater to Kathleen, but within limits. And the limits, it should be noted are mutually understood. Kathleen, it was concluded, has a right to privacy, to her reading, but not to the extent that she does not fulfill her admitted responsibility of having the supper ready.

A second point to be made, and one which I myself didn't realize until after the session, was that Francis never talked about any personal rights of his own. Now, he was very much involved in the session. That was obvious. Unlike Kathleen however, his only concerns seemed not so much personal as intra-familial. He is a genuinely unselfish guy.

This focus upon the familial and lack of concern for the personal is very consistent with his view, "that when you got a family your life isn't your own life completely." What this means, he indicates later, is that "—we all of us got a responsibility to make each other better." What more can any therapist ask for a family goal?

Francis left little doubt in any of our minds that he would continue to live up to his familial commitments. The difference, he made clear to us, was that now he would communicate congruently, his personal feelings would gibe with both his words and his behavior.

Chapter 14
Outcomes and Final Notes

After Therapy: Francis (via a tape)

"Things are better now, much better. They're much better with me and my wife. We can make it now, if you know what I mean. I'm more relaxed about everything. (chuckle) 'Course that was part of the problem. I always *looked* too relaxed, too quiet. I *wasn't* relaxed though. I was all tied up in knots. I never could seem to get my tongue untied to talk even when I had to. I guess it was my head that was mostly in a big knot, all tangled up.

"It's not like that anymore. I look more relaxed because I am more relaxed. I talk much easier especially at home and I gotta' admit that I'm a pretty good wit. Outside the house I'm still quiet, mostly 'cause I think I'm basically a shy guy. I always will be. I don't care about that. My wife and I talked about it a couple of times. She doesn't either. That's the big thing, the big difference. She and I talk and a lot.

"The biggest change is in her. She seems to care about the kids, and me and the house. She almost never nags me about anything. She's keeping a neat house, mostly I think 'cause she knows I prefer it that way. Her cooking is better or at least it's very steady, and she's doing it rather than my daughter.

"Things are better much better. We even had Tom and Frank over for dinner last Sunday. Things are good."

About Me:

"What I learned about me is that I'm more able than I thought I was. What I learned is that if I have to I can handle things, not just my work 'cause I could always do that. I mean like in the area of people, the people that matter the most, my family.

"I learned that I can be a good father to my son. He taught me that I'm worth his respect. I think my daughter Alice helped out even more there than he did. It's important for a father to feel that he's a good father. I never had that feeling until after therapy.

"I learned that I can show and tell my feelings to my kids and to my wife. I still can't outside too much, but I don't usually feel like I have to there anyway.

"I've always loved my wife. I really like her now mostly 'cause she makes me feel so good.

"I've learned that I enjoy being a stronger personality. I was weak. I feel strong now. What I've learned is that life is better when you're strong."

After Therapy: Alice

"Since we finished our family counseling things are better, in fact they are much better. Mostly because everybody's talking to everybody. Daddy's still quiet, but it's a different kind of quiet. He'll always be a quiet man. The original quiet man, that's Daddy. But it's different now. When he talks he usually says something funny, Daddy's a riot. I never knew that before the counseling. Supper is so much fun. Last night I thought I'd split my sides laughing. Daddy recited a poem he learned as a kid.

Jack and Jill went up the hill
Each with a dollar and a quarter
Jill came down with two and a half
Did they go up for water?

Even Mom laughed. And John, the original angry young man smiled.

"We seem to like each other. Maybe we did before the counseling. The difference is that we show it. Daddy bought Mom some purple plums. She's wild about them! He bought them on his way home from work. He never did things like that before. Daddy's a part of the family, a basic and important part. It didn't seem like he was even in it before.

"Mom is happy now, at least most of the time. Sometimes she's even radiant. She still yells though and mostly at me or John. I notice she almost never yells at Daddy. Better me and John. And this is going to sound a little crazy I know, but what I notice most about Mom is that she *looks* beautiful. She's always been pretty but now she looks *beautiful*.

"John talks to me now. Sometimes he's even nice to me. And believe me, that's a real switch.

"What I learned about me.

"I learned that even though I'm very young I can be helpful to others if I'm honest with them. Being honest means to be yourself. Mostly it means letting other people see how you feel without being a regular pain about it all. I learned that it's important to learn what to keep in and what to say.

"I also learned that I've got a lot to learn. I don't feel bad or scared about that. I'll learn. After all Rome wasn't built in a day. I'm only 12½."

After Therapy: Kathleen

"The major difference between before and after is that I feel loved and I can love-out. My husband loves me. I guess it's true that he always did, but now he shows it to me. *What a difference! !* The difference between feeling loved and not feeling loved is the difference between living and vegetating. I was vegetating before. I'm living now.

"I like getting up in the morning. I enjoy making different kinds of breakfasts, from strawberry pancakes, to grilled sausages, to scrambled eggs and toast. I even tried jellied pigs feet two weeks ago. I enjoy creating and giving to my family.(Although I think my husband might be getting up a little more fearfully each morning!) Mostly I get an awful lot of satisfaction and pleasure when I give. (I had my two older boys for dinner last Sunday.)

"I love talking. I always did. Now I like to think all day when I'm working. I love being alone for that reason and I love working all day in the house. Then when the kids and my husband come home I tell them what I've been thinking. They seem so interested. I get such a boot out of that. They are so interested! It makes me feel so great that they are. They tell me in so many ways.

"I recognize that this isn't going to last—staying home, working and thinking. I'm starting even now to feel I want a job outside. But I'm not worried about it. I'll get something, I've thought about clerking in a dress shop. I'd be good at that! I have a flair for clothes and I like them.

"We were all so distant. We're close now. I don't know what else to say. Yes, we're all so very much closer than we were before therapy. About Me:

I'm optimistic where I used to be very pessimistic. I used to be bored, angry, yelling all the time and I hated myself. I have none of those feelings anymore. My family respects me. I know that. I don't have to yell to be noticed anymore. I'm not completely satisfied with myself, but I do like me. My husband and my children could have done much worse!

"I'm going to continue to change, I'm sure. Especially after I go out to work which I plan to do. I'm excited about that—and I'm a little scared."

After Therapy: John

"Generally things are much better. I think the biggest change is in Ma. Very rare when she yells. She talks fast still, but it's a *happy* fast not an angry fast. She looks better too. She's always been good looking but she's even prettier now. Sometimes I even hear her singing around the house. It's nice.

"I used to think my father was like a ghost in the house. Well, it's like he came back to life. Still quiet, but his quiet is a different kind, like Ma's talking is a happy fast, his quiet is a happy, *comfortable* quiet. At least it doesn't make me up-tight. I sit in the same room with him now a lot in fact. We sit there and he smokes his pipe. We talk a little. I talk more. He listens, nods his head a lot. Hard to explain. It all makes *me feel* comfortable, 'cause I know he's comfortable. I like my father now, a lot.

"Tom and Frank were over last Sunday. I find it real hard talking to them. I wish they'd been with us in therapy.

"I guess that's the biggest change in the family. We all seem to like each other a lot. And we show it. Alice always seemed to be able to show it, but nobody else. Last night my father went by me where I was sitting and mussed up my hair. First time that ever happened. Made me feel good.

About Me:

"Biggest change in me that I notice is that I'm not so mad anymore. I used to be mad, I mean like all the time. I didn't like anybody except my girlfriend Dee. She was the only one I wanted to be with. I didn't have my friends.

"I go out with guys sometimes now. I see Dee. I've got to know my father, pretty good I think. I even like to talk to Alice. To Alice! That's a real change.

"This morning when I was on my way out to school I stopped and kissed my mother. She looked surprised. I don't blame her. I'd never done that before. Then she grabbed me and hugged me and then she said, "Oh John, I'm so glad." I knew what she meant. I'm glad too.

"I go to school now without a "chip on my shoulder" as Dad would say. School's better. It's school and I'm not exactly an outstanding student, but I'll graduate."

TWO MONTHS LATER FINAL NOTES

We never had a follow-up session. Francis telephoned me several days before the scheduled date to cancel for his family. He and Kathleen were going away for a two-week vacation. His succinct explanation was, "First vacation we've had alone since we got married."

Cancellation of the follow-up session is not unique. In fact, it is common both for those families which have profited from the therapy and for those families which have not.

All the reports about John are very encouraging. He completed his probation without undue incident. He is presently in his last year of high school and according to Mr. Dalton, "obtaining very respectable grades." Of even more significance, he is working part-time with his father. "The boy's good with wood," was the laconic comment from Francis.

If John's progress is any barometer for forecasting the Whiting domestic climate, and I believe it is, then the prognosis for the Whitings is good. According to Kathleen, who has phoned me periodically to chat, Francis continues to be relatively quiet, unemotional, and uninvolved outside the family circle. Within the family, however, Francis has modified his behavior markedly. For one thing, he confronts Kathleen when he feels that she behaves inappropriately. In her last call she had implied that Francis' bout with impotence had dissipated. I had suspected this. His comments and behavior at our last session were those of a competent man, a man with strong feelings of adequacy. His ability to be sexually attentive in turn has rewarded Kathleen's sexual needs, which quite properly she interprets as appropriately feminine. The sum effect upon Kathleen is to make her feel more adequate as a person. The maternal role has apparently become very tolerable as her children are grown. Her role as a wife, always less threatening, may well have become rewarding.

I'm convinced that one reason for the relatively speedy and continuing success of the Whitings has been the family conscience. It is strong in all of them. What this means, of course, is that they are all very much identified not only with the social and moral taboos, but with each other too. It is conscience which arouses feelings of guilt. And it is precisely conscience and the fear of the guilt which it precipitates which has inhibited John from more violent acting out. As I think about it, it is probably conscience which has kept Kathleen from becoming involved in an extra-marital affair and thereby becoming further, perhaps permanently alienated from her family. Doubtless it is conscience, too, which forms the foundation for the commitment which Francis is so fond of explaining. I learned a long time ago that people without a conscience are not capable of loving. The Whitings, I have learned, are very loving people.

Index

The Mapmakers' Quest

The Mapmakers' Quest

Depicting New Worlds in Renaissance Europe

DAVID BUISSERET

OXFORD
UNIVERSITY PRESS

OXFORD
UNIVERSITY PRESS

Great Clarendon Street, Oxford OX2 6DP

Oxford University Press is a department of the University of Oxford.
It furthers the University's objective of excellence in research, scholarship,
and education by publishing worldwide in

Oxford New York

Auckland Bangkok Buenos Aires Cape Town Chennai
Dar es Salaam Delhi Hong Kong Istanbul Karachi Kolkata
Kuala Lumpur Madrid Melbourne Mexico City Mumbai Nairobi
São Paulo Shanghai Singapore Taipei Tokyo Toronto

Oxford is a registered trade mark of Oxford University Press
in the UK and in certain other countries

British Library Cataloguing in Publication Data

Data available

Library of Congress Cataloging in Publication Data

Data available

ISBN 0-19-210053-X

10 9 8 7 6 5 4 3 2 1

Printed in Great Britain by T. J. International Ltd,
Padstow, Cornwall

Dedicated to my friends and former colleagues at The Newberry Library, Chicago, where I have worked with much delight since 1965.

ACKNOWLEDGEMENTS

This whole business began in the spring of 1980, when I had walked home for lunch from my office in the History Department at the University of the West Indies, with its wonderful views of Jamaica's Blue Mountains. Astonishingly enough—for this was in the days before the repairs from the hurricane of 1988 gave the island good communications—my wife had received a telephone message from Chicago, asking if I were interested in applying for a position at the Newberry Library there. I was in fact quite content to be working in French and West Indian history at the University of the West Indies. But the island was entering a period of intensified tumult, and my children were growing up, so we decided to leave.

My first Newberry job as Director of the Hermon Dunlap Smith Center for the History of Cartography was operating the projector for one of the Center's periodic Nebenzahl Lectures, on 'Art and cartography'. This was an appropriate task, for I certainly knew little about the history of cartography. Indeed, the whole field was about to be taken in hand by Brian Harley, then of the University of Exeter, and David Woodward, my predecessor at the Smith

Center, who had migrated to the University of Wisconsin at Madison. There they eventually began publishing a multi-volume *History of cartography*, which has become indispensable for studies in this field.

Meanwhile I had begun reading my way into the subject, using the rich collections of the Newberry Library, and the continuing advice of Robert Karrow, Director of Special Collections there. For more general questions, I also learned to use the encyclopaedic range of John Aubrey, master of the Ayer Collection; later, James Akerman and Pat Morris also joined, to furnish still more cartographic expertise. Coming to the field as a historian of early modern Europe, and of its expansion into the wider world, I was interested from the start by an apparently simple problem: why was it that there were so few maps in Europe in 1400, and yet so many by 1650?

Much of my time at the Newberry (1980–95) was spent in trying out various ways to understand this problem, with the wholehearted support of Richard Brown, Director of Research and Education. I was able to continue these ventures when in 1995

I went to the University of Texas at Arlington, to take up the new Jenkins and Virginia Garrett chair in the history of cartography (and Southwestern studies) there. Both the Newberry and UTA are privileged places to study the history of cartography, for each has a critical mass of staff members interested in our rather obscure field, and each has specialized collections.

PLAN OF THE BOOK

Although this book attempts to tackle its theme by subject area, it also tries to move forward in time, beginning with the time when the cartographic ideas of classical European antiquity began to affect the thought of the dawning Renaissance, towards 1400. This first chapter was largely written using the resources of Northwestern University's Library in Evanston, as well as a six-month fellowship grant from the National Endowment for the Humanities, in 1996. I have also profited from the advice of Richard Talbert of the University of North Carolina, even though I fear that he will not agree with some of my conclusions.

Northwestern University has an extraordinary collection of art books in its Deering Library, which I used for the second chapter. This takes up the theme of the relationship, as I see it, between art and cartography in early fifteenth-century Europe. It is an area in which I am rather ignorant, but I have profited not only from the art seminar of the University of Chicago, but also from an invitation to write the introduction to the catalogue of an exhibition held in 2000 at the Musées Royaux des Beaux-Arts at Brussels. This exhibit, called *Le peintre et l'arpenteur*, offered an occasion on which I received many helpful corrections from colleagues in the field of art history.

When the time came to think of a theme for the Nebenzahl Lectures, it seemed appropriate to try to imagine how early modern European kings and their ministers had reacted to a dawning cartographic consciousness; this is the theme of Chapter 3. Peter Barber of the British Library contributed two lectures on map-use among the sixteenth-century English elite, and in their published form these two lectures have been particularly widely quoted. Peter Barber has continued to help me to understand the riches of his library, and to counsel students sent to him for advice.

The fourth chapter concerns the cartographic activities of the various European powers, and I greatly profited in this area from conversations with the late Professor David Quinn, and with other colleagues of the Society for the History of Discoveries. In 2001 the European University Institute at Florence invited me to offer a lecture on this theme, and this was an excellent opportunity to gather in the reactions of the many young scholars who attended this lecture series.

The theme of the fifth chapter is military history, and here I had the good fortune to pay two visits to the Herzog August Bibliothek, in Wolfenbüttel (Saxony). This splendid collection includes much early modern military material. The Newberry Library is also strong in this field, and I have sometimes profited from the advice of a Newberry reader, Martha Pollak of the University of Illinois at Chicago. In Paris, Monique Pelletier was always ready with good advice concerning the massive holdings of the Bibliothèque nationale de France. It has also been salutary to have to explain the nature of 'the military revolution' to my students in Texas, many of whom are well acquainted with much more recent developments.

Finally, Chapter 6 attempts to explain the cartographic significance of early modern economic developments. Here I was able to organize two relevant Nebenzahl Lectures, on 'The estate map in the Old and New Worlds' and on 'Envisioning the city'. It will be seen that I have greatly profited from the contributions of the lecturers, including particularly Professor P. D. A. Harvey, Sarah Bendall, Naomi Miller, and Richard Kagan. In a project that has now lasted over twenty years, I am sure to have received help and advice that I have not cited. But I ask pardon for this, and indeed for the way in which some old friends may find that I have misunderstood or contorted their ideas.

DAVID BUISSERET

Arlington, Texas / Chicago, Illinois
May 2002

PREFACE

During the past two or three decades, there has been a sharp increase in the number of scholars interested in the history of cartography, with numbers in the *International Directory* (published periodically by Map Collector Publications Ltd of Tring) rising from fewer than 400 in 1992 to about 650 in 1998. There has been a corresponding development in our understanding of the historical significance of maps. Many new lines of argument have been put forward, and three of these are of particular importance for the present work. Firstly, the definition of maps has been made both more extensive and more precise. Secondly, there has been a prolonged attempt to put maps into their social and economic framework; and thirdly, scholars have succeeded in showing that the mapping impulse seems to be universal among human societies. Each of these new patterns of understanding has a contribution to make to the present work, which essentially seeks to explain why there were so few maps in Europe in 1400, and so many by 1650, and to track down some of the consequences of this major intellectual shift. This is not a theme that has hitherto attracted any single work, though Professor P. D. A. Harvey began asking some of the relevant questions in his *The history of topographical maps*, published in London in 1980.

DEFINITIONS OF A MAP

In redefining what a map is, scholars have largely departed from the early twentieth-century *Encyclopaedia Britannica* definition of it as 'a graphic representation of part of the earth's surface'. We have come to realize that a map need neither be graphic, nor represent the earth's surface. For instance, the stick charts of the Pacific islanders, though generally accepted as maps, are not graphic, any more than city models are. Moreover, we have made maps of the surface of the moon and of other heavenly bodies, as well as, for example, of terrestrial weather systems. What in fact makes a map a map seems to be its quality of representing a locality; perhaps indeed we should call it a 'locational image', or even a 'locational surrogate'. The primary function of such an image is to convey locational information, thus distinguishing it, for instance, from some landscape painting which, while conveying such information incidentally, primarily seeks aesthetic effect. In cognitive terms, the map has to rely upon the brain's perception of space rather than of sequence. Thus this list (used in teaching students in the United States):

AL

CA

FL

NY

WA

is plainly not a map, though this arrangement :

WA   NY

CA   AL

FL

begins to possess a cartographic element, because it appeals to a kind of locational imagery intended to allow us to visualize the spatial relationship between the states of the United States of America. It may be that in its central function of representing, the map is necessarily an analogue rather than a digital device.

This revision in the definition of maps has an important bearing on our understanding of how cartography developed in late medieval Europe. Once we begin looking for signs of map consciousness not merely in the production of what have long been recognized as maps, but also in the emergence of other forms of locational imagery, then we can much more convincingly trace back the roots of what otherwise would seem an inexplicable efflorescence of cartography. When medieval people carved orbs, or modelled palaces, or drew elaborate plans of abbatial compounds, they were moving towards a type of locational imagery that only later found full expression. This precocious mapping impulse needs to be tracked through into early modern Europe, when bird's-eye views, architectural drawings, fortification models, and even military diagrams exemplify the emergent need to understand and control the world by producing locational images of it.

THE STUDY OF MAPS IN SOCIETY

If the redefined map is a first key to understanding the cartographic history of early modern Europe, a second is the powerful tendency among scholars to reinsert maps into the societies and economies which generated them, often following the ideas of Brian Harley, much of whose work has recently been edited by Paul Laxton in *The new nature of maps: essays in the history of cartography*, published by The Johns Hopkins University Press in 2001. It was possible, sixty years ago, for an excellent introductory work such as R. V. Tooley's *Maps and mapmakers*, which ran through many editions, to study the map merely as artefact, and mostly a printed European artefact. We have come to believe, though, that it is indispensable to relate cartographic evidence to the wider human experience, reinserting the artefact into history at large. In this respect, historians of cartography are taking up an approach that has long been common among art historians, one of whose major concerns has been to reintegrate the objects of their study into the societies that produced them.

In terms of our present theme, the need to relate maps to their social origins leads to a radically fresh approach. It is no longer sufficient to study maps in terms of their 'national schools', say, or of their material types; now we have to consider the nature of the economic, social, and cultural developments that brought fresh cartographic forms to life. Indeed, it is hardly an exaggeration to say that we now need to ask: 'to what new types of map will this new cultural development give rise?' In Marxist terms, we have to stand old Hegel on his head. So the development of a new interest in classical antiquity gave rise to a whole new perception of the role played by maps in the ancient—and consequently soon in the modern—world (Chapter 1). The theological developments of the thirteenth century, with their emphasis on the primacy and excellence of the faculty of vision, gave birth to a whole new way of 'seeing' and mapping the world (Chapter 2). Similarly, a fresh

understanding of the possibilities of arithmetic led to its application to the problems of perspective, and thence to developments in the way of portraying not only figures but also landscapes.

Eventually, around 1500, a precocious map consciousness came to pervade the elites of many parts of western Europe, as we have tried to demonstrate in Chapter 3, and after that time each new societal development had its cartographic counterpart. Thus there are cartographies of the Reformation and Counter Reformation (Conclusion), of the Military Revolution (Chapter 5), of the expansion of Europe into the wider world (Chapter 4), and so forth. In this book, we attempt to analyse these cartographies not so much in terms of the map-objects produced as in terms of the societal changes that gave birth to them. By thus inverting the normal order of proceeding—turning Hegel on his head—we hope to show how cartography has both influenced and exemplified the course of modern European history in many hitherto unsuspected ways.

WORLD AND EUROPEAN MAPPING

If the reinsertion of maps into the wider social context, which is our second major concern, enables us better to understand the significance of cartography in early modern Europe, our third major theme, a revised understanding of the incidence of maps in the world, enables us to put this European development into the context of world history. Here we come to understand that in 1400 Europe was remarkably backward, in cartographic terms, by the side of such leaders as China and Japan: this emerges clearly from volume 2, book 2, of the pathbreaking *History of cartography* edited by Brian Harley and David Woodward. Yet by 1700 Europe had drawn ahead of the rest of the world in virtually every kind of mapping. Considering the importance of cartography to almost every aspect of life in western Europe by that time, we are led to ask if it did not play an important and so far rather neglected role in the rise of the West, that enigmatic process by which a small area of islands and archipelagos has imposed its cultural patterns, and until recently its political power, on the rest of the world. Seen in this light, the 'cartographic revolution', which had so powerful an effect upon European societies, may be said to have had an influence that became worldwide.

CONTENTS

LIST OF PLATES

LIST OF FIGURES

The author would like to thank all those who gave permission to reproduce the pictures.

Introduction: Mapping during the Middle Ages

ABOUT 1980, it would have seemed easy to describe the state of mapping in medieval Europe. Apart from the portolan charts of the Mediterranean Sea, which appeared anachronistic in the accuracy of their coastal outlines (Fig. 4), it seemed to most scholars that there were basically only rather crude and inaccurate religiously inspired world maps, with here and there startlingly innovative cartographic ventures like those of the English monk Matthew Paris (Fig. 2). This static and traditional world of maps, the story continued, endured more or less unchanging until the sharp impact of the classical atlas of Claudius Ptolemy, rediscovered in the early fifteenth century. By offering over twenty maps of the ancient known world, it suddenly brought Europeans into contact with the geographical learning of the ancient worlds of Greece and Rome (Figs 7, 8).

MAPPÆMUNDI, OR WORLD MAPS

This simple story has been completely overturned by the work since the 1980s, which has revealed—and is revealing—a medieval scene that was hugely more varied in every respect. This new assessment was probably initiated by the publication in 1987 of the first volume of a new *History of cartography*, edited by J. B. Harley and David Woodward.[1] This volume put on to an entirely new footing the study of the *mappæmundi*, or main group of medieval world maps (Fig. 1). A new classification of *mappæmundi* was formulated, as a result of an exceptionally full recension of them; more importantly, it was forcefully suggested that these maps needed to be seen in their social context, and not judged by the preoccupations of our own day. These images were generally composed by clerics, concerned to offer compendia of what was known about the outline of the Christian world; they were not designed for navigation, for raising taxes, or for accurately dropping bombs. It is therefore foolish to complain that they were not suitable for these purposes.

This new approach to *mappæmundi* has been most fruitfully developed by authors like Peter Barber, Evelyn Edson, Patrick Gautier Dalché, and Scott Westrem. In his short work on *Medieval world maps*, essentially an introduction to the exhibition of the Hereford Map (a wonderful example of the type, preserved at Hereford Cathedral in England) held in 1999, Barber begins from the idea that *mappæmundi* have to be understood on their own terms, and in those of the society that produced them. Thus the Hereford Map, which seems to have hung for many years in the cathedral there, was designed to give the parishioners an idea of the geographical layout of Christendom and its neighbours, complete with its main scripturally described features. Centred on Jerusalem, the map describes a huge variety of places in Asia, Africa, and Europe, relating them to biblical writings so as to compose a sort of geographic encyclopædia. Seen in this perspective,

Fig. 1. World map from the *Etymologiæ* of Isidore of Seville, Augsburg, 1472. *Mappæmundi* vary greatly in their complexity, and this is an example of the simplest kind. Deriving originally from remote antiquity, it shows the world in shorthand. On this disc (or sphere) are seen the three continents, divided by the 'great sea or Mediterranean', and surrounded by the 'Ocean Sea'. There is little doubt that most medieval people interested in geography carried this diagram in their heads, though it could often be greatly elaborated.

the Hereford Map seems a remarkably successful example of locational imagery.

Barber also points out that 'from the very first, medieval maps charted time as well as space' in their numerous historical images,[2] and suggests that medieval scholars salvaged much more than has been thought from the ancient world, the Hereford Map being a good example of this. Combined with the idea that much information on *mappæmundi* derived from the ancient world is the belief that their origin was often less purely religious than has been thought. For instance, Marcia Kupfer has attacked the idea that these great maps were necessarily associated with the high altar in medieval churches, arguing instead that we should consider more closely the fact that large *mappæmundi* were sometimes found in secular courts, where they were presumably of interest to the kings and their retainers.[3] This is an idea also developed by Daniel Birkholz, particularly in association with the great map that once decorated Westminster Hall in the time of Henry II.[4]

Fig. 2. Matthew Paris, Map of England, Wales, and Scotland, *c*.1250. This monk of Saint Albans seems to have had a unique faculty for drawing regional maps like this one, which shows a large number of recognizable place-names along the spine of England, and then some indication of Scottish cartography, beyond Hadrian's Wall.

OTHER MAP-TYPES: REGIONAL MAPS, BROAD-SIDES, AND JUDICIAL MAPS

Scholars like Professor Harvey have also been concerned to emphasize the wealth of other map-types that existed during the Middle Ages.[5] England seems to be exceptional in having the regional maps of Matthew Paris (*c.*1250, Fig. 2), as well as the map of Britain known (after one of its owners) as the Gough Map (*c.*1360). It has always puzzled historians that Matthew Paris, a monk of Saint Albans, should have been able to produce such detailed maps of England, Scotland, and Wales, and recent writers like Birkholz have tried to explain the appearance of his maps as something more than a stroke of individual genius, wondering instead if his work formed part of a now-lost cartographic tradition.[6] There has been more general agreement about the significance of the Gough Map, which with its network of roads and well-placed towns clearly seems to have emerged from some early 'bureaucratic' service at Westminster. This is all the more believ-

Fig. 3. Anon., Woodcut of Saint Augustine, *c.*1450. This 'popular' broadside contains a map as one of its main features, reminding us that much work needs to be done in tracking down cartographic images embedded in other medieval documents and objects.

able, since England was unusual in being a country where such a degree of centralization existed at that time.

During the fifteenth century, the printed pamphlets which began to circulate in western Europe often contained images of various parts of the world, to judge by the Italian woodcuts studied by Gerald Danzer (Fig. 3).[7] These woodcuts suggest that we should look further afield than has been customary for evidence of locational imagery during the Middle Ages, taking in what could be termed some of the earliest popular art. We should also look more closely at some material objects, like the world-images on the orbs so often carried by princes. In many ways, England seems to have been precocious in the production of early maps, but Professor Harvey has also shown that the island lagged behind parts of the Continent in producing maps to illustrate legal cases.[8] He found a text of 1395 from the *parlement* of Paris suggesting that a plan and image (*'figure et portrait'*) should be used to make a case clearer, thus confirming the idea of Père François de Dainville[9] that maps were by no means unknown in French courts of law in the fifteenth century; they may also have been found in Spain.

PORTOLAN CHARTS

Professor Harvey also offers us an interesting commentary on the origin of portolan charts, maps of the Mediterranean Sea, which were, he shows, in use by 1270. For in that year Louis XI, king of France, sailing across the Mediterranean to a crusade in Tunis, was apparently shown such a chart so that he could assess his vessel's progress.[10] Portolan charts have survived from around 1300, and continued to be produced right up until the seventeenth century. Although they show the Mediterranean with considerable accuracy from the start, their purpose has never been clear (Fig. 4). Some were drawn for the libraries of princes and merchants, but the ones taken on ship may have been used simply as harbour-references, since they contain large numbers of port-names that could remind a mariner of the lie of the coast. It seems most unlikely, at all events, that they were used to plot a course, in the way that charts would eventually come to be used.

LARGE-SCALE PLANS OF CITIES AND BUILDINGS

We find mention here and there in the literature of the existence of city plans: Charlemagne, for instance, is recorded as having had maps of Constantinople and of Rome.[11] Perhaps these had survived from the ancient world, and were like those which the Romans used, one of the most famous ones having been incised at Rome on stones set upright in a wall, measuring 13 by 18 metres.[12] The style of this map closely resembles that of one of the most remarkable architectural plans to survive from the Middle Ages

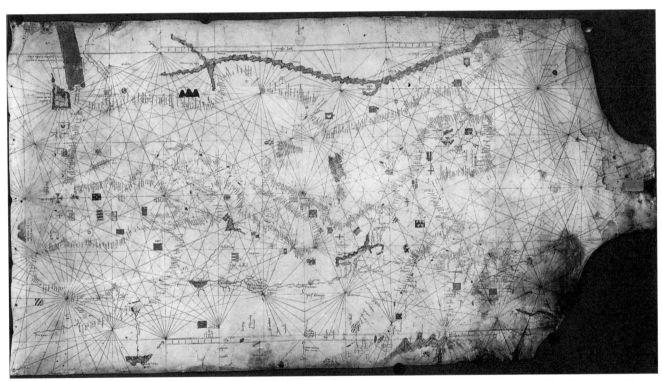

Fig. 4. Portolan chart of the Mediterranean Sea, attributed to Angelino Dulcert, *c.*1350. This chart is typical of a map-type that varied little from 1300 to the seventeenth century. The coasts of the Mediterranean Sea are delineated with remarkable accuracy, and the numerous port-names are inserted at right angles to the coast. The map is enmeshed in a system of rhumb-lines, and individual rulers' realms are marked with flags, though there is otherwise little internal detail.

(Fig. 5). This shows the work to be done at the Abbey of Saint Gall, in Switzerland, and is drawn using the style and conventions of the Roman surveyors. Such plans were probably composed as a matter of course when great buildings were to be undertaken, though sometimes models might have been used instead. Almost all of these plans —and models—seem to have perished, though we do have some from the *Sketchbook* of Villard de Honnecourt, active between 1225 and 1250.[13] This *Sketchbook* also contains many well-observed images of animals and humans, making one think of the rather similar sketches made by Matthew Paris. Perhaps the capacity of close observation and record was much less rare than we have imagined.

CONCLUSION

One way and another, then, there were in the Middle Ages many locational images, ranging in scale from the maps of the world down to the plans of abbeys. Moreover, it now seems likely that

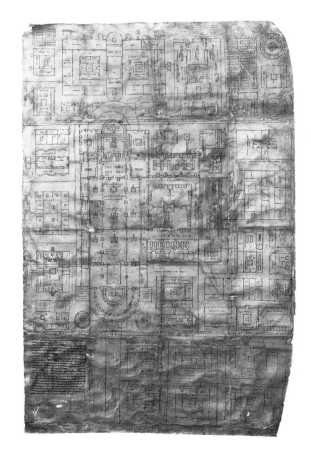

Fig. 5. Anon., Plan of the Abbey of Saint Gall, Switzerland, *c.*820. This wonderfully detailed image of work to be carried out at the monastery of Saint Gall reminds us of stylistically similar plans incised into upright stones in classical Rome. It suggests what other evidence also implies, that the cartographic traditions of antiquity remained alive in various parts of western Europe.

such images began to become more numerous earlier than we have previously thought. Whereas the date of such an increase used to be taken as about 1400, recent work by Catherine Delano-Smith and Roger Kain suggests that in England, at least, it began as early as 1200.[14] However, medieval maps emerged from medieval pre-occupations, and it will be well to end this introduction by setting out the types of map completely lacking before 1400.

To start with, there were apparently no world maps based upon an understanding of mathematical coordinates.[15] The *mappæmundi* were entirely innocent of this idea, and so, perhaps curiously to our eyes, were the portolan charts, whose coastal accuracy seems to belie their empirical composition. Larger-scale maps of regions were also almost totally lacking, probably because people did not have the habit of thinking regionally. In the Middle Ages, allegiances did not follow geographical boundaries, but were composed of myriad chances of marriage, war, and loyalty. War itself was as yet waged on a relatively small scale: the Black Prince needed no map in order to go on the rampage in France during the fifteenth century, for he had only a few thousand men, no supply-lines to guard, and no artillery to be conducted through difficult country.

For a long time, too, cities were content with the images that they seem to have inherited from the ancient world. It took time even for the burghers of rich and sophisticated cities to feel the need for images of their towns, and compilations like those of Hartmann Schedel in the late fifteenth century, as we shall see, often still offered the same image for a number of different cities.[16] If cities remained unmapped, so did the countryside. The Cistercians, great farmers, yet felt no need to delineate their cereal fields so as to exploit them as efficiently as possible; indeed, the very idea of 'exploiting' them for an urban market lay far in the future. The Roman surveyors had developed the idea of centuriation, dividing the flat lands around the Mediterranean Sea into those huge rectangular fields that still show up so well from the air. But the very idea of centuriation seems to have been lost, and in any case this precise and geometrical system was inappropriate for the rolling, broken countryside of much of western Europe.

Venturing outside Europe, travellers brought back their information in textual form. Even when they made long voyages, like the Vikings, they felt no need to record these travels in locational imagery. They often cast the record in the poetic form of sagas, for this was a time when the oral tradition remained supreme. So, consequently, was the power of memory. Mary Carruthers has reminded us of the power of memory in all aspects of medieval life,[17] and this faculty usually generated texts, or at most diagrams. The advent of very extensive mapping of overseas territories, to which we shall turn in Chapter 4, meant not only that the mind could now dwell in remote places that could be visited through maps, plans, and views, but also that the body could also return there, thanks to maps and charts which eventually made the whole world the Europeans' oyster.

I

The influence of ancient Greece and Rome

THE writers, artists, and statesmen of classical antiquity exercised a powerful influence upon the imagination of people in fifteenth- and sixteenth-century Europe. In each field, one writer came to be thought of as the master: Virgil for poetry, Quintilian for teaching, Aristotle for physics, and so forth. In mapmaking, the acknowledged master was Claudius Ptolemy (AD 87–150), and sometimes historians of cartography have limited themselves to a consideration of his undoubtedly extensive influence upon the mapmakers of early modern Europe. But this would be a mistake, for the classical world was influential in at least two other ways: in the texts mentioning cartography that it offered to perceptive readers, and in the cartographic ventures generated by the desire to map and describe the monuments of classical antiquity. Let us first consider the texts.

CLASSICAL TEXTS INVOLVING MAPMAKING

Herodotus, writing in the fifth century BC, has a wonderful cartographic story. Aristagoras, prince of Miletus, was anxious to bring the Spartans into war with the Persians. So he came to Sparta in order to interview the Spartan leader Cleomenes, 'having in his hand a bronze tablet with the whole map of the world engraved upon it, and all the sea, and all the rivers'.[1] Armed with this map, he engaged Cleomenes in conversation, describing the territories of the various Greek powers. And he said, 'here are the Lydians, right next to the Ionians, living in a fertile land, and they have much silver among them'. As he spoke, he pointed to these places on the map of the world that he carried around, engraved on his tablet. Aristagoras was plainly using his map, which perhaps had been compiled by the noted Anaximander of Miletus,[2] to make geographical points; by any definition, this was a cartographic exercise. Alas for the hopes of Aristagoras: Cleomenes did not at once answer, and in their next conversation, Aristagoras was imprudent enough to mention that the proposed campaign would take the Spartans three months' journey from the sea, whereupon he was at once sent packing. However, this first textual account of map use has a fully convincing context, which must have impressed the many fifteenth-century readers of *The history*.[3]

This sort of context is often missing from subsequent examples suggested by historians of cartography, partly because of the great possibilities of ambiguity in translation. For instance, in one of the later volumes of his great *History of Rome*, Livy describes how the conquest of Sardinia by Tiberius Sempronius Gracchus was celebrated: 'cuius rei ergo hanc tabulam domum Jovi dedit. Sardinia insulæ forma erat, atque in ea simulacra pugnarum picta.'[4] This passage was translated in 1814 by George Baker as: 'in commemoration of which event he presented this tablet, an offering to Jupiter: a map of the island of Sardinia was engraved on the tablet, and representations of the battles fought there were delineated on it.' However, the same passage was translated by Frank Moore in the Loeb Classical Library[5] as: 'in commemoration of this event he set up this tablet to Jupiter. It had the form of the island of Sardinia,

and on it representations of battles were painted.' Evidently, the earlier translation implies a much more developed kind of map than the later translation, which might suggest merely a tablet shaped in the distinctive form of Sardinia.

Historians dealing with the theme of maps in classical antiquity have relied on a wide variety of translations, generally interpreted in a sense favourable to the idea that cartography was widespread.[6] In this chapter, we shall try to avoid such over-optimistic examples, selecting only those passages which clearly show the reader that some object clearly definable as a map was in use. The aim is first to set out such passages in the ancient authors, and then to consider what use may have been made of them by authors of the fifteenth and sixteenth centuries, when the enthusiasm for classical examples was immense.

Somewhat younger than Herodotus was Aristophanes (445–388 BC), in whose play *The Clouds* there is a delightful passage, clearly bringing out the use of mapping as a satirical device.[7] Strepsiades is being shown a map by a student:

Student. Look, here's a chart of the whole world. Do you see? This city's Athens.
Strepsiades. Athens? I like that; I see no dicasts [jurymen] sitting. That's not Athens.
Student. In very truth, this is the Attic ground.

Strepsiades. And whereabouts are my townsmen of Cicynna?

Student. Why, thereabouts, and here, you see, Euboea; here, reaching out a long way by the shore.

Strepsiades. Yes, overreached by us and Pericles. But now, where's Sparta?

Student. Let me see. O, here.

Strepsiades. Heavens! How near us. Oh, please manage this, to shove her off from us, a long way further.

Student. We can't do that, by Zeus.

It is evident here that Aristophanes is inviting us to witness a thoroughly cartographic occasion, though this occasion seems to be unique in the playwright's repertoire. From a little later on we have an interesting disposition in the will of Theophrastus, one of the 'Eminent Philosophers' whose lives were described by Diogenes Lærtius in the third century.[8] Theophrastus asks that upon his death, 'the small portico adjoining the shrine of the Muses shall be rebuilt no worse than before, and that the panels showing maps of the world shall be put in the lower cloister'. The translations differ quite widely, but agree in referring to the maps in the panels.

A different kind of influence may be detected in the writings of the Latin poet Horace (65–8 BC), who became the chief literary figure in Rome after the death of Virgil. In his *Ars pœtica* he advanced the novel and intriguing argument that a painter might claim parity with a poet, in the sense that the art of each might be equally capable of imparting truth.[9] This, in an age when poetry was conceived of as the major way of transmitting knowledge and experience, was a revolutionary idea; the concept of a 'learned painter' was indeed seen as a contradiction in terms, rather as it would have been incongruous to speak of a 'learned surgeon'. Neither the painter nor the surgeon (who was also a barber) had before this time found a place among the men of learning. But Horace's attempt to 're-position visual knowledge within the realm of learning' made a great appeal to Renaissance thinkers like Alberti, as we shall see, and it was a short step from the kind of visual knowledge transmitted by the painter to that provided by the cartographer. So mapmaking came to be one of the kinds of visual knowledge that could reasonably be studied within the pantheon of learning.

Strabo (64/63 BC–*c.* 21 AD) was born a year or two after Horace, and his *Geography*, in seventeen books, would have been the single most important source for early modern readers to gain knowledge about the cartography of classical antiquity.[10] This work circulated in manuscript in western Europe from 1423 onwards and was first printed in 1469: its first two books give an unrivalled survey of ancient geography and cartography. We learn that Anaximander of Miletus (*c.*611–547 BC) was the first person to publish a geographical map (perhaps the one used by Aristagoras…), and that Hecateus of the third century BC left behind a work on geography. In this part of the *Geography*, Strabo insists on the importance of geographical knowledge for rulers and commanders, for without it they will make unnecessary mistakes. Strabo goes on to explain the role of Erastosthenes (c.276–196 BC), who established a map of the inhabited world, and made many corrections to existing maps.

In succeeding sections, Strabo is concerned to establish the relative excellence of the maps of Erastosthenes and of Hipparchus (c.160–125 BC), and mentions the work of Crates in constructing a globe showing the whole world. His own aim was to give 'the shape and size of that part of the earth which falls within our map, indicating at the same time what the nature of that part is and what portion it is of the whole earth'.[11] His concept of the inhabited world was rather as it is shown on the Ptolemaic map of Plate VI; for this area, he says, a map may be made upon a plane projection, rather as the portolan charts of the Middle Ages were. The work of Strabo was widely known during the fifteenth and sixteenth centuries, and surely was influential in forming Europeans' ideas about the mapping of antiquity.

Equally well known among architects was the work of Vitruvius, who was born about 25 BC and wrote *On architecture*, a ten-book compendium of all that was known about building. Book VIII concerns 'water-supply', and Vitruvius there went into an argument concerning the nature of winds, some of which bear water and some of which are dry. He adds, 'a proof of this is found in the sources of rivers, as they are painted on maps of the world, and as they are described'.[12] His readers would have no doubt about the existence of detailed regional maps in the world of Vitruvius.

Pliny the Elder (AD 23–79) was born fifty years later than Vitruvius, in the early imperial age, and is known for his great *Natural history*, in 37 books.[13] Books II–VI are particularly concerned with geography, and it is clear from certain passages that Pliny relied for much information on the great world map of Marcus Agrippa (63–12 BC) at Rome. In Book III he very specifically explains how this map came to be constructed, in a passage concerned with a question of geography:

Agrippa was a very painstaking man, and also a very careful geographer; who therefore could believe that when intending to set before the eyes of Rome a survey of the world he made a mistake, and with him the late lamented Augustus? For it was Augustus who completed the portico containing a plan of the world that had been begun by his sister in accordance with the design and memoranda of Marcus Agrippa.[14]

We have no idea of what this map looked like, though we may suppose that it was incised upon an upright wall, rather like the *Forma urbis Roma*, of which fragments survive.[15] It is not hard to imagine that the existence of public monuments like the map of Agrippa did lead to a certain degree of map knowledge among the citizens of Rome. There is a curious passage in the *Lives* of Plutarch (AD c.46–c.120) which suggests that such casual cartographic knowledge may also have existed among the Athenians during the fifth century BC. This was a time when Alcibiades, the subject of the 'Life', was trying to incite the young men of Athens to participate in a campaign in Sicily. Plutarch tells us, concerning this adventure, that 'many were they who sat in the palæstras [gymnasia] and lounging-places, mapping out in the sand the shape of Sicily and the position of Libya and Carthage'.[16] This evidence seems fairly conclusive, though it is true that the casual reader might not make much of it, buried as it is in the multi-volume set of *Lives*.

The final classical work that we should consider, leaving aside for the moment the *Geography* of Ptolemy, is the military treatise of Vegetius, compiled in the fourth century AD.[17] In the section concerning 'Marches near the enemy', Vegetius is very clear about the need for a map:

A general cannot be too careful and diligent in taking necessary precautions to prevent a surprise on the march… In the first place, he should have an exact description of the country that is the seat of war, in which the distances between places, the nature of the roads, the shortest routes, by-roads, mountains and rivers should be correctly noted. We are told

that the greatest generals carried their precautions on this head so far that, not satisfied with the simple description of the country wherein they were engaged, they caused plans of it to be made on the spot, that they might regulate their marches by the eye with greater safety…

As we shall see, the text of Vegetius, which was printed for the first time about 1475, became extremely influential among early military thinkers of the Renaissance.

These, then, were the main texts that might have caught the attention of early modern readers of the classics. Of course, there were other evidences of map use in antiquity, such as the texts of the *agrimensores*, or land-surveyors,[18] the manuscripts of the *Notitia dignitatum*, which set out the official posts of the empire in cartographic form,[19] or the Peutinger Table itself, a highly idiosyncratic road-map of the Roman Empire which was then known only to a few enthusiasts in the humanist circles of imperial Vienna (Fig. 6).[20] But this and other evidence was as yet unknown to the great mass of readers, as Germaine Aujac has pointed out.[21]

THE WORK OF CLAUDIUS PTOLEMY

The ancient writer who had the most obvious influence on map use in early modern Europe was undoubtedly Claudius Ptolemy, who flourished at Alexandria around 140 AD. Ptolemy was primarily

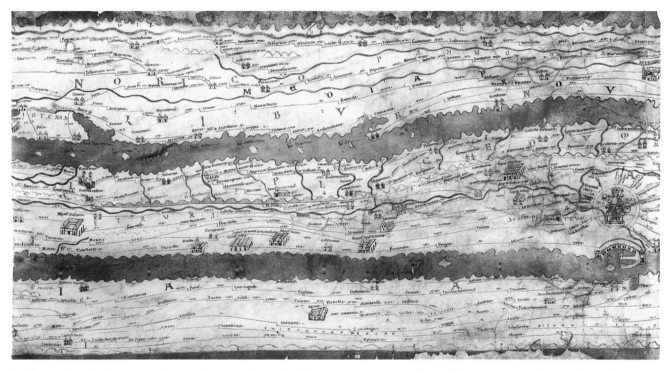

Fig. 6. Detail from the Peutinger Table. Konrad Peutinger (1508–47) of Augsburg once owned this elongated Roman map named after him. Originally compiled in the fourth century, it measured 6.75m x 34cm, as a long scroll, which is now divided up into 11 (once 12) segments. It was based on the Roman road-system, giving a highly squashed view of the Roman world from Britain to Syria. Our figure shows segment IV, with an elongated Italy across the middle. Rome on the right (with all the roads leading to it) is seen with its port of Ostia, and Ravenna (twin towers) appears at the middle left.

known for his work in astronomy and optics, and it was in the course of his astronomical *Almagest* that he mentioned his intention to write a 'Geography'.[22] This eventually took the form of eight books, of which the first two contained the principles according to which world maps might be drawn, and the latter six enumerated the latitude and longitude coordinates of about 8,000 places in the *oikumene*, or known world. Ptolemy acknowledged that much of his information came from previous scholars, in particular Marinos of Tyre. He also wanted to insist that his were directions for drawing a map of the known world, and not local maps. As he put it, local cartography depends on landscape drawing and needs no mathematical method.

His manuscript seems to have sunk into obscurity after his death, though in the ninth century it was translated into Arabic, and studied in the great Islamic centres. Towards the end of the thirteenth century it was rediscovered by the Byzantine scholar Maximus Planudes, who seems to have used Ptolemy's instructions in order to construct a series of twenty-seven maps.[23] After that time a good many Greek manuscript copies were produced,[24] and the *Geography* must have been studied in the Byzantine world up to the time of the fall of Constantinople to the Turks in 1453. Before then, though, in 1406, a Latin translation had been made, and versions of this translation were reproduced in western Europe in considerable numbers during the fifteenth century; from 1427 onwards there are even additional maps and plans to supplement the original twenty-seven of the main version.[25] Many of the great European libraries contain copies of this Latin manuscript version, which with its maps became an object of great beauty, and highly desirable to collectors. During the twentieth century, a number of facsimiles were made of these manuscript atlases, from such depositories as the Bibliothèque nationale de France at Paris, the Biblioteca Nazionale at Naples, and the University Library at Valencia.[26]

Famous scribes such as Henricus Martellus and Nicolas Germanus came to be associated with the manuscript copies of the *Geography*, and it was the Germanus version of the work which served as the model for the first printed version with maps, published at Bologna in 1477.[27] This printed version proved to be as irresistible to collectors as the manuscript copies had been, and it went through many editions, constantly acquiring new maps, or *tabulæ novæ*, which often contradicted the information on the original maps (Figs. 7 and 8). Thus the Ulm edition of 1482 had four new maps, the Rome edition of 1507 seven new ones, and the Strasbourg edition of 1513 twenty new ones. By then, with the information coming in from the new worlds outside the *oikumene*, the original maps were beginning to be retained purely for historical reasons.

The original twenty-seven maps showed an astonishing knowledge of the world for a scholar based in second-century Alexandria.

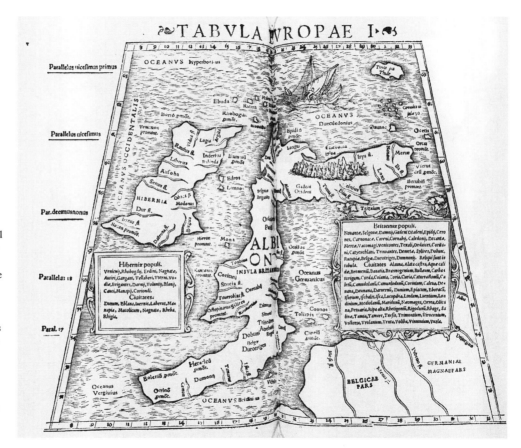

Fig. 7. Claudius Ptolemy, Original map of the British Isles, from the *Geographia* (Basel, 1540). This is from the first series of maps in the atlas, compiled from Ptolemy's coordinates. It gives an approximate outline of Britain and Ireland, and offers quite long lists (in the cartouches) of the peoples and cities of the two islands. The border contains the coordinates according to which the position of the cities was plotted, following the lists given in the first part of the *Geographia*.

Fig. 8. Claudius Ptolemy, *Tabula nova* of the British Isles, from the *Geographia* (Basel, 1540). This map comes from the same edition of the *Geographia*, and is one of the 20 *tabulæ novæ* ('new maps') which follow the 27 original ones. Its image of England is slightly more accurate and detailed, and it is curiously adorned with flags in the tradition of the portolan charts, to mark the realms of the kings of Scotland and England.

The centre of Ptolemy's east–west world was Rhodes, and yet he was able to give remarkably precise details of the towns and rivers of the British Isles, which indeed come first in his sequence of maps. He was not at all interested in political boundaries, or indeed in charting the seas, but he did try to give an impression of the main mountain chains. His influence lies in the astonishing originality of two of the elements discussed in his first two books: the idea of constructing a world map based on latitude and longitude, and the possibility of adopting different projections in order best to render a round earth on flat paper. The maps of the European Middle Ages had in the case of the portolan charts succeeded in giving remarkably precise impressions of the Mediterranean Sea and sometimes of the area around it, but these were entirely lacking any general coordinates, and proved to be impossible to adapt to the requirements of mapping the world beyond the *oikumene*. It was then, when the Europeans began to penetrate the northern and southern latitudes, that the principles enunciated by Ptolemy came into their full application; they were indeed an essential aspect of European cartographic expansion.

RENAISSANCE READERS AND CLASSICAL TEXTS

It is clear, then, that a good many suggestive texts were circulating in manuscript during the fifteenth century. But the case of Ptolemy is typical in that his work, like many others, began to have a powerful influence on the writings of contemporaries chiefly after it had been printed.[28] A good example of this was the great humanist scholar Desiderius Erasmus (1467–1536), who had a wonderful faculty for identifying and distilling the most remarkable new ideas of his time: as early as 1514 he published two works on the art of teaching, *De copia verborum et rerum* and *De ratione studii*.[29] Erasmus believed that education should begin with language studies, without any attempt at what he calls *eruditio*.[30] But then, he wrote, 'real' studies could be intermingled with language, and these real studies were best approached by using examples of *evidentia*, or vividness, often presented in a visual form such as a wall-chart. Erasmus makes no specific mention of maps, but his advocacy of 'what the Greeks call topographies' clearly shows that he had some such locational imagery in mind. Reading his admonitions, we are reminded of the later techniques of Saint Ignatius Loyola (1491–1556), who also wished to make the maximum use of the different senses. Thus in his *Spiritual exercises* he advocated the importance not only of the textual narrative, but also of the imaginative use of sight, taste, and smell in meditating on the Christian life.[31]

Seven years later, in 1521, Niccolò Machiavelli (1469–1527) published his treatise *L'arte della guerra*, which ran into numerous editions in various languages. It was translated into English in 1573 by Peter Whithorne as *The arte of warre*, and some way into this

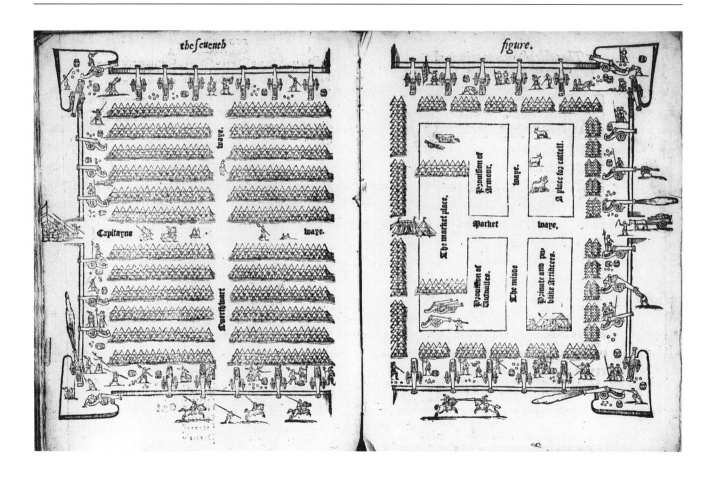

work (fo. lxxxiii), Whithorne observes in the margin that 'The description of the countrie where an enemie must march, is most requisite for a captaine to have'. This marginal note refers to Machiavelli's assertion that when marching in enemy country 'the first thing [the Captaine] ought to do, is to get described, and painted out, all the countrie through which he must marche, so that he may know the places, the number, the distances, the waies, the hills, the rivers, the fennes, and all qualities of them'. Clearly, Machiavelli had been reading his Vegetius, even if, as we shall see in Chapter 5, it would be many years before such large-scale topographical maps could actually be constructed at a commander's need. Whithorne's book is also interesting for the way in which it called forth the editor's expertise in providing maps and diagrams: in the plates, many different formations are diagrammed, and there is a bird's-eye view of the ideal fortified camp (Fig. 9).

Fig. 9. Plate from Peter Whithorne's translation of Machiavelli's *L'arte della guerra* (London, 1573); the 'seventh figure', showing 'the manner how to incampe an army'. The Byzantines had inherited from the Romans their ideas for encamping armies, and these were taken over by sixteenth-century military theorists. Here Whithorne sets out a quadrilateral with heart-shaped bastions at each corner, and places inside set apart for 'a place for cattell', 'Provision of armour', 'a market place', and so forth. If such an arrangement were generally followed, all the soldiers would know their way about every camp.

Machiavelli's work on war was widely read, but could not compare with the Europe-wide influence of the *Cortegiano*, or 'Courtier', first published in 1528 by Baldassare Castiglione (1478–1529).[32] It was translated into English in 1561 as *The boke of the courtier*, and took the form of a dialogue so conceived as to bring out the qualities desirable in a courtier. Of course, military skill and the defence of honour play a prominent role, but Castiglione also insisted that 'our Courtier ought in no wise to leave out ... cunning in drawing, and the knowledge of the verie art of painting'.[33] Like all humanists, he justified this need by referring to the customs of classical antiquity:

Wonder ye not if I wish this feate in him, which now adayes perhappes is counted an handicraft and full little to become [i.e. suit] a gentleman, for I remember that I have read that the men of old time, and especially in old Greece, would have gentlemen's children in the scholes to apply painting, as a matter both honest and necessary ... Among the Romans in like manner it was in verie great reputation ....

We are reminded here of the Horatian attempt to reposition the visual arts among the learned disciplines.

For Castiglione, 'painting' had 'many commodities, and especially in warre, to draw out countries, plateformes [i.e. fortifications], rivers, bridges, castels, holds [i.e. strongholds], fortresses and other such matters, the which though a man were able to keep in mind (and that is a hard matter to doe), yet can he not show them to others'. Clearly, he is here following the ideas of Machiavelli and Vegetius, but he carries the idea further in then asserting that there is a moral element to the delineation, for the whole earth is indeed 'a noble and great painting, drawn with the hand of nature and of God'. Painting, he adds, is less permanent than sculpture, but much better able to convey topographical information. Castiglione is estimated to have had around 300,000 readers during the early modern period, and certainly the *Book of the courtier* went through over 150 editions between 1528 and 1850;[34] its influence in enhancing the role of the 'painter' or topographer must have been huge.

Among educationists, the influence of Juan Luis Vives (1493–1540) was also great. In his *De tradendis disciplinis*,[35] he tried like Erasmus to set out the whole programme through which a student could most effectively learn. In book IV, chapter 1, he comes to 'Logic and nature study', which involves 'a general explanation, an exposition or, as it were, a picture of the whole of nature … so that a full representation and description of the whole world is included as in a picture'. For this, he adds, the works of Pliny and of Pomponius Mela will be needed.[36]

After that, 'The pupil should read Strabo, who wrote a descrip-

tion of the world and gave its history at the same time. Let him also consider the maps of Ptolemy, if he can get a corrected edition. Let him add the discoveries of our countrymen on the borders of the East and the West.'[37] Presumably by a 'corrected edition' Vives means an edition with as many *tabulæ modernæ* as possible. His phrase about 'the borders of the East and the West' is interesting, because it shows that he was at first thinking in terms of the Ptolemaic *oikumene*, which indeed had had borders not only on the east and west, but also to the south and north. It was precisely the mariners of Spain and Portugal who were in the process of enlarging these borders, as we shall see in Chapter 4.

In the same year that Vives published his great work, Sir Thomas Elyot (c.1490–1546) published *The boke named the governour*, which most fully sets out the utility of maps in the mind of early modern humanists.[38] First, Elyot needed to establish 'that it is commendable in a gentleman to paint and carve exactly, if nature thereto do induce him'.[39] To sustain this claim, he named 'Claudius, Titus, Hadrian and both Antonines' as examples of ancient rulers who had also been considerable 'painters'. He went on to advance the usual arguments about the military utility of maps, pointing out that Alexander the Great

Caused the countries whereunto he purposed any enterprise diligently

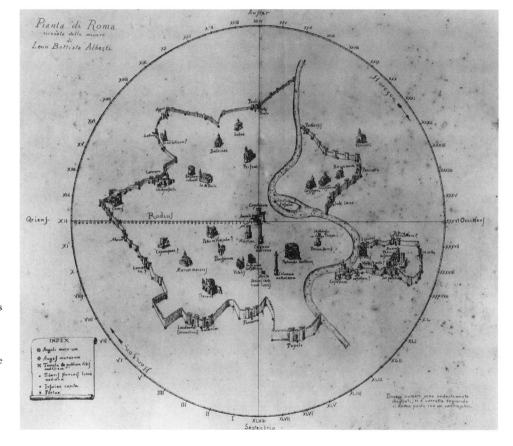

Fig. 10. Plan of Rome, constructed according to Leon Battista Alberti's instructions in his *Descriptio urbis Romæ*, c.1440. Oriented southwards, this plan was constructed according to Alberti's scheme for measuring angled distances from about the site of the present Piazza Venezia. The result is a plan siting many of Rome's ancient monuments within a frame that is still quite recognizable: the present Vatican City within its walls on the lower right, the walled enclave to the west of the Tiber River above it, and then the mass of the walled city to the east of the river.

and cunningly to be described and painted, that beholding the picture he might perceive which places were most dangerous and where he and his host might have most easy and convenient passage. Semblable [i.e. similarly] did the Romans in the rebellion of France and the insurrection of their confederates, setting up a table openly, wherein Italy was painted, to the extent that the people looking in it should reason and consult in which places it were best to resist or invade the enemie.

It is not clear to which classical texts Elyot was referring, but it is evident that he was using them to promote the use of maps,[40] as Machiavelli had done. Elyot, however, carried the possibilities of map use further. For historical studies, he added, 'It should be a convenient lesson to behold the olde tables [*tabulæ*] of Ptolemie, wherein all the world is painted', thus adding a spatial element to the student's understanding. Nor was the use of maps to be entirely studious, for what could be more delightful than following voyages on maps through the imagination 'in a warme studie or parlor'?

Finally, Elyot took the idea of map use a large step further, in suggesting the administrative uses of cartography. By consulting a map, the governor might see 'where he shall employ his study and treasure'; we are reminded of Lord Burghley (1520–95), Queen Elizabeth's statesman, annotating his maps of England to show where dangerous Recusants (Catholics) might be found, or eventu-

ally of French finance ministers studying maps of the fiscal districts called *généralités*, with a view no doubt to trying to squeeze out the maximum in taxation. Elyot made constant use of classical examples in his argumentation, whether or not these examples really represented what actually happened in classical antiquity, and his book represents a high point in the imaginative adaptation of map use in affairs of state.

RENAISSANCE ARCHAEOLOGISTS AND MAPMAKING

The influence of classical antiquity was not felt only in the way in which early modern authors chose to interpret cartographic references in classical writers. The very process of uncovering the material remains of antiquity also called for the production of maps and plans. There had been medieval scholars who were interested in what would be called classical archaeology,[41] but in the time of Leon Battista Alberti (1404–72) the study made huge advances.

Fig. 11. Bird's-eye view of Nola from Ambrogio Leone, *De Nola*, 1514. This plan of the circular ancient city of Nola sets out the positions of the Roman amphitheatre and temples. But it also superimposes on this plan the outline of present-day Nola ('Nola presens') within its walls, showing how Renaissance archaeologists could use maps to relate classical antiquities to present-day buildings.

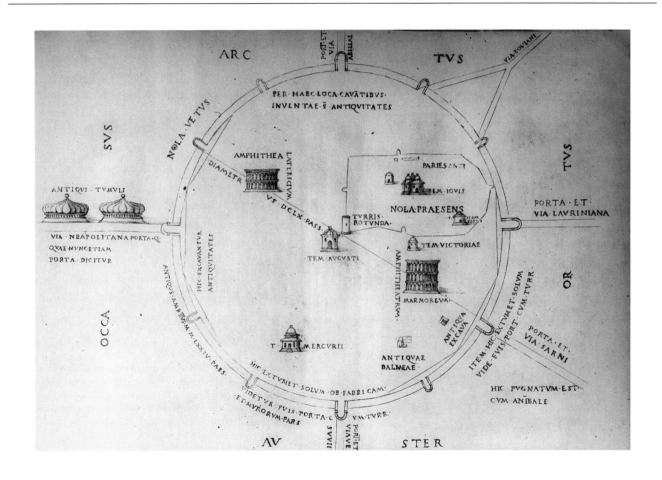

ARC TVS

VIA ROVIANI

PORTET VIA ABELLAE

PER HAEC LOCA CAVATIBVS INVENTAE S ANTIQVITATES

NOLA VETVS

SVS TVS

DIAMETR

AMPHITHEA LATERICIVM VS DCLX PASS

PARIESANTI

TEM IOVIS

NOLA PRAESENS

ANTIQVI TVMVLI

VIA NEAPOLITANA PORTA Q QVAE NVNC ETIAM PORTA DICITVR

TVRRIS ROTVNDA

PORTA ET VIA LAVRINIANA

HIC EXCAVANTVR ANTIQVITATES

TEM AVGVSTI

TEM VICTORIAE

ANTIQVS AMBITVS IN M LXXIV PASS

AMPHITHEATRVM MARMOREVM

OR

OCCA

T MERCVRII

ANTIQVA EXCAVA

PORTA ET VIA SARNI

ITEM HIC EXTVM ET SOLVM CVM TVRR VIDE EVIS PORT CVM TVRR

HIC EXTVM ET SOLVM OB FABRI CAM

ANTIQVAE BALNEAE

HIC PVGNATVM EST CVM ANIBALE

VIDETVR FVIS PORTA C ET MVRORVM PARS

VM TVRR

PORTET VIAVE

SAVII

AV STER

Already during the 1430s Alberti had come to a new understanding of surveying and mapping,[42] which he used in his great work, the *De re ædificatoria*, a survey of classical architecture which circulated widely in manuscript during the 1440s and thereafter, and was eventually printed posthumously in 1485. During the 1440s Alberti's archaeological research also gave rise to his *Descriptio urbis Romæ*, a little treatise in which he explained how to draw a correctly-scaled map of Rome, using a system of angle-measurements and paces. He does not seem to have put this system into effect, but his treatise has allowed others to reconstruct ancient Rome according to his theory (Fig. 10). The contrast with earlier delineations of the city, such as the one by the Limbourg brothers (Fig. 14), is very striking; the basis had here been laid for a systematic archaeology based on accurate topographical knowledge. As Gadol puts it, this new exactitude 'was due not to sharper observations but to the mathematising of observation and representation alike'.[43] Although Alberti was a commanding figure, whose work demands attention, he was working along with the currents of thought of the time, which also gave rise to the kind of map provided by Flavio Biondo in his *Roma instaurata* in the 1480s;[44] it was as if the new passion for classical archaeology could not thrive without newly accurate plans of the cities under study.

Other works confirmed this truth in the later fifteenth century,

and it was most strikingly demonstrated in Ambrogio Leone's *De Nola*, published in 1514. Leone made use of plans of Nola to bring out its archaeological history. First came a general view of the area, to put the town into its geographical context. Then came a plan of ancient Nola, superimposed on a plan of the existing town, followed by a plan and then a bird's-eye view of the present town (Fig. 11). Clearly, by the early sixteenth century a scholar like Leone was capable of using a wide variety of mapping techniques to bring out whatever aspects he wished to emphasize. Five years later, the great Raphael perished (see Chapter 2) just as he was about to undertake a new plan of Rome: 'he had devised a new and wonderful way of doing this, so as to present the city as he saw it, as if new, before the eyes of the architect'.[45]

It was not only cities that were the object of these archaeological surveys. The emperor Charles V (1500–58), we are assured by the German historian Hans Delbrück,[46] studied the camps of

Fig. 12. Drawing of a city and a Roman camp from Andrea Palladio (ed.), *I commentari di C. Giulio Cesare* (Venice, 1575). Here Palladio uses his imagination to reconstruct a circular city on a river, with another city away to the right. Ships on the river seem to blockade the town, outside of which are two strikingly different camps, and an army drawn up for battle. To complete the narrative, letters on the plan refer back to an accompanying key.

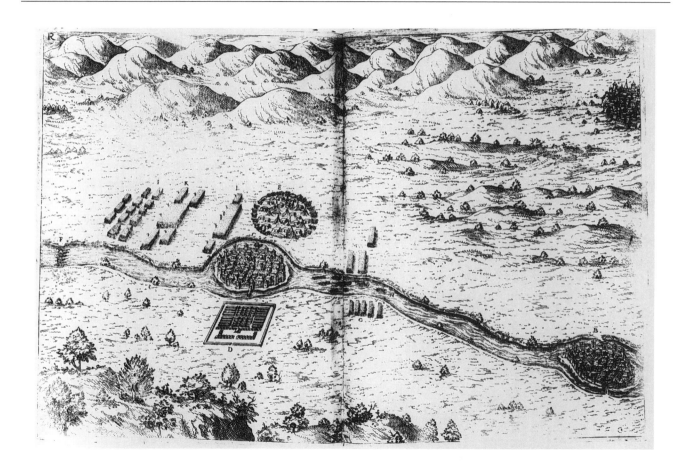

Caesar and made a plan of one in France. As we shall see in Chapter 5, early modern military men were very interested in the encampment-methods of the Romans, and developed the camp-plan into a type all of its own. It is also true that the Roman camp is of extraordinary interest as a type, since many of them set out the main lines for the towns, and even great cities, which often succeeded them.

At least one major cartographer came to his trade through an interest in classical antiquities: this was Pietro Ligorio (*c.* 1510–1583), who graduated into general mapping after he had developed his skills in delineating Roman sites.[47] Abraham Ortelius (1527–98) was also fascinated by the remains of classical antiquity, and in successive editions of his great *Theatrum orbis terrarum* (first edition, Antwerp, 1570) provided plans of interesting sites. One way and another, many of the cartographic contributors to the Ortelian work were also concerned to map the material remains of classical antiquity.[48]

By the late sixteenth century, the provision of maps had become inseparable from the textual editions of many classical works. When, for instance, the great architect Andrea Palladio (1518–80) decided to edit Caesar's *Commentaries*, he provided thirty-nine plates to accompany the roughly 400 pages of text. The plates in this work, *I commentari di C. Giulio Cesare* (Venice, 1575), cover a wide variety of phenomena. There is the usual plan of a Roman camp, but also imaginary bird's-eye views of particular battles (Fig. 12). There is also a bird's-eye view of a mobile Roman bridge; by the later sixteenth century, classical scholars knew how to use visual, often cartographic, material to illustrate many aspects of the history of antiquity that they sought to elucidate. In this, as in other respects, the new-found enthusiasms for Greek and Latin antiquity had widespread consequences for cartography.

2

The painterly origins of some European mapping,
1420–1650

HISTORIANS of art have long agreed that there was a major stylistic change in western European art between 1400 and 1500. Whether they call it 'the advent of a new realism', or 'the coming of the Renaissance', or even the 'age of discovery', they agree that some great wind of change blew through the fifteenth century. What has not been so well understood is that this new way of 'seeing' the world applied as well to the production of maps, where entirely new styles emerged, often in fact developed by those long recognized as painterly innovators. It was as if painting and mapping were simply different means of rendering the same newly-visioned reality, for artists like the Limbourgs and Van Eycks.

The origins of this development are not easy to track down, in part because historians of art have not been able to come to any agreed understanding of the life and works of such figures as the Boucicaut Master, the Limbourgs, and the Van Eyck brothers.[1] Still, it seems to be clear that some of the earliest examples of the new style are the books of hours produced in the early fifteenth century by the Limbourg brothers.[2] The Turin–Milan Hours have been largely lost, but from the *Très riches heures* produced for the Duc de Berry (1340–1416) we gain an excellent idea of the nature of the innovations.[3]

The manuscript begins with a calendar of the seasons, and for each month a castle is portrayed against a background of rural activity. Whereas in previous books of hours these buildings would have been generic, in the *Très riches heures* they are portrayed with almost startling fidelity. We have no difficulty in recognizing the

Louvre in Paris, or the *châteaux* at Saumur and Vincennes, the latter shown in Fig. 13, the image for December. In the foreground the huntsmen supervise the dogs as they destroy the unfortunate boar; the man on the right sounds the mort on his horn. In the background loom the towers of Vincennes, most faithfully represented; the Duke had been born in the great central tower in late November, 1340. Each castle in the series is represented with such fidelity that it is as if the Limbourgs were trying to offer us topographical guides to these great buildings.

Plate I shows a different kind of site, from the cycle of Offices of the Saints in the same book of hours. Here Saint Michael, having just wounded the dragon, hovers over the Abbey of Mont Saint Michel. As before, the scene is meticulously observed, and has in fact changed little to the present day. The great abbey looms over the town, reached through a pair of gates from the causeway, flooded at high tide. Some boats lie high and dry upon the sand, where a few pools remain. In the background is the distant island

Fig. 13. The Limbourg brothers, The December image, showing the *château* of Vincennes, from the *Très riches heures*. This is one of the earliest European images to offer an accurate delineation of a particular place. It was probably drawn from the south-west of the *château*, in what is still the Bois de Vincennes, the old royal hunting forest. The keep looms high above the six lesser towers, with the royal chapel to its right, and the whole site emerges from a dense wood.

of Tombelaine. In the town, each house seems to have been individually drawn, and we readily recognize the Norman half-timbering; in short, this image seems to be the result of close and accurate observation.

The idea that this startlingly innovative style has something to do with a newly 'cartographic' way of seeing the world is encouraged by the Limbourgs' inclusion in the *Très riches heures* of a map of Rome (Fig. 14). For this, as Millard Meiss emphasizes, is the first surviving example of a book of hours to include a map; it may also be relevant that the Duc de Berry is said to have possessed several *mappaemundi*.[4] In Figure 14 the representation is quite conventional, taking its place in a long tradition of plans of Rome.[5] But it is thoroughly practical, if the idea was to portray the main monuments of the city. At the upper right, outside the walls, is the church of San Paolo fuori le Mura, and at the bottom centre, between the two bridges, we see the Castel Sant'Angelo. Many classical and medieval monuments are shown more or less in their correct positions within the city: it is a convincing, if naive, bird's-eye view.

The work of the Limbourgs bears a close relationship to that of the Van Eyck brothers, who indeed upon occasion completed work begun by them. Jan Van Eyck, too, was a master of topographical 'realism', producing paintings whose topographical details seem to take us right into the world of the early fifteenth-century Low

Fig. 14. The Limbourg brothers, Plan of Rome from the *Très riches heures*. This south-orientated bird's-eye view shows the main monuments of Rome, in an exaggerated and sometimes fanciful way. Nevertheless, a comparison with Fig. 10, taken from the same angle, shows that both artists had well caught the curve of the River Tiber, the circular sweep of the walls to the east, and, to the west, both the papal enclave (bottom right) and the small walled area on the west bank.

Countries, even if none of the actual sites has been positively identified.[6] More remarkably, he also seems to have 'painted' a terrestrial globe.[7] His near-contemporary, the historian Bartolomeo Facio, describes it as 'the most perfect work of our time, on which one can distinguish not only the places and continents, but also the distances which separate them'. If indeed this globe was the work of Van Eyck, it is a further demonstration of the way in which a leading painter was simultaneously 'seeing' the world in what we would call cartographic terms.

There have been numerous attempts to track down the philosophical and theological background to the artistic development exemplified by the Limbourgs and Van Eycks. The most obvious, but mistaken, explanation is that it was an aspect of 'the Renaissance'. Several authors have conclusively demonstrated, however, that these developments in the Low Countries were pre-humanist, relying rather on the declining Middle Ages for their inspiration than on Renaissance Italy.[8] Indeed, when Italian artists (somewhat later) began to master the illusion of reality, it was using different techniques and achieving quite different results; moreover, they did not have the same interest in depicting precise and identifiable sites.[9]

There seem to be two main strands in the complex variety of historians' reasoning on this matter. For Erwin Panofsky, the meticulous delineation of 'the particular' demonstrated by the Limbourgs was an outcome of the nominalist strain of thought, strikingly represented by William of Ockham (*c.*1295–*c.*1350). If, as the nominalists maintained, reality was to be apprehended only in the discrete and particular, then the minute description of individual objects would be the most worthy task of the painter[10]. As Millard Meiss put it, the Limbourgs were 'champions of a pictorial nominalism'.

A somewhat different approach is taken by those historians of philosophy who emphasize the importance of Neoplatonism in the thought of the fourteenth century.[11] For them, a key element in the Neoplatonic tradition was the importance of mathematics as a way of 'seeing' God's immanence in the universe. As Cosgrove puts it, this faith in the mathematical foundation of Christian (and other) morality 'placed considerable emphasis on graphic representation, whether in the visual arts or mapping and survey, which depended upon visual measurement'.[12]

Whether those who emphasize the role of Neoplatonism, or those who insist upon the importance of nominalism, are nearer the truth, it seems undeniable that the waning Middle Ages was a time when the sense of sight had attained a new importance. As Johan Huizinga puts it, in his masterly *The autumn of the Middle Ages*, 'The basic characteristic of the late medieval mind is its predominantly visual nature. This characteristic is closely related to the atrophy of the mind. Thought takes place exclusively through visual conceptions. Everything that is expressed is couched in visual terms.'[13]

It is in the writings of Nicholas of Cusa, who flourished in the 1440s and 1450s, that these ideas are most fully and revealingly worked out. Nicholas led a busy diplomatic life, as papal representative to the princes of Germany, but he also wrote a good deal of theology, of which the 'Vision of God' is the most relevant to us.[14] A central message of this work is that God pervades all things, and that the essence of God's presence is sight (and not, as with Thomas Aquinas, being). Nicholas explains the function of the human intellect in terms of a mapmaker.[15] We are, he says, like a cartographer living in a city with five gates, analogous to the five senses. Through these gates come messengers bearing different reports, and one of the most important of the gates controls the messengers of light and colour, who inform us about all things visible. Having received the reports, the intellect reduces them to a well-ordered and measured map, which is in itself a reflection of the Creator of the sensible world thus delineated. It is remarkable that Cusa should adopt the metaphor of the sense-driven mapmaker, when he comes to explain the nature of human mind and intellect. This metaphor draws him as far as possible from the twelfth-century notion of Saint Anselm, that things are harmful 'in proportion to the number of senses that they gratify'.[16]

Knowing his background, we are not surprised to discover that Nicholas of Cusa drew one of the earliest maps of Germany, which was also a very early example of a regional map. No copy of the manuscript original now exists, but there is a printed version from the late fifteenth century. The original was made about 1450, and was no doubt the fruit of his many travels on papal business. For its construction he seems to have used a *torquetum*, an instrument for measuring both horizontal and vertical angles, rather as a modern transit does. Such instruments had long been known in theory to medieval Europe, but their use for practical surveying was new. In his later years Nicholas finished several important treatises on scientific themes, including one (now lost) entitled 'De figura mundi';[17] his life seems to have been a rare blend of original speculation and practical achievement.

It is possible that Nicholas of Cusa derived some of his ideas about cartography from Italy, where he was acquainted with the learned circles of Florence, and in particular with Leon Battista Alberti.[18] The latter was not only a remarkable essayist, poet, architect, and mathematician, but also could be taken to personify the unity of painting and cartography, in developing a new way of seeing the world. For painting, he recommended the use of the *velo*,

essentially a device for rendering a mathematically correct image of any subject, by viewing it through a transparent grid, whose information could then be transferred square by square to a smaller grid on paper. Albrecht Dürer made a famous drawing of this simple but effective system, showing the artist's eye fixed at one point, as he transcribes the complex image of the model on to a lattice similar in proportion to the one through which he is gazing.

It would have been possible, of course, to apply the *velo* principle to the delineation of a city, but here Alberti proposed a more elegant, mathematically based solution (Fig. 10). The cartographer was to take sightings in degrees of various landmarks from a central elevated position, and then, having paced the distances, was to transfer these figures to a map. Alberti's own map has not survived, but a nineteenth-century reconstruction was made from his notes, and gave a highly accurate result.[19] In cartography, as in painting, Alberti had in effect described techniques that would serve many mapmakers and artists in the centuries to come.

Fig. 15. Jean Fouquet, View of Notre-Dame de Paris from the Etienne Chevalier book of hours, *c.*1450. Fouquet here leads us into fifteenth-century Paris, looking at the west façade of Notre-Dame from a point on the south bank, perhaps where the Pont Neuf now begins to cross the river. The visible bridge still has its houses on it, and parts of the river-bank are still open and lined with trees, before the great expansion of the sixteenth century.

Back in northern Europe, the tradition inaugurated by the Limbourgs and Van Eycks found followers, even if the majority of artists continued to paint in the older tradition. Probably the most remarkable follower was Jean Fouquet, who served the French kings between about 1440 and 1480.[20] Fouquet was widely known not only in France but also in Italy, and in the precision of his topographical detail he excelled even the great Italians. The view of Vincennes in the background of his 'Job' is remarkable, as is the distant image of Orléans on one of the folios of the 'Grands chroniques de France'. This manuscript, now preserved at the Bibliothèque nationale de France, contains equally convincing views of such towns as Clichy, Montpensier, Rheims, Tours, and so forth.

Even more astonishing is the view of Notre-Dame of Paris from the dismembered Etienne Chevalier book of hours (Fig. 15). This page comes from the Hours of the Holy Spirit, and shows 'The Descent of the Holy Spirit upon the Faithful'. The Holy Spirit, visualized as the right hand of God, descends upon a circle of faithful, clustered before the River Seine, behind which rises the great cathedral of Notre-Dame. This building dwarfs the houses and even the other churches; note the Pont Saint-Michel on the right, a bridge which was still then—like the other bridges of Paris—covered with houses. As far as we can tell, Fouquet was not associated with any specifically cartographic activity: we have to return to Italy for fresh examples of artists in whom the painterly and map-making urges coexisted.

The most spectacular of them all was of course Leonardo da Vinci (1452–1519). Not content with attaining pre-eminence as painter, sculptor, architect, musician, and natural scientist, Leonardo was also a master cartographer. He could delineate large areas of countryside either planimetrically or in bird's-eye view, so that there is a continuum between the bird's-eye views like his 'View of the Alps' and his map of Tuscany.[21] These images show a pass in the Alps during a furious rainstorm, and almost equally mountainous country in central Italy. The sea is in blue, as are the lakes, and the mountains are indicated with a brown wash, which conveys a most effective impression of their location and height. The map includes over 200 names, and covers the region from the Po Valley in the north to Umbria in the south-west.

Leonardo could also portray towns, either in strict planimetry (as seen directly from above), or in bird's-eye view. Figure 16 shows a little-known sketch of Milan, drawn about 1508, when Leonardo was working on his study of the city's renewal. The roughly circular sketch at the top shows three-quarters of the city's perimeter, and the rapid bird's-eye view below it sets out the main buildings, including the castle and the lazzaretto (hospital for contagious diseases); clearly Leonardo used both angles in formulating his image

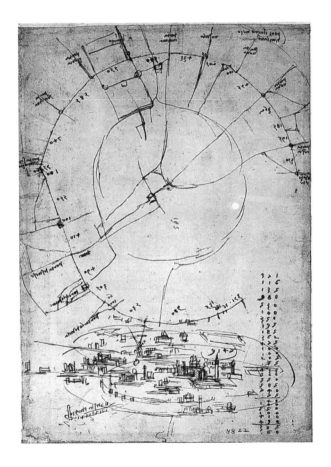

of the city and the work to be done there. He also produced a purely planimetric (rigorously vertical) view of Imola, a celebrated *tour de force* for the time. It would be many decades yet before most plan-makers could follow him, for instance, in showing all a town's features in this way. Even the most accomplished draughtsmen of the sixteenth century could rarely resist showing large buildings in bird's-eye view, on an otherwise planimetric map.

Leonardo had such an instinctive grasp both of natural forces and of cartographic possibilities that upon at least one occasion his work poses a tricky problem to the historian of cartography: should his 'view' of the Arno, for instance, be regarded as a map or a diagram? It is a map in the sense that it represents a locality, but it goes beyond the normal understanding of a map in trying to explicate the forces underlying the appearance of the water.[22] The fact is that Leonardo was capable of using an extraordinarily wide range of 'locational imaging' in order to translate what he saw as reality.[23]

Fig. 16. Leonardo da Vinci, Plan and elevation of Milan *c.* 1500. Normally, we have to deal with the finished work of artists and cartographers, who have thrown away the scraps of paper that might have allowed us to see their inspiration. But here we have a scribbled plan straight out of the head of Leonardo, famous indeed for the extent of his surviving notebooks. We see how he visualized the city in plan at the top, then switched to a bird's-eye view, at the same scale, on the bottom.

His two great rivals and contemporaries, Raphael Sanzio (1483–1520) and Michelangelo Buonarroti (1475–1564), were less obviously alert to the possibilities of cartography: indeed, Michelangelo is often described as being contemptuous of the descriptive topography/cartography of northern art.[24] However, he had mastered certain aspects of the cartographer's craft, being capable not only of drawing plans and elevations of buildings, but also of producing plans for fortifying the walls of Florence.[25] For his part, Raphael seems to have been drawn into urban cartography by the need to preserve the rapidly disappearing monuments of ancient Rome. According to Roberto Weiss, Pope Leo X commissioned him to draw an idealized plan of the city;[26] it is certain that he drew many site-plans of the buildings. As a letter published after his death in 1520 puts it,

he had set forth in a book—as Ptolemy set forth the configuration of the world—the ancient buildings of Rome, with their proportions, forms and ornaments, so faithfully that he who has seen these drawings might fairly contend that he has seen ancient Rome … he reproduced not only the plans and locations of the buildings … but also the elevations.[27]

In northern Europe, the only figure of stature comparable to that of the three great Italians was Albrecht Dürer (1471–1528), who also proved susceptible to the mapping impulse, particularly in the latter part of his life.[28] In his earlier years he was content to compose paintings and woodcuts—for the latter of which he was chiefly famous—within the traditional limitations of subject and technique, which did not include topographical views. When he went to Italy in 1494, though, it was as if he felt compelled to record the countryside, in a series of hauntingly beautiful watercolours (Plate II). Thereafter, his interests veered more and more towards the accurate depiction of topography, until in 1525 we find him publishing the *Instruction in mensuration with compass and triangle*, part of his insistence that young German painters should no longer grow up like 'wild, ungrafted trees', but should master those elements of perspective which would enable them to produce accurate topographical drawings.

In his own work, his interest in measurement and accurate delineation was shown in his *Treaty of fortification* (1527), and in woodcuts like the superb *Army beleaguering a city* (1527), where the constituent elements of the army are set into a very realistically observed landscape.[29] Throughout his life, Dürer maintained friendships at Nürnberg with the leaders of scientific thought there, collaborating in 1515 with Johann Stabius on the engraving of two celestial spheres and a world map, and contributing the folio with the armillary sphere to Pirckheimer's edition of Ptolemy (1525).[30]

Dürer's career was marked by many-sided activity in painting, etching, engraving, woodcutting, and writing that almost entitles him to rank with the many-talented Italians of the period. Like them, he began his career preoccupied by the themes of late medieval art, but also like many of them, he became more and more interested in the theory and practice of representing localities. In range of interests, his nearest counterpart in the German-speaking regions was probably Augustin Hirschvogel (1503–53). Born in Nürnberg, Hirschvogel lived most of his life in Vienna, where he produced innumerable engravings covering a wide variety of themes—biblical scenes, portraits of princes, hunting and village scenes, decorative vessels, coats of arms, and so forth.[31] His many sketches of perspective designs and geometrical forms make us believe that he was interested in problems of representation, which he worked out in numerous landscapes, some of which showed specific locations ('The castle of Murano', for instance); in 1543 he also published *Geometria*, 'bringing architecture and perspective together', as the subtitle claims.[32] As a cartographer, Hirschvogel

Fig. 17. Augustin Hirschvogel, Self-portrait (Adam von Bartsch, *Le peintre graveur*, 21 vols., Leipzig, 1854–76). When Augustin Hirschvogel chose to represent himself, it was not as a painter, as we might expect, but rather as a geometer, with globe and compass. It means that he wished to be thought of as a natural scientist, able to bring measurement and so understanding to all phenomena.

was capable of composing a wide range of maps. Upper Austria and Muscovy were the areas of his early maps, but his fame rests chiefly upon the great plan of Vienna published in 1552. This was a circular planimetric map, preceded by two large views of the city: clearly Hirschvogel was master of a wide range of representational imaging. His self-portrait (Fig. 17) shows him with globe and dividers, with the interesting legend 'circulus mensurat omnia'—suggesting that everything can be measured.

In the Low Countries, we might take Cornelis Anthonisz (c.1499–c.1556) as our first example of a painter-cartographer. Working in Amsterdam during the 1530s, 1540s, and 1550s, he is chiefly known not so much for his paintings as for his woodcut portraits of princes.[33] His life is very obscure, but he must have had some training in cartography, for he produced a very wide range of images. On the large scale was the woodcut 'Siege of Terwaen [Thérouanne]' and the magnificent woodcut bird's-eye view of Amsterdam (Fig. 18), generated in twelve sheets in 1544 from his similar painting of 1538. He also produced other town-plans and a navigation-manual with landfall views. On the small scale he produced a map of Europe, now lost (though praised by none other than Abraham Ortelius), and the 1543 *Caerte van Oostland*, a woodcut on nine sheets showing the northern Netherlands, Germany, and the Scandinavian countries in greater detail than ever before.

We know very little about Cornelis's life or sources, but we may imagine that at Amsterdam, even before the days of its glory after the collapse of Antwerp in the 1570s, there was a circle of learned people to which he belonged, and from which he could generate his astonishing cartographic information.

The learned circles of sixteenth-century Antwerp are easier to reconstruct. Here the most prominent painter was Pieter Bruegel the Elder (c.1525–1569), familiar of Ortelius and of the painter and printseller Hieronymous Cock.[34] He is well known for his paintings of the Flemish countryside, some of which can be shown to represent actual places; versions of them also circulated widely as engravings. When he went down into Italy in 1552, he seems to have made many topographical sketches, some of which afterwards appeared as engravings.[35] Passing through Rome, he probably gathered material for the view of the city identified by Marcel Destombes;[36] in short, although he made no maps, he was a highly competent topographer.

Adjacent to Antwerp lies Bruges, and here the best example of a sixteenth-century artist-cartographer was Pierre Pourbus (1524–84).[37] Born in Gouda, he spent most of his life in Bruges, where he painted many religious scenes in an unexceptional and unmemorable style. He also compiled about twenty-eight maps, of which six survive. They range very widely in scale and technique, from

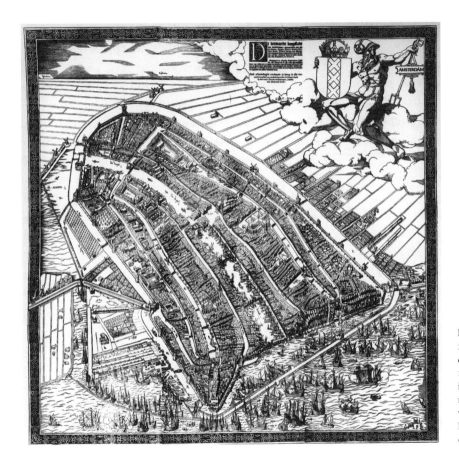

Fig. 18. Cornelis Anthonisz, Plan of Amsterdam, 1544. Cornelis Anthonisz began his career by producing woodcuts of princes during the 1530s and 1540s in Amsterdam. But he soon became interested in maps, compiling a small-scale map of Europe, regional maps of the Low Countries, and a superb view of the burgeoning city of Amsterdam, shown here with its bustling quays and its numerous ocean-going ships.

the bird's-eye view of the 'Vue panoramique de l'Abbaye des Dunes' of 1580, to a bird's-eye view of the same region taking in a much larger area, to the 'Grande Carte' of the Bruges region finished in 1571, for which many of the earlier maps were preparatory studies. These preparatory maps were sometimes mere sketches, without scale or orientation, but they often covered areas where there were old or new dyke-works, and so were important in establishing property-rights. Pourbus may have learned his mapping skills from his father-in-law; at all events, he could draw a wide range of maps, and evidently received commissions from many of the landowners around Bruges.

It would be tedious to enumerate the various French painters whom we know also to have been cartographers.[38] But we ought to notice the remarkable combination of art and cartography in the maps of the so-called 'Dieppe School', whose members thrived in that Channel seaport between about 1540 and 1570.[39] The French mapmakers seem to have learned their skills from the Portuguese, who often took 'painters' with them on their early sixteenth-century voyages, and who were associated with the mariners of Dieppe in the Brazil trade.[40] Not many examples of these Portuguese artists' work survive, though the so-called 'Miller Atlas', now preserved at the Bibliothèque Nationale in Paris, gives us a good idea of the nature of their work. The page showing the central 'New World' offers a remarkable pair of sketches (Fig. 32). To the north, in the land of 'Bimini', now more or less Florida, we see an Edenic scene in which fox, deer, and bear subsist peacefully; it has sometimes been remarked that this imagery preserves much medieval lore, and we have here perhaps an echo of prelapsarian zoology, appropriately enough in a land near the presumed Fountain of Youth. The lower scene takes in 'the Antilles, where men go to seek gold', and here a languid female figure indicates to her vigorous mining-companion where he is to dig. The poses of these figures seem irresistibly classical, reminding us that the artists' minds contained much baggage from Greece and Rome, as well as from the Middle Ages. The lower part of the map also contains very well observed outlines of the coasts of the Caribbean islands and of north-eastern South America; it is a remarkable fusion of two modes of perceiving the new-found lands.

A similar fusion may be found on many of the maps from Dieppe. The most spectacular assembly of them is that found in the so-called 'Vallard Atlas', now at the Huntington Library.[41] Created in 1547, this atlas contains fifteen maps showing different parts of the world; all are oriented southwards, as was common with the work of the Dieppe School. Plate III shows the map of the mouth of the Saint Lawrence River, marked 'Rio do Canada' in the middle of the estuary. In the foreground we see the party led there by the

Sieur de Roberval in 1542; the clothing both of French women and of men is particularly well observed. The men carry halberds and arquebusses, and this group is watched at a distance by skin-clad Indians; in the background a palisaded fort is under construction, and a pair of bears completes the picture. This kind of imagery is clearly neither pure art nor pure cartography, but a cunning blend of the two, calculated to convey the essence of a strange land.

The best studied of the Dieppe atlases is probably the one compiled about 1540 by Jean Rotz, presented to Henry VIII of England, and now preserved at the British Library.[42] The Rotz maps cover virtually the whole world, showing for each area not only the outlines of the coasts and the main ports, but also the main activities of the inhabitants. In North America, we thus see Indians, rather unconvincingly shown resembling ancient Greeks, and what is probably the first European representation of a tepee, the characteristic hut of many Plains Indians. In southeast Asia, we have well-observed houses on stilts, and local rulers riding in state on canopied litters. In South America, we see the Tupinamba villages, with their palisades and longhouses, and the gathering of log-wood for export to France. A scale of latitude borders this scene, and outside it is a charming floral border, of the type found in medieval French miniatures. In short, the work of Rotz is not only a marvellous combination of the two ways of

'seeing' but also reminds us constantly of the medieval roots of this new vision.

Jean Rotz was for a time in the service of Henry VIII, the first of the English monarchs to take a great interest in maps (see Chapter 3). There was a good deal of cartographic actvity at his court, and its greatest artist, Hans Holbein (1497–1543), seems to have been peripherally associated with cartography, making some contribution to the world map published at Basel in 1532,[43] and painting maps for the king's pageants.[44] Holbein demonstrated his awareness of the new significance of cartography in his painting of 1533 generally known as 'The Ambassadors'. On the left is Jean de Dinteville, French representative in London, and on the right Georges de Selve, visiting him from Paris; they were heavily involved with problematic negotiations concerning Henry's marriage, and with French policy towards the emerging Protestants in France. Between them, on various shelves, lies a great variety of geometrical instruments and a pair of globes: presumably Holbein meant these to stand for the complicated geopolitical problems that the two statesmen were trying to unravel. The painting shows Holbein's keen awareness of the importance of maps in the new European order. He would have been able to learn about the various instruments from court figures like the mathematician Nikolaus Kratzer (1487–1550), whom he also painted.[45]

Plate I The Limbourg brothers, View of Mont Saint-Michel from the *Très riches heures*. When the Duc de Berry leafed over his *Très riches heures*, and came to this folio devoted to Saint Michael, he did not see simply a generic version of the saint's activities, as was often the case in Italian painting of the time, but could locate Saint Michael above the monastery that bore (and bears) his name, on his tide-girt crag off the coast of Normandy.

Plate II Albrecht Dürer, Watercolour view of the Trent valley. This watercolour, unhappily lost during the Second World War, is hard to appreciate unless we understand how it represents a radical change in the interests of Albrecht Dürer, away from the religious and courtly paintings and woodcuts of his early years, towards the landscape-delineations, eventually based on precise mensuration, of his later ones.

Plate III Anon., Detail from the map of North America, the 'Vallard' atlas, 1547. The maps of the Dieppe School contain the most remarkable combination of cartography and iconography, and this is a fine example of that mixture. In the foreground is a well-observed group of sixteenth-century French people, standing on the north side of the Saint-Lawrence River, whose course and estuary are shown in the background, which includes the coastline stretching down to Florida at the top right.

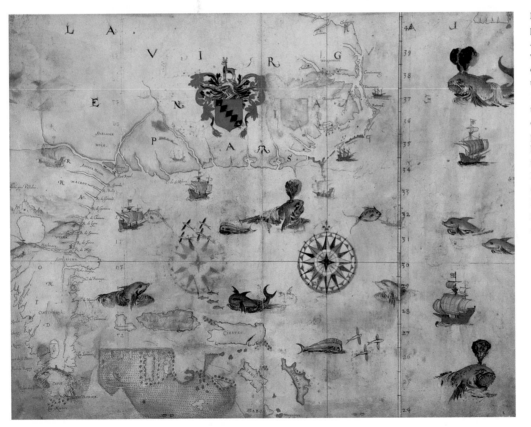

Plate IV John White, Map of part of the east coast of North America, 1585. John White was the English equivalent of Jacques Le Moyne in that, taken to the New World in 1585 on an English expedition as illustrator, he turned out to be not only an excellent portrayer of the local Indians, but also an accomplished cartographer, as this map shows. It stretches from Florida (lower left) to the Outer Banks, showing the coastline, reefs, and islands in some detail.

Henry's court, in whose circles Holbein moved from 1526 to 1528, and again from 1532 to 1543, was full of map-conscious individuals like Kratzer, Sir Thomas Elyot (see Chapters 1 and 3), the lawyer John Rastell (d. 1536), and the cartographer George Lily. The latter was the son of one of Thomas More's closest friends, and it is possible that the maps in the Basel, 1518 edition of More's *Utopia* (first edition, 1516) were the work of Holbein's brother Ambrosius.[46] As we read about the circles of acquaintance in these early modern courts, or in great cities like Antwerp and Nürnberg (see above), Rome and Venice, we are bound to reflect upon the smallness and intimacy of the sixteenth-century learned world, which often seems like a group of like-minded friends sharing the excitement of the heady rediscovery of classical antiquity. In later centuries, this sense of intimacy would fade, replaced to some degree by learned academies and journals. The frequent informal contacts, which must have encouraged interchange between 'artists' and 'mapmakers', blurring the line between them, would also have been lost.

We have so far been considering mostly established artists who

Fig. 19. Paul Pfinzing, Study for a staircase from his 'Studies in Perspective' c.1590. Pfinzing has long been known to historians of cartography as composer of local Nürnberg maps and a substantial survey-manual (see Fig. 71). But a hitherto unknown collection of 'Studies in Perspective' preserved at Harvard University shows that he was also interested in questions of artistic representation, as in this careful drawing delineating a staircase.

also drew maps. There is also one sixteenth-century cartographer who, rather surprisingly, turns out to have been interested in problems of perspective. This is Paul Pfinzing (1554–99), celebrated not only for his many maps of the Nürnberg region, but also for his survey-manual known as the *Methodus geometrica* (Nürnberg, 1598).[47] His biographer knows nothing of it, but Pfinzing was the author of extensive 'Studies in Perspective', now preserved at Harvard's Houghton Library (MS typ 117H). This large notebook contains a considerable number of drawings of squares, cubes, and so forth, as well as some more complicated sketches. Figure 19 shows a drawing of a spiral staircase from Pfinzing's notebook: clearly he was interested in advanced problems of perspective and shading (note his distinctive if diminutive signature at the foot of the staircase).

Two curious instances of artists turning cartographer come from the early European settlement of the east coast of the United States.[48] When the French decided to establish a colony on the Saint John's River (in Florida) in 1564, they recruited Jacques Le Moyne, Sieur de Morgues. Until then he had been, as Quinn puts it, 'trained to paint flowers and fruit in the manner of traditional miniaturists', but on the expedition 'he had perforce to become a cartographer and found himself making sketches of river entries and eventually compiling a general map of the areas the French

reached'. This map was eventually printed by Theodor de Bry in *America*, part I (1591) (Fig. 20), together with a dozen or so of the sketches of smaller areas. The manuscript original of the map has not survived, but from the printed copy it is clear that Le Moyne was quite capable of offering a novel and reasonably accurate delineation of a part of the coast that until then had not been well known to Europeans.[49]

Much the same could be said of John White, who as a journeyman painter accompanied Martin Frobisher on the voyage to Baffin Island in 1577. There he made excellent sketches of Eskimos,[50] which is no doubt why he was then assigned to Sir Walter Raleigh's expedition to Virginia in 1585. Here he collaborated with Thomas Harriott upon a quite extensive mapping programme, from which several manuscript maps and sketches survive (Plate IV). The area round the Outer Banks, which White knew personally, is best shown, but the delineation of Florida and the islands is also passable. Like Le Moyne, White seems to have been able to switch quite

Fig. 20. Jacques Le Moyne, Map of the Florida region, *c.*1565, from Theodor de Bry, *America* (Frankfurt, 1591). Jacques Le Moyne had been known for his delicate drawings of plants and fruits when he was recruited for a French expedition to Florida in 1564. Once there, he produced not only remarkable images of the country and of the native people, but also this detailed map of the French and Spanish settlements in the area; his imaging covered both drawings and maps.

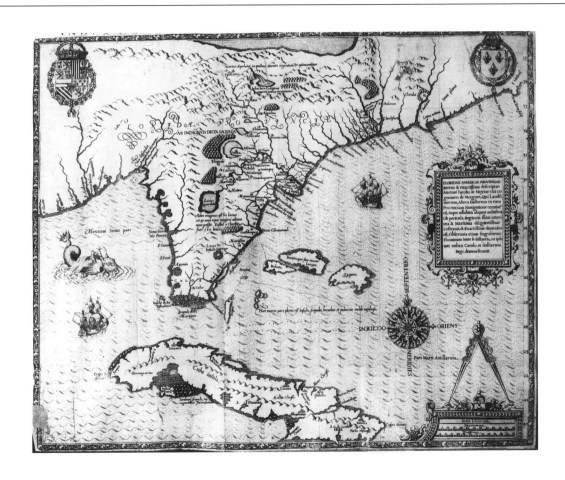

easily from one mode of representation to the other: as Svetlana Alpers puts it, mapping was still 'a casually acquired skill'.[51] We do not know much about White's later life, but he does not seem to have drawn any more maps; as for Le Moyne, having escaped the murderous Spanish attack upon the French settlement, he went back to his exquisite studies of plants and insects.

During the sixteenth century, then, many painters could turn their hands to mapmaking, and many cartographers were also painters. Some links between the two activities may still be found in the seventeenth century, but as time went by they became fewer. In the early part of the century, Jacques Callot (1592–1635) may be taken as a representative of the older tradition.[52] Famous for his etchings of such themes as saints and sinners, the miseries of war, and scenes in town and countryside, he also produced three huge engraving of sieges, covering Breda (1627–8), La Rochelle (1631), and the Île de Ré (1631). These engravings are remarkable both in their mastery of the general scene and in their detail and seem to respond to a particular sensibility of the time. Figure 21 shows a detail from the engraving of the siege of Breda: the Spanish general Ambrosio Spinola is in the foreground, with the Infanta Isabella (both on horseback). Into the background stretch the well-observed units and lines of communication of the Spanish army. Images like this were remarkably accurate, in that approximate orders of battle may often be recon-

structed from them; they were also impressive works of art, often measuring as much as ten feet on their longest sides.

The only other seventeenth-century figures who seem to possess the remarkable range of the sixteenth-century artist-cartographers are the four sons of the Amsterdam painter David Vingboons (1576–1632).[53] All mapmakers, they all also pursued adjacent careers. The most interesting from our point of view was Johannes (1616/17–70), who supplied many of the maps and views for the atlases of the Dutch East and West India Companies (Fig. 47).[54] These marvellous volumes are rather like the great compendium of city-plans published by Georg Braun and Franz Hogenberg between 1572 and 1617, in that each page seems to attack the problem of representation from a different angle. Sometimes the maps are purely planimetric, but often they are oblique bird's-eye views, sometimes covering huge areas of territory. The latter have a strongly painterly quality, reminding us of the origins of much mapmaking. The great Dutch printed atlases of the seventeenth century

Fig. 21. Jacques Callot, Detail from the *Siege of Breda*, *c.*1628. Jacques Callot was famous in early seventeenth-century France not only for his striking images of the horrors of war, but also for his huge engravings of siege-scenes which combined artistic and cartographic elements. Here we witness the siege of Breda in 1628, with fashionable spectators in the foreground, and in the background the fortified city and its attackers' circumvallation.

were also remarkable for their ornamental use of art, in which the figures were less conventionalized than once was thought.[55]

In European art of the late sixteenth and seventeenth centuries, the pervading presence of cartography is often felt. When El Greco came to delineate Toledo, he included with his astonishing view of the city a largish map, held out by a ruffed figure (Plate V).[56] It is as if the artist wanted to remind us that this was another possible way of seeing the city, the different modes having not yet become quite separate. The work of Jan Vermeer (1632–75) also makes much use of maps as decorative and perhaps as symbolic elements.[57] Diego Velásquez (1599–1660) included maps in some of his work, notably in *The Siege of Breda*.[58] For the same siege, Pieter Snayers painted his *Landscape with horsemen at the Siege of Breda*, now at the Prado Museum in Madrid. Maps, then, often found a place in paintings at this time. But that was not to say that the painters were in any sense cartographers; it was merely that cartography had so penetrated the mindset of people in some regions, particularly the Netherlands, that maps were naturally used in the normal form of representation.

In fact, it is hard to imagine any leading painter of the late seventeenth or eighteenth century having the old easy familiarity with mapmaking. We can hardly conceive of Rembrandt or Rubens compiling maps on the side, still less of Watteau or Gainsborough doing so. The learned world was much larger, and the days were gone when a city like Nürnberg could bring together painters and mapmakers with astronomers and mathematicians, all interested in new ways of delineating 'the real'. As a symbol of this change, truly an example of 'thick symbolism', we could cite the fascinating observation of Jean Boutier,[59] that in the second half of the seventeenth century the Parisian mapsellers migrated from the Quartier Saint-Jacques, where for many years they had shared stalls with merchants of paintings, and took up new quarters in the area frequented by the salesmen of scientific instruments. This was a change rich with meaning, symbolizing the divorce of cartography from art, and the end of an association that went back to the early fifteenth century, and had been of great importance in the development of mapmaking.[60]

Cartography among the ruling European elites,
1450–1650

THE ruling elites of early modern Europe had mostly chosen themselves through heredity, and exercised power in a very personal way, without the intervention of what would eventually be called 'bureaucracies', still less that of elected officials. Their influence on the way in which affairs were conducted was therefore very great, and this is one reason why it is important to know when they began to see how maps could be used to govern more effectively. Of course, it is not easy to discern the attitudes towards maps of fifteenth- and sixteenth-century rulers. Ideally, we look to direct testimony about their tastes, such as exists for the Emperor Charles V (ruled 1519–58). Failing this, it is sometimes useful to observe the nature of the learned circles in which they moved: the Emperor Maximilian I (ruled 1493–1519), for instance, was constantly surrounded by people who composed and used maps. Almost all the rulers had libraries, and here the purchase of atlases and other cartographic items, as well as some instruments, may indicate an interest in mapping. Finally, we may obtain some idea of rulers' tendencies by considering the nature of their patronage, whether this involved map-galleries, urban surveys, or large-scale maps of their territories.

THE PAPACY

The rulers of the principalities of Italy do not seem to have been as precocious in map use as was once thought;[1] still, it is among them that the earliest stirrings of map-consciousness are to be found. When Eugenius IV (1431–47) had re-established the papacy at Rome, after the exile in Avignon, his successor Nicholas V (1447–55) was able fully to embrace the ideas of the Renaissance. Thus in his time the Vatican library was greatly expanded, and acquired a copy of Ptolemy's *Geography*.[2] The Apostolic secretary, Poggio Bracciolini, was encouraged to hunt down manuscripts for this library, which also employed many copyists. Nicholas was the enthusiastic patron of humanists like Leon Battista Alberti, one of the earliest advocates of a new type of city mapping, as we have noted in Chapter 1; he also encouraged Guarino of Verona (1374–1460), an early Hellenist who translated the *Geography* of Strabo.[3]

The papacy of Pius II (1458–64) was also remarkable for the patronage of humanists, for its protection of ancient monuments, and for the collection of antiquities.[4] This pope commissioned *mappæmundi* for the cathedral of his native town, Pienza, and also for his city palace, the Palazzo Venezia in Rome.[5] Described as 'an excellent geographer', he was much struck by reading the *Geography* of Ptolemy, 'and wrote a lengthy commentary on it, stressing particularly the importance of [the mathematical network of figures of latitude and longitude]'. His writings were widely read in the sixteenth century, even in Protestant lands, and his complete works were published in Zürich in 1551 and again in 1571.[6] During the rest of the century, other popes continued to patronize human-

ists and to collect ancient manuscripts: in the time of Sixtus IV (1471–84), for instance, three copies of the *Geography* entered the Vatican library,[7] while in the late 1480s Innocent VIII (1484–92) caused the Villa Belvedere at the Vatican to be decorated with views of the main cities in Italy.[8]

Early in the sixteenth century, the papacy of Julius II (1503–13) was particularly remarkable for its patronage of artists and architects like Bramante, Michelangelo, and Raphael, and during this pontificate a very precocious series of painted wall-maps was begun at the Vatican in the long gallery known as the Loggia del Cosmografia. Work on it continued under the pontificates of Pius IV (1559–65), Gregory XIII (1572–85), and Sixtus V (1585–90).[9] Gregory XIII seems to have been particularly interested in cartography, as part of his general concern for the natural sciences. In 1580 he called to Rome Ignazio Danti (1536–86), professor of mathematics at Bologna since 1576. Danti came to advise on the reform of the calendar, accomplished in 1582 (the so-called 'Gregorian calendar' used today); he stayed to work on a new Galleria Geografica, or gallery of wall-painted maps. This was at first to be a 'true representation of the papal states', but was eventually enlarged to include the whole of Italy.[10] This gallery testified to Gregory's wide-ranging scientific curiosity, which extended as well to the construction of an astronomical observatory, the 'tower of the winds'. This observatory allowed celestial observations that were of importance to terrestrial cartography.

THE VENETIAN REPUBLIC

Venice was another part of Italy in which rulers early saw the potential of maps. Denis Cosgrove has argued convincingly that 'maps held a place in the Venetian patrician culture close to the heart of a number of its central concerns', including not only maps of marine defences, and charts of trading regions, but also maps of *Terraferma* (the mainland possessions of the Republic) upon which items of military interest were shown.[11] As early as 1460, the Venetian Council of Ten commissioned maps of the territories around Padua, Brescia, and Verona.[12] In the first half of the sixteenth century, maps were generated by such specialized Venetian bodies as the Rural Land Office and the Office of Border Commissioners;[13] the latter half of the century was chiefly remarkable for the work of Cristoforo Sorte (*c.*1510–*c.*1590) and Giacomo Gastaldi (*c.*1500–*c.*1565). Both had originally worked as hydraulic engineers, concerned with the vast network of canals that regulated life in *Terraferma*. In the 1580s, Sorte was commissioned by the Council of Ten to make a set of maps of *Terraferma* and the rest of the empire for the Sala del Senato in the ducal palace; Gastaldi published many engraved maps, some at a relatively large scale.[14]

All in all, Venice provides an interesting example of the precocious use of maps; perhaps, as Cosgrove speculates, this may have been the result of its early and continuing contacts with Byzantium.[15]

THE KINGDOM OF NAPLES

The other part of Italy that was in frequent contact with the Byzantine and the Muslim worlds was the kingdom of Naples. During the fifteenth century, its rulers were also kings of Aragón, thus controlling two of the main areas of portolan chart production (see Introduction). They were heirs to a long tradition of learning, which they maintained during the fifteenth century: for instance, Alfonso of Aragón (ruled 1416–58) greatly expanded the library at Naples, in 1454 acquiring a copy of Ptolemy's *Geography*.[16] Late in the sixteenth century, the kingdom was intensively mapped by Mario Cartaro (1540–1614), official cartographer from 1583 to 1594.[17] Cartaro produced a remarkable image of the kingdom, consisting of a general map, accompanied by twelve subsidiary maps, showing each province in detail. Figure 22 shows his map of the province of 'Terra d'Otranto'. This map has scale and orientation and is tied to the graticule of latitude and longitude; in some cases it mentions the number of 'hearths' in a town, and so could be the basis for valuation for taxation purposes. The maps remained in manuscript, and have only recently been reproduced in facsimile.[18]

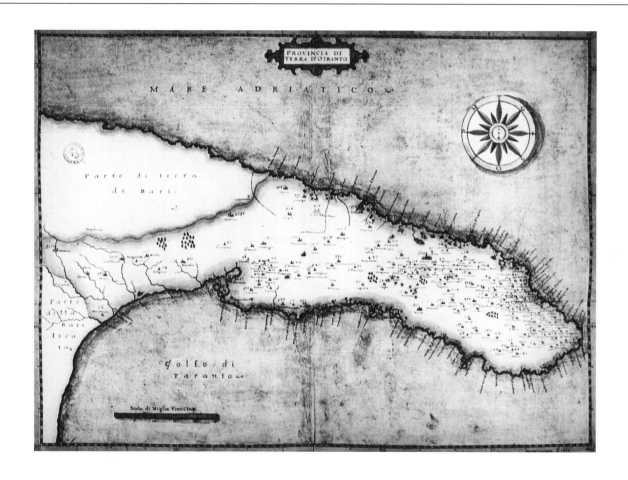

THE DUCHY OF FLORENCE

In Florence, leading thinkers showed an interest in maps from the beginning of the sixteenth century onwards. Grand Duke Ferdinand I of Tuscany (1544–1604) was particularly interested in cartography. He filled one room of his Uffizi Palace with maps and scientific instruments, and decorated another room with frescoes by Giulio Perigi (1540–1635) of cherubs holding 'astrolabes, compasses and other instruments'.[19] It must have been an acquaintance with this milieu that made Catherine de Medici, wife of Henri II of France, so active in French cartography (see below). Towards the middle of the seventeenth century, it was the duke of Tuscany who encouraged Sir Robert Dudley (1573–1649) to come to Florence from war-torn England. In the Italian city, Dudley created the extraordinary six volumes of sea-charts comprising the *Arcano del mare* (Florence 1646–7); the Tuscan court long remained a centre for scientific patronage.

Fig. 22. Mario Cartaro, Map of the province of Otranto, c.1590. This manuscript map is one of twelve such subsidiary maps showing the kingdom of Naples. The area may be found on the initial general, or master map, though it is not there indicated by a frame, as on a key-map. These detailed maps give the number of 'hearths' in a town, and so could be used to visualize the demographic structure of the kingdom.

There was, of course, no concept of a unified cartography of Italy. When, around 1600, Giovanni Antonio Magini (1555–1617) was collecting maps for the atlas *Italia*, eventually published in 1617, he had to 'ask, and re-ask of all the princes and heads of state in Italy, and their engineers, for the necessary designs'.[20] In *Italia*, the Cartaro maps stand out for their accuracy and detail; few of the other principalities had anything to rival them. On the other hand, as Marino has shown,[21] many detailed maps were being commissioned by administrative bodies during the 1560s and 1570s, not only in Venice but also in centres like Milan and Florence. Marino ascribes this greatly increased volume of state cartography to the economic upturn which followed the end of the wars in 1559, allowing the newly strong bureaucracies to tap into a longstanding tradition of large-scale mapping.

THE KINGDOM OF PORTUGAL AND THE DUCHY OF BURGUNDY

Outside Italy, the fifteenth-century rulers most interested in cartography were probably the kings of Portugal, who keenly followed the charting of their seamen's progress down the west coast of Africa (see Chapter 4). Philip the Good, Duke of Burgundy (ruled 1419–67) also presided over a court acquainted with the newest developments in art. Jan Van Eyck, whose combination of iconographic and cartographic skill we have considered in Chapter 2, was his *valet de chambre* and secret agent. When Jean Germain, bishop of Chalon-sur-Saône (1400–60), wished to make a special gift to the Duke, he composed a *mappemonde spirituelle* (or 'spiritual world-map') setting out the places made famous by incidents in the life of Christ, the Virgin, and the Apostles.[22] This gift is illustrated in a fine illumination (Plate VII), and it is unimaginable that Jean Germain would have thought of such a gift had Philip the Good not been well acquainted with the conventional notion of a *mappa-mundi*. His successor as duke, Charles the Rash (ruled 1467–77), came to a violent end on the battlefield of Nancy, but his daughter Mary of Burgundy married Maximilian of Austria, who was Holy Roman Emperor between 1493 and 1519, and extraordinarily alert to the possibilities of cartography.

THE HOLY ROMAN EMPIRE

Well aware of the rising tide of humanism in Italy, Maximilian was keenly resolved to play the role of the literate prince. His name is associated with four major publications: the *Geheimes Jagdbuch*, which is a treatise on hunting; the *Teuerdank*, an allegorical poem about his courtship of his wife Mary; the *Weisskunig*, describing his early upbringing and life; and the *Zeugbücher*, which describe the contents of his arsenals.[23] The texts of these works may sometimes

seem uninspired, but they are marvellously illustrated by craftsmen whom Maximilian had carefully chosen. Another fine example of his patronage of imagery is *The triumph of the Emperor Maximilian*, for which Hans Burgkmair provided woodcuts of magical delicacy.[24]

Knowing that he was so attuned to the visual arts, we are not surprised by the assertion of the bishop of Chiemsee, writing to the cardinal of Siena in January of 1491, that Maximilian knew the topography of his lands so well that he could jot down an impromptu map of any region.[25] He numbered many artists and some cartographers among his close friends. One of his physicians, for instance, was Konrad Türst (1450–1503), the early cartographer of Switzerland.[26] His librarian in Vienna was Conrad Celtis (1459–1508), famous as the discoverer of the Roman Peutinger Table (Chapter 1). Celtis was a leading humanist and a fervent German nationalist; he lectured on the *Geography* of Ptolemy and 'is believed to be the first person to use globes as a teaching aid'.[27] He was one of a circle of humanists at the University of Vienna, most of whom were interested in geography and in cartography. One of them was Johann Cuspinianus (1473–1529), who served in Hungary and worked on the geography of that region.[28] Another was Jacob Ziegler (1471–*c.*1549), contributor to the *Theatrum orbis terrarum* of Abraham Ortelius in 1570. Perhaps the most celebrated member of this group was Johann Stabius (d. 1522), a mathematician who by order of the emperor had 'painted' a map of Austria, which has not come down to us. From this circle of scholars, which also for a time included Johannes Aventinus (1477–1534) and Georg Tanstetter (1482–1535), Maximilian could thus call upon a variety of cartographic talent unrivalled anywhere else in Europe at that time.

The successor to Maximilian as Holy Roman Emperor was Charles V, whose inheritance brought together Castile and Aragón, the Netherlands, the Habsburg lands in Germany, and extensive holdings in Italy. To each of these areas the new emperor brought the use of maps in government. In the Spanish kingdoms, Ferdinand (ruled 1479–1516) and Isabella (ruled 1479–1504) had greatly encouraged the mapping of overseas expansion (Chapter 4), but they had not initiated any peninsular cartography. Shortly after Charles's accession, in 1517, Fernando Colón (1488–1539), son of Christopher Columbus, began a 'Description of the geography of Spain' that included both written texts and maps.[29] This work went on for six years, and eventually covered almost 7,000 villages in Castile. But it was stopped by order of the government in 1523, perhaps because it came to be associated with the Comuneros revolt of that year.

In the Netherlands, as Kain and Baigent put it, 'mapping … became increasingly important in the sixteenth century under Charles V'.[30] As count of Holland, he was determined to discover the extent of his domain lands, and for this purpose in 1523 appointed a commission under Adriaan Stalpaert. Maps were drawn up by Maarten Corneliszoon from the Rhineland, and eventually 1,300 land parcels were plotted. The villagers were well aware of the purpose of this survey, and went so far as to threaten Stalpaert with death; their suspicions were correct, for once the extent and value of the lands were fully understood, they were taxed at much higher rates.[31]

During the 1530s, Charles V maintained his interest in using maps to administer the Netherlands. In 1533 he commissioned a survey of the north quarter of Holland in order to reassess the incidence of dyke taxes: the survey showed that fresh assessments were needed.[32] In the next year, 1534, Charles turned his attention to the polder authorities, responsible for land reclaimed from the sea. They had been producing maps since the middle of the fifteenth century, but Charles now required that each polder authority 'engage surveyors as regular employees'.[33] He seems to have acted in much the same way in the Milanese, where he instituted a land survey that was completed in 1568, and would not be revised before the eighteenth century.[34]

Charles V, then, made extensive use of maps in civil administration. He was also aware of their military use, as we know from a remarkable passage of the *Mémoires* of Martin Du Bellay concerning the Provence campaign of 1536.[35] The emperor, writes Du Bellay, 'normally had in his hand or before his eyes a map of the Alps and lower Provence, which the marquis of Saluzzo had given him. He studied it so often and so intently, using it to further his designs and his desires, that he began to think that he had the country in his grasp, instead of just the maps.' Charles used not only maps to chart and record his military progress, but also sketches. As Robert Karrow notes, 'Cornelis Anthonisz [author of a famous view of Amsterdam, Fig. 18] accompanied the imperial troops as a topographic artist on at least two expeditions, to Algiers in 1542 and to Thérouanne ten years later.' Unfortunately, none of his sketches seems to survive, though there are engravings of them.[36]

In spite of his many diversions in central Europe, Charles kept abreast of the work being done at the school of navigation in Seville, work more fully described in Chapter 4. Indeed, our main way of knowing about this cartography is from copies of the master map that Charles gave to other European rulers, for the copies once kept at Seville have all perished.[37] In 1525, for instance, he gave the 'Castiglione map' to Baldassare Castiglione (1478–1529), papal nuncio, possibly for presentation to Pope Clement VII. A year later he gave another copy to Cardinal Giovanni Salviati (1490–1553), special papal nuncio in Spain, and in 1529 he presented to Clement VII a magnificent world map by Diogo Ribeiro.[38] He seems to have thought of maps and atlases as particularly appropriate gifts, and in 1542 gave his son Philip the superb atlas by Battista Agnese (1514–64) that is now preserved at the John Carter Brown Library in Providence.[39] We know that his interest in these world maps was more than merely formal, for in May 1541 Cardinal Gasparo Contarini (1453–1542) wrote to Pope Paul III that he had been having long conversations with the emperor, who 'showed remarkable geographical knowledge in speaking of maritime charts'.[40] He also took a close interest in the navigation school, and in particular supported Sebastian Cabot after appointing him as pilot major in 1518. From 1526 to 1530 Cabot was involved in a disastrous South American expedition, and upon his return fell (deservedly, it would seem) into disgrace. But, as Robert Karrow puts it, Cabot 'must have had an extraordinary relationship with Charles V, for in the same year the emperor recalled him from exile, cancelled the sentence, forgave the fines and reinstalled him in the office of pilot major'.[41]

Charles had access to the best cosmographers in his empire, and there are several testimonies to his close relations with them. In 1539, for instance, when the emperor was laid up with gout at Toledo, the cosmographer Alonso de Santa Cruz (1500–72) noted that Charles spent 'most of his days with me, his royal cosmographer, learning about astrology, the earth and theory of the planets, and other things about sea charts and cosmographical globes, from which he derived much amusement and delight'.[42] The next year, Charles was shown a world map recently compiled by the celebrated cartographer Gemma Frisius (1508–58): the emperor pointed out an error on this first version, which was duly corrected.[43] In 1546 Charles was with his court mathematician, Peter Apian (1495–1552), when Ingolstadt was besieged by the Protestants. As the story goes, the emperor calmly discussed mathematics with Apian, while the mathematician showed more concern for the missiles flying around them.[44]. We do not know much about Charles V's library, but he probably collected atlases and maps, and sometimes had them copied. As Liévin Algoet (d. 1547), his court scribe, put it, part of his scribal work consisted in 'composing geographical works and maps, of which [the emperor] is most fond'.[45]

Charles shared these interests with his wife, the Empress Isabel, daughter of Manoel I of Portugal. In 1536 she wrote to the viceroy of Mexico that 'we very much want to have a plan or pictures of the principal cities, ports and coastlines of that land';[46] as we shall see in Chapter 4, such a programme was initiated in the 1570s. In 1555 the emperor abdicated, retiring to Yuste, his remote retreat in the hills of northern Spain. Here, free from the cares of state, he could

indulge his hobbies, and 'maps, clocks and books filled the leisure hours'.[47] This is confirmed by the (relatively scanty) list of possessions taken after his death: they included among the books a 'Tolomeo' (probably the *Geography*), 'maps of Italy, Flanders, Germany and the Indies', and 'three large books of paper, with drawings of trees, flowers, men and other objects from the Indies'.[48]

PHILIP II OF SPAIN

With such a father and mother, it is not surprising that the son, Philip II of Spain, was also convinced of the importance of maps in administering his empire, which now extended over most of Central and South America, as well as over Pacific islands like the Philippines. In the peninsula, Philip seems to have initiated the ambitious project directed in the 1560s by Pedro de Esquivel (d. 1575), professor of mathematics at the University of Alcalá de Henares.[49] Before his death, Esquivel had largely completed this venture, covering the territory of Spain at a scale of about 1 : 430,000, using mathematical instruments in an extensive on-the-ground survey. After his death, the work seems to have been carried on by the royal cosmographers Juan López de Velasco and Joáo Baptista Lavanha (*c*.1550–1625), ending in the compilation of the so-called 'Escorial Atlas'. This atlas, which consists of a key

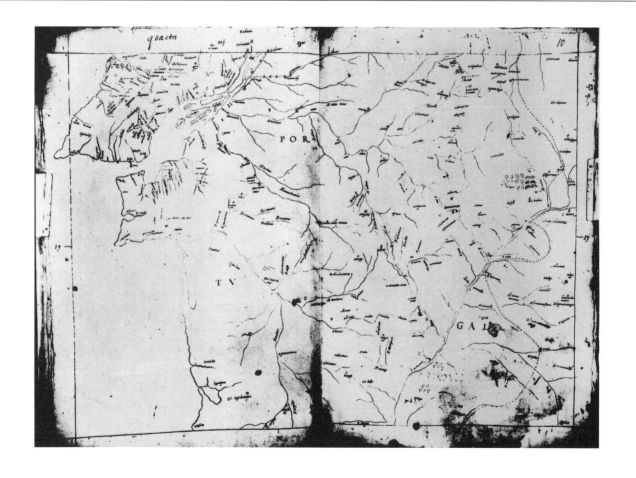

map of the whole peninsula (for maps of Portugal became available after the union of 1580) and twenty sub-maps, gave Philip a better representation of the region than any other European area of comparable size. Figure 23 shows the fourth map of the sequence, and gives much accurate detail of Portuguese rivers and towns. Curiously, the work was abandoned in the 1590s and the atlas was then left in the library of the Escorial.

In 1561 or 1562 Anton van den Wyngærde (d. 1571) arrived in Spain to undertake a remarkable series of views of her cities.[50] He had been recruited by Philip in the Low Countries in 1557, and for about ten years worked in the peninsula, with a commission from the king enjoining the towns to offer him every assistance. Some of his images eventually decorated the walls of Philip's hunting lodge at El Pardo, outside Madrid, and others could be found on the walls of the Madrid Alcázar. But the great body of his work was sent to the Low Countries after his death in 1571, presumably for publication. In fact, these plans for publication fell through, and the draw-

Fig. 23. Pedro de Esquivel, Map from the Escorial Atlas, *c.*1580. This map comes from a set of twenty maps covering the whole Iberian peninsula. They are keyed in to a first, general map, which sets out these maps on the peninsula, numbering them from 1 to 20. This is map 4 ('quarta', top left) and shows the Atlantic coast near Lisbon, with a detailed image of its hinterland. All the subsidiary maps conform to the latitude and longitude figures on the main map; this is very systematic, mathematically based work.

ings were eventually dispersed to collections in Vienna, London, and Oxford, entering an obscurity from which they have only recently been rescued.[51]

The counterpart in the Low Countries to van Wyngærde's work in the peninsula was the vast project commissioned from Jacob van Deventer (d. 1575) in 1558 or 1559.[52] From then until 1572, van Deventer worked on his delineation of cities and towns of the region, eventually producing some 320 maps, of which 228 have survived (Fig. 24).[53] These beautiful, delicate, and precise drawings allowed the king to obtain a remarkably extensive and accurate idea of the towns owing him allegiance (some only for a time) in the Low Countries. They were not published as a group in the sixteenth century, but some, as we shall see in Chapter 6, found their way into volumes 3 and 4 of the *Civitates orbis terrarum* of Georg Braun and Franz Hogenberg (6 vols, Cologne, 1572–1618).

The other major project commissioned by Philip in the Low Countries was the general map undertaken by Christian Sgrooten (*c.*1532–1608), who was appointed royal geographer in 1558.[53] Ten years later he began his great work, handing it over in 1573, not quite finished; this manuscript is now at the Bibliothèque Royale in Brussels. He seems to have continued to work after that, for by 1590 he was writing to Philip about 'certain new maps' in an atlas that considerably expanded the scope of the work undertaken in

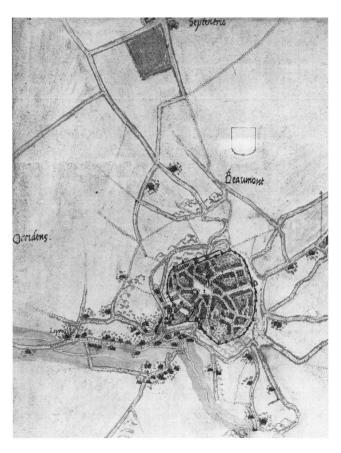

Fig. 24. Jacob van Deventer, Plan of the town of Beaumont, *c.*1560. This little town in what is now south-western Belgium has been shown with great precision, probably as a result of pacing with a compass. The centre of Beaumont, in the heart of the area that remained loyal to the Habsburgs, has changed little to the present day. This image was eventually used in the great printed collection of Braun and Hogenberg (Fig. 78).

1568–72. Philip ordered that Sgrooten be paid, but forbade publication of the atlas, which is now at the Biblioteca Nacional in Madrid.

In all the parts of his European empire, then, Philip personally encouraged the production of maps, and it was the same for his overseas possessions (Chapter 4). All this cartographic activity generated a mass of maps, which from 1565 onwards were often kept in the library of the newly constructed palace of El Escorial, in the foothills outside Madrid. Here Philip's librarian, Benito Arias Montanus (1537–98), collected geographical books from all over Europe, as well as maps and mathematical instruments. Many other rooms in the Escorial also contained maps: in 1592, for instance, the throne room was hung with more than seventy of them.[54] It is striking that very little of this vast cartographic effort ever appeared in print. The later atlas of Sgrooten was, as we have seen, deliberately suppressed, but there seems to have been no such attempt to suppress the work of van Wyngærde or of the compilers of the Escorial Atlas. Indeed, the van Wyngærde drawings were deliberately sent to the Netherlands for publication, and this reminds us how backward Spanish printing was during this century. It was impossible in the peninsula to find the large presses capable of taking huge map-plates, such as could be found in Germany, in the Netherlands, and in Italy. Perhaps this weakness of the native technology explains in some degree the failure of these mapping schemes to reach a wide public.

In thinking about the mindsets of Maximilian, his son Charles, and grandson Philip, we are bound to be struck by their intensely visual nature. As well as encouraging a large number of cartographers, Maximilian also patronized a very wide range of engravers and painters, including great masters like Albrecht Dürer. Charles, too, was famous for the excellence of his taste in the visual arts, and Philip was a faithful patron of painters like El Greco. It is tempting to believe that these Habsburgs encapsulated, as it were, the new way of 'seeing' that we tried to set out in Chapter 2. At all events, it is sure that their patronage over the course of the sixteenth century did much to encourage the work of cartographers in their lands.

THE KINGDOM OF FRANCE

The Habsburgs' great enemy was the Valois dynasty of France, represented at the beginning of the century by Louis XII (ruled 1498–1515). He did acquire a manuscript copy of Ptolemy's *Geography* for the royal library, but it was his successor, Francis I (ruled 1515–47), who first showed a serious interest in maps.[55] Francis was anxious to be seen as patron of the new learning coming out of Italy, and one of its leading practitioners was Oronce Fine (1494–1555), mathematician, engineer, and cartographer. The king supported Fine throughout his career, during which he seems for some time to have been incarcerated. After his release, he was in 1531 appointed to the Chair of Mathematics at the newly instituted Collège de France. Fine was remarkable for the extent of his publications, including many maps, though some scholars take him to be more of a popularizer than an original thinker.[56]

The two areas in which Francis saw the practical usefulness of maps were in fortification, more fully investigated in Chapter 5, and in overseas expansion, considered in Chapter 4. He hired many Italian engineers to work on the north-eastern frontier during the 1530s and 1540s, and we may be sure that their precise and scaled maps influenced their French counterparts. He also encouraged French expansion into what became Canada, no doubt becoming conversant with the maps and charts produced by the Dieppe School. In 1541, for instance, before Jacques Cartier's third voyage to Canada, the king held a planning session attended by a Portuguese pilot, Joao Lagarto. The pilot brought with him two marine charts and an astrolabe, reporting afterwards that the king discussed the project 'with understanding and intelligence'. The following evening the king showed Lagarto two charts of his own, which the pilot described as 'well painted and illuminated, but not very accurate': this is a fair description of much of the work of the Dieppe School (Chapter 4).

Francis was succeeded by Henri II (ruled 1547–59), who continued to use maps in fortifications and in planning overseas ventures. He also on at least one occasion used them in the field, for Marshal Vieilleville describes how in 1552, campaigning in the Rhône valley, he showed Henri a map of the area, 'which His Majesty carefully examined, although it was very late', and agreed with the marshal's assessment of the situation, later observing that a military commander should never march without a map. Henri also began the practice of trying to control the growth of Paris by mapping its unregulated growth outside the walls (in the 'faubourgs', or 'false towns'). The town council had become worried about this problem in 1550, and so the king ordered its members to meet with Girolamo Bellarmato (1493–1555), an Italian engineer then working at Le Havre, so that Bellarmato could first sketch the areas newly occupied and then, in collaboration with the council, make a map of what expansion would be allowed. It is not clear from the records if this procedure was actually followed, but it is plain that the king well understood how useful mapping could be for the problem.[57]

Henri died accidentally in a tournament in 1559, and the government fell into the hands of his widow, Catherine de Medici (1519–89) and her sons, Francis II (ruled 1559–60), Charles IX (ruled 1560–74), and Henri III (ruled 1574–89). Catherine had grown up in Florence, and was familiar with the way maps were being used there. She brought with her Florentines like Gabriello Symeone (1509–75): he was primarily an astrologer, but also made an early map of the province of Auvergne. Another member of her entourage was Pierre Hamon (d. 1569), calligrapher, typographer, and writing-master to the *dauphin*; Hamon drew for Catherine a superb map of France, now in the Pierpont Morgan Library of New York.[58]

Henri II had in 1552 named as *géographe du roi* a certain Nicholas de Nicolay (1517–83), a cartographer who had also been a great traveller and secret agent. About 1560, Catherine commissioned Nicolay to 'draw up and set out in volumes the maps and geographical descriptions of all the provinces in this kingdom'. Local officials were enjoined to offer him every help in this project, allowing him, for instance, access to *clochers*, or bell-towers. Nicolay eventually completed maps for Berry (1567), Bourbonnais (1569), and Lyonnais (1573), a small part of his total task. Figure 25 shows his map of Berry; it provides some detail, but entirely lacks any kind of mathematical reference. Nicolay did not get very far with his task, but it was probably impossible for a single person to

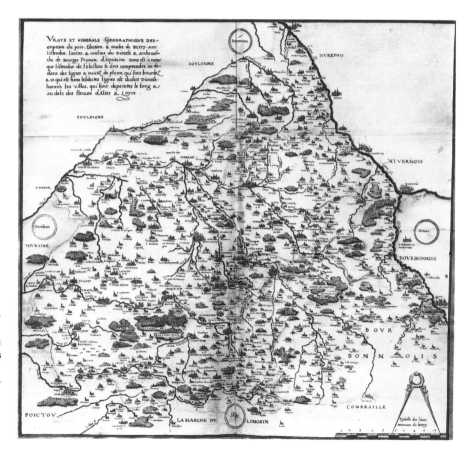

Fig. 25. Nicolas de Nicolay, Map of the Duchy of Berry, 1567. Nicolas de Nicolay was commissioned about 1560 by Catherine de Medici to compile an atlas of France. He began in the area that he knew best, in the centre, and in six years compiled three maps, of which this is one. Nicolay worked by provinces, and gave no indication of latitude and longitude; his work is a great deal less sophisticated mathematically than that of Esquivel (Fig. 23).

cover as vast an area as the whole of France, particularly when it was wracked by civil war. It is significant, though, that Catherine felt the need to start such a project.

She died in 1589, and her son Henri III was assassinated in the same year, being succeeded by Henri IV (ruled 1589–1610). This king was, as the Père François de Dainville put it, 'a man who thought everything out in images'. He had come to the throne after twenty years or so of campaigning, and was himself capable of making a field-sketch for a proposed fort. Five years after his accession, and no doubt in response to his known taste for maps, a collection of maps of France was published by Maurice Bouguereau of Tours. This *Théâtre François*, as it was called, was the first atlas to gather together maps of the French provinces, though the coverage was far from complete, and the scale and accuracy very variable.[59]

During Henri's reign a great deal of mapping was undertaken by the royal engineers and lodgings-masters, whose work is analysed in Chapter 5; the king was also a great patron of Samuel de Champlain (1567–1635), who would soon be compiling his astonishing maps of north-eastern America (Chapter 4). At Paris, Henri powerfully encouraged the establishment of a scientific milieu in which cartography and similar skills could flourish. At the newly built section of the Louvre palace he set aside a whole gallery (the basement of the *grande gallerie*) where painters, engravers, gun-

smiths, and other craftsmen could work: here might be found experts like Philippe Danfrie, engraver and inventor of scientific instruments like the *graphomètre*, a new device for surveying.

Henri also wished to set up at the Louvre a geographical and hydrographical museum, in which there would have been six huge maps showing France, the continents, and the oceans. This echo of the great Italian geographical galleries also had a counterpart at the palace of Fontainebleau, where one gallery was given over to views of the royal *châteaux*; Henri's chief minister, the Duc de Sully (1559–1641), also had one room of his house at Villebon decorated in this way. At the newly built Place Royale (now the Place des Vosges), Henri and Sully provided town houses for a variety of technicians and administrators. They included the engineer-cartographer Claude de Chastillon (d. 1616) and the lodgings-master Pierre Fougeu, both of whom drew many maps. Henri only had twelve years in which to pursue his ambitious projects, but it is clear both that mapping lay at the heart of his preoccupations, and that he and Sully laid the foundations for state cartography in France.

THE KINGDOM OF ENGLAND

Across the Channel, as we have seen, the English had shown early signs of using maps in Crown administrative affairs (see the

Introduction). But by the end of the fifteenth century, as we know from the exhaustive study of Peter Barber,[60] this early promise had not endured: indeed, as Barber puts it, 'king and country were rather backward by German and Italian standards in respect of the new geography and cartography in the early sixteenth century'. Henry VIII (ruled 1509–47) did not for a decade or so after his accession show any sign of using maps more effectively than his father had done. But the 1520s saw the coming to power of royal advisers who were powerfully influenced by the ideas that they found in their reading of the classical authors of Greece and Rome, and they greatly influenced the king. Sir Thomas Elyot was only the most prominent of these cartophiles, numerous at court (see Chapter 1). The reign of Edward VI (1547–53) saw an intensification of map use, so that 'by the middle of the century [maps] had become a fully integrated aid in the formulation of policy and an instrument of administration'.[61]

During the reign of Elizabeth I (1558–1603), maps continued to be used for a wide variety of purposes, even though the queen herself was no cartophile. Very few fortifications were now constructed, but the growing impetus towards overseas expansion led eventually to the compiling of maps of the wider world (Chapter 4). Moreover, two of the queen's principal ministers, Francis Walsingham (secretary of state 1573–90) and William Cecil, Lord Burghley (secretary

of state 1558–62 and lord treasurer 1572–98), were great cartographic enthusiasts, using maps in their official work and surrounding themselves with maps in their private lives.[62]

Major cartographic projects were undertaken at home as well as overseas. From 1568 onwards a series of surveyors worked in Ireland, until the English dominion over that unfortunate land was firmly based on extensive geographical knowledge.[63] In England, too, a series of surveys was undertaken, of which the most famous was the one carried out by Christopher Saxton (c.1542–1606). From the early 1570s onwards, using privileges provided by the central government, Saxton traversed the whole country, until in 1579 he could publish an atlas containing maps of all the counties;[64] these maps were then consolidated into his wall-map of 1583, and the county maps continued for many years to form English people's idea of their country. Saxton's work was in some ways rather primitive. His county maps, for instance, were conceived simply to fit the page of the atlas, and were consequently drawn at a variety of scales; they had no indication of latitude or longitude (Fig. 26). Moreover, they showed no roads, and gave sketchy coverage to some counties.

In the 1590s official encouragement was given to John Norden to undertake a fresh survey, but this in the end covered only a few counties.[65] Both Saxton and Norden were also well known as

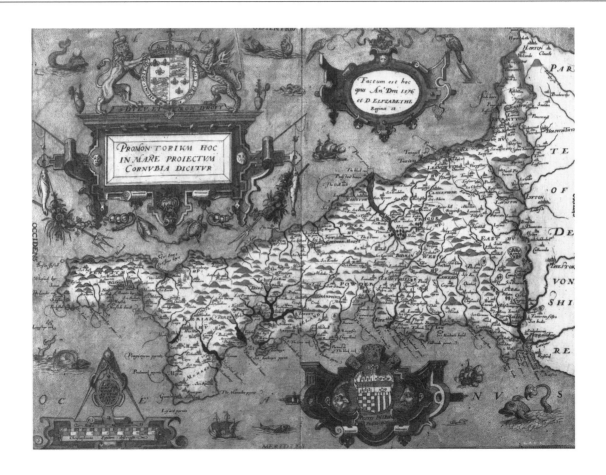

estate surveyors (see Chapter 6), and the estate map as a type continued to flourish during the seventeenth century. But during that time the role of the monarchy was often disputed and somewhat muted. Even after the restoration of Charles II in 1660 there was nothing in England to rival the great encouragement given to cartography by all the French kings, from Henri IV to Louis XIII (ruled 1610–43) and Louis XIV (ruled 1643–1715). The consequence was that English mapping and map publication were generally outstripped by the French during the seventeenth century.

THE KINGDOM OF SWEDEN

The chronology of map-consciousness among the elites was quite different in the Scandinavian countries from that of western Europe. In Sweden, it was only in the early seventeenth century that Karl IX (1550–1611) commissioned a general topographical map from Anders Bure; the country was poor and sparsely inhabited, so that this was in fact a remarkable development. Karl's son was the

Fig. 26. Christopher Saxton, Map of the County of Cornwall, c.1576. Saxton's work was rather like that of Nicolay, in that he chose to work by local units, in this case counties, without reference to any general mathematical scheme. However, England was at peace in the 1570s, and he was able to complete his task remarkably quickly. In spite of their technical weakness, Saxton's county maps were very influential in forming the idea that English people could now have of their county and country.

famous Gustav II Adolf ('Gustavus Adolphus', ruled 1611–32), and in his time Bure's map was completed, and a new general survey, or *Landmateriet*, was initiated in 1628.[66] This survey was very sophisticated in its methods, for surveyors were specially trained, and were instructed to suggest improvements that could be made in agricultural regions. They used plane tables and had a standardized colour scheme for fields, meadows, and so forth. They began work in 1633, and the results are today preserved in a remarkable series of 'geometric landbooks', which provide more abundant information than is available from any other European country.

By 1633 Gustav Adolf was dead, killed at the battle of Lützen the year before, but it was clearly his driving vision that had led to the establishment of the *Landmateriet*. He personally used maps chiefly in war, setting up the corps of military engineers in 1613, but this military mapping became in effect civilian cartography, when engineers like Olaf Hansson were set to surveying the German lands captured by the Swedish army.[67] They also worked in Pomerania, but were hampered by the resistance of the German inhabitants, who correctly perceived that such surveys would be the prelude to more effective government. The *Landmateriet* established by Gustav Adolf survived into the eighteenth century, when it actively collaborated in the widespread enclosures that were part of the new agricultural practices. In historical perspective, it was

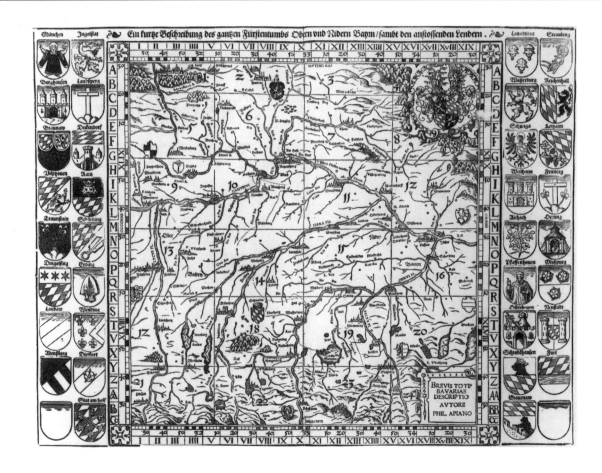

part of the concept of *storgöticism*, or the notion that the original Gothic people were now regaining their rightful heritage; this was a central element in the propaganda of Gustav Adolf. Kain and Baigent summarize Swedish developments in this way: 'When this colonial mapping [i.e. mapping of the conquered territories] is combined with the production at home … the extraordinary achievement of Swedish seventeenth-century cartography can be appreciated; it is without parallel in the Western world.'[68]

In central Europe there is one remarkable example of precocity in map use. Duke Albrecht V of Bavaria (1528–74) in the 1560s commissioned Philip Apian (1531–89) to compile a map of his duchy. This map was published in 1568, and consisted of a key-map, with quadrilaterals numbered from 1 to 24, to form the detailed maps. Figure 27 shows this key-map, with armorial bearings decorating each side, and a detailed graticule of latitude and longitude. The twenty-four individual maps then fit into this graticule, each indicating its coordinates as appropriate. Apian was

Fig. 27. Philip Apian, Key-map to his survey of the Duchy of Bavaria, 1568. This printed key-map of Bavaria, showing the divisions of its 24 subsidiary maps, resembles the manuscript key-map that Esquivel made for the Iberian peninsula. Like Esquivel, Apian was an accomplished mathematician, and so produced a map clearly showing the relationship of Bavaria to the general graticule of the world.

a remarkable mathematician, and this map, even if it covers only a relatively limited area, testifies to his skill. Albrecht also employed as court painter in Munich Hans Mielich (1516–73), celebrated among other achievements for his 1549 view of Ingolstadt.[69]

In general, mapping was not viewed with enthusiasm by nobles in the German-speaking area. We have seen how the inhabitants of Pomerania resisted the Swedish surveyors, and in Brandenburg-Prussia as well the Junkers were hostile towards the rulers' attempts to map their lands. No doubt they too saw that thorough and comprehensive cartographic coverage would help Berlin to extend its power into regions where it was feebly felt. All this would change during the seventeenth century, largely under the influence of war.[70]

CONCLUSION

In summary, then, it is possible quite accurately to discern the stages by which map-consciousness reached the elites of early modern Europe. Like so much else, this development began in Italy, and spread first to Germany, in the time of Maximilian, and then, with a short delay, to the northern 'new monarchs' such as Francis I and Henry VIII. It came late but powerfully to Sweden, and even later to Russia, in the time of Peter the Great (ruled 1696–1725).[71] The general surveys commissioned by monarchs differed greatly in their sophistication. Sometimes, as in the cases of Magini in Italy and Bouguereau in France, the surveys consisted merely of assembling the best existing provincial maps, and then printing them in a uniform atlas. Sometimes the operation was more complex, involving state support of a cartographer who then mapped the country according to the existing provincial divisions: this was the case for the counties of England mapped by Saxton, and for the provinces of France and Naples mapped by Nicolay and Cartaro respectively. Finally, the most complete and complex survey involved the establishment of a key-map, like the ones drawn by Apian in Bavaria and Esquivel in Spain. The subsidiary maps indicated on this key-map were then surveyed, so that there was a complete and mathematically defined map of the whole territory.

All this activity and patronage by the rulers of early modern Europe generated a much higher level of map-consciousness among their peoples. It is hard to imagine the formation of widespread English map-consciousness without the mapping of Saxton, and easy to see how powerfully the mapping of Sweden by Gustav Adolf was bound up with the ideology of *storgöticism*. In an age when the example of quite small elites had an effect much greater than it might have now, the adoption of maps by monarchs and ministers powerfully encouraged their diffusion in society at large.

Mapping in the expansion of Europe,

1400–1700

As we have seen, portolan charts originated in the Mediterranean Sea around the end of the twelfth century. Those from the main Italian centres—Genoa, Venice, and Ancona—generally showed only the Mediterranean and a limited part of western Europe. But the charts from the Catalan centres—Majorca and Barcelona—sometimes went north as far as Scandinavia, and the Catalan atlas of 1375 even covered parts of the Far East.[1] This charting system offered a remarkably accurate outline of coasts, based as it was on both long experience of the routes and frequent compass-observations. However, its great weakness was its lack of any system of location by mathematical coordinates. Clearly, if its system of delineating coastlines could be combined with the worldwide system of latitudes and longitudes provided by the Ptolemaic system, then the Europeans would have a charting system of great potential power.

This combination is just what came about during the fifteenth century, in a series of mostly Venetian world maps dating from the 1440s and 1450s. Four of these were drawn by Giovanni Leardo, and the most famous of them by Fra Mauro (Fig. 28). He came from the Camaldolian monastery on the island of Murano, by Venice, and the account-books from the abbey show that he was in effect directing a cartographic workshop there: buying materials, hiring draughtsmen, and directing their work. He received information from a variety of sources, including Lisbon, and succeeded in producing a *mappamundi* which combines a portolan-chart-style image of the Mediterranean with a Ptolemaic version of the Indian

Fig. 28. Fra Mauro, World map of 1459. As we noted in the Introduction, the portolan chart emerged in the thirteenth century of the Mediterranean Sea, and gave a wonderfully true image of that region. We also noted in Chapter 1 that from the early fifteenth century onwards, manuscript copies of Ptolemy's *Geographia* were circulating in western Europe. It is therefore not surprising that by the mid-fifteenth century maps like this one emerged, combining features from the two previous traditions.

subcontinent, and an early delineation of the slow Portuguese progression round the north-west coast of Africa.[2]

PORTUGAL

It was in the delineation of this Portuguese expansion that the portolan chart style was first tested in a systematic way in the wider world. The Portuguese monarchy expelled the Muslims from the kingdom very early, about 1340, and this brought into being a realm that was relatively united, well protected from its enemies, and yet open to the Atlantic world. So the Portuguese, having discovered the Canary Islands as early as the 1330s, in 1415 took the decisive step of occupying Ceuta, in north Africa (against the advice of King John I, described as 'prudent and tired …'). About this time Prince Henry (1394–1460), later known as 'the Navigator', was becoming increasingly influential, and seems to have been behind the Portuguese push down the coast of Africa, even if he was far from being the sort of 'research institute director' that some historians

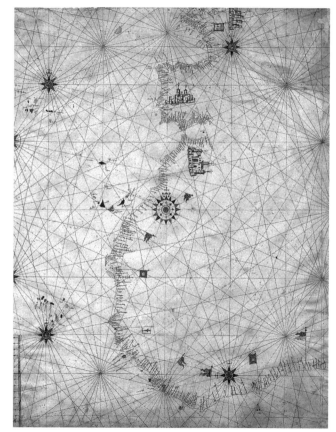

Fig. 29. Anonymous Portuguese chart of the north-west African coast, *c*.1471. This chart shows how the Portuguese recorded their progress round the west African coast, using the portolan-chart style to show their discovery of the Gulf of Guinea. Sixteen windroses radiate from an elaborate central rose, and the ports along the coast are not only written in, at right angles to the coast, but also marked from time to time with the flag of the Portuguese king; one or two cities are also shown with images.

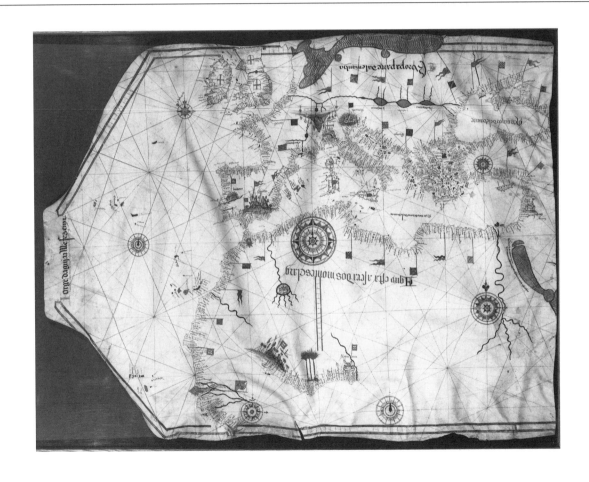

have made him.[3] About 1440 he brought the Majorcan mapmaker Jafuda Cresques to Portugal, and at the same time was calling for charts to be made of the lands now discovered beyond the formerly impassable Cape Bojador, on the west African coast.

As the years went by, the Portuguese progress was systematic: in the 1450s the Cape Verde Islands were reached, and the Azores were settled, in the 1460s the Gulf of Guinea was explored, and by 1488 Bartholomew Diaz (d. 1500) had reached the Cape [of Good Hope]. These yearly increments of knowledge were recorded on maps, though for the earliest years we have only those of the Venetian Grazioso Benincasa (active 1450–82), no doubt relying on Portuguese informants.[4] The earliest surviving Portuguese map is probably an anonymous chart of the 1470s now preserved in the Biblioteca Estense, at Modena (Fig. 29).[5] This chart is drawn in typically portolan style, no doubt following at a distance the teaching of Jafuda Cresques of Majorca: note the sixteen

Fig. 30. Jorge de Aguiar, Chart of north Africa and the Mediterranean Sea, 1492. This elegant chart shows how the Portuguese were extending the portolan-chart style delineation not only around the coast of Africa, but also up into Scandinavia. The Danube River is prominently shown, though it improbably reaches the North Sea, and the Atlantic islands are also featured. There is an attempt to show not only latitude, on the scale in the middle of Africa, but also, it would seem, longitude along the top and bottom edges of the chart.

windroses (compass cards showing the direction of the eight main Mediterranean winds), the rhumb-lines, the flags, and the city-sketches.

Two other surviving charts predate 1500: one by Pedro Reinel (active 1485–1555) in the Archives Départementales of the Gironde, and another by Jorge de Aguiar (active 1490) in the Beinecke Library at Yale (Fig. 30).[6] The Aguiar chart is slightly more elaborate than the one preserved at Modena; it interestingly shows the continuing line of the Gulf of Guinea as an insert in the middle of the African continent, and shows both the Red Sea and the Baltic Sea in medieval style, the latter just above the 'parte d'Alemanha' ('part of Germany').

One capital source of information about Portuguese cartographic knowledge at the end of the fifteenth century is the globe made by Martin Behaim (c.1459–1507) in 1492 at Nürnberg, and still preserved there.[7] Probably the most remarkable aspect of this globe, one of the earliest known to have been made in Europe since classical antiquity, is its delineation of the Atlantic Ocean (though it was not then called that). When the globe was constructed, the Portuguese thought of the middle Atlantic as being studded with islands, to the west of which was the considerable land of Cipangu, or Japan, with its distinctive upright rectangular shape. There were, indeed, fifteenth-century Portuguese maps, like the famous

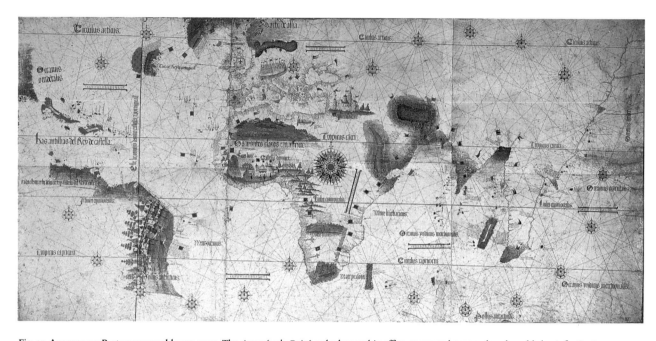

Fig. 31. Anonymous Portuguese world map, 1502. The *Armazém da Guiné*, or hydrographic office, seems to have produced world charts for Portuguese mariners from the beginning of the sixteenth century. These would have been functional charts, and seem to have disappeared. But they surely looked like this elegant world chart, spirited back to Italy by an agent of the duke of Modena. Note how quickly the Portuguese cartographers have mastered the main outlines of their new empire in the East.

Pizzigano chart,[8] which clearly showed large islands a little to the west and south of the Azores. Small wonder that Christopher Columbus, relying on cartographic information of this nature, as well as on the Ptolemaic abbreviation of the distance between Europe and Asia to the west, thought that Cipangu was well within range of his fleet. In fact, Cipangu is about ten thousand miles from Spain, an impossibly long distance but for the fortunate barrier formed by the American continent.

Perhaps as early as 1500, the Portuguese set up a body known as the *Armazém da Guiné*, or later the *Armazém da Guiné, Mina e Indias*, one of whose functions was to act as a charting centre for Portuguese overseas voyages. The documents bearing on these origins are scarce, but we do know that by 1517 the ships of the Portuguese East India trade were being issued with two nautical charts as they left Lisbon, to be handed back upon their return.[9] The so-called 'Cantino map' of 1502 is probably a product of this Portuguese navigation centre (Fig. 31).[10] It is a world map with a greatly enlarged version of what would be Brazil, which had been assigned to Portugal by the treaty of Tordesillas (1493). To the north and east are the Spanish Antilles; above them may be seen the 'terra del rey de Portugall' ('land of the king of Portugal') somewhere near Newfoundland. The African coast and India are shown with extraordinary accuracy, considering that Vasco da Gama (c.1460–1524) had rounded the Cape less than five years earlier. Note that there is no mention of where the line of Tordesillas (which ran right around the globe as a north–south line) would fall in the east; in the 1520s there would be much disputation between Spain and Portugal over this cartographic problem, which was very difficult to solve in the absence of good readings of longitude. This east–west measurement could not be accurately made until a good maritime chronometer became available, in the eighteenth century.

Virtually no Portuguese maps survive from the ensuing period of great expansion, when a settlement would be made at Mozambique (1505), Affonso de Albuquerque (1452–1515) would found Goa (1510), and the Portuguese would establish themselves at Malacca. Our only Portuguese cartographic testimony of this period is an anonymous chart in Dijon,[11] and the astonishing world map preserved at the Bavarian State Library in Munich.[12] Like the Cantino map, this comes from a time when the area east of Aden was beginning to be quite well known, but when a great gulf of ignorance separated the Portuguese possessions by what is now Newfoundland from those in the southern part of the newly found American continent. Of course, it was still by no means clear that this was a new continent: perhaps it would turn out to be a mere collection of islands, with Cipangu to be found as the most westerly of them.

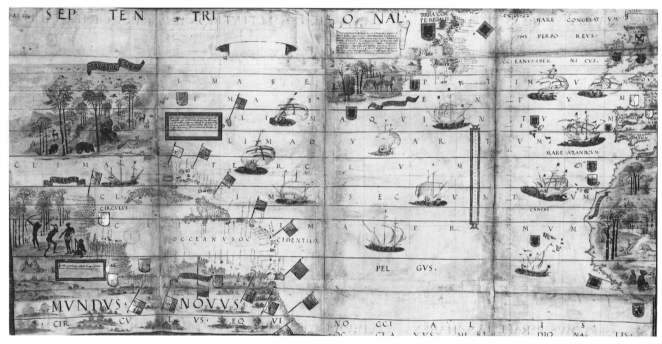

Fig. 32. Map of the north Atlantic Ocean from the 'Miller Atlas', 1519. The atlas from which this map comes takes its name from one of its recent owners, though it was composed about 1519 by Portuguese cartographers. On the right is Europe, and on the left, at a larger scale, the 'Mundus Novus' of South America and the Antilles. The cartographer wanted to identify the lands of the king of Spain—or of 'Castille', as he put it—and so has freely scattered his flag both on the islands and on the mainland.

The uncertainty about the general shape of central America had been largely dispelled by the time of the so-called 'Miller Atlas', now also preserved at the Bibliothèque nationale in Paris.[13] Its most famous page (Fig. 32) is the one showing the central Atlantic, with some Portuguese lands up towards Newfoundland, and the 'lands of the king of Spain' in and around the Caribbean. Among these Castilian lands are found two wonderful examples of iconography, for the Portuguese mariners customarily included 'painters' on their journeys;[14] these two images are analysed in Chapter 2. It is important to note here that Portuguese charts often produce a wonderful alliance of the cartographic with the iconographic.

Portuguese overseas cartography of the sixteenth century is thus remarkable for the great number of beautifully produced world atlases created by a relatively small group of cartographers: the Homem family, the Reinels, Bartolomeu Velho, Sebastiao Lopez, Fernao Vaz Dourado, the Teixeira family, and Pedro Fernandez de Quiros.[15] These atlases were often sent out of the country, to the libraries of Europe's great princes and rich merchants, and so they escaped the devastating effects of the Lisbon earthquake of 1755, in which almost all the cartographic material left in Portugal perished. One of the most beautiful of these atlases ended up in the Newberry Library, in Chicago. Drawn by Sebástiao Lopes, about 1565, it epitomizes the main features of these charts. Plate VIII shows the page containing the map of western Europe, north Africa, and the western approaches. It is clearly still in the portolan chart style, with its place-names at right angles to the coast, its windroses, the arms showing the possessions of the rulers, and the vignettes showing 'Argin' and 'Mazaguao'. But now a set of figures along the chart's western edge sets out the latitudes.

Very few of the functional, workaday maps produced in the heyday of Portuguese cartography have survived. Indeed, perhaps there was not anything like the variety that we shall encounter among the Spanish cartographers, for the settlements of Portugal were mostly commercial bases: the Portuguese, partly as a matter of policy and partly because of their small population, were not generally interested in extensive settlement of the territories in which they operated. Brazil was one of the few areas in which they established what used to be called a 'colony of settlement', and this huge area thus came to be quite thoroughly mapped. Figure 33 shows the Bay of Todos os Santos from the remarkable atlas by Joáo Teixeira Albernaz I (c.1575–1660). Between 1616 and 1643 Albernaz produced six manuscript atlases of Brazil, in which the number of maps rose from sixteen to more than thirty: this was a cartographic sequence which marked a major advance in Portuguese knowledge of their great transatlantic colony.[16]

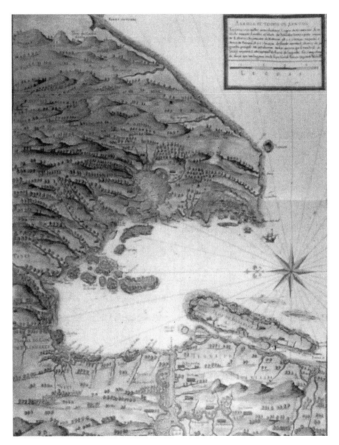

For navigation, the Portuguese produced some remarkable manuscript collections of charts, though again very few have survived. The charts of João de Castro (1500–48) might stand as examples of this work. He was an astonishing figure in the history of Portuguese eastward expansion, combining a profound knowledge of history with great maritime skills; he became governor of the Indian territory in 1545. The image from his *Roteiro* of the course between Goa and Diu (Fig. 34) gives an idea of the nature of his style, with its concentration on safe anchorages and their approaches. Our figure comes from a seventeenth-century copy of one of the charts of his *Roteiro*, but the original charts, concerning the Red Sea as well as the course by the Cape of Good Hope, are finely drawn and tinted with delicate watercolours, mostly using browns and greens.[17]

The overseas cartography of Portugal has often been underestimated, partly because during the 1520s many of her best chartmakers

Fig. 33. João Teixeira Albernaz I, Map of the Bay of Todos os Santos, Brazil, *c.*1626. This cartographer was a member of the large Teixeira family, much involved in the mapping of Portuguese possessions during the late sixteenth and seventeenth centuries. Joao Teixeira was active both in the East and in the West, producing both large- and small-scale maps and charts. This map of the Bay of Todos os Santos in Brazil shows how he was concerned to offer general views of the land that was being occupied, as well as detailed charts of anchorages.

Fig. 34. Joáo de Castro, View of Goa from his *Roteiro desde Goa al Diu*, *c.*1520. In the Middle Ages, northern European seamen had produced what the English called 'rutters', or navigation-guides. Joao de Castro gave the same name to his *roteiros*, which were manuscript collections of charts, designed to enable Portuguese seamen to navigate the new routes between Lisbon and the Eastern possessions, many of them shown on Fig. 31.

defected to Spain, where opportunities were more abundant. After the union of the two crowns in 1580, moreover, many Portuguese were absorbed into the service of the Spanish crown. Among the most celebrated of these were Pedro Fernandez de Quiros and Joáo Baptista Lavanha, celebrated for his work on the cartography of Aragón. When Portugal again became independent, after the revolt of 1640, her overseas empire had to contend with the rivalry not only of the Spaniards, but also of the French, the English, and the Dutch. It is astonishing that in the face of these rivals, the Portuguese succeeded longest of all of them in retaining part of their overseas empire. The part played in this by cartography, though, is very hard to assess following the earthquake of 1755, as we have seen.

SPANISH MAPMAKING

In Spain there was no such single catastrophe, but even here the holdings of the Archivo de Indias in Seville have huge gaps, no doubt incurred in times of civil unrest. The union of the crowns of Castille and Aragón in 1479, which gave rise to the rule of the 'Catholic Kings' Ferdinand and Isabella, meant that the united kingdom could call upon the cartographic resources of Barcelona, long a centre of portolan chart making, as well as of Majorca. In spite of the expulsion of the Moors and Jews after 1492, the kingdom also continued to profit from the great contribution which these peoples

had made to astronomy and mathematics in medieval Spain. The arrival of Christopher Columbus in his New World presented the Spaniards with an astonishing problem of cartography. The brother of Columbus was a cartographer, and so perhaps was Columbus himself, and one of his works may be preserved at the Bibliothèque nationale de France in Paris.[18] A small sketch of part of the north coast of what is now Haiti may indeed be the first European attempt at representing part of the New World. It bears the inscription 'la Española', or Hispaniola, and is thought by some scholars to be by the hand of Columbus himself, during his first voyage.[19]

Even more remarkable is the 'Juan de La Cosa' map of 1500, now preserved at the Museo Naval in Madrid.[20] Thought to be the work of a captain who had accompanied Columbus on his second voyage (1493–4), this astonishing map covers both the Old World and the region to which Columbus had come (Fig. 35). Europe is portrayed in an absolutely conventional portolan-chart style, as indeed are Africa and parts of Asia. Across the 'Mare Oceanum' (the 'Ocean Sea' of Columbus) to the west, though, the left-hand side of the map shows two huge jaws of land, in between which is a remarkably accurate delineation of the Caribbean islands. It seems incredible that the Spaniards could so soon have come to so accurate an understanding of the main features of the great arc from Trinidad to Cuba, and it is tempting to believe that this delineation owes

Fig. 35. Juan de La Cosa, Detail from his world map, *c.*1500. This figure shows the left-hand, western half of a world map drawn about 1500, apparently by a captain who had accompanied Columbus on his second voyage in 1493. It has a fine compass rose, with the eight subsidiary roses in the traditional style, and the enigmatic figure of Saint Christopher, perhaps to be interpreted as the 'Christo-ferens', or Christ-bearer, of Christianity to the peoples of the new-found world.

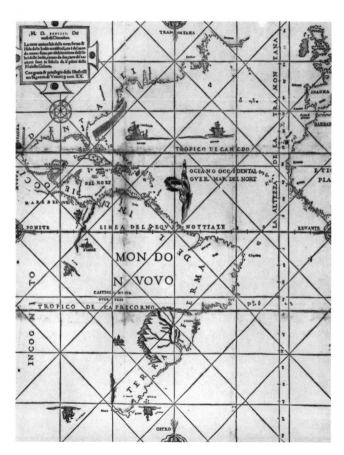

something to informants from the islands. We know, for instance, that a Lucayan Indian taken back to Spain by Columbus, in the course of an interview with King Ferdinand of Aragón, was able to lay out on a table the outline of the Caribbean, using stones, and it is certainly possible that La Cosa was able to call upon expertise of this kind. To the north he shows the 'sea discovered by the English', marked by appropriate flags; on the rest of the map, Castilian flags fly. A cartouche containing an image of Saint Christopher occupies the western end of the Caribbean Sea, which might, for all La Cosa knew, lead directly into the sea in which lay Cipangu and China. The map of La Cosa seems to have been constructed more or less

Fig. 36. The 'Ramusio map' of the New World, 1534. This map gets its name from Giovanni Battista Ramusio (1485–1557), the Venetian publisher of the *Summario* of 1534 (a history of the West Indies) in which the map was bound. It represents the current state of knowledge of the Spanish *Casa de Contratación* (hydrographic office) at Seville, and is presented without any characteristics of the portolan-chart style. The east coast of North America is now well known, but huge areas of coastline are not, and these are left blank.

Fig. 37. Alonso de Santa Cruz, Map of Cuba from the 'Islario', 1542. Using information from the *Casa de Contratación,* Santa Cruz in 1542 generated his 'Islario', so named because the world was still imagined as a series of islands. This atlas contained nine general maps, followed by about 100 more detailed maps of different parts of the world. This image of Cuba has a well-observed coastline, and inserts the main cities, including Havana (top left) and Santiago (bottom right), as well as the central ridge of mountains.

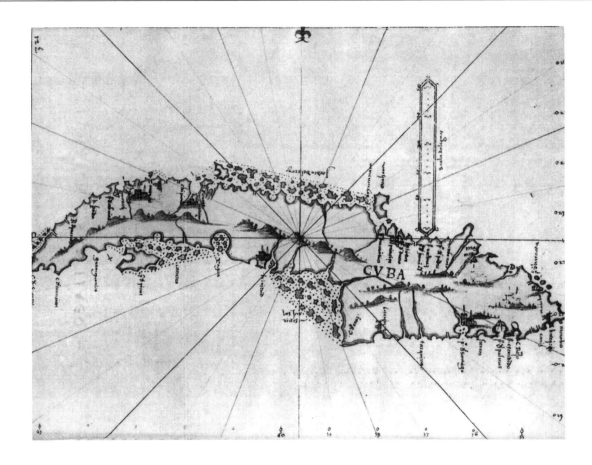

informally, or at any rate without the help of any sort of theoretical cartographic organization. This would change in 1508, when a school of navigation was founded in the *Casa de Contratación*, or 'House of Trade', in Seville.[21] From that time onward, the Spanish crown supported an elaborate staff of cosmographers and pilots, one of whose main functions was to develop a general map, the *padrón real*, and to make sure that Spanish mariners leaving Seville were equipped with appropriate charts. This Spanish organization in effect imitated the Portuguese *Armazém da Guiné, Mina e Indias*, and during the 1510s, 1520s, and 1530s drew together the best cartographic expertise available in the peninsula.

No copies of the early *padrón real* are now known to survive in Spain, but examples may be seen in various libraries on both sides of the Atlantic. They were all sent out to princely allies of Spain, and greatly diminish the notion that the information of the *padrón real* was a closely-guarded state secret.[22] Some of the finest are attributed to the originally Portuguese Diogo Ribeiro (d. 1533), who became *cosmógrafo mayor* in 1523. He seems to have worked closely with Nuño Garcia Torreño, named pilot in 1519, who was the author of the printed map of 1534 shown in Figure 36. This map, included here because it is much easier to reproduce than its manuscript precursors, summarizes the progress of Spanish cartography at its most creative period, and was well described by Boies

Penrose as 'notable alike for its delicacy and accuracy'.[23]

Information derived from the *padrón real* was summarized in the compendious 'Islario' of Alonso de Santa Cruz (c.1505–72). After accompanying Sebastian Cabot on his voyage of 1526–30, Santa Cruz settled back at Seville, where he was named *cosmógrafo real* in 1536. Six years later he produced not only a world-map in gores (triangular sections that fitted together to make a globe), now at Stockholm,[24] but also this world-atlas known as the 'Islario', now preserved at the Biblioteca Nacional in Madrid. It bears this rather curious title because, following the medieval fashion, the world was conceived as being a series of islands. The atlas consists of nine general maps, followed by about 100 maps of different parts of the world. These maps often show the Spanish world with remarkable fidelity (Fig. 37), and became the basis for much other cartographic work. By the time of his death in 1572, Santa Cruz had amassed a large collection of maps of various parts of the world, and this great resource was passed on to his successor, Juan López de Velasco; alas, it seems eventually to have perished in the great fire at the Escorial in 1677.[25]

The maps of the 'Islario' do not show very much detail about internal regions of the New World, but this was a feature of the map published in 1562 by Diego Gutiérrez, and now known only in two copies, at the Library of Congress in Washington and at the

British Library.[26] Diego Gutiérrez succeeded his father (of the same name) at the navigation-school in 1554, and was still alive in 1569. His map, which surely derived from the latest version of the *padrón real*, seems designed to set out the respective holdings of the Spaniards and the French in America, and was perhaps conceived to mark the rapprochement of 1559 between the two countries, when the Peace of Cateau-Cambrésis put an end to several decades of war, and Philip II of Spain married Elizabeth of Valois. It curiously lacks a latitude scale (Fig. 38), and makes no mention of the line between the Spanish and Portuguese possessions agreed at Tordesillas in 1493. But it does mark a certain stage in the Spanish understanding of their overseas territories, when the interior of the continent was beginning to give up its secrets.

Juan López de Velasco, who received the Santa Cruz archive in 1572, had been appointed in 1571 as *cosmógrafo-cronista*, precisely in order to advance Spanish understanding of the overseas territories.

He seems to have been largely responsible for issuing the requests for the colonial administrators to produce the *relaciones geográficas* (geographical reports) and their accompanying *pinturas* (maps: see

Fig. 38. Diego Gutiérrez, Detail from his map of the New World, 1562. This detail shows how the Spaniards were beginning to sketch in the land behind the coastline, setting out the main line of great rivers like the Amazon (bottom right), and identifying many of the local tribes, like the 'Chichimeci' and the 'Cossa' in what is now Texas. In the north, the 'Tierra Francisca' marks the area where the French had tried to settle in the 1530s and 1540s, in the Saint Lawrence River Valley; the Spaniards evidently regarded this still as the French area of influence.

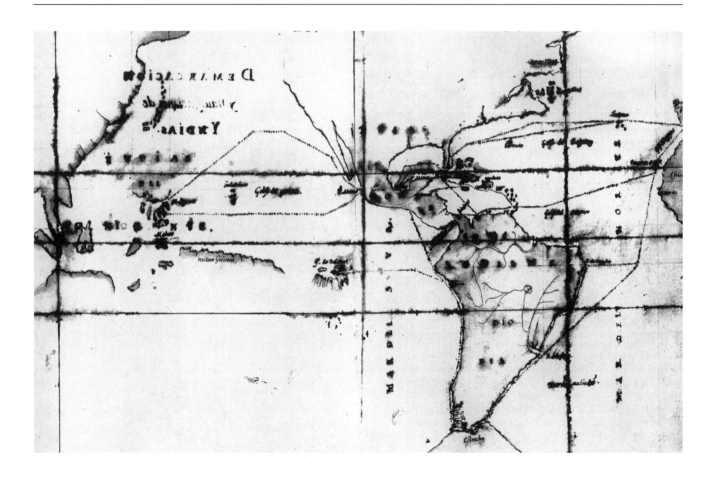

below). By 1574 he had accumulated a vast amount of information, which he summarized in the text of his 'Geografía y descripción universel de las Indias', a manuscript that was not printed until 1894.[27] To accompany the text he also produced a partial world map, and twelve regional maps, showing the Spanish empire generally by *audiencias*, or judicial districts. The maps are not particularly detailed, or even particularly accurate, but taken together they are startling evidence of the way in which a Spanish administrator could envision the empire as a whole, for the benefit of the very map-conscious Philip II. The manuscript maps seem to survive in an atlas at the John Carter Brown Library (Fig. 39); a version of them was printed in 1601 by Antonio de Herrera in his *Décadas*, and this work, often reprinted, must have strongly influenced people's ideas of the nature and extent of the Spanish overseas empire.

Philip II was a great enthusiast not only for maps, but also for written reports of any kind, and it was no doubt he who incited López de Velasco to send out the requests for information in 1571

Fig. 39. Juan López de Velasco, Map of the Spanish world, 1575. This map is a little hard to read, because some writing from other pages has been offset on to it. Showing the Spanish world with its main trade routes, it is the master map for the twelve detailed regional maps which follow. Composed by López de Velasco about 1575, it was printed by Antonio de Herrera in his *Décadas* of 1601, most efficiently summarizing the extent of Spanish power in cartographic form.

and 1577.[28] Philip insisted that a map should accompany each report, and these *pinturas* which accompanied the *relaciones* offer an extraordinary and unique example of cartographic syncretism, for they were compiled by a great variety of draughtsmen, and consequently range stylistically from those that are almost purely indigenous in style to those that show only European influences. Plate IX shows a good example of this syncretic style. It is the *pintura* which accompanied the *relación* for Mexicaltingo, in the archdiocese of Mexico, and is now preserved in Austin, Texas.[29] There is a large church towards the top left, and this is identified as 'San Juan Evangelista, that is, Culhuacan'. As is so often the case with the *pinturas*, secondary churches dot the countryside, linked by Aztec-style roads with the marks of feet; these roads bridge the rivers with a distinctive sign. In the centre is an indigenous building sign and a mountain 'glyph', or symbol; as the accompanying text explains, 'because of this hill the place is named Culhuacan.' The *pintura* was the work of Pedro de San Augustín, but we know nothing of his background, or what led him to this conflation of the two styles.

Just how successful López de Velasco was in absorbing the content of the hundred or so *pinturas* is not clear: many of them, though full of information, would not have been easily understood by a sixteenth-century Spaniard.[30] The cosmographers of the *Casa de*

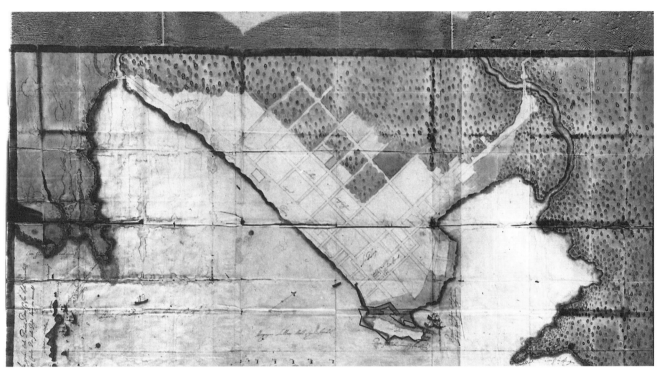

Fig. 40. Cristóbal de Rojas, Plan of Panamá, 1609. Rojas seems to have been the leading Spanish engineer around 1600, and played a large part in the fortification of Spanish sites in the New World after Drake's raid of 1586. This plan of what is now Old Panama sets the little town very well into its surroundings, though one may wonder if the square fields around it really existed. This first settlement was sacked by Sir Henry Morgan in 1671, and the new Panama City was built to the west of it.

Contratación continued their labours into the seventeenth century, but their work became less and less original, and by the turn of the sixteenth century some of the most interesting maps came from the military engineers. They had been working in Europe from the first half of the sixteenth century, at first for Charles V (ruled 1516–56), and then for Philip II (ruled 1556–98); it was after the raid of Francis Drake in 1586, when he sacked many cities around the Caribbean,[31] that these engineers began their labours in the New World.

Some were Spaniards, like Cristóbal de Rojas (active 1580–1614), though about half were foreigners like the Italian Juan-Bautista Antonelli (active 1580–1604).[32] The plan which Rojas drew of Panamá in 1609 is very typical of their work (Fig. 40). Rojas was an instructor at the Academy of Mathematics in Madrid, had published a manual of fortification, and had worked a good deal in Europe. So when he came to the New World in the early seventeenth century, he produced very polished maps, with scale and orientation, and

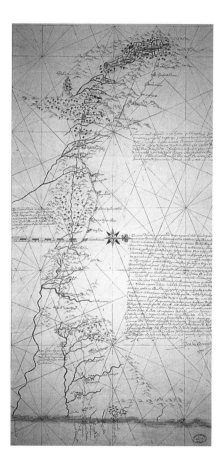

Fig. 41. Juan-Bautista Antonelli, Map of the road from Vera Cruz to Mexico City, 1590. The Antonelli family from Italy worked for the Spanish monarchy from the 1580s onwards. Juan-Bautista Antonelli was active in the Americas from 1580 to 1616, mostly working on fortifications, but also producing this very unusual map of the road from Vera Cruz (at the bottom) to Mexico City (at the top). Antonelli accompanies the map with an extensive commentary, for the route from the capital to the treasure-fleet port was a central strategic lifeline.

sometimes an indication of the surrounding countryside. Antonelli was also capable of drawing this kind of plan,[33] but he also on occasion drew smaller-scale maps. Figure 41 shows his delineation of the road between Vera Cruz, on the Gulf of Mexico (bottom of the map), and Mexico City. The map showed all the most important towns on the way, and also indicated the major *estancias* (estates) and *ingenios* (sugar works), as well as such spectacular sites as the 'bolcan' (volcano) that looms over the plain of Mexico City. Antonelli could turn his hand to a variety of civil engineering projects, like many of his successors; a good number of maps and plans of their projects survive in the archives.[34]

The cosmographers, then, had given a general coastal outline of Spain's new possessions, and plans of the greater towns had been provided by the royal engineers.[35] The attempt to cover the provinces in detail through the *pinturas* had partially failed, since there does not seem to be any evidence that this manuscript material was ever incorporated into general maps. So, for the time being, there were no maps showing the countryside in any detail; that would come in the time of the Jesuit cartographers, beginning at the end of the seventeenth century. Still, the cartographic effort put out by Spain during the sixteenth century, helped to some degree by the indigenous contribution, had resulted in a remarkable knowledge of the main features of the new possessions.

FRANCE

The early possessions of France across the Atlantic were small and few, but they did give rise to some remarkable maps, under the patronage of the Portuguese cartographers. As early as 1529, mariners from Dieppe went to Brazil, where they were seeking wood for the textile-manufacturers of Rouen.[36] Following Portuguese example, they were accompanied by a *peintre* (literally, painter), whose job it was to record the scene in the New World. It is also possible that such an artist accompanied Jacques Cartier (1491–1557) to the Saint Lawrence River in the 1530s and 1540s, and Plate III is probably his work. The maps of the Dieppe School, which appeared for about twenty years from the late 1530s, are remarkable not only for their information about the latest discoveries, but also for their imagery: they are in sharp contrast to the austere and almost always undecorated work of the Spanish *Casa de Contratación*.

Fig. 42. Samuel de Champlain, Plan of Quebec from *Les voyages* (Paris, 1613). Champlain, founder of French Canada, was a very active cartographer, whose style owed nothing to that of the portolan charts. In *Les voyages* of 1613 he provided large-scale sketch-maps of the major sites in the Saint Lawrence River Valley, taking care to indicate not only French settlements, but also the longhouses and fish-traps of the Indian tribes who surrounded them. There is no doubt that this empathy with the local peoples made him a very successful leader.

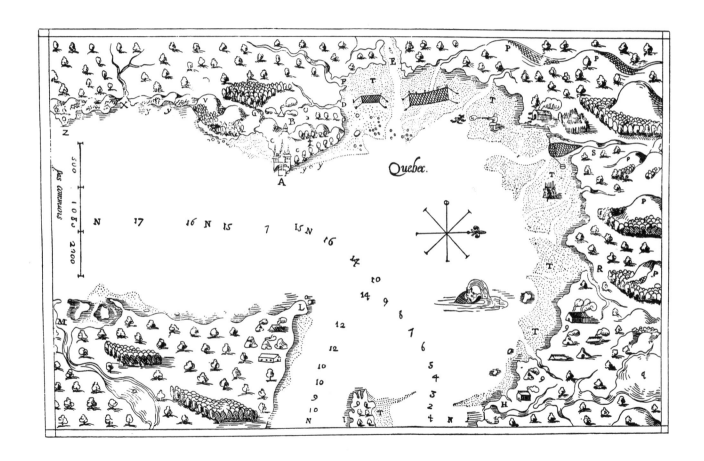

Virtually nothing survives of them at Dieppe itself, probably following the disastrous English bombardment of 1696. But scattered around the great libraries of the world are perhaps a dozen world maps and half a dozen atlases.[37] Plate X shows a page from one of these atlases, by Jean Rotz (*c.*1505–*c.*1550). He was a Dieppe mapmaker who in 1541 decided that he would like to enter the service of Henry VIII of England, and so he crossed the Channel and took with him a characteristic atlas. The title-page, with a large image of the English royal arms, explains this ambition. There are about twelve maps in the atlas, and the one chosen here shows the east coast of South America, where French interest was strong. The map is oriented southwards, with splendid portolan-chart-like windroses in the sea. The dwellings and stockaded villages of the Tupinamba Indians are carefully shown; they themselves are cutting redwood and taking it down to the coast, where a Frenchman rather improbably waits for it in a canoe. No doubt so that Henry VIII can better understand the map, some legends have been added in English: 'the cost of the Brazil', 'the ryver of Plata', and 'the distroit of Magellan'. Maps of this kind show a remarkable fusion of traditions, for the portolan chart style derived from the Portuguese has been combined with elements of medieval French illuminated manuscripts, shown in the wonderfully decorative flowery borders. Having emerged from the collab-

oration with the Portuguese, the cartographers of Dieppe prospered for only about twenty years, until their port was caught up in the French civil wars, after about 1560.

There ensued a period during which the French produced little colonial cartography,[38] but then in 1603 Samuel de Champlain (1567–1635) made the first of his several voyages to the Saint Lawrence River valley, founding Quebec in 1608. Champlain came from Brouage, in western France near La Rochelle, and proved to be not only a very skilful leader but also a master cartographer. Whereas previous expeditions, like the ones headed by Jacques Cartier, had been unable to contend with the rigours of the Canadian winter, Champlain brought his group through the difficult season by attending to both their physical and psychological needs: indigenous plants against scurvy, for instance, and hunting-competitions to pass the time in the cold and dreary weather.[39]

He produced a good many publications, many of which contained maps; some of his manuscript material has also survived.

Fig. 43. Samuel de Champlain, Chart of Acadia and Norumbega, 1607. This remarkable map of the coast between Boston (lower left) and Nova Scotia (upper right) seems to have been compiled from a series of observations made from a small boat working along the coast. In its presentation it is in marked contrast to the work of John Smith (Fig. 49), who seems much more concerned to put a European imprint upon the land.

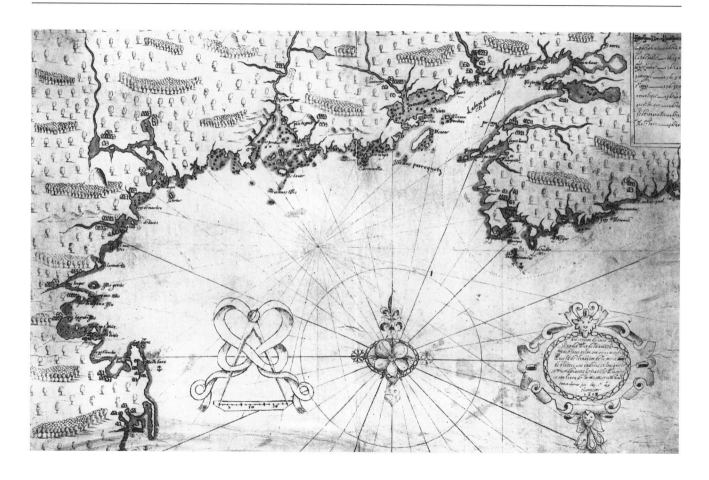

Figure 42 shows one of the large-scale maps from his *Les voyages* of 1613. It sets out the early site of Quebec, which is at 'A', 'where the *habitation* is built'. The succeeding letters on the key often refer to the local resources—gardens, fields for wheat, and so forth—and the map itself shows such features as Indian villages and fish-traps. One has the feeling, in looking at this little map, one of about twenty in the book, that Champlain is thinking about how to survive in this country, which others had found so unfriendly.

As well as making these little large-scale sketches for publication, he also seems to have used them in combination to produce small-scale maps of large areas. Figure 43 shows his manuscript map of the east coast of North America between Nova Scotia and Boston. It dates from 1607, and gives a detailed image of about 400 miles of coastline. Champlain may have constructed it partly from native informants, but it is likely that much of it was compiled from a small boat, by taking successive compass-readings of the features on the shoreline during his visits between 1603 and 1607. This map marks a total break from the tradition of the Dieppe School maps, with their strong influence from the Middle Ages, including both the portolan chart style and the decorative borders. It is possible that Champlain was a pupil of the Jesuits, and that his maps show the application of their mathematical teaching, but this is not known.

In 1612 Champlain published *La carte géographique de la Nouvelle France*, stretching from Newfoundland in the east to Lake Erie in the west, with a border containing much information about the products of the country. It also contains information about the local peoples, with a handsome pair of 'Almouchicois'.[40] The woman is bearing a gourd and an ear of corn, while the man carries his weapons. This illustration brings out the difficulty of transforming manuscript material into convincing printed illustrations, without allowing the ideas already in the head of the engraver to play too large a part. For the pair advance with a curiously classical gait, and while the woman looks much like Marie de Médicis (1573–1642), the man curiously resembles her husband, King Henri IV (ruled 1589–1610).

During the 1630s, the most original colonial cartography in France was probably centred on Le Havre, where Guillaume Le Testu had practised in the days of the Dieppe School. The de Vaulx

Fig. 44. Jean Guérard, World map, 1634. Le Havre had been founded at the mouth of the River Seine by François I in the early sixteenth century, and became the great centre from which French overseas expansion was directed. Jean Guérard, based in Le Havre, produced this manuscript map in 1634 to set out the most recent discoveries for Cardinal Richelieu. The coasts of the Pacific Ocean remain largely unknown, but the rest of the world is well delineated, and Australia is beginning to appear (bottom right).

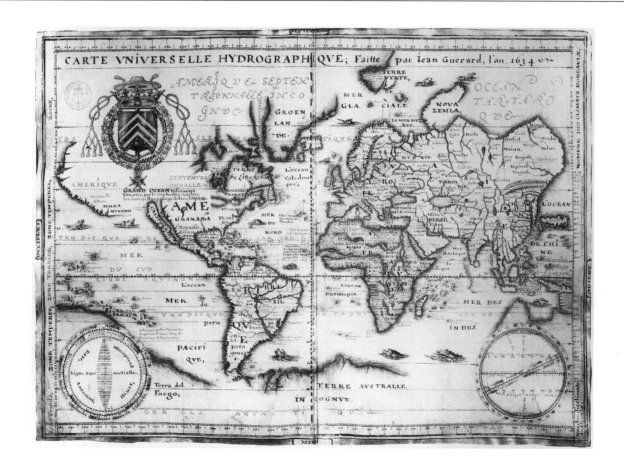

brothers, Jacques and Pierre, were succeeded by Jean Guérard, responsible for a number of Atlantic charts and then, in 1634, for a world map dedicated to the Cardinal Richelieu (1585–1642) (Fig. 44). This map, bearing the cardinal's arms, was clearly designed to show him, as minister in charge of navigation, what the possibilities were for colonial expansion. French settlements are carefully shown, and so are the latest ventures of the English. Above California, for instance, the legend tells us that this is the 'great ocean, discovered in the year 1612 by the Englishman Henry Hudson; it is believed that from here there is a passage to Japan'. There remain considerable omissions and mistakes, but this is all the same a map from which quite accurately informed decisions could be made.[41]

During the second half of the seventeenth century, French cartographers continued to be active, particularly in North America. The Jesuits undertook a certain amount of cartography there, including a remarkably accurate map of the top part of Lake Michigan, and the whole of Lake Superior. On the whole, the French tended to publish small-scale maps covering the whole world in great atlases, and large-scale maps of the French provinces and their fortifications, without venturing into specialized maritime cartography.[42] At the end of the century, though, the *Neptune Français* was published, and this was the first of those French maritime atlases that would become common during the eighteenth century.

THE LOW COUNTRIES

During the most productive period of Iberian chartmaking, in the first half of the sixteenth century, the Low Countries had been part of the Habsburg empire. When the northern region, known as the United Provinces, revolted about 1564, a new power came into being that was centrally dependent upon the sea and upon trade. The southern region, which continued to be held by the Spaniards, contained the great cartographic centre of Antwerp, but after the split many of its mapmakers migrated northwards, to places like The Hague, Amsterdam, and Leyden. It was in the latter city that in 1584 Lucas Janz Waghenær (c.1534–1605) published the first edition of his *Spiegel der Zeevært*, the first printed sea atlas.[43] It was at first confined to the waters around Europe, but set the pattern for atlases that would eventually cover the whole world.

Fig. 45. Lucas Janz Waghenær, Map of the English Channel from his *Spiegel der Zeevært* (Leyden, 1584). The map from this earliest of printed sea atlases shows the English Channel off the Isle of Wight, and the coast to the east of it. When the Spanish Armada came up the Channel in 1588, many of their ships were equipped with manuscript copies of this map. It would have told them how to take shelter in the area between the Isle of Wight and the mainland. But they missed this chance, and pressed on to Flanders and eventual destruction in the course of their flight round the British Isles.

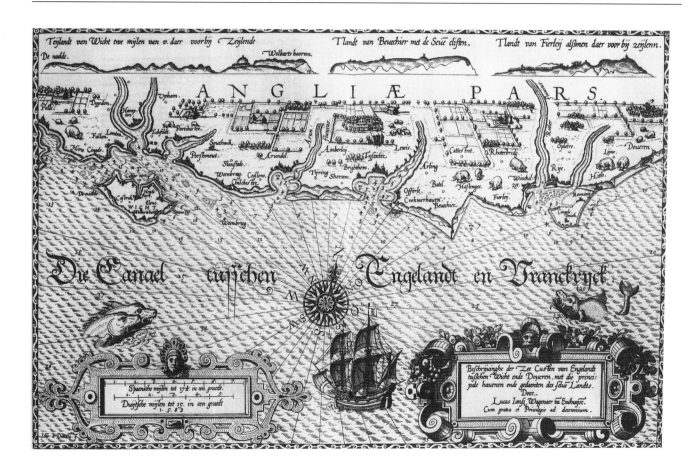

Teijlandt van Wicht twe mijlen van v. daer voorbij Zeijlende   Tlandt van Beuechier met de Seue cliften.   Tlandt van Fierleij alfmen daer voor bij zeijlenn.

De noelde.   Wolbarts hoornn.

A N G L I Æ P A R S.

Die Canael tusschen Engelandt en Vranckryck

Spaensche mijlen tot 17½. in een graedt.
Duytsche mijlen tot 15. in een graedt.
1 5 8 3

Beschrijuinghe der Zee Custen van Engelandt
tusschen Wicht ende Doueren, met die princi-
pale hauenen ende gedaenten des selue Landts.
Doer.
Lucas Ianſz Wagenaer uū Enthuyſē.
Cum gratia et Priuilegio ad decennium.

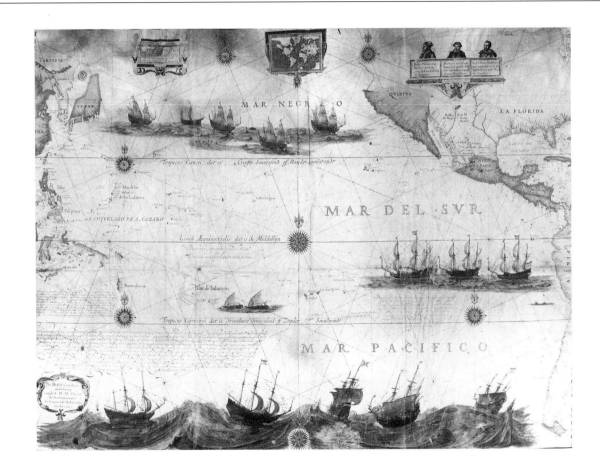

Figure 45 shows a page from the *Spiegel*, covering part of 'the channel between England and France'. The Isle of Wight is at the upper left, and Dover on the extreme right. Most of the main towns are marked, as well as such features as the Needles ('de Nælde') on the west end of the Isle of Wight. Some soundings are indicated, particularly for entering harbours like Arundel, Brighton, and Rye. At the top of the page is a series of 'landfall' images, to help the mariner when approaching the coast. Evidently, this first attempt at a printed atlas is quite crude, but it would be a certain help in navigating the Channel, and succeeding editions both added maps and improved accuracy. With atlases like this, the way was clear for the day when every vessel could carry relatively cheap printed charts of any part of the world.

During the 1580s and 1590s, the Dutch also produced many manuscript charts, relying on a procedure rather like that of the Portuguese and Spaniards.[44] At Amsterdam there was a hydro-graphic office, where the East India Company, founded in 1602, ran a chartmaking branch that supplied captains with charts when they left, and received them back upon their return, together with their comments. From 1617 onwards the official chartmaker for the East India Company (the 'VOC') was Hessel Gerritsz (1571–1622), and after 1621 he held a similar position with the newly founded West India Company (the 'WIC'). Figure 46 shows his wonderfully elegant chart of the Pacific Ocean of 1622. Although the ships in the northern regions ride peacefully enough, those in the southern seas are fearfully tossed about, to remind the viewer of the perils suffered by many expeditions there. There is a latitude scale, but no indication of longitude, though in general the latest discoveries are entered. There was as yet no indication of the shape of Australia, but the islands of the western Pacific are well represented. When he died in 1622, Gerritsz was replaced by members of the Blæu family, who used their monopolistic position to strengthen their commercial ties, which enabled them to produce hugely expensive ventures like Joan Blæu's *Atlas Maior* (11 vols, Amsterdam, 1662–72). Dutch society seems to have been particularly well attuned to the use of maps, whether in atlases or as wall-maps, for they were used not only as instructional tools, showing the extent of the empire, but also adorned places like the city hall of Amsterdam as a demonstration of power.

Fig. 46. Hessel Gerritsz, Map of the Pacific Ocean, 1622. This evocative map retains a faint echo of the portolan chart in its central compass-rose, with lines radiating out to subsidiary ones. It was drawn at a time of confusion in the nomenclature of the great ocean, for in the north it is the 'Mar Negro', in the middle the 'Mar del Sur' (so it at first seemed, from the isthmus of Panama), and in the south (the least pacific part) the 'Mar Pacifico'. Eventually, of course, the whole ocean would be the oddly named Pacific.

They also provided essential information for the directors of the East and West India Companies. Satellite hydrographic offices were established in Batavia (1618) and in Recife (1630), and much of the information generated by these offices was processed by Johannes Vingboons, leading member of a large family of artists, into wonderfully evocative maps, plans, and views. The view of the entrance to the harbour at Havana (Fig. 47) was thus generated from a series of drawings, and this was often the case, some such preliminary drawings coming from foreign sources. The work of Vingboons was of such elegance that even when it had become outdated, it was not thrown away, and now his remarkable images of the Dutch empire may be found scattered among a great many European archives.[45] Brazil, which had been captured by the Dutch, was recovered by the Portuguese in 1654, and in other parts of the world the Dutch came under increasing pressure from the emergent power of the English and the French. But there can be

little doubt that their extraordinary maps and plans had not only had a major effect on the Dutch people's idea of empire, but had also enabled the directors of the overseas companies to come to rational conclusions about expenditure on ports and fortifications.

ENGLISH OVERSEAS MAPPING

Throughout most of the sixteenth century, the English lagged behind the Iberian powers in their overseas cartography. They knew about what was going on in Spain: indeed, Sebastian Cabot (c.1485–c.1557), whose world map printed in 1541 publicized the work of the *Casa de Contratación*, returned to live in England between 1547 and 1557, and in 1556 Stephen Borough (1535–84) tried to establish a navigation school in England on the lines of the one in Seville.[46] In 1563 John Dee (1527–1608) advised the new Queen Elizabeth to the same effect, and in 1574 William Bourne, in his *A regiment for the sea*, lamented that English navigators had to rely on charts made in Portugal, Spain, or France. In practical terms, when Francis Drake was preparing in 1576 for his world voyage, he had to go to Lisbon to buy suitable charts.

Towards the end of the century, though, things began to change. When John White was assigned to accompany Sir Walter Raleigh's expedition to Virginia in 1585, he not only produced remarkable sketches of the scenery and people, but also drew passable maps

Fig. 47. Johannes Vingboons, View of Havana, Cuba, c.1630. A Dutch ship is here seen approaching the heavily-fortified harbour of Havana. Vingboons could make images like this, or in bird's-eye view, or as maps. He belonged to a large family of artists, and was closely connected to other Amsterdam chart-makers; for instance, some of his drawings were engraved by Hessel Gerritsz. The manuscript maps compiled in the early seventeenth century often formed the basis for the great Dutch atlases that were published later in the century.

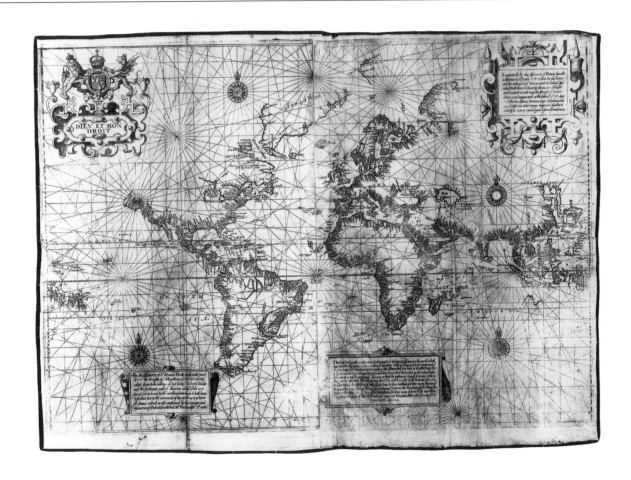

(Plate IV). The influence of Richard Hakluyt (*c.*1552–1616) and John Dee has long been known, and Lesley Cormack has more recently shown how the young men at Oxford and Cambridge universities were drawn at this time towards geographical thinking, essential to the new imperial ambitions that were particularly prominent at the court of James I's son, Prince Henry, who died prematurely in 1612.[47] The map which epitomizes this new expansionism is the 1599 world map of Edward Wright (Fig. 48). He was a Cambridge mathematician, concerned to produce a map which would not only be drawn according to the new principles of Mercator (world map, 1569), but could also set out the discoveries described in Richard Hakluyt's *Principal navigations.*

Wright is less well informed about the western Pacific Ocean than Hessel Gerritsz would be, a little more than twenty years later (Fig. 46), but he is otherwise abreast of the latest discoveries, as the three informative cartouches explain. The splendid royal arms might stand as an affirmation that England was now determined to venture out into the wider world, still largely the pre-

Fig. 48. Edward Wright, World map, London, 1599. **This extraordinary map marks the coming of age of English cartography, in its conflation of the Mercator projection and the portolan-chart-style windroses. The latest discoveries are described in the three long cartouches, but the insistence on writing the place-names at right angles to the coast gives the map a strangely old-fashioned feel.**

serve of the Iberians. Unlike many of the Iberian cartographers, Wright, like Jean Guérard (Fig. 44), gives a certain emphasis to northerly climes by moving the Equator downwards from the centre of his chart, which is equipped with figures for both latitude and longitude. Note, though, that Wright expresses these thoroughly modern concepts in a markedly medieval form, for his map still owes much to the portolan chart, with its ring of compass-roses and its arrangement of place-names at right angles to the coast.

The English determination to take possession of lands claimed by other powers, and of course actually occupied by Indian tribes, was nowhere better expressed than in Captain John Smith's map of *New England,* 'observed and described' in 1614 (Fig. 49). This map, which went through many editions, was designed to draw English settlers to the region by (falsely) emphasizing its Englishness.[48] The indigenous names have been totally eradicated (though some would eventually creep back), and a large portrait of Smith, tutelary deity of the new colony, occupies far more space than the royal arms. The verse under the portrait sets out his aims: 'Thy faire-discoveries and fowle-overthrowes of salvages, much civilized by thee, best shew thy spirit, and to it glory win.' A posse of large vessels approaches this inviting land, thus Englished beyond recognition. The contrast in place-naming with the relatively unobtrusive 1585

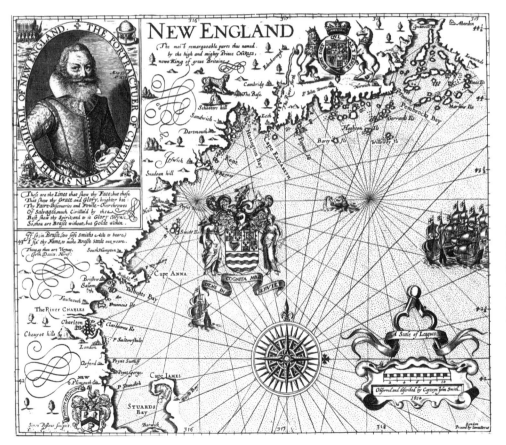

Fig. 49. John Smith, *New England* (London, 1614). This is a map that has been very much commentated on, because it so clearly expresses not only the ambitions of England, but also those of John Smith. It is instructive to compare this boastful map with the sober work of Champlain, in Fig. 43. Whereas Smith seems determined to impose his presence on the land about to be seized, Champlain gives the impression that he is concerned simply to set out the main geographical features; in other maps, he also gives fair prominence to the Indian tribes.

Plate V El Greco, View and plan of Toledo, *c.*1610. This view of Toledo, though somewhat distorted in the interest of artistic balance, nevertheless recognizably shows the main monuments of the great city behind its wall. It is all the more curious that El Greco should have chosen to accompany it with a map, as much as to say, there are two ways of showing a city, and I have mastered both of them.

Plate VI Claudius Ptolemy, An Image of the known world superimposed on a globe. This map from a manuscript of Ptolemy's *Geography*, produced at Florence around 1470, shows the world very much as Strabo wished to portray it, showing the known world in relation to that (much larger) part of the world which remained unknown. Of course, the land extends much too far from east to west, and it was this type of imaging that gave Christopher Columbus the false notion that he could sail from Spain directly to Asia; luckily, America was in the way.

Plate VII Jean Germain, Illuminated page showing the author presenting his 'Spiritual *mappamundi*' to Philip the Good, duke of Burgundy, *c.*1450. This most unusual illuminated page was commissioned – or perhaps even drawn – by Jean Germain, bishop of Chalon-sur-Saône, as a special gift to the duke of Burgundy. It is of interest to our argument, because it shows that at the Burgundian court, a courtier would expect the mighty duke to appreciate a very unusual cartographic gift.

Plate VIII Sebástiao Lopes, Map of the North Atlantic, 1565. This map comes from an atlas of 1565 by Sebástiao Lopes, one of the most skilled of Portuguese chartmakers. A certain amount of new information filtered through to these charts, but they were chiefly remarkable not for their utilitarian qualities, but for the beauty of their execution, with superb coats-of-arms, windroses, cartouches, and city views.

work of John White (Plate IV) is remarkable, and seems to testify to the new spirit of bravado among the English.

A whole school of chartmakers appeared in London to serve the overseas ventures. Emerging in the 1590s, they continued to produce manuscript maps for about 100 years. These maps are stylistically distinctive, though this 'Thames' or 'Drapers' School was entirely unorganized. Something like 500 maps survive in this style, over 300 of them by William Hack (active 1680–1710). Figure 50 shows a chart of the North Atlantic, drawn by Andrew Welch in 1674.[49] The legacy of the portolan charts is still present, with the windroses and rhumb-lines, but the new style has very distinctive cartouches and a well-organized system of distinguishing by letter-size between sites of greater or lesser importance. Other maps of the Thames School would show these characteristics, and also a curiously archaic way of delineating coastlines, with a sort of crudity and exaggeration reminiscent of the portolan charts.

The chartmakers of the Thames School differed sharply from those of the Dieppe School in that they often also participated in the production of printed maps. This is interestingly illustrated by the contents of the Blathwayt atlas.[50] William Blathwayt (1649–1717) had entered the service of the Plantation Office in London in 1674, and became secretary to the Committee of the Lords of Trade and Plantations. This body was responsible for encouraging overseas ventures, and so its secretary needed a good set of maps to guide its deliberations. Blathwayt put together forty-eight maps, of which thirteen were manuscript and thirty-five printed, all bound up in a single volume. Ten of the manuscripts were by members of the Thames School, and so were some of the printed ones: the first in the volume, for instance, is a world map published by John Thornton. Blathwayt did not confine himself to English cartographers in his search for useful maps, but included work by the Frenchman Nicolas Sanson and the Dutchman William Blæu. Almost all his material concerns the western hemisphere, and as a whole gives us an excellent idea of what was available in England towards the end of the seventeenth century.[51]

The book of sea-charts produced by Waghenær in 1584, known in England as *The mariner's mirror* (translation of the *Spiegel der Zeevært*), had long served English mariners in various editions and under various titles. In 1669 the Thames School chartmaker John Seller (active 1658–98) announced that he intended to produce 'a Sea Waggoner ['Waghenaer' in approximate English] for the whole world', and in 1689 he published the first part of it, confusingly enough the fourth book of *The English pilot*.[52] This first part was followed by four others, some under different editors, until the whole world was indeed covered. Seller was much criticized for his fourth volume, which seemed to be largely copied from Dutch

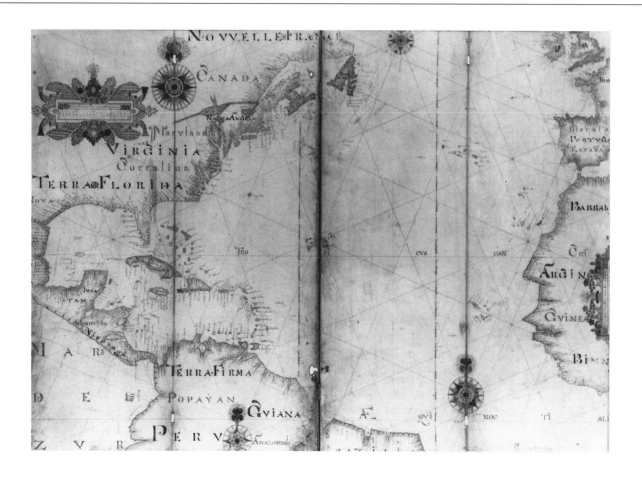

sources. But the coming of *The English pilot* established a basis from which subsequent and improved editions could be generated, until eventually books of charts existed to enable captains to navigate through the whole world in comparative safety.

ITALY

The English, starting slowly, had eventually caught up with the French and the Dutch. The mapmakers of Italy, on the other hand, were prominent during the fifteenth century, but during the sixteenth century produced less and less original material. This is entirely comprehensible, for the Italian states were not well placed geographically to participate fully in the expansion of Europe into the wider world. Thus even their great navigators had to serve Atlantic powers: one thinks of Columbus himself and the Cabots from Genoa, or Vespucci and Verrazzano from Florence. All the same, the sixteenth-century cartographers of Italy performed a great service in popularizing Iberian discoveries through the

Fig. 50. Andrew Welch, Chart of the North Atlantic, 1674. This is a characteristic chart of the Thames School, with its very distinctive capitalization and its generally accurate coastlines. It represents the cartographic expression of the era when English navigators were beginning to feel their oats, even if in some respects (the windroses and the exaggerated embayments) it harks back to earlier times.

printed maps produced in centres like Venice, Florence, and Rome.[53] Their manuscript material consisted essentially of portolan-chart-style atlases summarizing these discoveries and destined for princely libraries, as in the work of Battista Agnese, who compiled about fifty of them. Still, as Lawrence Wroth has shown, the series of atlases by Agnese does show evidence of incorporating new information, apart from their often being extraordinary works of art. One, as we have seen, was chosen by Charles V as a present for Philip II (Chapter 2).[54]

During the seventeenth century, Italy produced two great monuments of colonial cartography: the *Arcano del mare* (3 vols, Florence, 1646–7) of the Englishman Sir Robert Dudley (1573–1649), and the globes of the Venetian friar Vincenzo Coronelli (1650–1718). The latter began his career by producing for Louis XIV of France the amazing 15-foot manuscript globe still to be seen in France, but then, rather like Fra Mauro, organized at Venice a substantial enterprise which in his case produced smaller printed globes.[55] Figure 51 shows a gore from one of these globes, and demonstrates how well Coronelli could keep up with the latest discoveries of the mid-1680s. He knew that La Salle (1643–87) had in 1682 established that the Mississippi River ran into the Gulf of Mexico, even if he placed this river many hundreds of miles too far to the west. He also knew about the general disposition of the

Great Lakes, and illustrated his map with many images drawn from previous cartographers. The position of many Indian tribes is shown, and a series of notes sets out historical events at different points on the map. The globes of Coronelli, which came to occupy a prominent place in many palaces and substantial houses, greatly contributed to Europeans' knowledge of the wider world.

CONCLUSION

In general, there was a great variety in the Europeans' approaches to delineating this world. Such delineation was an essential part of the expansion, for though the Vikings, for instance, had been able to reach the New World without maps, their colonizing venture had nothing of the geographical complexity encountered by the sixteenth-century mariners and settlers. For the latter, maps were essential: like the Polynesian sailors with their stick-charts, they

Fig. 51. Vincenzo Coronelli, Gore from his world globe of *c.*1685. This is a detail from one of a series of globe-gores produced by Coronelli in Venice about 1685; assembled together, the gores could be attached to a sphere in order to form an image of the globe. Many such globes have survived, for they were from the start beautiful and precious objects. Their extraordinary importance in making strategic decisions was well understood by President Roosevelt, who during the Second World War caused several large identical globes to be constructed; he sent one to Churchill and one to Stalin, so that in their discussions of strategy they all might have the same grasp of geography.

simply had to devise some locational imagery in order to return to the lands that they coveted.

The Iberians organized this cartography in a centralized way, setting up centres at Lisbon and Seville through which all information could be filtered, assessed, and then made available to chosen captains. The great difference between their mapping styles is that the Portuguese were also master iconographers, whose charts were often as rich in imagery as the Spanish charts were bare and austere. They passed this style on to the chartmakers of the Dieppe School in France, and it survived to some degree even in the Dutch printed charts of the seventeenth century. The Portuguese and Spaniards had begun by using the portolan-chart techniques inherited from the medieval Mediterranean, and this style endured for an astonishingly long time, up to the manuscripts of the Thames School in England, and even into many of the printed charts produced in the seventeenth century by the Blæus. It took a mapmaker trained in some external tradition, like Samuel de Champlain, completely to abandon this style, so powerful was the influence of the medieval Mediterranean.

Whereas the Iberians had organized their chartmaking in a highly centralized way, the northern powers allowed the various centres to develop as they would. In fact, the Iberian centres were hard pressed fully to control their cosmographers, who would often sell their knowledge if the price were right. This distinction between the private and the public was even vaguer in the north, where the Dutch cartographers of the East and West India Companies, for instance, were often also commercial publishers. This mixing of manuscript and printed material for profit was also characteristic of England, where many members of the Thames School came to publish printed maps. It is hard to imagine this taking place in the Iberian peninsula, not least because of the undeveloped state of the printing industry there.

In fact, many of the new ideas about the shape of the world made their way from Portugal and Spain during the sixteenth century to Germany and Italy, where enterprising publishers transformed them into printed maps. Eventually, printed maps produced by contending nations like the English and the Dutch formed an important part of national propaganda, when it came to territorial claims in the New World.[56] Just as the Englishman John Smith used cartography to efface native claims in New England, so all over the New World European powers used mapping to cast a Ptolemaic grid over the lands that they coveted. In requesting the *pinturas* that accompanied the *relaciones geográficas*, the Spaniards inadvertently reversed this process, by allowing a different image of the world to make itself seen. But, as time went by, the cartography of the Europeans everywhere gained the upper hand, and proved to be an important element in the seizure and settlement of the wider world.

Apart from this ideological element in colonial cartography, which in a sense validated for early modern Europeans their seizure of overseas territories, there is also a highly practical element. By the eighteenth century, arising out of the developments that we have been describing in this chapter, any European vessel of any size would be carrying a set of charts that would permit it to sail more or less safely into almost any part of the world. This was a development comparable, in conflictual terms, to an army equipped with guns opposing a group armed only with spears. Or, to make the analogy closer, it was like an army with access to satellite imagery opposing one using only the intelligence-gathering capacities of the Second World War. The ships of the European powers were by the eighteenth century so well equipped in spatial information that we might consider rephrasing the famous phrase of Carlo Cipolla, and attribute their success to their superiority in 'guns, sails—and maps'.[57]

The maps drawn during the Military Revolution, 1500–1800

MANY historians write about a 'Military Revolution' in early modern European history. The set of changes to which they refer offers one of the best examples of the way in which transformations in one part of the historical process produce changes in the nature of mapping. There has been much debate about the exact nature and precise timing of the 'Military Revolution',[1] but it is undeniable both that there *were* great changes in the art of war in early modern Europe, and that these developments profoundly influenced many different societies, economies, and political structures, both within Europe and outside it. The chief changes in the way that war was waged can be summarized under six main themes.

THE NATURE OF THE MILITARY REVOLUTION

Firstly, armies grew very greatly in size between 1500 and 1700. Whereas the army of the Emperor Charles V, at the siege of Metz in 1552, seemed unprecedently large at 50,000 men, by the end of the next century some countries had eight times that number of men under arms.[2] Secondly, the artillery emerged as a distinct arm, alongside the traditional cavalry and infantry, and this in turn led to the development of an entirely new type of fortification.[3] These new defences could not be extemporized by nobles or city councils, but had to be specially designed and constructed by a new group of officers, who came to be known as 'engineers'.

The third great change was that the infantry began from the late fifteenth century onwards to be trained—or 'drilled', as the phrase went—very intensively in the handling not only of pikes but also of firearms, great and small.[4] From being almost indistinguishable from what continued to be known as a 'mob', they came to form distinct and controllable 'units', part of a hierarchy.

The fourth development was that these new-style armies began to acquire new specialists, such as lodgings-officers and supply-officers.[5] Like the engineers, they emerged as a result of the change in size and type of armies. These changes in size and type led to the fifth great change, which involved the need to exercise a new type of control over the three arms—cavalry, infantry, and now artillery. The art of a commander now consisted in maximizing their very different strengths, making optimum use as well of the terrain and of the weather.[6] Finally, a corresponding development took place at sea. The crowds of hired merchantmen were replaced in the sixteenth century by fleets of specialized warships, armed with heavy guns. Their aim was no longer simply to close with their opponents and board them, but to perform uniform tactical manoeuvres in such a way that they could most effectively bring their guns to bear.[7]

Taken together, these changes were nothing less than a revolution in the way that wars were fought. They also proved to have revolutionary social and economic effects, reducing some societies to widespread poverty, and destroying the power of some political groups, but greatly accelerating European world dominance, stimulating economic development in some regions, and firmly establishing the power of rulers skilful and lucky enough to profit from them. The changes in the art of war also had deep and far-reaching effects upon mapmaking: as R. A. Skelton once put it, 'the extent to which the mapping of the land surface of the globe was accelerated and enriched by the military surveyor cannot be exaggerated'.[8]

GROWTH IN THE SIZE OF ARMIES AND THE DEVELOPMENT OF TOPOGRAPHICAL MAPPING

The relatively small armies of the Middle Ages had not needed to make elaborate plans for their passage through the countryside. When the Black Prince (1330–78) and Henry V (ruled 1413–22), for instance, made their destructive incursions into France, they took no maps, for their forces could slip inconspicuously through the countryside, and were accustomed to live off the land. In general, late-medieval armies relied for geographical information upon spies, whose reports were verbal; they were sent out in front of armies, and, if they returned, were 'debriefed' by commanders.[9] Indeed, map-consciousness in Europe was still poorly developed, so that the very idea of using graphic aids would not have crossed commanders' minds.

All this began to change in the late fifteenth century, when the French armies began their campaigns in Italy. Around 1495, for instance, Jacques Signot drew a map showing the French King Charles V (ruled 1483–98) the best way to take his artillery down into Italy,[10] and in that same year the besiegers of Novara equipped themselves with a map which showed the roads, marshes, woods, rivers, and villages around the city.[11] These precocious stirrings received powerful theoretical reinforcement from the writings of Niccoló Machiavelli, Baldassare Castiglione, and Sir Thomas Elyot, all of whom, as we have seen, thought that they detected map use in the writings of the military authors of classical antiquity (Chapter 1). Some military commanders took all this advice seriously: in 1520 Henry VIII (ruled 1509–47) is said to have commissioned a map of Gascony and Guyenne for the invading English army,[12] and the French memorialist Martin Du Bellay (c.1495–1559) described the Emperor Charles V in 1536 as having in his hand a map of Provence (a region of southern France) so effective that, in looking at it, he felt as if he had already captured the territory.[13]

However, it was one thing to imagine the potential use of maps for armies on the move, and another thing to provide them at a scale which could take into account individual buildings, strong bridges, impenetrable thickets, boggy patches, and so forth. After the publication of the *Theatrum orbis terrarum* of Abraham Ortelius in 1570, the whole of Europe was for the first time covered in an easily portable atlas. But the Ortelian maps were too small-scale to offer anything but a gross impression of the geography. When, for instance, the Spanish duke of Alba (1508–82) was planning his campaigns in the Netherlands against the Dutch rebels in the 1560s, he could only find maps of remarkable crudity to delineate his passage from the Mediterranean Sea northwards along France's eastern frontier, and once in the Netherlands he had to commission Christian Sgrooten (c.1532–1608) to prepare large-scale maps of the area. This skilful mapmaker did indeed eventually cover the area in thirty-four large sheets, with sufficient detail to be of some use for operations.[14]

The new military schools from the late sixteenth century onwards often offered mapmaking in their curriculum. For instance, when Sir Humphrey Gilbert (1539–83) set out the syllabus for his proposed academy of 1570, he provided for a teacher 'who shall teache to drawe mappes, sea charts etc., and to take by view of eye the platte of any thinge'. Similarly, in the academy of Antoine de Pluvinel (1555–1620), established at Paris in the early seventeenth century, young nobles were to learn not only riding but 'enough drawing to design a fort and map a plan of campaign'.[15] Clearly, there was a feeling that officers ought now to be able to make manuscript maps of the military operations that they commanded.

In spite of these and other academic projects, printed maps continued to lag far behind what was necessary, even in the seventeenth-century editions of Mercator and the Blæu family.[16] Thus when Henri IV of France was planning an offensive into the German regions in 1610, he had to rely upon sending spies forward, to tell him where his army with its artillery might easily pass: we know this from the secret accounts, where the payments are recorded.[17] When, in 1631, Gustav Adolf II of Sweden (ruled 1611–32) wished to take advantage of his crushing victory at Breitenfeld, he hardly knew how to proceed, for he had no detailed maps of the lands south of Brandenburg or west of Magdeburg;[18] he was in the dark.

From about the middle of the century onwards, France began to be mapped in ever greater detail by the Sanson and Cassini dynasties.[19] But it would not appear that the generals of Louis XIV (ruled 1643–1715) made great use of large-scale topographical maps for field operations, any more than did their adversaries, Prince Eugene of Savoy (1663–1736) and the Duke of Marlborough (1650–1722).[20] The standard practice of the time appears to have been to obtain the best maps available, and then to amplify their information from local informants. As the celebrated French engineer

Vauban (1633–1707) puts it in his manual,[21] to learn about territory 'you must obtain the best topographical maps available, and then annotate them canton by canton [roughly 'county' by 'county'], generating information from people living there'.

This combination of graphic and oral information lasted into the eighteenth century, but seems to have begun to change in the 1740s. It is possible to examine a long and rich chronological slice of English eighteenth-century mapping from the Cumberland Collection of military maps at Windsor Castle. They were assembled by the Duke of Cumberland (1721–65), who was more successful as a map-collector than as a general, and are available on microfilm and as microfiche.[22] To judge from this collection, it was in the 1740s that the English army began to use special draughtsmen, who went into the field and compiled large-scale manuscript maps with titles like 'Plan of the lines near Oudenbosch'. These mapmakers, with names like Robert Barker, D. Paterson, and William Eyres, have not been closely studied.[23] But their work marked a radical departure in military cartography, for now a commander could order up a detailed map of an area over which he intended to fight. In a document like the 'Sketch of the ground between Herenthout and Beringen', made by Eyres and Paterson in the 1740s, the woods are carefully inserted and there is some attempt to show relief, so that with a map of this kind a commander could make a rational dispos-

Fig. 52. War games in an eighteenth-century German military academy, Hans Friedrich von Fleming, *Der vollkommene teutsche Soldat* (Leipzig, 1726). In this elegant room, four sets of instructions seem to be going on at the various tables. Above the tables on the right, there are on the wall two large panels setting out the calibres of the artillery, and on the wall at the end, five instructors seem to be discussing the best way to assault a well-defended sea port, looking something like La Rochelle.

ition of his troops, and see both where the artillery could pass, and also where it might best be sited to harass the enemy.

In France much the same sort of development was taking place. In *Le parfait aide de camp*, published at Paris in 1770, Georges-Louis Le Rouge (active 1730–70), 'ingénieur et géographe du roi', explains how during the 1740s and 1750s it had been found necessary to train young aides-de-camp in bringing the most recent topographical and military information to the general officers whom they served, often using maps. Probably the leading exponent of military map use in France at this time was Pierre Bourcet (1700–80), whose book entitled *Les principes de la guerre de montagne* (Paris, 1775) explained how 'a commander should plan troop manoeuvres and supply on a day-to-day basis from maps'.[24] As yet, though, these relatively detailed maps relied on hachures (striations marking hills) to indicate the terrain: there were no contour lines until quite far into the nineteenth century.

Meanwhile the same type of development was taking place in Brandenburg-Prussia, where Frederick the Great (ruled 1740–86) used officers like Major Von Wrede and Major Von Griese to manage a travelling *Plankammer*, or map-office, from which material could be generated for most contingencies.[25] Frederick's own *Instructions for his generals*[26] insist upon the use of 'the most detailed and exact maps that can be found', for 'knowledge of the country

is to a general what a rifle is to an infantryman and what the rules of arithmetic are to a geometrician'. Frederick was of course in close touch with what was going on in France and England, and probably used specialists from these countries.

Figure 52, taken from *Der vollkommene teutsche Soldat*, published at Leipzig in 1726, shows how thoroughly the study of maps was penetrating the German military academies. Groups of students are seen examining them at tables alongside the walls, while at the end of the room a large map sets out the details of a siege. Such an image is impossible to imagine for the sixteenth century, but by the middle of the eighteenth century armies had become so large that some form of cartographic control had become absolutely indispensable, along with standardized written orders, fighting groups of about 12,000 men, and trained general staffs; this was all part of a process of growing bureaucratization.[27] Indeed, the military

Fig. 53. C. Chapin, 'Sketch of the ground upon which was fought the battle of Waterloo', 1815. This map, commissioned by Wellington a few weeks before the battle of Waterloo in 1815, shows the characteristics of the military topographical maps developed from the middle of the eighteenth century onwards. The scale is relatively large, enabling roads, tracks, buildings, and fields to be shown in some detail. From a military point of view, its deficiency is that the commander could not use the hachure-type marking of elevation accurately to site his artillery. Contour lines would eventually solve this problem.

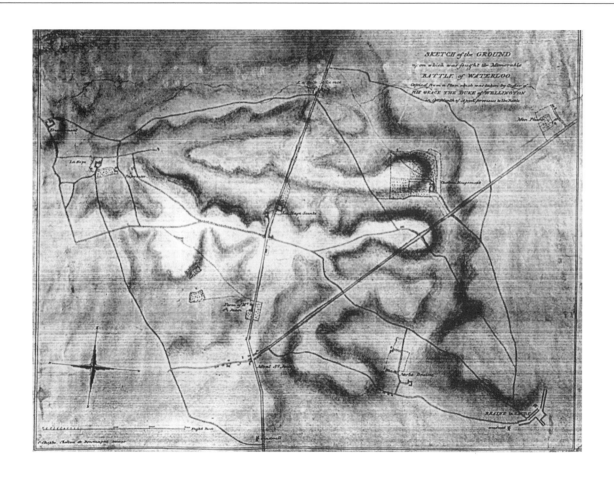

hierarchy and procedures that developed at this time would have been quite recognizable to twentieth-century soldiers.

The grasp of topography was to be tested in the French and British armies by the unusual circumstances of the American Revolutionary war (1776–83). In this transatlantic terrain, as a British general wrote to his principal surveyor in 1767, 'there is no map of the inhabited provinces of any use, for there is none correct; even the roads are not marked'.[28] On the whole, both armies rose well to the occasion: the French generated uniform and effective maps through their topographical engineers, while the British used a wider range of officers to produce an immense quantity of quite accurate cartographic information.[29] The forces under the command of the American general George Washington (1732–99) also developed a cartographic capability; he had complained in 1777 about 'the want of accurate maps of the country', and that very year set up a map-making unit within the Continental Army, which seems to have performed creditably.[30]

By the late eighteenth century, then, Machiavelli's hope that a commander would be able to 'paint out the country through which he must march' had been largely fulfilled. During the wars at the end of the century, with their even larger armies, maps were used even more effectively. Napoleon Bonaparte (1769–1821) never went on campaign without his mobile map collection, which accompan-

ied him in a special cart, and he used it frequently, spending a good deal of each day down on his hands and knees, minutely examining the maps supplied by his cartographic expert, General Louis Bacler d'Albe (1761–1824).[31] On these maps he plotted not only his own dispositions, but also those of the enemy, as reported by spies. Eugène Carrias explains the arrangement like this:

General Sanson was head of the topographic office for the *Grande Armée*; he was responsible for preparing maps relating to the theatres of war in Germany and Italy. Berthier had to see to the construction of two mobile compartmented boxes which were assigned to the Emperor and his chief of staff. They were so arranged that at a single glance you could take in the movement of all the Austrian troops, regiment by regiment and battalion by battalion … The maps were divided up so that each section corresponded to one of the Austrian armies.[32]

It is easy to understand the great advantage that this specialized information would have given the French armies.

Napoleon's nemesis, the British general Wellington (1769–1852), also relied heavily upon his cartographic staff, which for instance supplied him with a detailed map of the site of the Waterloo battle some weeks before it took place (Fig. 53).[33] Knowing that Napoleon would soon march northwards against the British and their allies around Brussels, Wellington had seen to it that maps were drawn of four or five possible battlegrounds. It was the

Waterloo map which turned out to be the crucial one, allowing Wellington to set out his defensive position with his usual skill, so that repeated and furious French attacks were eventually repulsed, and Napoleon's defeat and exile became inevitable.

THE EMERGENCE OF ARTILLERY AND THE DEVELOPMENT OF NEW-STYLE FORTIFICATIONS

Various kinds of firearm had been used in Europe as far back as the early fourteenth century. As time went by, the tendency was for these weapons, both large and small, to become more mobile, quicker-firing, and more accurate at longer ranges. Thus musketeers, as we shall see, came to join pike-armed infantrymen in the classical squares, and heavy firearms slowly emerged from their original role as massive stationary adjuncts to a siege. A decisive step in this latter respect came with the French invasion of Italy in 1494. The French brought with them an artillery train of hitherto unimagined power

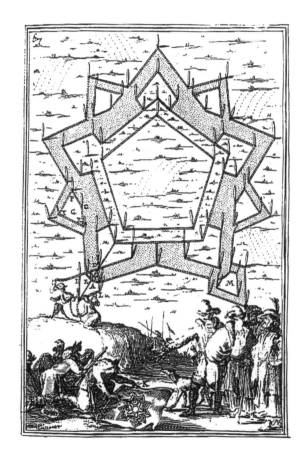

Fig. 54. Alain Manesson-Mallet, Plate of an engineer with a map supervising the construction of a fortress, from *Les travaux de Mars* (3 vols., Paris, 1684–5). At the bottom right, the engineer explains his work to a group of well-clad visitors. At his feet is the plan of the fortress, held down against the breeze by a figure with a gun slung across his back. In the background, workmen peg out the lines of the pentagon, to be constructed on flat land happily devoid of farm-buildings. Just behind the hill, an armed force seems ready to protect the proceedings.

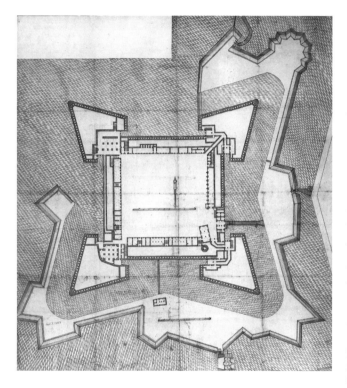

and mobility, which soon proved that the high walls of the Italian medieval cities were no match for their destructive power.[34]

The curtain-walled cities that were found all over western Europe at that time proved very vulnerable to attack by cannon-launched projectiles, made at first of stone and then of iron. A whole section of the defences would rapidly be reduced to rubble, and then the town would be at the mercy of the assailant. Some means had to be found both to reduce the vulnerability of the defences, and to offer the possibility of a counter-battery. The architectural solution was found in 'bastioned traces': from the early sixteenth century onwards, towns came to be surrounded not by high walls, but by a series of thick low walls and bastions, upon which artillery could be sited. Figures 54, 55, and 56 show the shape of these bastions, projecting from the walls. The bastions and walls were so conceived that an attacker could be caught in cross-fire no matter what the direction of approach, and a ditch usually completed the defences. Supplementary bastions, or outworks,

Fig. 55. Rochus Guerini, Graf von Linar, Manuscript plan of the fortress at Spandau, *c.*1578. The citadel of Spandau is situated at the confluence of the Spree and Havel rivers, a few kilometres west of the centre of Berlin. It became the leading Prussian fortress, and was besieged at various times by Swedish, French, and Russian forces; after 1945 it held for a while Nazi leaders accused of war crimes. Spandau, whose central area survives, was also an arsenal, and gave its name to a particularly devastating machine-gun.

might be added to force the attacker to begin the assault even further back from the town proper (Fig. 55).

Such bastioned traces were immensely costly to construct, requiring the purchase of a huge band of land, not only for the works themselves, but also for the extensive fields of fire needed outside them. They also demanded entirely new construction techniques: whereas it was possible to undertake the construction of quite elaborate curtain-walls around a city, without first preparing a plan, it was impossible to set out a bastioned trace without first working it out on paper, plotting out the walls and bastions in such a way that their protective weapons could come into maximum play. Needless to say, the configuration of such traces changed as weapons increased in range. Figure 54, from the French engineer Manesson-Mallet's *Les travaux de Mars* of 1684–5, symbolically illustrates the process: the engineer on the right explains the plan, while workmen stake out the shape of the new fortification upon the ground.

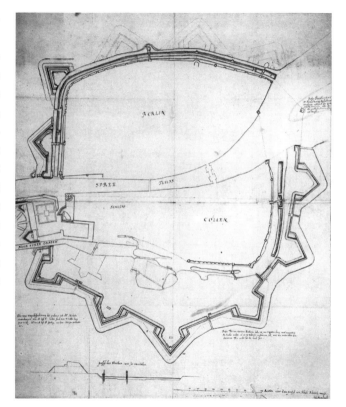

Fig. 56. Johann Gregor Membhard, Manuscript plan of Berlin, 1659. This little-known manuscript plan should be compared with Membhard's slightly earlier printed plan (Fig. 59).
Both show the River Spree curving across the centre of the image, with a branch of it enclosing the town of 'Kölln' to the south. The Electors' castle and *Lustgarten* then appear to the west. They had not fitted very well into the medieval walls (Fig. 59), and it was even more difficult to include them in the bastioned trace; this clearly remained a vulnerable part of the city's defences.

It was the engineers of the Italian states who had taken the shock of the French artillery in 1494, and it was they who developed the first bastioned traces, which indeed were first known as 'traces italiennes'.[35] Relatively few of their early manuscript plans have survived, perhaps because they became so stained and torn in the course of use that they were thrown away once the work was complete.[36] In *Firearms and fortifications*,[37] Pepper and Adams reproduce one of the earliest plans, drawn about 1529 by Baldassare Peruzzi, an architect who was associated with the Sangallo family of Florence, famous builders of fortifications. At the top is a large citadel, from which the bastioned walls stretch to enclose a large area. There is some indication of buildings within this area, and some indication also (in the shape of faint pencil-lines) that Peruzzi had calculated the angles of fire in laying out his project. In the end it was never built, which indeed may account for the survival of the plan. During the first half of the sixteenth century fortifications of this kind were built in Italy at Genoa, Florence, Palmanova, Piacenza, Siena, Rome, and Turin, to name only the most prominent.

Just as the Italians learned from the French about the new power of artillery, so the French learned from the Italians about the new style of fortification. During the late 1530s and early 1540s, François I employed Italian engineers in strengthening his north-eastern frontier. They worked at Boulogne, Hesdin, Landrecies, Montreuil, St-Pol, Thérouanne, Villefranche, and Vitry-le-François, to name only the most important and costly sites. No doubt they created many plans, but, in spite of intensive research, it is not clear that any of their paperwork survives, except in the archives of Turin.[38]

The situation was very different in England, where the activity of Henry VIII left a great deal of evidence, which has been extensively studied.[39] Henry decided in 1539 that he needed a vast system of coastal defence for protection against the French, and by the end of 1540 as many as twenty-four new forts were being garrisoned—a huge effort, made possible by lavish use of the money made available by the plunder of the monasteries during the 1530s. These new forts, many-gunned round towers like the one at St Mawes, taken from German and some Italian examples, were already out of date when they were planned. By the middle 1540s Henry realized that they might not be the best way to defend cities, and so he turned to the bastioned trace for protecting cities like Berwick and Portsmouth. For the latter there survives a very significant and well-studied plan, perhaps by the English engineer Sir Richard Lee (1513–1575).[40]

This plan shows the whole city planimetrically, with the streets and houses included, and the walls carefully delineated; two bastions have been pencilled in, to supplement the existing defences. The map has no scale-bar, but it bears the inscription that 'this plat is in every inch an 100 foot', or in other words that its scale is 1 : 1,200. Scholars have debated much over the origins of this scaled drawing, trying in vain to establish the exact mode of transmission from Italy, where scaled plans were known from the early sixteenth century, to England.[41] Common sense would suggest that the transmission occurred through contacts between Italian and English engineers, jointly engaged in Henry's fortification-schemes, for which such scaled drawings were indispensable. At all events, the scaled drawing would now have a long history in England, being crucial not only for fortification plans but also for the estate maps that began to emerge in the late 1560s (see Chapter 6).

During the sixteenth century, Italian engineers could be found at most of the European princely courts, serving a variety of masters. Once such engineer was J. B. Guerini (1525–96), who after working for the kings of France (as 'Roche Guérin') went in the 1560s, at the outbreak of the religious wars in France, to serve various German princes.[42] In 1578 he entered the service of Johan Georg of Brandenburg (ruled 1571–98), and as *Baumeister*, or head architect, for the citadel at Spandau, produced a remarkably elegant plan of the work there (Fig. 55). The bold blocking of the bas-tions and outer works contrasts with the elegant penmanship of the inner details; this is a working drawing, but a most delicate one, showing the cartographic sophistication now required in drawing up plans from which fortifications could be constructed.

As in the other European countries, the Italian engineers in the German lands gave way in the seventeenth century to native-born experts. One such expert was Johann Gregor Membhard (1607–78), whom we shall encounter later in this chapter. Figure 56 shows his 1659 plan of the new works at Berlin. This plan does not appear in the usual listings of Berlin plans, perhaps because it is now preserved (rather unexpectedly) in the ducal library at Wolfenbüttel.[43] It shows the twin towns of Berlin-Cölln, divided by the River Spree, for which a new canal is proposed (middle left, 'Neue Spree graben'). It is carefully scaled, and three proposed new bastions are pencilled in at the top; in fact, they would soon be built. J. B. Guerini, alias Roche Guérin, alias Graf von Linar, had many counterparts in the Spanish-speaking world, where Italian architects like the Antonelli dynasty were particularly active in fortifying Spain's New World possessions.[44]

Manuscript plans of fortifications continued to be produced in great numbers for the next 200 years, as Europe came to be liberally sprinkled with bastioned traces; they were also common in the European overseas empires.[45] As the great French engineer

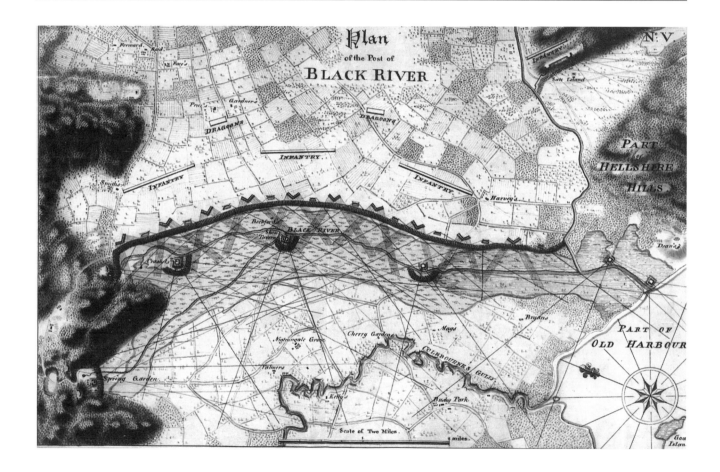

Vauban put it, writing about 1700, 'there are now few strongholds in Europe of which we do not possess plans; most of them, indeed, have printed versions'.[46] Many of these plans were collected into atlases that were very widely disseminated; the work of Christophe Tassin (active 1630–45) in France, for instance, provided a huge readership with plans of the major French fortifications,[47] and Tassin had his counterparts in both Germany and Italy.[48]

On the whole, these manuscript and printed plans did not show much development as time went by. But by the late seventeenth century they did often show the fields of fire from the various gun-plaforms, and this in turn often drew the cartographers into showing quite extensive areas of countryside outside the fortified area. Figure 57, for instance, drawn in 1780, shows the fields of fire from the gun-platforms defending the post of Black River in Jamaica, offering as well some idea of the surrounding countryside. In general, the delineation of the fields of fire reveals to the historian exactly what the engineer had in mind when designing the fortification. It also offers a way of estimating the range of the heavy weapons being used.

The fortification plans were originally designed for a limited purpose. But those which survive are of interest not only for what they tell us about military history, but also for the information that they contain about the development of cities. Many plans set out the pattern of streets, and are sometimes a unique source for this information.[49] Other plans reveal the sequence of development of modern cities, in whose street-patterns and green spaces may often be detected the influence of long-abandoned ramparts and bastions. The work of urban archaeologists and architects would be severely hampered without the existence of these generally accurate plans of early modern towns.

GRAPHIC REPRESENTATIONS OF MILITARY FORMATIONS AND PROCEDURES

One of the aspects of Roman warfare that most interested Renaissance commentators was the way in which infantry had been trained to carry out maoeuvres in unison. The fifteenth-century Swiss were among the earliest in modern times to practise similar uniform movements, and it seemed that there were further lessons to be learned from the engagements of antiquity. As Peter Whithorne put it in *Certaine waies for the ordering of souldiers in battel-*

Fig. 57. Archibald Campbell, 'Plan of the post at Black River', 1780. Major-General Archibald Campbell prepared an atlas of maps of the British defences of Jamaica, at a time when a French invasion seemed imminent in 1780. This is 'no. V' in the series, and is a good example of military mapping of the period. Roads, marshy areas, and fields are well shown, as are the hills which hem the plain in to east and west. Such a map gives a rather sanitized look to the countryside, but it does describe the main features convincingly.

ray, published at London in 1588, the question was, 'what advertisement ought to be used in turning about a whole band of men, after such a sort as though it were but one body';[50] in short, what was the best way to organize drill-squads?

Such manoeuvres could be explained in words, but were much more effectively set out in the form of maps and diagrams. There had been such diagrams in medieval works on geometry, astronomy, and medicine, but Machiavelli seems to have been the first to apply them to military matters.[51] In *The arte of warre* he uses many figures to set out the correct position of each soldier on the line of march. The many translations of *The arte of warre* added to this store of visual material. For instance, Peter Whithorne's edition of 1573 not only used many drawings of formations, but also included 'plattes' or plans of different types of fortification, and a 'figure' showing 'the manner how to incampe an army' (Fig. 9).

This use of imagery to explain the new military procedures continued to flourish in the seventeenth century. In 1616, for instance, Count John of Nassau opened a military academy at Siegen, and the first director of the *schola militaris*, Johann Jacob von Wallhausen, in 1621 published his *Defensio patriæ oder Landstrettung*, based on the precepts taught in the academy.[52] This sumptuous work contained many fold-out plates showing how infantry formations ought to be manoeuvred, with each soldier's place shown;

it also had plates of individual infantrymen performing various drills with the musket. About the same time, Antoine de Pluvinel (1555–1620) was running an academy for young nobles in the Paris of Louis XIII (ruled 1610–43). Here too one of the objects was to explain graphically how to adopt the latest military principles, or, as a contemporary puts it, 'how the students may best arrange the battalions, and provide a regular fortification for strongpoints'.[53]

The diagrammatic approach was also applied to the production and operation of heavy artillery. There had been sixteenth-century German artillery manuals, but one of the most elegant was that produced by Benedit de Vassallieu (active 1585–1615), French royal engineer, in 1613.[54] Here all the elements needed to put a gun into the field—wooden carriages and tools, powder of various types, gun-barrels, and so forth—were drawn out in their correct dimensions. The idea was not only that any gunner could now operate any weapon, but also that the various parts were interchangeable and could be manufactured uniformly. Vassallieu's manual, which had counterparts in the German lands, was in fact a primer for the mass production of weapons, using techniques that went back at least as far as the sixteenth-century Venetian Arsenal, and stretched forward to Mr Ford of Detroit and beyond.

In this development of illustrated military manuals, techniques of book manufacture played an important part. In the Middle Ages, it would perhaps have been desirable to have set out graphically the part played by each archer in an army, and how the bow should be handled. But if such a manual had been composed, it could only have been circulated in manuscript, to a limited number of people. By the end of the sixteenth century the Europeans had not only mastered the mass production of printed books, but had also developed copper-engraving to a stage at which such books could provide large pictorial pages. The need to explain the new military developments to as large an audience as possible made it inevitable that authors would have recourse not only to printed books but also to a wealth of imagery within them, since so many of the new theories and techniques could best be illustrated in the form of images.

THE EMERGENCE OF NEW MILITARY SPECIALISTS: ENGINEERS

The title of 'engineer'goes far back in European history: the English army of Edward III, in the middle of the fourteenth century, numbered a good many of them on its payrolls. But they took on a whole new significance during the sixteenth century, because it was they who designed the new fortifications. At first most of them came from Italy, but the northern powers soon developed their own engineers, beginning in England in the 1530s, and rather later in France, Brandenburg-Prussia, and Spain, where Italian

engineers remained prominent down to the end of the sixteenth century.[55] The primary purpose of the engineers was to work on the new fortifications, and in England they remained largely confined to this task. But in France and Brandenburg-Prussia, where the fortification-programmes were much more extensive, the engineers became involved in mapping projects extending far beyond the mere drawing of fortification-plans. Sometimes these projects were associated with the building of public works, like canals, or with the construction of royal palaces. But they also seem often to have been undertaken because, in the shape of the engineers, the monarchs had a readily available group of skilled cartographers.

Their work in France is relatively well known.[56] Four of them were on the payroll in 1597, and six in 1611; all were by then of French origin. As they were assigned to provinces for their defensive works, it was natural that their mapping activity covered these areas. In Picardy, for instance, the engineer was Jean Errard (1554–1610), author of *La fortification réduicte en art*, published at Paris in 1600, the first French manual setting out the new methods of fortification.[57] His deputy was Jehan Martellier, who was responsible for compiling both large-scale maps of the various *gouvernements* (military districts), and also a newly accurate map of the province as a whole (Fig. 58). This set of maps was copied several times in the engineers' map-room (probably at the Arsenal in

Paris), and eventually served for the printed version engraved by the prolific map-publisher Christophe Tassin in the 1630s.[58]

To the south, in Champagne, the engineer was Claude Chastillon (active 1580–1616), author of the superb book of views known as the *Topographie française*, published at Paris in 1641, some years after his death. Chastillon probably drew his own maps, which closely paralleled those of Martellier in scope and style; his work was also adopted by Tassin for the atlases of the 1630s.[59] In Dauphiné the engineer was Jean de Beins (active 1589–1630), whose maps have been closely studied,[60] and who is acknowledged to have been the founder of accurate cartographic knowledge of this Alpine region. Once again, his work found its way into a variety of printed collections, profoundly influencing the early seventeenth-century cartographic image of south-eastern France.

In Provence, the engineers were Raymond and Jean de

Fig. 58. Map of Picardy composed by Jehan Martellier, *conducteur des desseins* for Jean Errard, *c.*1602. Jehan Martellier built this provincial map up from twenty or so large-scale maps showing the military districts called *gouvernments*; these maps covered areas roughly 10 miles (16 km) square. Combined into this general map, they offer an image of the province that is far more detailed than contemporary printed maps. Eventually, this map found its way into print in the atlas published by Christophe Tassin in 1634.

Bonnefons, but they did not undertake topographical mapping, confining their work to the delineation of towns like St Tropez, Toulon, and Marseille. The other engineer prominent under Henri IV was Benedit de Vassallieu, author of the artillery-manual that we have already mentioned. He was also the probable author of detailed maps of Brittany—which also found their way into the publications of Tassin—though his area of activity was officially Guyenne, away in the south-west of France. He was also the author of a magnificent printed plan of Paris, published in 1609. Whereas former views of the city had adopted an eastward orientation, with the River Seine rather woodenly and vertically bisecting the image, Vassallieu's view was taken from the north-east, and the most remarkable buildings—the Louvre, Notre-Dame, the Arsenal, and so forth—were shown very carefully and excessively large. Vassallieu succeeded in changing an image that had been unimaginative and static into one that caught the dynamism of the fast-expanding capital.[61]

Taken as a whole, the cartographic activity of these engineers resulted in the mapping of a large part of France in much greater detail than had hitherto been accomplished. Their work was interrupted by the assassination of Henri IV in 1610, and was not thereafter resumed at anything like the same intensity. But the dissemination of their work in the publications of Tassin marked a decisive advance over the provincial maps found in the 1594 atlas of Maurice Bouguereau.[62] After that, large-scale maps of France were produced first by Nicholas Sanson (1600–67), in the 1650s, and then, in the latter part of the century, by the Cassini dynasty.[63] The activity of the military engineers in large-scale manuscript mapping thus lasted for only about fifteen years (1595–1610), but their work in printed form then greatly extended cartographic knowledge of most of France's frontier provinces.

The pattern of events in Brandenburg-Prussia was somewhat different.[64] As in France, the leading figures of the sixteenth century were Italians, with Francesco Chiaramella of Venice and J. B. Guerini of Tuscany the most prominent[65] in building fortifications. Chiaramella worked in the 1550s for the rulers both of Braunschweig and of Brandenburg; Guerini, as we have seen, succeeded him in Brandenburg in 1578. Neither seems to have drawn any topographical maps, though we know that Guerini was an accomplished draughtsman (Fig. 55). In 1618 the territories of Prussia and Brandenburg were united under John Sigismund (ruled 1608–19) who seven years earlier had one engineer and four *Werkmeister* (clerks of works) on his payroll.[66]

John Sigismund was succeeded by George William (ruled 1613–40), after whom came Frederick William, the Great Elector (ruled 1640–88), in whose time the engineers were assigned to sur-veying, or *Landesvermessung*.[67] The nature of these duties is explained in a commission of 1649 for Christoph Friedrich Schmidt.[68] He is, of course, to make true and accurate surveys, and in a passage reminiscent of Queen Elizabeth's commission to Christopher Saxton (Chapter 3), local officials are enjoined to help him, just as he is advised to keep them in touch with his work. Schmidt had received similar commissions in 1642 and 1644, but we do not know what work he may have accomplished.

The most famous of the Great Elector's engineers was Johann Gregor Membhard (1607–78), who had been born at Linz and entered the Elector's service in 1638.[69] His first work was at Pillau, and then he was called to Berlin, where he drew the well-known plan reproduced in Matthæus Merian's *Topographia Electorat. Brandenburgici et Ducatus Pomeraniæ*, published at Frankfurt am Main in 1652. Reproduced as Figure 59, this plan shows the city of Berlin-Cölln before it had been equipped with a bastioned trace. The palace

Fig. 59. Johann Gregor Membhard, Plan of Berlin, reproduced in Matthæus Merian, *Topographia Electorat. Brandenburgici …* (Frankfurt am Main, 1652). This plan of Berlin is typical of those assembled by Matthæus Merian into his great printed urban collections of the mid-seventeenth century. The first such collection had been that of Braun and Hogenberg, begun in 1595 (see Chapter 6), and during the seventeenth century engineers' plans were published in this way in many European countries, until virtually every town of any size had appeared in print.

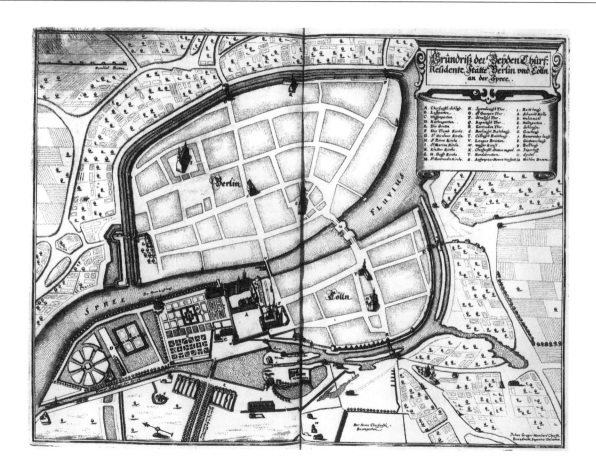

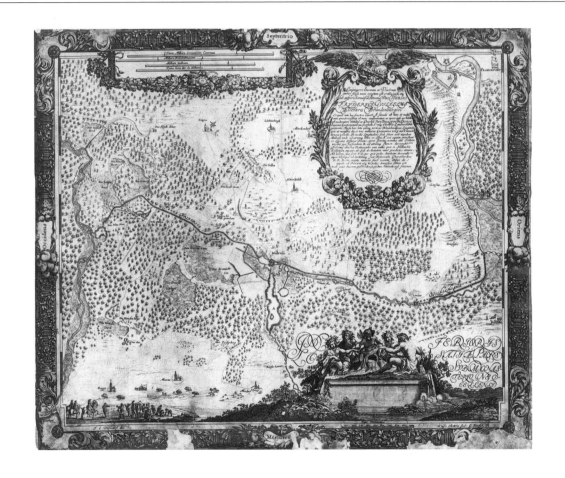

('A' on the key) and *Lustgarten* ('B') of the Elector are prominent, as is his kitchen garden ('D'). The medieval walls are pierced by a number of gates, and the internal pattern of streets is shown. This printed plan should be compared with Membhard's manuscript map of 1659 (Fig. 56), showing the bastions in place. Much of his time was taken up with work on the Elector's houses at Berlin and Potsdam, though after 1666 the work at Berlin was supervised by Philipp de Chieze,[70] who had come from Orange in France to become the Elector's *Generalquartiermeister* and first *Baumeister*.

Chieze collaborated with Joachim Ernst von Blesendorf (1640–77)[71] on the Oder–Spree Canal, just to the south-east of Berlin, for which a printed map survives (Fig. 60). The map is oriented northwards, with the River Oder on the right and the River Spree on the left; the canal leads through Müllrose in the centre. It is signed (lower left) 'J. E. Blesendorf', and was engraved by Bartsch; there is an elaborate cartouche and several scale-bars. The villages are easily identified on the modern map, as is the general

Fig. 60. Joachim Ernst von Blesendorf, Map of the Oder–Spree Canal, *c.*1670. The engineers of the Great Elector in Prussia seem to have been required to undertake more varied tasks than their contemporaries in other countries, and this elegant printed map shows how one of them saw the newly built Oder–Spree Canal, with a survey-party at work on the lower left. Such a map was probably printed as an exercise in public relations for the Great Elector.

topography. Blesendorf, who came from a Berlin family of painters, was sent to Rome in 1666–8, presumably to learn Italian engineering techniques, and upon his return was appointed *Oberingenieur* (chief engineer); when Chieze died in 1674 he succeeded him as *Generalquartiermeister*, only to be killed in 1677 at the siege of Stettin.

Two other engineers were best known for their works on fortification, illustrated by many plans. Christian Neubauer was *Ingenieur und Landmesser* in 1667 and at least until 1673; he was the author of the *Discoursus et vera architecturæ praxis* (Stargard in Pommern, 1679).[72] Matthias Dögen in 1647 published the *Architectura militaris moderna*, a treatise on military architecture remarkable for the aesthetic power and compositional skill of the plates.[73] Finally, we have to note the work of the engineer La Vigne, who in 1685 drew a magnificent plan of Berlin and its environs.[74] The city has now taken on its fully-bastioned shape, and the surrounding countryside is shown with care in what the author calls a 'Plan Géométral'. He shows the main roads, and distinguishes between field and forest; this was a map to bear comparison with the contemporary work in France of the Cassinis.

The Great Elector thus had a considerable number of trained engineers in his service, and it is likely that they produced many maps that are now lost. From 1661 onwards his library had a map collection, which eventually passed to the German national collection, though in a much reduced state.[75] One of the great curiosities of cartography is the huge atlas dedicated to him in 1666 by Johann Moritz of Nassau, and known as the *Atlas des grossen Kur-Fürsten*.[76] It mostly contains relatively small-scale printed Dutch maps, but bound in among them are two large-scale manuscript maps, of Brandenburg and East Prussia, that may well be the work of one of the Great Elector's engineers. By the time of his death in 1688 he had laid the foundations of an engineering service that would come to maturity in the next century.

The work of the engineers went on under his successor, King Frederick I (ruled 1688–1713). In 1704 an edict set out the pay-scale for the *Ingenieur-Conducteurs*, whose name reminds us of the French *conducteurs des dessins* (makers of maps and plans) who in the early seventeenth century were the engineering mapmakers. But the *Conducteur*'s patent of 1677 printed by Bonin curiously makes no mention of the drawing of maps as part of his duties. At all events, the engineers continued to draw maps, even if we have no copies of them. In 1706, for instance, Jean-François de La Monge mapped the region of Krossen, Friedrich Kreutz worked in the Neumark, and Alexander Blomerus produced maps defining the boundary between Braunschweig and Brandenburg.[77]

Early in the reign of King Frederick William I (ruled 1713–40) a *Plankammer* (map library) was established at Potsdam,[78] and in 1728 the *Ingenieurkorps* was put upon a formal administrative footing, with thirty officers on the rolls.[79] *Landesaufnahmen*, or topographical surveys, were among their duties, and we know for instance that *Landmesser* Balzer and *Konducteur* Bielitz worked at Stettin around 1726–7, and that *Kapitan* Embers was assigned to work at Düsseldorf in 1737.[80] Many of the engineers' names at this time were French (Du Moulin, Corbin, Guyonneau, and so forth); they were probably Huguenot refugees. One of the most prominent was General Peter von Montargues (1660–1733). He had become an engineer in 1689, and then rose steadily up the chain of command, becoming head of the engineering service in 1706.[81]

Many of Montargues's maps survive in the German National Library, and they range from plans of fortifications to extensive topographical surveys. One of the most remarkable is the 'Special-Karte von der Mittel-Marck', a coloured manuscript map at a scale

Fig. 61. Peter von Montargues, 'Particuliere Landkarte der Landstrasse von Ratzburg bis Neuburg …', 1709. Montargues had become head of the engineering service in 1706, and compiled a great many maps that survive in the German National Library. He was of French origin, and this map is a good example of the way in which French engineers now 'saw' the European countryside. It is too small-scale to offer much detail, but gives an excellent generalized impression; the key contains information on a variety of settlements, such as 'village without a church'.

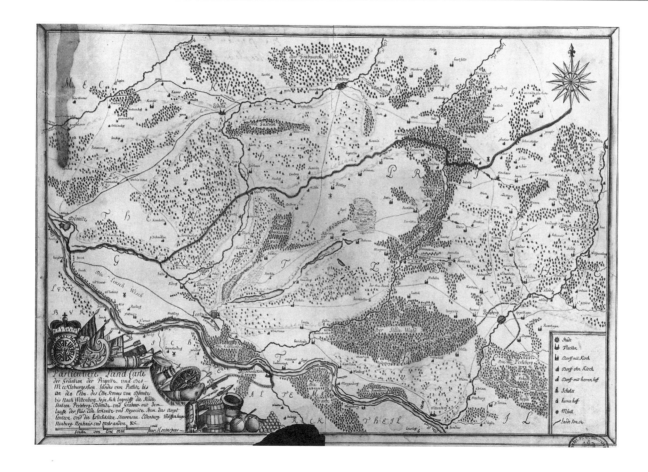

of about 1:100,000 that has recently been well reproduced.[82] This map, which shows interesting details of the growth of Berlin, was probably designed rather for civil administration than for military purposes. Figure 61 shows Montargues's delineation of the frontier between Mecklenburg (north, at the top) and the Prussian region of Prignitz. The River Elbe runs diagonally across the bottom left-hand part of the map, and Putlitz is seen on the right-hand margin: the map thus covers an area nearly forty miles across, locating towns, villages, and hydrographic features quite precisely.

King Frederick II, Frederick the Great (ruled 1740–86), thus inherited a thriving service in 1740. He was personally interested in maps, and capable of drawing his own cartographic sketches.[83] For greater convenience in directing his armies, he seems to have organized a mobile *Plankammer*,[84] and he enjoyed the company of the engineers who provided maps for it. Thus Johann Friedrich von Balbi (1700–79), who had entered Prussian service at an early age, and eventually survived nine battles and twenty-three sieges, was often the king's companion at Potsdam in his later years.[85] At least one map from Balbi's hand survives, the 'Geographische Special Karte von der Mittel Marck', dating from 1748.[86] This coloured manuscript map is at a scale of about 1:75,000, not large-scale enough for a military reconnaissance map, but ample for giving an idea of the lie of the land.[87]

Another engineer close to the king was Major von Wrede.[88] None of his maps survives, but we know that in 1746 he was working on the border with Schleswig-Holstein, and that between 1747 and 1753 he produced a detailed map of the Silesian border with Bohemia and Moravia. One of his colleagues was Major Griese, in charge of the travelling *Plankammer*. He worked in 1754 on the border of Schleswig and Poland, and on the morning of the battle of Kolin achieved a kind of immortality by failing to find a map of this site.[89] The general supervision of the engineers at this time was the responsibility of Field-Marshal Samuel von Schmettau (1684–1751), who in 1754 had begun a trigonometrical survey of Prussia: 'Frederick discouraged the experiment, because he feared the consequences if such accurate maps should fall into the hands of the enemy.'[90] Schmettau is best known for the superb new map of Berlin that he commissioned from Friedrich August Hildner (active 1740–70), and which was published in 1764.

The engineers of Frederick II were thus active in making maps. Many have been lost, and most were confined to the *Plankammer* from the time of their execution, for fear that they would fall into the hands of Prussia's enemies. It is therefore difficult to make an estimate of their full extent, but we may assume that many parts of the country were covered, at a relatively large scale. After

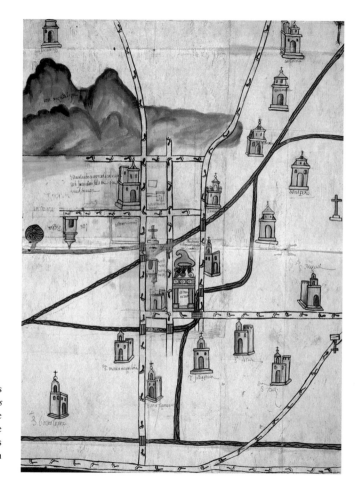

Plate IX Anon., *Pintura* from the *Relación* for Mexicaltingo, *c.*1580. This is a good example of a *pintura* sent back to Spain with one of the *relaciones geográficas* in response to the request of Philip II. Churches dot the countryside, and in the town is San Juan Evangelista. The whole image seems to be an exercise in evangelization, for Spanish roads and churches are superimposed on indigenous signs for roads, rivers and hills, just as a Spanish society would be superimposed on an Indian one.

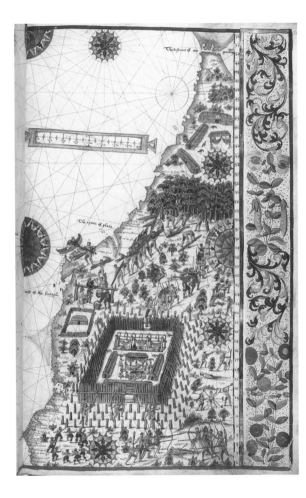

Plate X Jean Rotz, Detail from his map of South America in his *Boke of Yydrography*, 1541. Several atlases of the Dieppe School have survived, and this is one of the most elegant of them. This page, showing the east coast of South America looking southwards to the strait of Magellan, shows the accurate observation of Tupinamba villages, with their hammocks and longhouses within a stockade. Along the right-hand margin is not only a scale of latitude, but also a flowered border that irresistibly reminds us of the miniatures of late medieval France.

Plate XI John Norden, Plan of Orford and its surroundings, *c.*1600. John Norden (1548-?1625) resembled Christopher Saxton in that he too was an estate surveyor who also turned his hand to the making of county maps. Here is one of 28 maps in an atlas that he compiled to show the estates of Sir Michael Stanhope between Woodbridge, in Suffolk, and the sea. We see the River Alde lapping the quays of the old port, and the main street leading up to the church and castle. Since 1600, the fields have all been consolidated, but the layout of the streets, and the position of many individual buildings remain the same.

The figure below shows the areas mapped by John Norden's atlas.

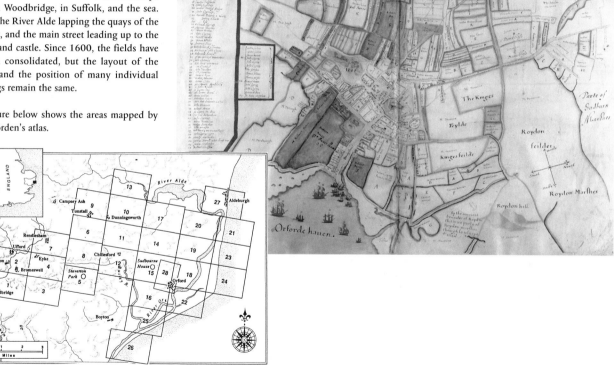

Plate XII John Walker, Detail from a map of the manor of Bishop's Hall, drawn for Sir Thomas Mildmay, 1591. John Walker was an exceptionally prolific Essex estate mapper, whose work has been well studied. Like John Norden, he drew maps that are scaled and planimetric, but neither of them could avoid from time to time relapsing into bird's-eye view images for particular buildings and objects like ships. No doubt this made their images more accessible to their patrons, though it also brings out the extraordinary skill of cartographers like Leonardo da Vinci, who could compile maps that were entirely planimetric, with no intrusion of 'painterly' views.

Frederick's death in 1786 the way was clear for a renewed map programme, and from 1815 onwards the so-called *Generalstabskarten* (general staff maps) began to appear.[91]

It would no doubt be possible to multiply examples of engineering services in early modern Europe that produced maps; after all, as early as the 1620s, when Magini was seeking maps of Italian provinces for his great atlas, it was to the local engineers that he appealed.[92] But one other example must suffice here. It comes from 'An officer serving the Duke of Braunschweig-Lüneburg', and was published at Leipzig in 1758.[93] The task of the engineer, he says, is to provide the commander with special maps. It is no use relying upon 'Schlechte Homanische und Seuterische Karten' (the 'bad' printed maps produced by the firms of Homann and Seutter), for these will lead to tactical errors. The engineer must make fresh maps showing streams, morasses, villages, roads, and so forth in detail, just as the French do in both peace and war. Indeed, says our officer, the French are so skilled at this work that they have better maps of our provinces than we do…

LODGINGS-OFFICERS AND SUPPLY-OFFICERS

The primary function of the engineers had originally been to design fortresses. In early modern armies, they had colleagues whose function was to attend to the soldiers on the line of march,

making sure that they were properly supplied, and found suitable lodgings at the end of the day. In English these officers were called lodgings-masters, and in French *maîtres des logis*.[94] The *maîtres des logis* in the time of Henri IV (ruled 1589–1610) produced more than 200 manuscript maps designed to help them in their task.[95] These maps eventually covered a large part of France at a hitherto unprecedented scale, containing about ten times as many place-names as the most detailed contemporary printed maps.

Figure 64 shows one of these maps, drawn by Pierre Fougeu. It covers the coast from Calais to Dunkirk, on the top right-hand border of the map. Offshore sandbanks are shown, as well as a large number of settlements, though on this particular map there is no mention by the town-names of the number of their *feux*, or hearths, where soldiers might be billeted. This map is unusual not only in making some indication of woods, but also in marking with a dotted line the boundary between the provinces of 'flandres' and 'artois'. With maps of this kind the king could, if he had wanted to, have constructed a very detailed administrative map of the whole kingdom. But they remained in manuscript in the archives of the lodgings-masters, and thus had little influence upon the general development of cartography.

The French lodgings-masters have not been intensively studied, least of all in their cartographic activities. But in his work

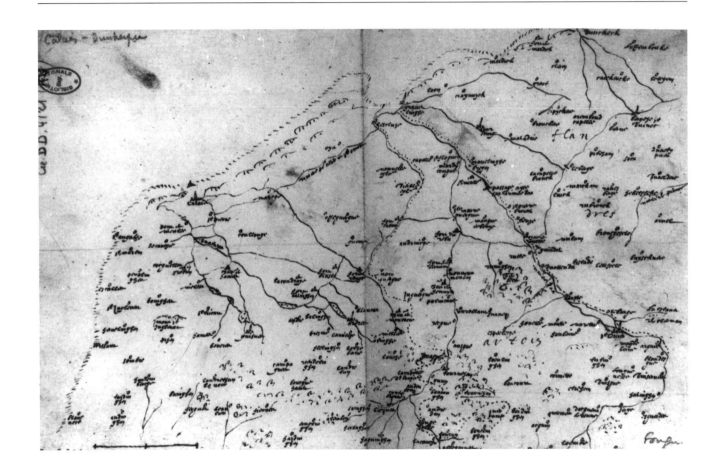

De l'attaque et défence des places (2 vols, The Hague, 1737 and 1742), the engineer Vauban gives an interesting summary of their duties (see also above). One essential thing for this office, he writes, is 'to know drawing, that is to say the art of drawing plans'.[96] The best way to set about this is to obtain the best available topographical maps, and then to work over them meticulously, consulting the local inhabitants about supplies of food, terrain, climate, and so forth. Then this information has to be inserted in a space specially left blank at the side of the map, ready for use when the army has to move.

We unfortunately do not have any atlases composed in this fashion by the *maîtres des logis*, but they would have been a curious combination of text and image. These officers were responsible for each night's lodging, and took the preparation of such encampments very seriously, following the Roman model (Chapter 1). By the middle of the eighteenth century we find in both English[97] and French map-collections special sections devoted to the manuscript cartography of camps. Indeed, in 1770 the sieur du Bois, 'ci-devant

Fig. 62. Pierre Fougeu, Map of part of Flanders and Artois, *c.*1609. This is one of over 200 maps that were generated by the lodgings-master Jacques Fougeu in the early seventeenth century. The collection seems to have survived largely intact because after the death of the Duc de Sully, in 1641, the cartographic workshop at his *château* of Bontin fell into neglect. In their day these were by far the most detailed maps drawn.

ingénieur-géographe de M. le comte de Maillebois' ('formerly M. le comte de Maillebois's engineer-geographer'), published a handsome volume entitled *Camps topographiques de la campagne de 1757 en Westphalie* ('Topographical views of the camps from the 1757 campaign in Westphalia') at The Hague. It is a fine example of a map-type that was once quite common and much appreciated.

We do not know much about the mapping activities of lodgings-masters outside France, but there is a faint echo of their work in England, where in 1641 Wenceslaus Hollar (1607–77) published the so-called 'Quartermaster's Map', presumably for the convenience of quartermasters involved in the Civil War.[98] However, unlike the French example, this was merely a small-scale version of maps already available in print, and could hardly have served its intended purpose of helping quartermasters to find food and lodging. In England, some of the functions of the lodgings-masters were covered by the Board of Ordnance, which had been reorganized in 1683, and from 1717 onwards seems to have directed the cartographic activities of a number of engineers based in the Drawing Room in the Tower of London.[99] It was these engineers who undertook the mapping of Scotland, when the Board was responsible for building roads and establishing posts after the revolt of 1745. The map was a great success, and by 1766 its main author, William Roy (1726–90), was already proposing 'A General

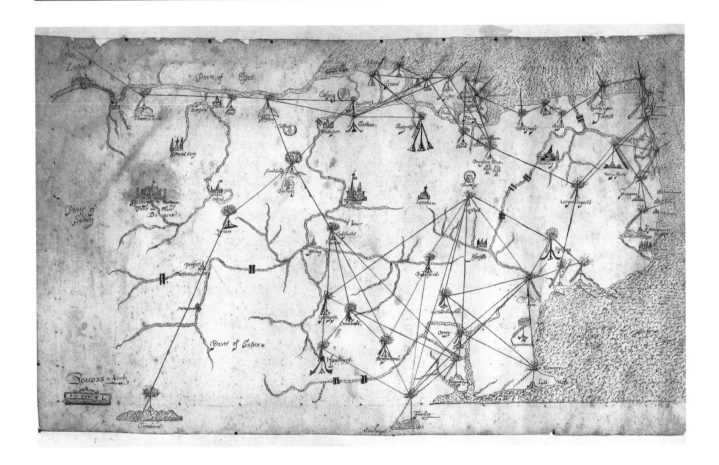

Military Map of England' as a sequel to it. This was the genesis of the British Ordnance Survey, whose first maps began to appear in the early nineteenth century.

Apart from the maps produced by these organized bodies, we also come across stray cartographic ventures sponsored for military purposes. Among the earliest are the maps of the Alpine passes drawn for the passage of the French artillery in 1515,[100] and the map of 1520 drawn by Sebastian Cabot to aid the English army in its invasion of Gascony and Guyenne,[101] both already mentioned. The remarkable bridging of the River Scheldt in the Netherlands by the engineers of the Spanish duke of Parma (1545–92) in 1585

Fig. 63. (opposite) William Lambarde, Map of the beacon system in south-east England *c.*1590. Before the heliograph, and long before the telegraph, the chief means of long-distance communication was the beacon-system, involving permanently stocked braziers on high poles that could be lighted in case of alarm. In England, such a system once existed all along the south coast, and William Lambarde here shows us the system extending into Kent, from the hills above Crowborough in Sussex (bottom left).

Fig. 64. Anon., Disposition of German princes' forces in the 1693 campaign. At first, it had been sufficient roughly to know where an army and its constituent groups were. But by the end of the seventeenth century, armies had grown so large that there had to be some way of locating their different elements; hence this map of 1693, enclosing elements like the dragoons and the artillery in balloon-like rings that showed more or less where they were on the ground.

also gave rise to a variety of imagery, including contemporary German prints setting out the way in which this bridge was anchored and protected.[102] The British lawyer and historian William Lambarde (1536–1601) in the 1590s produced a remarkable manuscript map of the beacon system in south-east England (Fig. 63).[103] During the 1630s a good many maps were drawn of the French north-eastern frontier, menaced by Spanish forces; in the Low Countries one of the most interesting of these is an atlas of the course of the River Somme, carefully indicating the points where crossings could be made.[104] As a final example we might take Figure 64, which shows the various units of the army of the German princes in 1693, as they are encamped in the vast region to the south-east of Frankfurt-am-Main.[105] The author has ingeniously used rather modern-looking 'balloons' to indicate the approximate locations of the various elements in the army, such as 'dragoner' and 'artillerie'; this is a technique that would become common in the nineteenth century, and indeed still survives.

MAPPING THE TACTICAL MOVEMENTS OF ARMIES AND NAVIES

As we have noted, the fifteenth century had seen the emergence of one distinctly new arm, the artillery, and the tactical transformation of an old one, the infantry. Whereas medieval engagements had normally involved a relatively incoherent conflict between cavalry and infantry—with the latter generally getting the worse of it—the new form of warfare often brought the three arms into play, in a variety of combinations and on different terrains. Cartography soon reflected this change. Medieval battle-scenes are fairly chaotic, with the artists striving chiefly to convey the terror and feudal magnificence of the occasion.[106] By the early sixteenth century this was changing, and artists like Hans Burgkmair the Elder, in his version of the Emperor Maximilian's victory at Schönberg in 1504,[107] begin to show distinct forces of cavalry and infantry, sometimes naming the leaders.

One of the earliest and most elegant of these new-style maps was Albrecht Dürer's 1527 woodcut called 'Siege of a fortified town', whose right-hand half is shown in Figure 65.[108] The town is not identified, but the forces are shown in their different components with remarkable clarity. On the right, an army advances to

Fig. 65. Albrecht Dürer, Detail from a woodcut showing an army advancing to attack a town, 1527. This is the right-hand section of a long woodcut, and shows an army on the march. There are two great blocks of pikemen, with their long weapons cradled on their shoulders, and a formidable crescent of supply-wagons, followed by the cattle that would provide food. At the side of these forces may be seen three guns, with their attendant horses and the wagons containing gunpowder and spare parts and a forge, just as the manuals showed them.

Den 2 September A.º 1590. hat Herzog von *Parma* in der Persohn die gewaltige Statt *Paris* proviantirt ünd Sie aus ihrer grossen Hüngers Noth errettet.

support its artillery. Groups of cavalry flank the army, which is followed by its supply-wagons and then by three droves of cattle; villages hideously blaze on the skyline. On the left (not shown on the figure), a defending army prepares to receive the attackers; its cavalry is nearest to us, in front of the dense group of pikemen massed in front of the fortress gate. Skirmishes are already taking place between the two armies, and before long battle will no doubt be joined.

Representations of this kind, which at first seemed so original, became quite commonplace during the sixteenth century. One of the most prolific campaign-illustrators was Franz Hogenberg, whose view of the Duke of Parma's relief of Paris in 1590 is reproduced as Figure 66. Here the carefully named elements of Parma's army advance towards the waiting gates of Paris at the top. The artillery, followed by its supply-carts, leads the way; then come distinct units of infantry and cavalry, all apparently in apple-pie order.

Fig. 66. Franz Hogenberg, Engraving showing the relief of Paris by the Duke of Parma in 1590 (Cologne, 1597) (The Newberry Library, Chicago). Hogenberg's military images are inevitably too tidy, but they do break the military forces down into their constituent parts. Here, the Spanish army of the Duke of Parma is about to relieve Paris (top left) from the besieging forces of Henri IV (top right). Infantry, cavalry, artillery, and supply-carts may all be seen moving forward, as the orders are trumpeted by the two figures on horseback in the centre of the image.

This, of course, is one of the great weaknesses of images of this kind, that they entirely fail to capture the terror, squalor, and disorder of the scene,[109] just as eighteenth-century images of town and countryside inevitably lend their themes an improbably orderly and romantic air. Still, artists like Hogenberg did succeed in conveying the military elements of the occasion.

This type of image was eventually replaced by a more abstract rendering of formations. We see a foreshadowing of this development in the plates engraved for Andrea Palladio's edition of Caesar's *Commentaries* (Venice, 1575) (Fig. 12). Here the columns have become almost abstract, and the individual soldiers have been lost to view. By the 1630s and 1640s, fully abstract formation-maps have begun to appear in manuscripts. Figure 67, for instance, shows a map setting out the order of battle of the Swedish army at the battle of Lützen (1632). The different units are named and use some conventional symbolism; this map comes from the Cumberland Collection, which contains a rather similar map of the English royal army's order of battle for Edgehill (1642).[110] Eventually, these abstract battle-plans began to emerge in printed form, and to adopt certain conventions.[111] Figure 68 thus shows an eighteenth-century French drawing of the battle of Hastembeck (1757). The different units—infantry, cavalry, and artillery—of the opposing armies are shown in various phases of the battle, by means of numbers keyed

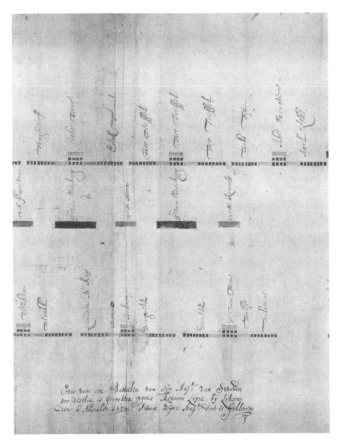

in to the 'Explication'. Often, cartographers began to show movement on maps like this by setting out the different positions of the formations at different times by means of varying colours. Sometimes a whole series of such maps was needed, to show the development of a complicated battle. Of course, these are all plans after the event: we do not seem to be able to tell how Frederick the Great or Napoleon plotted the position of the various formations as the battle actually raged. Eventually such plots would be made on transparent overlays, with some erasable material like wax crayon, but it is not clear when this practice began.

Fig. 67. Anon., Detail of the order of battle at Lützen, 1632. It seems to have been in the 1630s and 1640s that commanders began using maps like this, designed to show in conventional signs the different elements in an army. Sometimes, as in Figure 57, words like 'infantry' and 'dragoons' would identify what would now be called 'units'; eventually, they often came to be delineated either by different signs, or sometimes by colour.

Fig. 68. (opposite) Anon., 'Bataille d'Hastembeck', 1757. This is a battle-plan of the type that eventually became very common. The countryside and towns are indicated quite grossly, and the military formations are numbered, in accordance with a key. Sometimes two or three different movements could be shown on a map like this, or sometimes there would be a sequence of maps, to show the progress of the engagement. The slaughter and chaos had been neatly subsumed into decent and manageable images.

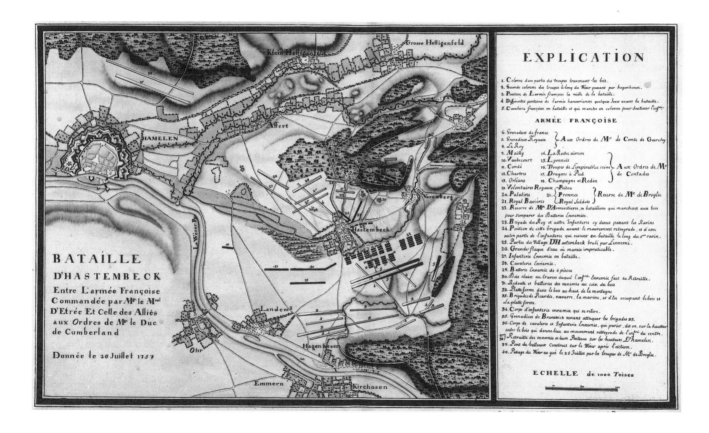

BATAILLE
D'HASTEMBECK

Entre L'armée Françoise
Commandée par Mr le Mal
D'Etrée Et Celle des Alliés
aux Ordres de Mr le Duc
de Cumberland

Donnée le 26 Juillet 1757

EXPLICATION

1. Colonne d'une partie des troupes traversant les bois.
2. Seconde colonne des troupes le long du Weser passant par Hagenhosen.
3. Position de L'armée françoise la veille de la bataille.
4. Differentes positions de l'armée hanoverienne quelques jours avant la bataille.
5. Cavalerie françoise en bataille et qui marche en colonne pour soutenir l'Infrie

ARMÉE FRANÇOISE

6. Grenadiers de France
7. Grenadiers Royaux   } Aux Ordres de Mr le Comte de Guerchy
8. Le Roy
9. Mailly   14. La Roche aimon
10. Vaubecourt   15. Lyonnois   } Aux Ordres de Mr
11. Condé   16. Troupes de l'impératrice reine   de Contades
12. Chartres   17. Dragons à Pied
13. Orléans   18. Champagne et Redin
19. Volontaires Royaux   Poitou
20. Palatins   21. Provence   } Reserve de Mr de Broglie
21. Royal Bavières   Royal Soldés
22. Reserve de Mr D'Armentières, 12 bataillons qui marchent aux bois
    pour s'emparer des Batteries Ennemies.
23. Brigade du Roy et autre Infanterie cy devant penant les Ravins.
24. Position de cette brigade avant le mouvement retrograde, et d'une
    autre partie de l'infanterie qui revient en bataille le long du 1er ravin.
25. Partie du Village D'Hastembeck brulé par l'ennemi.
26. Grande flaque d'eau ou marais impraticable.
27. Infanterie Ennemie en bataille.
28. Cavalerie Ennemie.
29. Batterie Ennemie de 4 pieces.
30. Bois clair au travers duquel l'Infrie Ennemie fait sa Retraitte.
31. Redoute et batteries des ennemis au coin du bois.
32. Platteforme dans le bois au haut de la montagne.
33. Brigades de Picardie, navarre, la marine, et d'un occupant lebois et
    la platte forme.
34. Corps d'infanterie ennemie qui se retire.
35. Grenadiers de Brunswick venant attaquer les brigades 33.
36. Corps de cavalerie et Infanterie Ennemie, qui paroit, dit on, sur la hauteur
    entre le bois qui donne lieu au mouvement retrograde de l'infrie du centre.
37. Retraitte des ennemis à leurs Positions sur les hauteurs D'hamelen.
38. Pont de bateaux Construit sur le Weser après l'action.
40. Passage du Weser au gué le 25 Juillet par les troupes de Mr de Broglie.

ECHELLE de 1000 Toises

The delineation of naval engagements followed much the same course as that of those on land. Major fleet engagements began in the second half of the sixteenth century, and it is precisely from the battle of Lepanto off Greece (1572) that a first group of maps survives. These maps show the ships of the Christian fleet in bird's-eye view, setting out part of the huge crescent, with the galleys in front of the 'round ships', or sailing-ships as opposed to galleys.[112] This type of representation was common throughout the seventeenth and eighteenth centuries, but towards the 1780s much more stylized maps began to appear. Often the vessels are shown by conventional symbols, differently coloured to show their positions at different stages in the battle. Maps of this kind, like their land counterparts, were much better at showing the course of a battle than the earlier maps, even if they too gave the chaos and diversity of an engagement a sort of spurious organization and tidiness.

CONCLUSION

The effects of the military revolution upon the development of cartography were thus far-reaching. Moreover, these cartographic developments, primed by military concerns, in many cases spread into general mapmaking, with very extensive effects. This is most obvious in the case of large-scale topographical mapping, which in many countries was first undertaken for military purposes, but then became an indispensable tool for a great variety of civilian activities, from town-planning to the reconstruction of ancient landscapes. We are constantly reminded of this by the ubiquitous survival in England of the maps of the Ordnance Survey, but we ought to remember as well that the standard map in France was for long the *Carte de l'état major*, and in Germany the *Generalstabskarte*. Both titles are translatable as the 'general staff map'.

The maps drawn for fortifying towns also had a far-reaching influence. This is most evident in England, where the idea of scaled maps seems to emerge from the military plans of the 1540s, but the same concern with scale probably led in many other countries to its adoption for civilian purposes. The ubiquity of military town plans also had a great effect upon city planners: not only were fortifications of great importance in any alterations that might be envisaged for a city, but the maps drawn by the military engineers often formed the basis upon which such decisions could be made. Arcaeologists, too, use these plans to discern the remains of buildings constructed long before the sixteenth century.

Finally, the various publications in which highly organized military activities were made graphic no doubt had their effect upon the populace at large. Here we should think not so much of drill-manuals as of plates showing how weapons should be handled; the idea that there was one best way to handle a musket surely must have influenced the way that people came to handle civilian firearms, or, for instance, to train horses for civilian purposes. Manuals like Vassallieu's, which set out the exact way in which heavy weapons were to be manufactured and operated, also must have contributed to the growing realization that the most effective form of manufacture depended upon mass production and standardization of parts. In all these different ways, the military manuals and the military mindset made their contribution to an increasingly industrialized society.

6

Mapping countryside and town in the new economies,
1570–1800

CHANGES in the art of war, as we have seen, led to related developments in cartography. Once armies reached a certain size and complexity, for instance, their manoeuvres could hardly be controlled except by maps. Much the same connection between certain historical developments and types of cartography can be seen in the case of the estate map, which first emerged as an English phenomenon in the 1570s. As we shall see, though, the coming of city maps appears to have been the consequence of a quite different kind of development, more technical than strictly historical. Whereas manuscript maps of the countryside emerged as a result of developments in the mode of agricultural production, maps of cities flourished because of the new opportunities offered by new printing techniques.[1]

ESTATE MAPS

In early sixteenth-century England, the ascertaining of landholding was carried out in a time-honoured way. There are a few medieval field-maps, but in general the concept of 'naming and bounding' in order to define property involved the practical identification of 'metes and bounds', and gave rise to those parish perambulations in which, it is said, up-ended choirboys' heads were used to tap the ground and so designate significant locations: hence 'beating the bounds'. In case of dispute, twelve 'good and lawful' men would be called upon to swear to the truth of verbal statements about boundaries, and their testimony would be textually recorded.[2]

Towards the middle of the sixteenth century, publications like those of Richard Benese (1537) and Leonard Digges (1556) began to appear, in which methods of land surveying were recommended;[3] this was all part of the growing English concern to advance 'good husbandrie',[4] but it did not at first involve the construction of maps. Traditional English 'surveyors' were literally 'overseers', whose information was normally compiled into a written survey, or terrier (straight from the French *terrier*, or 'book of land'). These surveyors were in fact generating textual registers of landed property in much the same way as their ancestors had done during the Middle Ages, and indeed at the time of the Domesday Book, about 1085.

THE ESTATE MAP IN ENGLAND

This began to change in the 1570s, when an entirely new cartographic form emerged, the estate map. This was a type of map which would eventually spread to many different parts of Europe and indeed of the world, but it retained certain characteristics, which allow us to distinguish it from other map-forms. Probably the most important is that it delineated only one economic unit, whether it was a cereal farm or a sugar plantation or some other form of rural enterprise. Estate maps often give a rather odd sense of the countryside, for they show only one proprietor's holdings,

leaving the adjacent land blank. If the holdings are scattered, as they often were, this can give the map the look of a half-completed jigsaw.

Such maps were also almost always manuscript, for this was not information that needed to be widely disseminated. Often they were collected together into atlases, which generally contained as well a written register of this property. Such atlases are relatively common in the English county record offices, and some, like William Senior's survey of the scattered Cavendish estates around Derbyshire and Yorkshire, finished about 1640, have been published.[5] In fact, they bring the reader so powerfully into the Tudor and Stuart countryside that it is a great pity that more have not been reproduced and annotated. Of course, some contain inaccuracies, but by and large they are astonishingly true to the ground, as indeed they had to be, in order to be useful.

The estate maps are of a fairly large scale, often around 1:5,000, and this allows them to show not only individual fields but also sometimes individual buildings. They are always drawn to scale, and their rapid spread shows that many English landowners by the late sixteenth century could appreciate this unfamiliar mathematical method of showing land; as we shall see, it took less practice to appreciate *Landtafeln*, or 'country pictures', generally adopted in German-speaking countries. It surely must be significant that

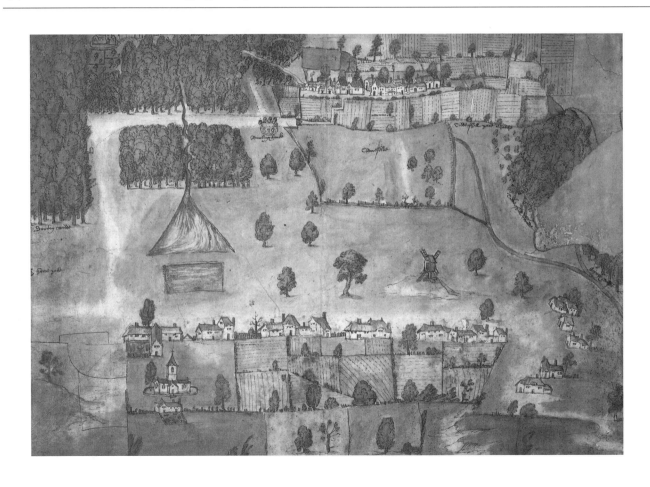

Henry VIII, as we have seen, had in the early sixteenth century employed large numbers of military engineers well acquainted with scaled maps. It seems likely that their knowledge percolated into civilian life, particularly as so many landowners had been military officers. Indeed, there are even cases like those of John Rogers and Federigo Genebelli (active 1580–1600), where a military engineer went on to become a land surveyor.[6] Certainly, by the late sixteenth century there seems to have been no shortage in England of surveyors skilled enough to draw scaled maps, and patrons who knew how to interpret them.[7]

The estate map must be distinguished from maps drawn in the course of legal cases; often these, like Figure 69, took the form of what Professor Harvey has called 'picture-maps',[8] setting out the appearance of the land in dispute. The purpose of the estate map, as David Fletcher has put it, was instead 'clarification of ownership',[9] and from this could come such other advantages as more

Fig. 69. Anon., *View of Wotton Underwood*, 1565. This elegant watercolour is a good example of the kind of 'picture-maps' that were sometimes drawn in the fifteenth and sixteenth centuries in the course of judicial disputes. The two Buckinghamshire villages of Wotton Underwood and Ludgershall face each other across a disputed common. Very few roads enter the area, and each dwelling has its own quite substantial plot of land. All would eventually be swallowed up by the building of Wotton House, with its extensive grounds.

efficient collection of rents and more logical disposition of crops. Often, then, these maps were simply used as administrative tools, hanging on the wall in the estate manager's office (where, indeed, their descendants may sometimes still be seen). But sometimes they also had a celebratory quality, as much as to affirm the extent and excellence of the landowner's possessions. Sarah Bendall quotes in this respect the magnificent map that has hung for many years in the main entrance to Long Melford Hall in Suffolk,[10] but there are many other examples, including some from the New World.[11] Of course, these maps are of extraordinary interest to modern historians for, as Plates XI and XII show, they can lead the perceptive viewer into the heart of early modern European towns and countrysides.

Plate XI comes from an atlas of some 'landes of the Right Worshipful Sir Michael Stanhope', made 'by ye perambulation, view and dimensuration of John Norden, accompanied by divers tenants of the same, whoe were sworn to give their best knowledge and direction in that behalfe, begun, continued and finished in ye years 1600 and 1601'.[12] The atlas eventually contained twenty-eight maps, covering the areas shown in the accompanying figure, and was preceded by a written 'table containing all the perticulers of this booke'. John Norden (1548–1625) was a many-talented surveyor, religious writer, and topographer; Sir Michael Stanhope no doubt perched somewhere in the very complicated genealogical tree of the extensive and influential Stanhope family.

The atlas contains a section on 'The use of the table following', where instructions are given for using the text and maps. These instructions were fairly elementary: the reader was, for example, told that 'by the maps yow may also see the buttes and boundes of some particular parcel of land. On your right hande the map spred before you is east, on your lefte west. The upper side from the eye is north, and that next the eye south.' As our breakdown map shows, these directions were approximate, but each of the maps fits well with its neighbour, as Norden worked his way steadily eastwards from Woodbridge, on the River Deben, to Aldeburgh by the North Sea.

Plate XI shows the small map numbered '28', which is centred on the town of Orford. Some of the surrounding fields are quite large, and were probably pasture; in places the fields were still divided into what look like survivals of the medieval strip system. The fields were delineated with considerable care, and even the small and irregularly-shaped meadows down by the river, salt-marsh taken in by medieval monks, can be shown to have been traced meticulously, since they retain much the same shape today.[13] The streets of the town are clearly shown, with the quay and the major landmarks of the Norman castle and the parish church. Contemporary features like the gallows, at the entrance to the town, are shown, and so are

many surviving elements, like distinctively named farms and ancient woodlands like Staverton Park. In short, by combining the text and images of this atlas, the landowner and his agents would have a very good idea of their holdings.

Many estate maps are primarily useful to modern historians for the way in which they show field-systems at a time when they were in transition from medieval strips to early modern enclosed fields. Some, though, also show early modern towns, and Plate XII is a good example of these. It shows the centre of the town of Chelmsford, and although much building has taken place in the four centuries since the map was made, John Walker (active 1584–1626) would still easily recognize the main elements of his work. The fields are distinguished by a variety of names: 'yeardes', 'croftes', 'landes', and so forth. Most numerous are the 'meads', or meadows; some belong to taverns like 'Bell meade' or 'Boreshead meade', while others commemorate times recently past. 'Fryers meade' marks a meadow just by the former friary ('Fryers'), dissolved by Henry VIII in the 1530s, where there is now a 'Fre schoole howse'. In the centre of the town are the parish church and the open market; maps like this re-create small-town early modern England as few other documents can.

A very large number of these estate maps were commissioned in England between the 1570s and the 1840s,[14] and it would seem that rather particular historical circumstances gave rise to them. The region had to sustain a good number of substantial economic units, and in this respect the map of surveyors (and so, generally, of maps) compiled by Delano-Smith and Kain is extraordinarily interesting[15]. It shows little estate mapping in the western half of the country, and a considerable concentration in the south-east; if it had taken in Scotland, that area too would have been largely lacking these maps. This south-eastern concentration exactly takes in the most developed farmland, and not coincidentally indicates the area (south of a line from the Wash to Bristol) where the parliamentary forces would be strongest during the Civil War.

This was an area already getting tied into the market, not only in the sense that proprietors here might produce for urban sales, but also in the sense that the land market, still much affected by the Dissolution of the Monasteries of the 1530s, was exceptionally lively, with many new proprietors wishing to know the exact extent of their estates. These proprietors had often encountered maps, whether at court or in the army, and found a ready pool of surveyors to carry out their commissions. There was, moreover, no existing tradition of land-depiction as existed in certain areas of continental Europe, like Germany and Switzerland. Finally, there was no central agency generating large-scale maps. When such an agency came into existence, in the days of the Ordnance Survey

during the nineteenth century, the time of the estate maps was over. For now such maps at an acceptable level of accuracy could be compiled by enlargement from the Ordnance Survey, even if this was not entirely gentlemanly. During the period between 1570 and 1840, though, much of England precisely combined the economic and social features that encouraged estate maps. This is not to say that such maps were bound to appear everywhere that conditions appeared to be propitious: as David Fletcher has shown, the drawing of estate maps sometimes depended to a great extent on individual initiative.[16] Still, conditions were present in England that were for some time lacking almost everywhere else in Europe.

THE NETHERLANDS

In the northern Netherlands, for instance, careful examination of a variety of cartographic histories fails to turn up any substantial number of estate maps.[17] Large-scale maps were indeed drawn to summarize progress on polder (land reclamation) schemes, and there was no shortage of skilled surveyors. It would seem, though, as Bendall puts it, that 'the system of land ownership in the Netherlands led to weak seigneurial power and a large number of very small landowners',[18] unlikely to commission estate maps. It may also be important that the northern Netherlands was a very small area, with few absentee landowners: there was nothing to

compare, for instance, with the treasurers of Oxbridge colleges, who often had to manage estates that might be 200 miles distant, and that they might never have visited.

For the southern Netherlands, on the other hand, we have the extraordinary work commissioned by Duke Charles de Croy (d. 1612), who succeeded his father in 1595 as the owner of vast estates in what are now Belgium and northern France. He seems chiefly to have employed 'Maistre Pierre Bersaques', an engineer and sworn surveyor who could produce both maps, plans, and views (*cartes, plantz [et] pourtraitz*) of the duke's possessions.[19] He and his colleagues eventually produced something like 2,500 images, which were stored in the ducal library at Beaumont (southern Belgium: see Figs. 24 and 78). Some of these were bird's-eye views, but many were exactly what we have defined as estate plans; together, they give an extraordinary image of the duke's extensive lands. Alas, the library was dispersed upon Charles's death in 1612, and the images have only recently begun to be edited and published.[20]

Fig. 70. Jacob Köbel, Illustration from *Geometrei: von künstlichen Messen* (Frankfurt, 1536). Here sixteen 'good men and true' have emerged from church, and lined themselves up in order to establish the length of a 16-*Schuh* rod. It is, as Köbel claims, a handsome image, with each person individually observed (note the different kinds of hat), and the surveyor standing by in the background with his assistants. But one wonders by how much such measures varied, from church to church.

GERMANY

In many parts of the German-speaking regions, conditions in the late sixteenth century seemed ideal for the production of estate maps: there were rich estates, sometimes producing for the market, an abundance of potential surveyors, and many cartographically sophisticated proprietors. But the German authors of survey-manuals seem generally to have recommended rather archaic methods of measurement. Thus in his *Geometria* of 1531, many times reprinted, Jacob Köbel advocates taking 'sixteen men, large and small', as they come out of church, and lining them up with one foot upon a rod (Fig. 70). This rod then becomes the surveyor's 16-*Schuh* staff, with which fields of various sizes can be measured. Here we recognize the English 'rod, pole, or perch', normally cited as 16.5 feet long, and a standard measure in England for many years. In contrast with the English writers who begin to appear later in the century, Köbel does not write as if for a lord desiring to know the bounds of his property, but as if for a tenant-farmer anxious to avoid squabbles with his neighbours. His is a sort of do-it-yourself book for smallholders, which no doubt explains its great popularity[21].

Manuals appearing later in the sixteenth century share this rustic quality, and they do not represent much technical advance over the ideas of Köbel; this is the case with Christoff Pühler (1563), for

Fig. 71. Paul Pfinzing, Illustration from his *Methodus Geometrica* (Nürnberg, 1598). At the top, a heavy, unsprung cart has been designed for the surveyor; below, we see him ensconced in it, sitting above his assistant, who is counting the distance travelled. They both have hats a cut above that of the coachman, whom the surveyor seems to be directing: 'walk on' and so forth. In the background, there is a landscape rather like the one that this method of survey would eventually produce.

78

instance, and Erasmus Reinhold (1574). When Herman Widekind published his *Bewirte Feldmessung und Theilung* (a survey manual) in 1578 in Heidelberg, he began with the down-to-earth comment: 'Herman Widekind wunschet dem Ackerman' ('Herman Widekind greets the husbandman'), and although he does advocate fuller use of the compass than does Köbel, his work is largely taken up in explaining various measures. Even Paul Pfinzing's splendidly produced *Methodus geometrica* of 1598 shares this slightly amateurish quality.

For measuring distance, Pfinzing recommends counting the number of paces that a horse made, or even a mechanical measuring cart. Figure 71 shows one of these, with its box for calculating the number of revolutions made by the cart's wheels. The surveyor himself rides in delicious comfort, his compass in his hand, no doubt calling out bearings and distances to his assistant. When one considers the alternative, which was slogging through often muddy fields with chains, it is not surprising that Pfinzing remarks that 'one finds measuring from a cart the best way'. For measuring

Fig. 72. Daniel Schwenter, An ideal field plan from his *Geometriæ practicæ novæ* (Nürnberg, 1617). This is a fairly typical *Landtafel*, with its impressionistic view of a large area of countryside. Letters mark the main features: thus at 'A' there is a fortified town, at 'B' a citadel, at 'C' a bridge, and so forth. An image like this was perfectly satisfactory for giving the reader an idea of the land on each side of the river winding down the centre.

irregular fields, he suggests the ingenious expedient of cutting out a paper map of the field, and then weighing it against a paper cut-out of known size. All in all, we are not surprised by his remark that 'land ought not to be measured out as carefully as saffron'.

Figure 72 shows an example of the kind of map that Pfinzing was going to construct. It comes from the *Geometriæ practicæ novæ* ('New practical geometry') of Daniel Schwenter, published at Nürnberg in 1617. The most notable features of the countryside are designated by letters explained in a key: the fortified town, the citadel, the villages, the fields, the woods, and so forth. There is no scale, and some of the fields may be little more than approximations. But the reader could use this *Landtafel oder Mappam* to get a good general idea of the lie of the land, portrayed, as Pfinzing puts it, 'as if in a mirror'. During the sixteenth and seventeenth centuries, this was the way in which the countryside was portrayed in areas like Rhineland/Westphalia, Bavaria, and Saxony.[22] There were many surveyors who could have produced—and occasionally did produce—larger-scale, planimetric maps, but in general their patrons were well content with the *Landtafel*, and its impressionistic image of the countryside.

It is not easy to understand why German landowners were satisfied with this kind of image. Perhaps the land market was relatively sluggish, and German agriculture slow to be permeated by capital-

istic ideas and practices. Perhaps it also had something to do with the fragmented nature of political authority. It surely had something to do with the rural chaos induced by the civil unrest of the early sixteenth century, and still more by the even more widespread disorder encountered during the Thirty Years' War (1618–48). For whatever reasons, it was not until the eighteenth century that a majority of large German landlords began to use the planimetric estate map as a tool of management.

ITALY

The same was true for most parts of Italy, to judge by the evidence of the many illustrated catalogues that describe recent map-exhibits from various parts of the peninsula. In Basilicata, Reggio Emilia, and the kingdom of Naples, for instance, we encounter some estate maps during the seventeenth century, but have to wait until the eighteenth century for their general adoption by improving landlords.[23] The only area for which this was not true is the republic of Venice, as several authors have shown.[24] This had long been known as a centre for cartographers, and between 1540 and 1580 the expansion of the Venetian patriciate into *terra ferma* (the mainland behind the city) led to a brisk market in land, and consequently to a good deal of mapping of it.[25] Both Kubelik, *Die Villa im Veneto* and Puppi, *Andrea Palladio*, offer a good many examples of estate maps, a genre which was clearly at home in the conditions of the sixteenth-century Venetian republic, with its prosperous estates and rich and cartographically sophisticated proprietors.

SPAIN

The Iberian peninsula offers a striking contrast with this area. There were vast estates in Spain's river valleys, and a governing elite well aware of the value of maps, as we have seen; moreover, she long enjoyed internal peace. However, Spanish agriculture also long remained primarily geared to production for very local markets, with little incentive for her landholders to introduce the kinds of innovation eventually associated with the improving landlords of the eighteenth century. It is true that the Mesta, or guild of sheep-owners, produced wool on a massive scale for the international market, but the passage of their transhumant herds was not a phenomenon likely to be mapped. Such large-scale provincial maps as existed generally showed towns and their rural possessions.[26]

FRANCE

In France, too, early modern agriculture was usually an affair of either self-sufficiency or of local supply; capitalist methods were slow to penetrate the French countryside, where a series of civil wars marked the century after 1560. Many members of the French nobility had been trained in Jesuit high schools, where cartography was often taught, but they generally commissioned detailed maps not of arable farms, but of forests, mines, and property-boundaries.[27] Figure 73 shows one of these forest plans, drawn in 1756 for the Duc de Brissac. This was probably the seventh duke (1698–1780) of that extensive family. He spent much of his life under arms for the French Crown, but when at home evidently wished to know the layout of the forests in which he hunted.

The historian Marc Bloch observed as long ago as 1929 that there seemed to be no seigneurial *plans parcellaires* (estate plans) before 1650, and not many in the century after that.[28] He continued by noting that estate plans became much more numerous after 1740, attributing this to the so-called 'feudal reaction' of the French nobility, who in many cases during the second half of the eighteenth century were taking their hereditary lands in hand, with a view to maximizing their output. Maps were an important part of this process: as the lawyer Joseph Rousselle observed in his *Instructions*

Fig. 73. N. Vincent, Plan of the forest of Brissac, 1756. Here is the forest in which the Duc de Brissac liked to hunt. Each separate wood is named and noted on the key; no doubt there were gamekeepers who could be instructed to encourage the deer in the best places. This map somewhat resembles an estate map, in that it shows only the land of the duke; adjacent 'seigneuries' or lordships are simply noted by name.

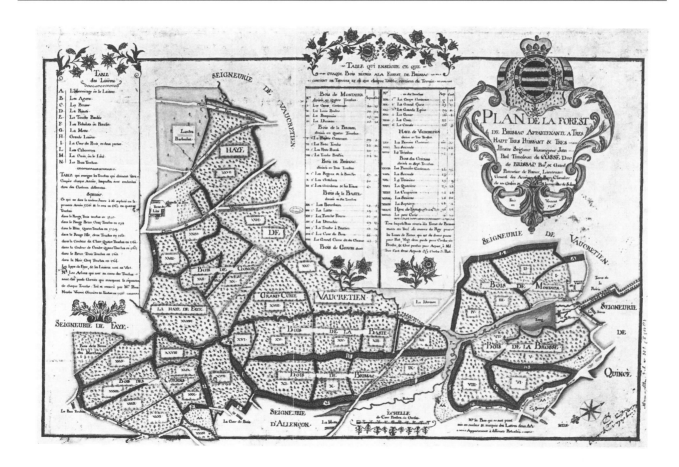

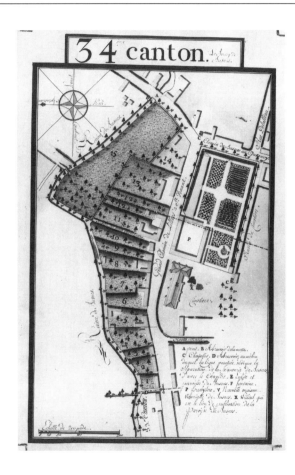

pour les seigneurs et leurs gens d'affaires ('Instructions for lords and their business people') (Paris, 1770), 'any land without a general survey and geometrical plan is never well known in all its details'.[29]

There was consequently a great increase of activity by *arpenteurs*, or surveyors, in late eighteenth-century France, and they were particularly active in the north-east, as the work of Abbé Roger Desrumeaux has shown.[30] Figure 74 shows one map from an atlas of 100 maps compiled in 1789 by the surveyor Christophe Verlet, to show the parish of Busnes, near Lille in northern France.[31] Each map shows one 'canton', fully filling the page; as the cantons were of different sizes, the maps in the atlas have a wide range of scales. On the map of canton 34 it is possible to distinguish not only the houses and fields of the peasants, but also the house of the *curé*, his church, and 'the lime-tree which is the place of publication of the parish of Busnes', where the king's edicts were read out, no doubt usually after Mass on Sunday. Other maps in this atlas show the roads, windmills, remnants of strip fields, and other features of the

Fig. 74. Christophe Verlet, Plan of the 34th *canton* at Busnes, 1789. This is a characteristic product of the *arpenteurs*, or surveyors, who thrived in north-eastern France in the later eighteenth century. The whole area has been carefully measured, and is shown in plan except for the trees, with their curiously conventional shadows (even the lime tree outside the church). Few studies have been made on these maps, but it would be most interesting to relate them to the modern countryside.

pre-revolutionary countryside; the lawyer Rousselle would surely have felt that such a closely-observed image would enable the land-lord to maximize the profits on this property.

THE NEW WORLD

Eventually, this Old World map form spread across the Atlantic Ocean to the New World, where it found a home in such areas of large, prosperous landholdings as the British West Indies and the states of South Carolina and Louisiana.[32] The archives of the National Library of Jamaica, and those of the Fireproof Building in Charleston, are full of maps of this kind. As in the Old World, estate maps here lost their function during the nineteenth century, when central mapping agencies produced large-scale maps of the countryside, so that landowners could use them to identify their property.

By the middle of the nineteenth century, then, estate maps had everywhere gone out of fashion. But they had fulfilled a useful role between 1570 and 1840, when in country after country they were adopted as part of what is sometimes called 'the agricultural revolution', and allowed landowners to manage their estates more rationally than had been the case when they had to rely only upon textual terriers. Indeed, they allowed landowners to manage their estates so efficiently that surveyors were sometimes menaced by peasants and yeomen who foresaw that the arrival of the surveyor often meant a rise in rent.

TOWN PLANS

We turn now to a form of map that cannot be shown to have emerged from changes in economic conditions, except in a very general sense. In order to understand how printed town plans became so popular in the late sixteenth century quite different con-siderations apply.[33] As we have seen, the Romans were well aware of the possibility of making city plans, which must have been par-ticularly easy to construct in towns planned upon a grid. Charlemagne is said to have possessed plans of Constantinople and of Rome, and there is a long tradition of mapping the city of Jerusalem.[34] As we have seen, the fifteenth-century revival of interest in the classical world led to enterprises like Alberti's pro-posal of *c.*1440 for working out a new plan of Rome (Fig. 10), and even earlier a rather similar plan was constructed for Vienna, though we have absolutely no idea who was responsible for it.[35] This plan too was based on distance measurements and is provided with a scale; it makes no attempt to set out the complex pattern of streets in Vienna, but does show where the main buildings were, indicating them in rudimentary perspective.

From the time that Ptolemy's *Geography* began circulating in western Europe, from the early fifteenth century onwards, various maps had sometimes been added to the original twenty-seven proposed by the master. In the extraordinary Ptolemaic atlas made for Federigo de Montefeltro of Urbino (1422–82) about 1470, there were not only seven 'modern' maps, but also ten city plans, showing Milan, Venice, Florence, Rome, Constantinople, Jerusalem, Damascus, Alexandria, Cairo, and Volterra.[36] These plans were all drawn in rather the same style as the earlier plans of Vienna and Florence, with the walls and internal rivers sharply delineated, and the main buildings set out in exaggeratedly large perspective views. It is possible to trace back the origin of some of them: the plan of Constantinople, for instance, clearly derives from that in the island book of Cristoforo Buondelmonte (active 1420).[37] However, it is difficult to know why this substantial collection of city plans should suddenly make its appearance: it is impossible to argue, for instance, that this was a period during which the towns rose to a new level of civic consciousness. Perhaps we should simply agree with Naomi Miller that these plans are 'a manifestation of an expanding world view', 'serving the growing demands for trade and travel', as well as being helpful for military purposes and guides for religious pilgrimage.[38]

At all events, they seem to have come at the beginning of a period when more and more city plans were being produced. In Florence, four large woodcut city views were produced at this time, showing Constantinople, Florence, Pisa, and Rome.[39] Even in faraway England, a town plan of Bristol was drawn in 1480, perhaps under Italian inspiration.[40] In Mainz, Bernard von Breydenbach published in 1486 his *Peregrinatio in terram sanctam* ('Pilgrimage to the Holy Land'), 'integrally illustrated with specific views, based on drawings by E. Reuwich'.[41] This work by Breydenbach was, however, very unusual; Hartmann Schedel's *Liber cronicarum*, published at Nürnberg in 1493, was much more typical of the time in that many of its views were non-specific. Indeed, seventeen woodblocks sufficed for fifty-seven different towns, since several were used more than once (Fig. 75).[42] As we have seen, the popes seem to have been remarkably sensitive to such new developments, and between 1484 and 1487 Innocent VIII commissioned a cycle of mural town-views that eventually included Florence, Genoa, Milan, Naples, Rome, and Venice. Six years later, Francesco II Gonzaga, Marquis of Mantua, commissioned a similar cycle for his

Fig. 75. Views of Mainz and Naples, from Hartmann Schedel, *Liber chronicarum* (Nürnberg, 1493). Although it is often asserted that the same image was used for different cities, it seemed a good idea actually to show two of these images, theoretically showing different cities. This way of proceeding is reminiscent of the images discussed in Chapter 2, when generic towns were regarded as perfectly satisfactory, before the coming of the idea of precisely observed locations.

Das drit alter

Mayntz

der werlt Blat XLII

Neapolis

palace at Gonzaga, including this time Cairo, Constantinople, Florence, Genoa, Naples, Rome, and Venice;[43] such cycles would thereafter often be a feature of European palaces.

City plans continued to be published during the early sixteenth century. In 1500 Jacopo de' Barbari produced the woodcut view of Venice that set entirely new standards for size, detail, and elegance

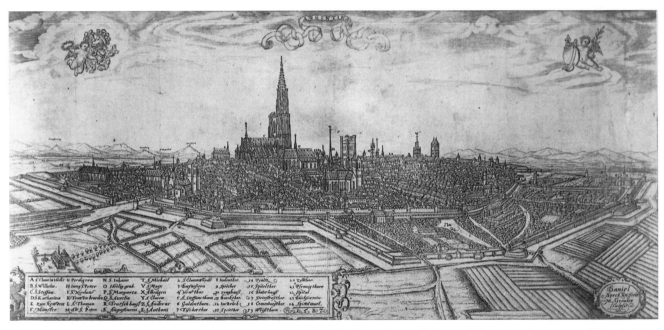

Fig. 76. Daniel Specklin, *Argentina* (Strasbourg, 1587). This is a characteristic profile, designed to set off the overwhelming visual importance of the cathedral in Strasbourg. Many people, of course, first saw cities from this angle, as they slowly made their way along the tracks leading to them and the welcoming pinnacles of the distant cathedral became ever clearer and larger.

of execution;[44] three years later, Leonardo da Vinci drew the plan of Imola which has often been taken to be one of the earliest purely planimetric images found in early modern Europe.[45] At this time the production of city plans was sporadic and unplanned, with fresh work appearing apparently at random, rather as other kinds of maps were produced without apparent plan, in the days of what were called the 'Italian atlases assembled to order'. These were atlases made up for each patron of whatever material happened to be available on the booksellers' shelves.[46]

PROFILES

At this time, the three possible ways of showing a city were all worked out for the great centres of western Europe, and then indeed of the world. The 'profile' showed it from ground level, as if approaching it on foot; this type of imaging was reminiscent of the 'landfall' sketches that came to accompany many nautical charts (Fig. 45). The Italian scholar Lucia Nuti, indeed, suggests that it was a 'northern' plan-type, born in those flat Netherlands where sea and land were barely distinguishable.[47] Figure 76 shows a modified image of this kind setting out the main features of Strasbourg, in 1587. Such an image makes it possible to give a powerful impression of the tall churches that often dominated sixteenth-century cities, and it can also show something of the sur-

rounding countryside. This sort of image has never gone entirely out of fashion, for it is also very effective for showing cities with a wealth of skyscrapers, like New York or Chicago.

BIRD'S-EYE VIEWS

More common was the diagonal image, also known as a 'bird's-eye view', or *vue cavalière*. Figure 18 shows Anthonisz's 1544 bird's-eye view of Amsterdam. It is not at all effective for showing the dominant tall buildings, but can give a remarkably full impression of the general layout of a city, in its industrial quarters as well as in its central administrative ones. In this case, too, it brings out very well the polders (reclaimed fields) in the surrounding countryside. Views like this did not require any technical skill on the part of the viewer, which is why they have remained popular for such purposes as giving tourists a general impression of a city, with its greater monuments usually given disproportionate prominence.

PLANIMETRIC IMAGES

The third way of showing a city is the very ancient planimetric method, by which the area is shown as if seen vertically from above, as the Romans had done, following the example of other ancient peoples. This type of imaging was not very suitable for popular consumption, as it requires a certain expertise to read plans

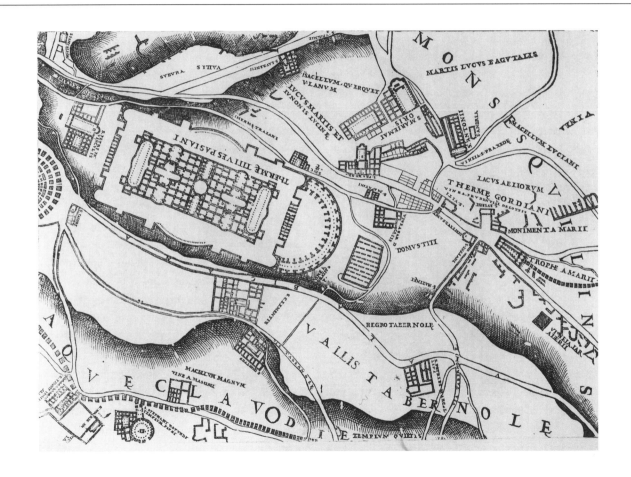

of this kind. One of the most famous examples made during the sixteenth century was the plan of Rome published by Leonardo Bufalini in 1555 (Fig. 77). This city had long been studied by archaeologists, anxious to make scaled plans in order to compile an accurate inventory of the many ancient buildings (Chapter 1), and Bufalini's plan was one in a long series.[48] Planimetric views have become indispensable for modern city planners, who use them as base maps upon which to plot the huge variety of urban services.

COLLECTIONS OF CITY VIEWS

Town plans embodying various combinations of these three styles were often published as single sheets during the mid-sixteenth century. Then, in the 1560s, the Catholic cleric Georg Braun (1541–1622) of Cologne had the idea of compiling a great standardized collection of such plans, just as Abraham Ortelius (1527–98) would in 1570 publish such a compendium of terrestrial small-scale maps, the *Theatrum orbis terrarum*. The first volume of Braun's *Civitates orbis terrarum* ('Cities of the world', a name clearly related to the Ortelian title) came out in 1572, to be followed by five more volumes up to 1617.[49] This collection of about 550 views, arranged in a slightly haphazard fashion, just as they came in from many contributors, enjoyed a huge success among the public, going through many translations and editions.[50] In later years this international collection would be succeeded by similar national collections, for the scope of the enterprise was vast, and it would hardly have been possible to expand the original idea. Thus for the German-speaking regions we have the wonderfully satisfying images of Matthæus Merian (Fig. 59).

The chief engraver for the *Civitates orbis terrarum* was the Protestant Franz Hogenberg (1538–90), no doubt with many assistants. He took the images as they came, and interpreted them in such a way that they do not differ very markedly in style from the original manuscripts. Many of these have not survived, but we do have the originals of a surprising number of the printed plates. R. A. Skelton, in his facsimile edition of the *Civitates*, divided the plates into the two classes, 'ichnographic' and 'scenographic'.[51] A prime example of the first would be the plates derived from the drawings of Jacob van Deventer (d. 1575), commissioned by Philip II to work on the cities of the Low Countries (Chapter 3 and Fig. 24). Deventer's drawings are very spare delineations, sometimes of quite

Fig. 77. Leonardo Bufalini, Detail from his map of Rome (Rome, 1555). This is one of the twenty sections into which Leonardo Bufalini's map of Rome was divided. It was mainly concerned to identify and locate the monuments of the ancient city, but in so doing it provided an excellent base map of the new Rome. The typography is curiously reminiscent of that found on fragments of city-plans surviving from Latin antiquity, and perhaps this resemblance is not accidental.

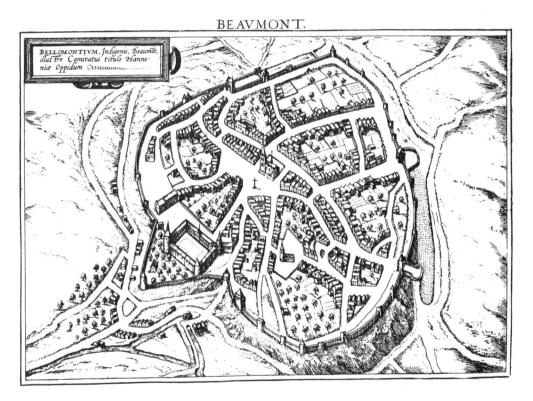

Fig. 78. Plan of Beaumont, from Georg Braun and Franz Hogenberg, *Civitates orbis terrarum* (6 vols., 1572–1617), iii. 26. Beaumont is the little town in southern Belgium near which the dukes of Croy had their famous castle, with its collection of countryside plans. This image was generated from the drawing of Jacob van Deventer (Fig. 24) and is characteristic of the 'ichnographic' or generally planimetric town plan.

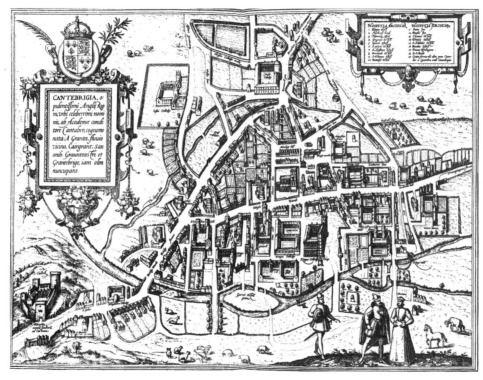

Fig. 79. Plan of Cambridge, from Georg Braun and Franz Hogenberg, *Civitates orbis terrarum*, ii. 1. This charming view of Cambridge shows the colleges clustered alongside the river, flowing from right to left across the foreground. The castle guards what are in fact the westward approaches (bottom left), but there is neither strict orientation nor scale to this 'scenographic' drawing. Even so, it is informative enough still to permit a visitor to navigate among the ancient colleges at the centre of Cambridge.

small towns, and they were translated by Hogenberg into plates that look somewhat more robust but are nevertheless little more than planimetric outlines (Fig. 78). As an example of a small town treated in a thoroughly 'scenographic' way we might take Cambridge (Fig. 79). Here the main outline of the streets is shown, but many of the buildings are also delineated as bird's-eye views; animals graze on the fenny Backs, and an elegant trio occupies the foreground. The 'ostells' are marked on the key, and the 'colledges' are clearly marked on the map, with a great many other features; the textual insertions greatly enhance an image of this kind.

Various explanations have been advanced to account for the reasons why Braun launched this ambitious and risky venture. The reading public was undoubtedly growing, and becoming richer; the printing presses were not only more numerous, but also better able to handle long runs of complicated images. The publication turned out to be a great commercial success, and contemporaries soon appreciated its simply pleasurable aspect; as Robert Burton (1577–1640) put it, in his *Anatomy of melancholy* (1621), 'a good prospect alone will ease melancholy … what greater pleasure can there be now than … to peruse those books of cities, put out by Braun and Hogenbergius?'[52] Braun himself writes in the introduction that his book 'presents to the view the site, the circumference of the walls, and the condition of those cities which were taken from the Christians by the most savage nations, with the greatest hope that they will be regained',[53] but this scarcely seems a very realistic aspiration. On the other hand, a much more convincing possible use has been ferreted out by recent German scholarship, which has laid stress upon what is called the *ars apodemica*, or discussion of the art of travelling.[54] It might not have been possible to leave for Italy with the bulky volumes of the *Civitates* under one's arm, but it would certainly have been possible to have acquainted oneself with the images and texts of Italian cities before departure, and then to have taken plans of them in the shape of the separate sheets that were made available by Braun; this, indeed, may well have been a major use of his publication.

THE NATURE OF CITY VIEWS

Scholars have of late also been interested in the way in which artists delineated the cities whose images they sent to Cologne for engraving and publication. Many of these scholars interpret the images as part of the concept of 'self-fashioning' that has thrown light on similar developments in the arts and literature. For John Pinto, the city views could be divided into those that are 'ichnographic' and those that are 'symbolic', a distinction close to that of Skelton mentioned above.[55] Evidently, the spare delineations of van Deventer were the least symbolic, and the most objective, whereas many bird's-eye views invited a highly emotional response, as Elliott also noted.[56] This idea has been most fully worked out by Richard Kagan, in his insistence on the contrast between '*urbs*-type', primarily topographic plans, and '*communitas*-type', symbol-oriented views. It is clear from his work that when carefully dissected, the most apparently objective city image will turn out to contain a good deal more 'communicentric' material than is at first obvious; each group of patrons, in short, will make sure that its images conform to the idea that it wishes to propagate of itself.[57]

At the same time that printed city images were thus being produced in large numbers, manuscript images of urban areas continued to be drawn. As we have seen (Plates XI and XII), many towns were carefully delineated in the course of estate mapping. Others were meticulously drawn out, as urban areas were remodelled in accordance with the new demands of warfare (Chapter 5). Martha Pollak has shown that many of these manuscript plans eventually found their way into print, in those huge collections of plans of fortified towns that were widely popular during the seventeenth and eighteenth centuries.[58]

Between 1500 and 1800, then, there had been a total change. Whereas at the beginning of the period images of both countryside and town were quite rare, by the end of it such plans were to be found in many parts of western Europe. The emergence of estate maps seems to correspond with quite specific changes in agricultural organization, whereas the proliferation of town plans resulted from a great variety of factors: from new printing possibilities, for instance, from the revival of interest in classical antiquity, from the needs of the military engineers, and from the new appreciation of imagery among influential groups. Perhaps both developments are best seen as a response to the growth of rural and urban economic structures, which constantly threw up new demands and new possibilities.

Conclusion: The accelerating use of maps

In the previous six chapters, I have tried to show how people in early modern Europe came to use maps in the everyday course of their business. By the beginning of the seventeenth century, they were in habitual use by soldiers, sailors, farmers, archaeologists, and administrators, to name only the most obvious users. Of course, I realize that some of these categories overlap, and that there are other areas where maps came to be used. To take only two of these, we might consider the use of maps by gardeners and by theologians.

GARDEN MAPS

As early as 1527, Baldassare Peruzzi (1481–1536) drew a plan for a proposed garden, complete with *casino*, pergola, and orchard.[1]

Renaissance architects generally considered the garden as an integral part of the house that they were designing, so that they often made plans and drawings showing the two together. Many such collections of plans and drawings were published during the sixteenth century, and one of the finest examples of this type of work, setting country houses into their surrounding gardens, is Jacques Androuet du Cerceau's *Les plus excellents bâtiments de France* ('The finest buildings in France') (Paris, 1576); similar examples could be found from all the western European countries. In *The world of André Le Nôtre* (Philadelphia, 1998), Thierry Mariage sets out the relationship between gardening and cartography in France, reproducing an interesting map by the great French gardener Le Nôtre himself,[2] and demonstrating that the art of gardening could hardly have grown as it did without the help of cartography. The construction of immense gardens like those at the palace of Versailles and elsewhere in Europe was dependent upon producing maps laying out not only their shape, but also the way in which they would intrude upon the surrounding countryside.

THEOLOGICAL MAPS

The 1520s also seem to have been the time when maps began to be used in Protestant bibles.[3] Martin Luther (1483–1546) had requested one (in vain) for the 1522 printing of the New Testament, and they were drawn for Protestant bibles from 1525 onwards, involving eminent artists such as Lucas Cranach, Hans Holbein, and Sebald Behaim. Interestingly enough, during the sixteenth century the use of maps in this way remained confined to Protestant, vernacular bibles, and they were very rarely found in Catholic, Latin bibles. It is curious that the ancient Church was thus unwilling to adopt what seems to us a powerful visual aid to understanding the scriptures.

In this, as in other respects, the Jesuits, founded in 1540, eventually represented a powerful reaction. For, in their desire to keep the ancient Church fully in touch with the latest learning, they laid particular emphasis in their schools, which spread rapidly over much of Europe in the late sixteenth century, on the natural sciences, including cartography. So it was that in the seventeenth and eighteenth centuries, their overseas missionaries, particularly in the Americas but also in China and other places, proved to be extraordinary mapmakers. After the coastal outline had been established by Iberian navigators, the mapping of the interior of South America was largely undertaken by Jesuit missionaries.[4]

PRINTING AND LITERACY

Mention of printed bibles recalls the fact that we have made no systematic attempt to summarize the impact of the coming of printing by movable type on the spread of map use, even though much work has been published on this theme.[5] Most of our discussion has concerned the manuscript precursors of printed maps, even though in each chapter we have eventually come to national atlases (Chapter 3), to volumes of printed charts (Chapter 4), to printed collections of fortification-plans (Chapter 5), and to the great printed collections of city plans (Chapter 6). Clearly, the spread of the printing press and the multiplication of atlases must have had a huge effect on the level of map use, as indeed did the slow growth of literacy. But it is extremely hard to quantify these effects, and for the sake of our present argument we should regard the advent of printing and of literacy as having chiefly a multiplier effect upon developments whose origins came long before the great

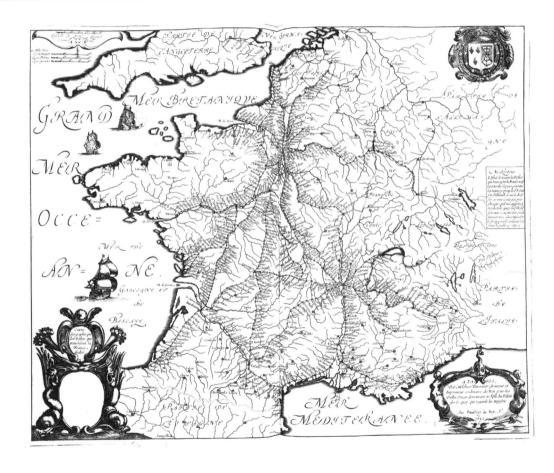

efflorescence of printed maps, in the late sixteenth century.

MAPS OF THE REALMS

After 1600, maps were constantly used for new purposes. When, for instance, Sir William Petty (1623–87) was assigned in 1654 to administer the 'pacification' of part of Ireland, one of his first acts was to get a spatial grip on the situation by commissioning the 'Down Survey' (apparently so called because it was written 'down').[6] This extensive and rapid survey of estates seized from Irish families during the English Interregnum (1649–60) demonstrated Petty's remarkable talents as an expeditious administrator. Having begun as a medical man (famous for having revived a woman apparently dead), he was able to turn his talents not only to the collection of statistics and the formulation of economic policy, but also—quite naturally it would seem—to cartography. His survey thus for many years formed the foundation of the British occupation of a large part of Ireland; it is a fine example of what

Fig. 80. Melchior Tavernier, Map of the French system of post-roads, 1632. This map of France is much the same as those later adopted as base maps, on which a variety of phenomena could be plotted. Here it is the post-roads which have been inserted, making us realize how far large areas of France— Brittany and the Pyrenean country most obviously—were from communications based on Paris.

Karl Marx might have called the map as the instrument of the possessing classes.

In France, state cartography was better developed than in England, so that as early as 1632 Melchior Tavernier could publish a map of France setting out its post-roads (Fig. 80). This map gives us a sort of X-ray of the centres of power in France at the time, with Paris and Lyons prominent. Each stage of the road is marked by a small circle, and the roads extend into Turin, Basel, and Brussels, though not of course into the land of the great enemy, Spain. When Jean-Baptiste Colbert (1619–83) became chief finance minister in France in 1661, at the beginning of the personal reign of Louis XIV, he announced his intention of basing his policies upon a thoroughgoing cartographic analysis of the realm.[7] He was greatly aided in this by Nicolas Sanson (1600–67) and his successors, who developed what would today be called a 'base map' of France, a sort of template (rather like Fig. 80 without the roads) upon which all matter of phenomena could be plotted: financial districts, religious jurisdictions, river-systems, and so forth. It eventually turned out that this particular base map had considerable inaccuracies, but the concept was remarkable and would eventually be very important all over the world.

Among the things that statesmen now wanted to know was exactly where their realms ended. In early modern times this had

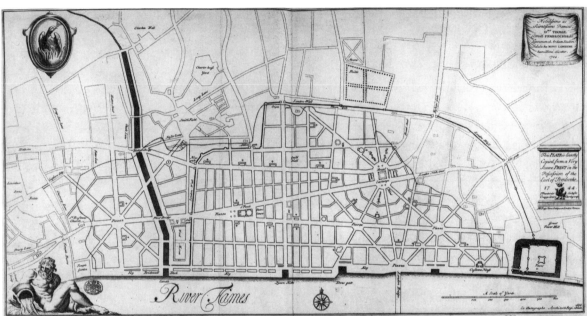

ICHNOGRAPHIA *Urbis* LONDINII, *post Magnum et fatale* INCENDIUM. *An°. D°.* MDCLXVI. *cum* IDEÂ. *Novæ Urbis* — A PLAN *of the City of* LONDON, *after the great* FIRE *in the Year of* OUR LORD 1666. *with the* MODELL *of the New*

EXPLANATION OF THE PLAN

not been a preoccupation: in the early sixteenth century, for instance, people knew that as you moved eastwards from Paris, you eventually came to estates owing allegiance to the emperor in Vienna; the further eastwards you went, crossing the Rhine River, the more numerous these estates were, until you had plainly left the kingdom of France. This sort of hazy frontier region would no longer do, in the days of growing central administrations, so that realms came to be precisely defined by cartographic frontiers. Rather approximate boundaries can be found on the sixteenth-century maps of Abraham Ortelius; in France, the attempt to identify and map a precise eastern frontier dates back to the first decade of the seventeenth century.[8] By the time of the treaty of Ryswick (1697), boundaries were agreed by the plenipotentiaries in accordance with the lines traced on an accompanying map.[9] During the eighteenth century, maps came to be an indispensable part of the negotiations concluding wars. When, for instance, Great Britain and the United States made peace at Paris in 1783, much of the

Fig. 81. Sir Christopher Wren, Plan for rebuilding London after the fire of 1666. Copied in 1744 from 'a very scarce print in the possession of the earl of Pembroke', this plan shows how, after the Restoration of 1660, English town-planners thought in terms of the grand baroque cities like Rome and Turin, which reflected their rulers' ambitions in wonderful vistas, piazzas, and avenues. In the end the medieval city was modified much less than might have been possible.

negotiators' time was taken up in marking out on the map (not a very accurate one …) the line that would henceforth separate Canada from the United States. Subsequent treaties always had this cartographic component, and sometimes, as in the case of the dispute between Venezuela and Great Britain in 1904, involved the creation of special atlases of historic maps in order to elucidate the respective claims.[10]

CITY PLANS

The sixteenth century had seen a great proliferation of town-plans, particularly in Braun and Hogenberg's *Civitates orbis terrarum* (Figs. 78 and 79). During the seventeenth century, printed plans came to delineate not only cities as they were, but as they might be. Thus, after the Great Fire of 1666, Sir Christopher Wren (1632–1723) produced his plan for rebuilding London (Fig. 81). We might be in some baroque southern city, with this provision for 'a round piazza', a 'usefull canal', and 'a triumphal arch to the founder of the New City, king Charles the second'. Very little of this splendid plan was carried out, Wren instead becoming fully employed with his many churches. But it is important that this map was the means by which citizens could now be brought to believe in the possibility of a new and better planned capital city. The work of Sir Christopher Wren thus foretold, in its cartographic component, such major exercises

in cartographic urban planning as the Burnham Plan, devised for Chicago by Daniel Burnham (1846–1912) in 1907.[11]

MAPS AND THE NATURAL SCIENCES

The seventeenth century was also the time when natural scientists naturally turned towards maps, whether celestial or terrestrial, to explain their theories.[12] When Galileo Galilei (1564–1642) wanted to set out his discoveries concerning the moon, he created a lunar sketch map, as did Johannes Helvetius in 1647. As for terrestrial maps, Fig. 82 shows a map of Athanasius Kircher (1601–80), by which the learned Jesuit polymath tried to explain his theory about the great water-currents which, he thought, swept about the world, only somewhat impeded by the existence of the land-masses. By this time scientists naturally used maps to explain such theories, which indeed were impossible to express in mere words.

As time went on, other natural scientists developed maps to elu-

Fig. 82. Athanasius Kircher, *Mappa fluxus* from his *Mundus subterraneus* (Amsterdam, 1668). This map shows how natural scientists could use cartography to set out the most problematic and complicated theories about the nature of the earth. It also shows how by the use of greatly enlarged ships, cartographers could reduce the impression of the huge distances involved in this sort of geography. But a map like this remains neutral in terms of European possession; it is simply an instrument to express a scientific theory.

cidate their theories. In physics, for instance, Edmond Halley (1656–1743) made a world chart of trade winds in 1686, following it up about 1700 with a chart showing magnetic variations in the Atlantic Ocean. In meteorology, the most famous early map is probably that of the Gulf Stream published by Benjamin Franklin (1706–90) in 1775. He had collaborated with his cousin, Timothy Fulges, a sea captain, to identify changes in water temperature over a vast area of ocean, and so to define the extent of the warm water emerging from the Gulf of Mexico, and spilling out across the Atlantic Ocean.

Early in the nineteenth century, William Smith (1769–1839) was at work on a geological map of England that essentially laid the basis of the new science of geology.[13] His is an extraordinary story: as the *Dictionary of national biography* archly puts it, Smith spent many years on those 'investigations into stratigraphy which ultimately brought him fame and poverty'. But the resultant map of 1834 is an extraordinary testimony to the expository power of cartography. Less spectacular, but ultimately almost as far-reaching in its implications, was the map compiled about 1855 by John Snow, who plotted on a base map of London the sites of cholera deaths. From this map, though not from merely textual evidence, it at once became clear that the incidence of cholera was highest among those 'who drank from the Broad Street water-

pump'. The science of epidemiology, or the incidence of health and disease, has come largely to rely on this kind of cartographic display of evidence.

In these many ways, then, the natural sciences came to rely on maps for the assessment of spatially based evidence, and a great variety of 'thematic maps' now emerged.[14] The eighteenth and nineteenth centuries have sometimes been described as 'the age of scientific cartography', but in truth they were marked simply by the refinement of cartographic methods. It is true that more of the world was mapped, more accurately, often using larger and more precise instruments, but the principles of this kind of cartography had long been worked out. Thematic maps came to be used much more widely and with greater sophistication, but these too could already be found in the seventeenth century.

Fig. 83. Engraving from Sir John Harington's translation of Ludovico Ariosto's *Orlando furioso* (facsimile published at Carbondale, 1966). This complicated plate shows numerous incidents in the convoluted Renaissance tale known as *Orlando furioso*. The whole plate takes the shape of a sort of fantastic bird's-eye view, and at the top of it Astolfo and Melissa are zooming over the sea, on their way to Scotia. Other editions have plates offering different versions of this remarkable flying beast.

THE EARLIEST AERIAL VIEWS

What completely changed the nature of locational imaging was the coming of the aerial view. This was a concept that had long exercised people's imagination. Among the Ancients, Cicero had remarked that the eye of God surely saw the world from space with great accuracy, and among the Renaissance writers Ludovico Ariosto (1474–1533) had put forward the idea of the Hippogriff, a marvellous creature that could fly over earthly kingdoms at will, and discover all their secrets.[15] The hero, Rogero, is thus described as flying from China to England, making observations on the way:

> A fairer place they saw not all the while
> That they had travelled in the air aloft,
> In all the world was not a fairer isle…

The first sign that these predictions might come true was the late eighteenth-century use of hot-air balloons: from vehicles like these, during the American Civil War of the mid-nineteenth century, photographs began to be taken. Then, in the early twentieth century, aeroplanes began to develop, with the result that during the First World War the first aerial images began to be habitually used. In Syria at this time, the French Jesuit Poidebard, in collaboration with a friendly local French squadron, began to use aerial surveys for archaeological purposes, and on the Western Front both sides used aircraft to generate images of the trenches that were much more telling than those derived from ground observation.[16]

TWENTIETH-CENTURY MAPPING

After the war, aerial survey slowly became an essential element in cartography. This process was greatly accelerated by the requirements of the Second World War. Now whole swathes of countryside could be accurately mapped, using overlapping images captured on a series of aerial runs. This aerial imagery did indeed give pilots the power of the Hippogriff, allowing them, for instance, to identify the sites from which Hitler was bombarding England with V-weapons. But in peacetime the results were as yet relatively unspectacular, resulting chiefly in the updating of existing maps and the mapping of remote and difficult regions of the world.

In the second half of the twentieth century, three developments allowed for an entirely new kind of aerial mapping to be possible. First, images now began to be made by spacecraft from many hundreds of miles above the earth. Then, they could be captured using a variety of different wavelengths, so as to identify not only visible light but also infra-red and radar imagery. Finally, the advent of powerful computers meant that the huge amounts of digital information amassed in this way could easily be manipulated into images accessible to the eye. Of course, these images were not always transferred to paper, but sometimes remained electronic, virtual delineations.

It is possible now to see that the types of maps that emerged in early modern Europe were in fact the precursors of these latest images. Instead of monarchs and ministers, we now have government agencies which use locational imaging for hitherto unimagined purposes: to monitor the flow of rivers, the growth of crops, the health of forests, the proliferation of buildings, and so forth. One of the most interesting uses concerns the pollution of natural resources. Whereas it was formerly a slow and laborious business to track down the pollution of rivers and the oceans, infra-red remote sensing now permits the ready identification of polluting sources. This can sometimes occur in real time, so that the polluting agent can not only be identified but also instantly confronted with the evidence.

ELECTRONIC CHARTS

The early charts, whose emergence is described in Chapter 4, are now represented by a great variety of navigational maps. Many of these images exist only in electronic form, like the devices now found in many cars and on most commercial aircraft. Perhaps the most advanced electronic charts are those used for navigating busy marine corridors like the strait of Dover and the Houston Ship Channel. Here, upon a conventional base chart, may be inserted in real time the state of the wind and tide, the pattern of other ships and wrecks, and any temporary hazards; this electronic image is of course constantly updated, and is normally not printed: it never reaches 'hard copy'.

The electronic maps most often used by the general public are the weather maps seen on television all over the world. These maps are also of great use to farmers, some of whom take satellite mapping a step further in subscribing to services that offer them periodic images of fields bearing crops that interest them. This allows them not only to plant at the right moment, but also to play the market in disposing of their harvests. In cities, too, electronic mapping has quite transformed the type of imagery described in Chapter 6. Urban areas have a huge variety of mappable elements: not only streets and buildings, but also gas lines, electricity lines, lines for fibre-optic cables, water lines, sewers, and so forth. Most great cities now have electronic maps, on which a chosen variety of these variables may be plotted, when some kind of repairs or renewal are planned.

It is probably in military mapping, whose origins are described in Chapter 5, that the advantages of the new kind of surveillance are most apparent. Armies with access to satellite imagery have instant images of the position of their own forces and those of the enemy. As the Gulf War showed, this capacity gives such armies operating in open country an overwhelming advantage over an adversary using the cartographic techniques inherited from the Second World War. The difference in effectiveness between the coalition forces and those of Iraq, based largely on different capacities in locational imaging, resembled the difference in nineteenth-century battles between forces armed with traditional spears and shields, and those (mostly European) already equipped with quick-firing guns.

There have thus been extraordinary advances in the technology of all the types of cartography that we identified as emerging in early modern Europe. It is difficult, perhaps even impossible, to assess the competitive edge that these developments had already given the Europeans by about 1700. But it is easy enough to imagine the impact that their maps brought to their agriculture, their city planning, their maritime navigation, and their military operations, to name only the most obvious areas. It is even easier to understand the effects of the continuing cartographic revolution, in a world where timely information has become the most indispensable commodity.

NOTES

INTRODUCTION

1. There is now a great compendium of references to medieval European cartography, with many suggestive references that need further research.
2. Barber, *Medieval world maps*, 8.
3. Kupfer, 'Medieval world maps', 271.
4. Birkholz, *The King's two maps*, in press.
5. Well, if briefly, described and beautifully illustrated in his *Medieval maps*.
6. Birkholz, *The King's two maps*, in press.
7. *Images of the earth* makes use of some very unusual woodcuts preserved in the Biblioteca Classense, Ravenna.
8. Harvey, *Maps in Tudor England*, 103.
9. See his 'Cartes et contestations'.
10. Harvey, *Medieval maps*, 39.
11. See Grant (ed.), *Einhard's Life of Charlemagne*, 54.
12. See Taub, 'The historical function of the *Forma Urbis Romæ*'.
13. Edited by Theodore Bowie; there are several plans.
14. Delano-Smith and Kain, *English maps*, 14.
15. In spite of the theoretical writings of Roger Bacon and some other scholars; see Woodward, 'Roger Bacon's terrestrial coordinate system'.
16. See Fig. 75.
17. See *The book of memory*.

CHAPTER 1

1. Herodotus, *The history*, book 5, 49.
2. Strabo, *Geography*, i 1, 10–12.
3. For manuscripts and subsequent editions, I have used the work of Bolgar, *The classical heritage*, though I suspect that this may no longer be the best source.
4. From George Baker, *The history of Rome by Titus Livius*, (Philadelphia, 1823).
5. Vol. XII, book XXVIII (28).
6. Nicolet's *Space, geography and politics* is a good example of this.
7. Aristophanes, *The Clouds*, i, 283.
8. There are considerable differences in translation between Harley and Woodward (eds.), *The history of cartography*, i, 158 and Hicks's version in his translation of the *Lives*, i, 505.
9. Hulse, *The rule of art*, 8 and elsewhere in the book.
10. The edition by Horace Leonard Jones is very helpfully edited.
11. Strabo, *Geography*, ii, 5, 12–14.
12. Vitruvius, *On architecture*, ii, 141; the Latin is 'quæ orbe terrarum chorographiis picta itemque scripta'.
13. I have used the edition by H. Rackham.
14. Pliny, *Natural history*, ii, 17 (book III, 2).

15. As explained by Taub in 'The historical function of the *Forma urbis Romæ*'.
16. Dilke, *Greek and Roman maps*, 25.
17. Vegetius, *Military institutions*, 76.
18. Classically explained in Dilke, *The Roman land surveyors*.
19. See Harley and Woodward (eds.), *The history of cartography*, i, 244–5.
20. Richard Talbert is presently working on a detailed study of this document.
21. Aujac, *Claude Ptolemée*, 140.
22. As explained by J. Lennart Berggren and Alexander Jones in the introductory essay to their indispensable new edition of the *Geography*.
23. For a description of this process see Grafton, *Rome reborn*, 158.
24. For a very full list, see Harley and Woodward (eds.), *The history of cartography*, i, 272.
25. See Grafton, *Rome reborn* and also Miller, 'Mapping the city'.
26. See Ptolemée, *La géographie*, ed. Aujac; Ptolomeus, *Cosmographia*, ed. Pagani; and Ptolomeo, *Cosmografia*, ed. Brotóns *et al.*
27. Facsimile edited by R. A. Skelton.
28. See Eisenstein, *The printing press*, 193 for a discussion on the influence of successive editions.
29. Edited in London in 1823.
30. According to Woodward, *Desiderius Erasmus*, 138–40.
31. See for instance Van Dyke, *Ignatius Loyola*, 273.
32. See Burke's full study, *The fortunes of 'The Courtier'*.
33. Castiglione, *The book of the courtier*, 77.
34. These figures are from Burke, *The fortunes of 'The Courtier'*.

35. I could find only the translation by Foster Watson (Cambridge, 1913).
36. Vives, *On education*, 168.
37. Ibid. 168.
38. Note that there are two editions, by Lehmberg and by Croft.
39. Elyot, ed. Lehmberg, *The book named the governor*, 23.
40. On this whole question, see Barber, 'England I: pageantry, defense and government'.
41. Weiss, *The Renaissance discovery of classical antiquity*, 3–4.
42. Gadol, *Leon Battista Alberti*, 167.
43. Ibid. 186 and Grafton, *Rome reborn*, 158.
44. Harvey, *The history of topographical maps*, 74.
45. Karrow, *Mapmakers of the sixteenth century*, 273.
46. Delbrück, *Geschichte der Kriegskunst*, iv, 117.
47. Karrow, *Mapmakers of the sixteenth century*, 347.
48. Ibid., 60, 272, 345, 349, etc.

CHAPTER 2

1. I have been chiefly guided by the works of Baldass, *Jan van Eyck*; Braider, *Refiguring the real*; Clark, *Landscape into art*; Dhanens, *Hubert und Jan Van Eyck*; and Links, *Townscape painting and drawing*.
2. Meiss, *The Limbourgs and their contemporaries*.
3. I have used the edition annotated by Jean Longnon; see Longnon, *Les Trés riches heures du Duc de Berry*.
4. Meiss, *The Limbourgs and their contemporaries*, i, 209, and Belozerskaya, 'Jean van Eyck's lost *mappamundi*'.

5. See Frutaz, *Le piante di Roma*.

6. Links, *Townscape painting and drawing*, 43–9.

7. According to the conventional wisdom, set out in Sterling, 'Jan van Eyck avant 1432'. But this has recently been challenged by Paviot, 'La mappemonde attribuée à Jan van Eyck par Facio'.

8. See for instance Braider, *Refiguring the real*, 10, and Links, *Townscape painting and drawing*, 56.

9. See for instance Bertelli, *Piero della Francesca*; Borsi, *Paolo Uccello*; Eisler, *The genius of Jacopo Bellini*; and Pons, *I Pollaiolo*; these painters were rarely concerned with the depiction of particular places.

10. Panofsky, *Early Netherlandish painting*, i, 12–18.

11. Cosgrove, 'Mapping new worlds', 76–80; Edgerton, *The heritage of Giotto's geometry*, 288–9; and Erickson, *The medieval vision*.

12. Cosgrove, 'Mapping new worlds', 76.

13. Huizinga, *The autumn of the Middle Ages*, 341.

14. There is a good analysis in Gardner, *Art through the ages*, 518–19.

15. Hopkins, *Nicolas of Cusa's dialectical mysticism*, 74.

16. Quotation from Clark, *Landscape into art*, 3.

17. Karrow, *Mapmakers of the sixteenth century*, 130.

18. For this all-embracing figure I have relied upon Gadol, *Leon Battista Alberti*.

19. This image (Fig 10) is reproduced by Frutaz, *Le piante di Rome*, pl. lxxix.

20. See Cox, *Jean Fouquet* and Plummer, *The last flowering*.

21. These maps are reproduced in Kish, 'Leonardo da Vinci, mapmaker'; Oberhummer, 'Leonardo da Vinci and the art of the Renaissance'; and the Montreal Museum of Fine Arts, *Leonardo da Vinci*.

22. See Gombrich, *The image and the eye*, 148.

23. See the observations of Clark, *Leonardo da Vinci*, and Reti, *The unknown Leonardo*.

24. Alpers, *The art of describing*, xxiii.

25. Tolnay *et al.* (eds.), *Michelangelo*, 452.

26. Weiss, *The Renaissance rediscovery of classical antiquity*, 95–6.

27. Published in Fraprie, *The Raphæl book*, 294.

28. For Dürer, I have relied heavily upon Levey, *Dürer*.

29. See the Fig. 65.

30. See Shirley, *The mapping of the world*, 44, and Wætzoldt, *Dürer and his times*, 211; some have also claimed that he had a part in the engraving of the 1524 plan of Mexico City (Germanisches Nationalmuseum, *1471 Albrecht Dürer 1971*, 358–9).

31. The best summary of his work is in Peters, *The illustrated Bartsch*, 95–363.

32. *Geometria … Ich bring Architectura und Perspectiva zusamen*, 1543, cited in Karrow, *Mapmakers of the sixteenth century*, 295.

33. See Armstrong, *The moralizing prints of Cornelis Anthonisz*.

34. On this massive *œuvre*, see Grossmann, *Bruegel, the paintings*; Klein and Klein, *Graphic worlds of Pieter Bruegel the Elder*; and Lebeer, *Bruegel, le stampe*; note also Popham, 'Brueghel and Ortelius'.

35. Well reproduced in Klein and Klein, *Graphic worlds of Pieter Bruegel the Elder*; Lebeer, *Bruegel, le stampe*.

36. Destombes, 'A panorama of the Sack of Rome by Pieter Bruegel the Elder'.

37. See Huvenne, *Pierre Pourbus*, and Smet, 'A note on the cartographic

work of Pierre Pourbus'.

38. For instance, Edouard Bredin and François Quesnel, cited by Boutier, 'Du plan cavalier au plan géométrique', 7–12.

39. There is no account of this school, but good material may be found in Wallis (ed.), *The boke of ydrography*; see particularly W. C. Sturtevant, 'The ethnographical illustrations', 67–72.

40. See Quinn, 'Artists and illustrators'.

41. Twelve of these marvellous maps are reproduced in the Library's calendar for 1992, the best source so far for them.

42. See Wallis (ed.), *The boke of ydrography*.

43. Shirley, *The mapping of the world*, 74.

44. See Buisseret (ed.), *Monarchs, ministers and maps* (Bibl.: Ch. 3) chapter by Peter Barber, 30.

45. On Holbein, see Strong, *Holbein and Henry VIII*; 'The Ambassadors' is extensively discussed in Jardine, *Wordly goods*, 425–6.

46. See Wooden and Wall, 'Thomas More and the painter's eye'.

47. See Gagel, *Pfinzing*.

48. For much of what follows, see Quinn, 'Artists and illustrators'.

49. For reproductions of his work, see Hulton, *The work of Jacques le Moyne de Morgues*, i, 45–54.

50. Reproduced in Cumming, Skelton, and Quinn (eds.), *The discovery of North America*.

51. Alpers, *The art of describing*, 127.

52. Dittrich (ed.), *Jacques Callot*, and Simone Zurawski, 'New Sources'.

53. The most recent work on the family is by Lammertse *et al.*, *Het kunstbedrijf van de familie Vingboons*.

54. Reproduced by Wieder, *Monumenta cartographica*.

55. See Bosters *et al.* (eds.), *Kunst in kaart*.

56. There is an interesting commentary in Links, *Townscape painting and drawing*, 116 ff.

57. See the chapter by Welu in Woodward (ed.), *Art and cartography*, 147–73.

58. Brown, *Velásquez*.

59. Boutier, 'Du plan cavalier au plan géométrique', 20.

60. Curiously, it enjoyed a temporary revival in the topographical drawings that engineer officers were trained to make in the late eighteenth century (Marshall, 'The British military engineers').

CHAPTER 3

1. According to John Marino in Buisseret (ed.), *Monarchs, ministers and maps*, 5–25.

2. See Müntz and Fabre, *La bibliothèque du Vatican*, 102–3, and Pastor, *The history of the popes*, i, 54–5.

3. Paschang, *The popes and the revival of learning*, 21–31.

4. Ibid. 51.

5. See the chapter by Juergen Schulz in Woodward (ed.), *Art and cartography* (Bibl.: Ch. 2), 115–16.

6. See the chapter by Samuel Edgerton, ibid. 43.

7. See Müntz and Fabre, *La bibliothèque du Vatican*, 223.

8. Following the new fashion described in Chapter 6.

9. See the references in Pastor, *The history of the popes*, xvi, 416–17, xx, 616, etc.

10. See Gambi and Pinelli (eds.), *La Galleria delle Carte geografiche*, and Pastor, *History of the popes*, xx, 618–19.

11. Cosgrove, 'Mapping new worlds', 65.

12. Harvey, *The history of topographical maps*, 58–60.

13. As explained by Marino, 'Administrative mapping in the Italian states', 6–10.

14. Cosgrove, 'Mapping new worlds', 71–4.

15. Ibid. 67.

16. Fryde, *The private library of Lorenzo de' Medici*, 571–2.

17. See Valerio, 'The Neapolitan Saxton', 14–17.

18. See Mazzetti (ed.), *Cartografia generale*.

19. Barber, 'Maps and monarchs in Europe', 99.

20. See the foreword to Magini, *Italia*.

21. Marino, 'Administrative mapping in the Italian states', 22.

22. Doutrepont, *La littérature française*, 228.

23. See Van Dyke, 'The literary activity of the emperor Maximilian I'.

24. See for instance Falk and von Bartsch, *Sixteenth-century German artists*.

25. Quoted by Ulmann, *Kaiser Maximilian I*, i, 206.

26. On many of these figures, see Strauss, *Sixteenth-century Germany*.

27. See Dreyer-Eimbcke, 'Conrad Celtis'.

28. This information on Cuspinianus and other savants comes from Karrow, *Sixteenth-century mapmakers*, 138–41 etc.

29. See Marín Martínez (ed.), *Memoria de las obras y libros de Hernando Colón*.

30. Kain and Baigent, *The cadastral map*, 24.

31. Ibid. 24–5.

32. Ibid. 13.

33. Ibid. 18.

34. Ibid. 18–19.

35. Quoted by Vann in 'Mapping under the Austrian Habsburgs', 158.

36. Karrow, *Mapmakers of the sixteenth century*, 42–8.

37. The best set of copies of these maps is now in Armando Cortesao and A. Teixeira da Mota, *Portugaliæ monumenta cartographica* (6 vols, Lisbon, 1960; see also the revised edition by Alfredo Pinheiro Marques (6 vols, Lisbon, 1987), i, 87–111; they are found in Mantua, in Weimar, in Wolfenbüttel, and in the Vatican.

38. Well reproduced in Cumming *et al.*, *The discovery of North America*, 106–7.

39. On this atlas, see Quinn, 'Artists and illustrators', 61.

40. Dittrich (ed.), *Registren und Briefe des Cardinals Gasparo Contarini*, 186.

41. Karrow, *Mapmakers of the sixteenth century*, 107.

42. Kagan, *Spanish cities of the Golden Age*, 41.

43. Karrow, *Mapmakers of the sixteenth century*, 210.

44. Ibid. 62.

45. Ibid. 36.

46. Kagan, *Spanish cities of the Golden Age*, 41.

47. Armstrong, *The emperor Charles V*, ii, 380.

48. Maxwell, *The cloister life of the emperor Charles the fifth*, 323.

49. For this project, see Buisseret on Spanish terrestrial mapping in the forthcoming Volume III of Harley and Woodward (eds.), *The history of cartography*.

50. Kagan, *Spanish cities of the Golden Age*, 11.

51. And well reproduced, ibid.

52. See van't Hoff, *Jacob van Deventer*.

53. For what follows, see Karrow, *Mapmakers of the sixteenth century*, 480.

54. Kagan, *Spanish cities of the Golden Age*, 48.
55. Much of what follows is minimally annotated, for it follows the argument of Chapter 4 in Buisseret (ed.), *Monarchs, ministers and maps*, 99–123.
56. On Fine see Karrow, *Mapmakers of the sixteenth century*, 168–90.
57. See Buisseret, *Ingénieurs et fortifications avant Vauban* (Bibl.: Ch. 5).
58. This remarkable map is reproduced in Buisseret (ed.), *Monarchs, ministers and maps*, 105.
59. See the analysis in Dainville, *Le premier atlas de France*.
60. 'England I: pageantry, defense and government'.
61. Ibid. 45.
62. Well demonstrated in Skelton and Summerson (eds.), *A description of maps*.
63. Barber, 'England II: monarchs, ministers and maps, 1550–1625', 61–2.
64. On this work, see Tyacke and Huddy, *Christopher Saxton*.
65. See Delano-Smith and Kain, *English maps*, 71–4.
66. Kain and Baigent, *The cadastral map*, 50.
67. Ibid. 57.
68. Ibid. 75.
69. Geisberg, *The German single-leaf woodcut*, vol. iv.
70. Kain and Baigent, *The cadastral map*, 72–3.
71. See Barber, 'Maps and monarchs in Europe', 103.

CHAPTER 4

1. On this famous atlas, see particularly Bagrow, *History of cartography*, 95.

2. On Leardo and Mauro, see Harley and Woodward (eds.), *The history of cartography*, i, 316–17.
3. See the views of Randles, 'The alleged nautical school … at Sagres'; of Russell, *Prince Henry 'the navigator'*; and of Teixeira da Mota, 'Some notes on the organization of hydrographical services in Portugal'.
4. On the maps of Grazioso Benincasa, see Harley and Woodward (eds.), *The history of cartography*, i, 433–4.
5. See Pinheiro Marques, 'The dating of the oldest Portuguese charts', and the same author's 'Portuguese cartography'.
6. Wonderfully reproduced in Cortesao, *History of Portuguese cartography*, frontispiece.
7. See Ravenstein (ed.), *Martin Behaims' Erdapfel*, 1492.
8. Analysed by Cortesao, *The nautical chart of 1424*.
9. Teixeira da Mota, 'Some notes on the organization of hydrographical services in Portugal', 54–8.
10. See the reproduction and commentary in Nebenzahl, *The atlas of Columbus*, 34–7.
11. See Du Jourdain and de La Roncière, *Sea charts*, 217–18.
12. For a good image, see Wolff (ed.), *America*, 135.
13. Ibid.; the name comes from a nineteenth-century owner.
14. See Wallis (ed.), *The boke of ydrography*, 7.
15. See the reproductions in Cortesao and Teixeira da Mota, *Portugaliæ monumenta cartographica*.
16. In addition to the *Portugaliæ monumenta cartographica*, we might note on these colonial maps the publication of the national commission, Comissao nacional, *Tesoros da cartografia portuguesa*, 153.

17. Reproduced in Wawrik, *Kartographische Zimelien*, 57 and *Tesoros da cartografia portuguesa*, 100.
18. See Du Jourdain and de La Roncière, *Sea charts*, 211–12. Recent work by Valerie Flint (*The imaginative world of Christopher Columbus*, Princeton, 1992) adds to earlier work to suggest that the Columbian attribution may not be altogether fanciful.
19. There is a good image in Berwick and Alba, *Mapas españoles*, 1: this work is a fine compendium of facsimiles of Spanish colonial maps.
20. This map has a puzzling history: see Nebenzahl, *The atlas of Columbus*, 30–1.
21. On this institution see the chapter by Alison Sandman in the forthcoming Volume III of Harley and Woodward (eds.), *The history of cartography*.
22. See the observations of Zandvliet, *Mapping for money*, 31.
23. Penrose, *Travel and discovery during the Renaissance*, 380; see also Holzheimer and Buisseret, *The 'Ramusio' map of 1534*.
24. See Dahlgren, *Map of the world, 1542*.
25. See Cuesta Domingo, *Santa Cruz y su obra cartográfica*.
26. Recently edited by John Hébert, *The 1562 map of America by Diego Gutiérrez*.
27. See Beltrán y Rozpide, *América en el tiempo de Felipe II*.
28. Recently explained in Mundy, *The mapping of New Spain*; see also González Rodríguez, 'Aprovechamiento informático de las relaciones geográficas'.
29. The *pinturas* have mostly been analysed by Acuña, in his series on the *Relaciones geográficas*.
30. Some historians, in particular Harley (*Maps and the Columbian encounter*), have taken this distinctive Indian style to be part of a plan for disinforming the Spaniards. But it seems more likely that this was simply their cartographic tradition.
31. And seems to have commissioned the remarkable 'Drake Manuscript', preserved at the Pierpont Morgan Library, and recently edited by Verlyn Klinkenborg as *Histoire naturelle des Indes* (New York and London, 1996).
32. On these engineers, see Buisseret, 'Spanish military engineers in the New World', Garrett Lectures (forthcoming).
33. See Angulo Iñiguez, *Bautista Antonelli*.
34. Particularly at Simancas: see Alvarez Terán, *Mapas, planos y dibujos*.
35. Listed and often reproduced in Chueca Goitia and Torres Balbés, *Planos de ciudades*.
36. On these origins see Wallis (ed.), *The boke of ydrography*.
37. Not only in the French national collections, but also in the British Library, the John Rylands Library (Manchester), and the Huntington Library (Pasadena, California).
38. This period is best covered in Du Jourdain and de La Roncière, *Sea charts*, 237–46.
39. On Champlain's survival skills, see Morison, *Samuel de Champlain*, and on his mapping work, see Heidenreich, *Explorations and mapping of Samuel de Champlain*.
40. See ibid. fig. 4 for an image of this map.
41. See Du Jourdain and de La Roncière, *Sea charts*, pl. 84.
42. See the entries in Pastoureau, *Les atlas français*.
43. A facsimile was published at Amsterdam in 1954.
44. See Schilder, 'Organization and evolution of the Dutch East India

Company's office', and more recently Zandvliet, *Mapping for money*.

45. For a fine reproduction of one of his atlases, see *Vingboons-Atlas*.

46. On these developments, see Zandvliet, *Mapping for money*, 26–32.

47. In *Charting an empire*.

48. As forcefully explained by Brian Harley, *Maps and the Columbian encounter*, 134–6.

49. They were analysed (with slightly different results) by Campbell, 'The Drapers' Company', and by Smith 'Manuscript and printed sea charts'.

50. Edited by Black, *The Blathwayt Atlas*.

51. See also the collection of Samuel Pepys, secretary to the Royal Navy, analysed by Wallis, 'Geographie is better than divinitie'.

52. See the facsimile edition by Verner, 1967.

53. See Woodward, *Maps and prints* (Bibl.: Ch. 7).

54. Wroth, 'The early cartography of the Pacific'.

55. An enterprise described by Wallis (ed.), *Libro dei globi*.

56. As explained by Schmidt, *Innocence abroad*.

57. Cipolla, *Guns, sails and empires*.

CHAPTER 5

1. Well explained in Rogers, *The Military Revolution debate*.

2. See for instance Parker, *The Military Revolution*.

3. Well described by Duffy, *Siege warfare*.

4. For an interesting summary, see McNeill, *Keeping together in time*.

5. Their activities are explained in Van Crefeld, *Technology and warfare*.

6. Oman's old *History of the art of war* still seems helpful.

7. See for instance Tunstall, *Naval warfare in the age of sail*.

8. Skelton, 'The military surveyor's contribution', 77–8.

9. A point several times made in Allmand (ed.), *War, literature and politics*.

10. Map reproduced in Buisseret (ed.), *Monarchs, ministers and maps*, 101.

11. Taylor, *The art of war in Italy*, 161.

12. See Skelton, 'The military surveyor's contribution', 81.

13. Quoted by James Vann in Buisseret (ed.), *Monarchs, ministers and maps*, 158.

14. See Parker, 'Maps and ministers: the Spanish Habsburgs', in Buisseret (ed.), *Monarchs, ministers and maps*, 140.

15. Quoted by Hale, 'The military education of the officer class', 442.

16. Meticulously catalogued by Kœman, *Atlantes neerlandici*, whose work is now being revised by Peter van den Krogt.

17. See Buisseret, 'Henri IV et l'art militaire', 348.

18. Parker (ed.), *The Thirty Years War*, 126.

19. See Pelletier, *La carte de Cassini*.

20. See for instance Duffy, *The army of Maria Theresa*, 118–20.

21. Vauban, *De l'attaque*, i, 94–5.

22. See Hodson, *The Cumberland Collection*. The call-numbers in this chapter refer to the earlier, microfilm version of the Cumberland micro-reproductions.

23. For an initial study, see Marshall, *The British military engineers*.

24. McNeill, *The pursuit of power*, 162.

25. Duffy, *The army of Frederick the Great*, 146.

26. Ibid. 47.

27. Irvine, 'The origins of Capital Staffs', 166.

28. Marshall and Peckham, *Campaigns of the American Revolution*, iv.
29. Harley, Petchenik, and Towner, *Mapping the American Revolutionary War*, 75.
30. Ibid. 47.
31. See for instance Vachée, *Napoleon at work*, 96–9.
32. See Carrias, *La pensée militaire française*, 222.
33. On this map see Buisseret, 'Newberry acquisitions'.
34. This development is well described in Taylor, *The art of war in Italy*.
35. Hale, *Renaissance war studies*.
36. In this they resemble working portolan charts, also subject to hard use.
37. Ibid. 179.
38. See Buisseret, *Ingénieurs et fortifications avant Vauban*.
39. By Colvin (ed.), *The history of the King's works*; Hale, *Renaissance war studies*; O'Neil, *Castles and cannon*; and Shelby, *John Rogers*.
40. It is well reproduced in Harvey, *The history of topographical maps*, 161.
41. See Merriman, 'Italian military engineers in Britain in the 1540s', in Tyacke (ed.), *English mapmaking*, 57–67.
42. Neumann, *Festungsbaukunst*, 48.
43. See for instance Scharfe, *Berlin und seine Umgebung*.
44. See Buisseret, 'Spanish engineers in the New World'.
45. See for instance A. W. Lawrence, *Trade castles and forts of West Africa* (London, 1963).
46. Vauban, *De l'attaque*, i, 21.
47. Enumerated in Pastoureau, *Les atlas français*.
48. Many are discussed in Pollak, *Military architecture*.
49. For an attempt to demonstrate this relationship, see Buisseret, 'Les plans de ville'.
50. Ibid. 47.
51. Hale, 'A humanistic visual aid', 283–7.
52. Parker (ed.), *The Thirty Years War*, 206.
53. Hale, 'The military education of the officer class', 460.
54. See Contamine (ed.), *Histoire militaire de la France*, i, 338–9.
55. For comparative figures, see Buisseret, 'L'œuvre des ingénieurs royaux dans les pays de l'Europe moderne' in Maroteaux and d' Orgeix (eds.), *Portefeuilles de plans*, 82–93.
56. See Buisseret, *Ingénieurs et fortifications avant Vauban* for a general survey.
57. For an analysis of this work, see Lallemand and Boinette, *Jean Errard*.
58. Described by Pastoureau, *Les atlas français*, 483.
59. Ibid. 454–5.
60. See Dainville, *Le Dauphiné et ses confins*.
61. Studied in Ballon, *The Paris of Henri IV*, 220–33.
62. Described by Dainville, 'Le premier atlas de la France'.
63. See Pelletier, *La carte de Cassini*.
64. The best general account still seems to be Bonin, *Geschichte der Ingenieurkorps*; he had access to many documents now destroyed.
65. See Mohrmann, 'Der "Welsche Pawmeister" Chiaramelli'.
66. Bonin, *Geschichte der Ingenieurkorps*, 6.
67. Ibid. 9.
68. Ibid. appendix, 253.
69. *Neue Deutsche Biographie*, 16 (1994).
70. Bonin, *Geschichte der Ingenieurkorps*, 14.

71. *Allgemeine deutsche Biographie*, ii, 1875.

72. Bonin, *Geschichte der Ingenieurkorps*, 13.

73. Pollak, *Military architecture*, 28–31.

74. Schulz, *Die ältesten Stadtpläne Berlins*, 27.

75. *Deutsche Staats Bibliothek*, 405–23.

76. A few facsimiles were produced at Stuttgart in 1971.

77. Bonin, *Geschichte der Ingenieurkorps*, 12–13 and 256.

78. *Deutsche Staats Bibliothek*, 40–6.

79. Bonin, *Geschichte der Ingenieurkorps*, 32.

80. Ibid. 42

81. Ibid. 24–5.

82. Scharfe, *Berlin und seine Umgebung*, 26.

83. Frederick the Great, *Instructions*, 49.

84. Duffy, *The army of Frederick the Great*, 146.

85. *Allgemeine Deutsche Biographie*, i (1875).

86. Scharfe, *Berlin und seine Umgebung*, 26.

87. SBPK (Berlin) Karte N 5435/10.

88. Bonin, *Geschichte der Ingenieurkorps*, 45 and Duffy, *The army of Frederick the Great*, 146.

89. Bonin, *Geschichte der Ingenieurkorps*, 45 and Duffy, *The army of Frederick the Great*, 146–7.

90. Duffy, *The army of Frederick the Great*, 146.

91. See Zögner and Zögner, *Preussens amtliche Kartenwerk*.

92. See Chapter 3.

93. *Gedanken*, 28–9.

94. Doucet, *Les institutions de la France*, ii, 642–9.

95. See Buisseret, 'L'atelier cartographique de Sully', and Desbrière,

'L'œuvre de Jacques Fougeu'.

96. *De l'attaque*, i, 94

97. See for instance the Cumberland Collection at Windsor Castle.

98. Van Eerde, *Wenceslaus Hollar*, 30–3.

99. According to Marshall, *The British military engineers*, and Seymour, *History of the Ordnance Survey*.

100. Good reproduction in Pelletier and Ozanne, *Portraits de la France*, 65.

101. Skelton, 'The military surveyor's contribution'.

102. Reproduced in Strauss, *The German single-leaf woodcut*, ii, 575.

103. See Delano-Smith and Kain, *English maps*, 250.

104. See Buisseret and Strove, 'A French engineer's atlas of the River Somme, 1644'.

105. Cumberland Collection, IV. 69.

106. Hale, *Artists and warfare in the Renaissance*.

107. Reproduced in Geisberg, *The German single-leaf woodcut*, i, 472.

108. Neumann, *Festungsbaukunst*, 210.

109. Jackson, *Discovering the vernacular landscape*, 136.

110. Cumberland Collection, II. 45.

111. Some of which are enumerated in Dainville, *Le langage des géographes*.

112. Cumberland Collection, I. 134.

CHAPTER 6

1. Described in Woodward, *Five centuries of map printing*.

2. Andrews, *Plantation acres*, 10. Sixteen such men may be seen on Figure 70.

3. Delano-Smith and Kain, *English maps*, 117–18.

4. See Darby, 'The agrarian contribution'.

5. See Fowkes and Potter (eds.), *William Senior's survey*.

6. Bendall, *Maps, land and society*, 78, and Bendall, 'Enquire "when the same platte was made"', 46.

7. See Sarah Bendall's *Dictionary of land surveyors*, a greatly expanded version of Peter Eden's original compilation.

8. In his *History of topographical maps*.

9. Fletcher, *The emergence of estate maps*, Ch. 2.

10. Described by D. P. Dymond, *Israel Amyce's map of Melford Manor* (booklet).

11. See plate 4 in Buisseret (ed.), *Rural images*.

12. Ipswich CRO, V5/22/1, vol. 1.

13. Buisseret, 'Perambulating the county of Suffolk with John Norden'.

14. See Bendall, *Dictionary of land surveyors*.

15. Delano-Smith and Kain, *English maps*, 118.

16. Fletcher, *The emergence of estate maps*, Ch. 7.

17. See, for instance, Donkersloot-de Vrij, *Topografische kaarten*; Fockema, *Geschiedenis der Kartografie*; and Heslinga *et al.*, *Nederland in Kaarten*.

18. Bendall, *Maps, land and society*, 9.

19. For an illustration, see Buisseret (ed.), *Rural images*, pl. 1.

20. In the sumptuous edition of the Société Royale des Bibliophiles et Iconophiles de Belgique.

21. See Buisseret (ed.), *Rural images*, 11.

22. Ibid. 11–20.

23. See for example the works by Angelini, *Il disegno del territorio*; Barichi (ed.), *Le mappe rurali*; and Faini and Majol, *La Romagna*.

24. See for instance Cosgrove, *The Palladian landscape*; Kubelik, *Die villa im Veneto*; and Puppi, *Andrea Palladio*.

25. Cosgrove, *The Palladian landscape*, 134.

26. See the chapter on Spanish terrestrial mapping in the forthcoming Vol. III of Harley and Woodward (eds.), *The history of cartography*.

27. See Archives de France, *Espace français*, 15–16.

28. Bloch, 'Les plans parcellaires', 66.

29. Quoted by Barbier (ed.), *La carte manuscrite*, 105.

30. In a great many articles, such as 'L'arpenteur, témoin du cadre social de son temps'.

31. This atlas found its way to the Newberry Library, in Chicago, but most remain in archives like the one attached to the cathedral at Tournai in Belgium.

32. See the map in Buisseret (ed.), *Rural images*, 109.

33. These printed town plans are listed by Bachmann, *Die alten Städtebilder* (Stuttgart, 1965), and Alois Fauser, *Repertorium älterer Topographie*, 2 vols (Wiesbaden, 1978).

34. See Uri Laor, *Maps of the Holy Land* (Jerusalem, 1985).

35. Reproduced in Harley and Woodward (eds.), *The history of cartography*, i, 474 (Bibl.: Introduction).

36. See the article by Miller, 'Mapping the city: Ptolemy's *Geography* in the Renaissance'.

37. See Manners, 'Constructing the image of a city'.

38. Miller, 'Mapping the city', 35.

39. Schulz, 'Jacopo de' Barbari's view of Venice', 429.

40. Harvey, *Medieval maps*, 67 (Bibl.: Introduction).

41. Schulz, 'Jacopo de' Barbari's view of Venice', 467.

42. Ibid. 464.

43. Ibid. 466.
44. As well as the article by Schulz, there is a passage in Harvey, *History of topographical maps*, 76.
45. For a good reproduction, see Reti, *The unknown Leonardo* (Bibl.: Ch. 2).
46. See Tooley, 'Maps in Italian atlases'.
47. Nuti, 'Mapping places'.
48. His twenty-sectioned plan is reproduced in Frutaz, *Le piante di Roma*, pl. cix/9.
49. Reproduced in a most serviceable facsimile edited by R. A. Skelton: *Civitates orbis terrarum*, 3 vols (Cleveland, 1966).
50. Ibid. I. xx.
51. Ibid. I. xi.
52. Cited by Elliott, *The city in maps*, 2.
53. *Civitates orbis terrarum*, Vol. I, 'Præfatio'.
54. Frangenberg, 'Chorographies of Florence', 49.
55. Pinto, 'Origins and development of the ichnographic city plan', 55.
56. Elliott, *The city in maps*, 1.
57. Kagan, '*Urbs* and *civitas* in sixteenth- and seventeenth-century Spain'; Kagan and Marias (eds.), *Urban images of the Hispanic world*.
58. See for instance the immense work of Pieter van der Aa, *La galerie agreeable du monde*, published in 66 parts at Leiden in 1729.

CONCLUSION

1. Reproduced in Hobhouse, *Gardening through the ages*, 55.
2. Ibid. 86.
3. On this theme see Delano-Smith and Ingram, *Maps in bibles*.

4. For this development see Buisseret, 'Jesuit cartography'.
5. See particularly Eisenstein, *The printing revolution*.
6. See Petty, *A geographicall description*.
7. Explained in Konvitz, *Cartography in France*.
8. See Buisseret, 'The cartographic definition of France's eastern frontier'.
9. According to Barber, 'Maps and monarchs', 82.
10. See for instance the British Government publication, *Maps to accompany documents and correspondence relating to the question of the boundary between British Guyana and Venezuela.* (London, 1896).
11. Known as the *Plan of Chicago*, by Daniel Burnham *et al.* (New York, 1909).
12. See Ch. 6 in Thrower, *Maps and civilization*, for much of what follows.
13. His work is recently described by Winchester, *The map that changed the world*.
14. Explained by Robinson in *Early thematic mapping*.
15. See the Hough reference.
16. For a good summary of these early developments, see Deuel, *Flights of fancy*.

BIBLIOGRAPHY

Introduction

Barber, Peter, *Medieval world maps: an exhibition at Hereford Cathedral,* (Mappæ Mundi, 1999).

Birkholz, Daniel, *The King's two maps: cartography and culture in thirteenth-century England*, Ph.D. dissertation, The University of Minnesota, 1999; now in the press for The University of Chicago Press.

Campbell, Tony, *The earliest printed maps* (Berkeley, 1987).

Carruthers, Mary, *The book of memory: a study of memory in medieval culture* (Cambridge, 1990).

Crone, G. R., *Early maps of the British Isles* (London, 1961).

Dainville, François de, 'Cartes et contestations', *Imago Mundi,* 24 (1970), 99–121.

Danzer, Gerald, *Images of the earth* (Chicago, 1991).

Delano-Smith, Catherine, and Kain, Roger, *English maps: a history* (London, 1999).

Du Jourdain, Michel Mollat, and de La Roncière, Monique, *Sea charts of the early explorers* (New York, 1984).

Edson, Evelyn, *Mapping time and space: how medieval mapmakers viewed their world* (London, 1997).

Gautier Dalché, Patrick, *Géographie et culture: la représentation de l'espace du VIe au XIIe siècle* (Aldershot, 1997).

Grant, A. J. (ed.), *Einhard's Life of Charlemagne* (London, 1907).

Harley, Brian, and Woodward, David (eds.), *The history of cartography,* Vol. I (Chicago and London, 1987) and Vol. II, book 2 (Chicago, 1994).

Harvey, P. D. A., *The history of topographical maps: symbols, pictures and surveys* (London, 1980).

Harvey, P. D. A., *Medieval maps* (Toronto, 1992).

Harvey, P. D. A., *Maps in Tudor England* (Chicago, 1993).

Harvey, P. D. A. and Skelton, R. A. (eds.), *Local maps and plans from medieval England* (Oxford, 1986).

Horn, Walter, and Born, Ernest, *The plan of St. Gall,* 3 vols (Berkeley, 1979).

Howse, Derek, and Sanderson, Michael, *The sea chart* (New York, 1973).

Kupfer, Marcia, 'Medieval world maps: embedded images, interpretative frames', *Word and Image,* 10/3 (1994), 262–82.

Lewis, Suzanne, *The art of Matthew Paris in the 'Chronica Maiora'* (Berkeley, 1987).

Parsons, E. J. S., *The map of Great Britain c.AD 1360 known as the Gough Map* (Oxford, 1958).

Taub. Liba, 'The historical junction of the Forma urbis Romae', *Imago Mundi,* 45 (1993), 9–19.

Vaughan, Richard, *Matthew Paris* (Cambridge, 1958).

Westrem, Scott, *The Hereford Map: a transcription and translation of the legends with commentary* (Turnhout, 2001).

Woodward, David, 'Roger Bacon's terrestrial coordinate system', *Annals of the Association of American Geographers,* 80/1 (1990), 108–22.

CHAPTER 1

Aristophanes, *The Clouds*, trans. Benjamin Rogers, 3 vols (London and New York, 1924).

Aujac, Germaine, *Claude Ptolemée: astronome, astrologue, géographe* (Paris, 1933).

Barber, Peter, 'England I: pageantry, defense and government: maps at court', in David Buisseret (ed.), *Monarchs, ministers and maps: the emergence of cartography as a tool of government in early modern Europe* (Chicago, 1992).

Biondo, Flavio, *Roma instaurata* (Verona, 1481).

Bolgar, R. R., *The classical heritage and its beneficiaries* (Cambridge, 1954).

Burke, Peter, *The fortunes of 'The Courtier': the European reception of Castiglione's 'Cortegiano'* (University Park, 1995).

Castiglione, Baldassare, *The book of the courtier* (1st edn., 1528; English translation, 1561; Everyman edn., London, 1948).

Delbrück, Hans, *Geschichte der Kriegskunst*, 7 vols (Berlin, 1900–36).

Dilke, Oswald, *The Roman land surveyors: an introduction to the 'agrimensores'* (Newton Abbot, 1971).

Dilke, Oswald, *Greek and Roman maps* (Ithaca, 1985).

Diogenes Lærtius, *Lives of famous philosophers*, trans. R. D. Hicks, 2 vols (Cambridge, Mass. and London, 1925).

Eisenstein, Elizabeth, *The printing press as an agent of change* (Cambridge, 1979).

Elyot, Sir Thomas, *The book named the governor* (editions of Henry Croft, London, 1883 and S. H. Lehmberg, London, 1982).

Erasmus, Desiderius, *De copia verborum et rerum* and *De ratione studii* (ed. London, 1823).

Gadol, Joan, *Leon Battista Alberti: universal man of the early Renaissance* (Chicago and London, 1969).

Grafton, Anthony (ed.), *Rome reborn: the Vatican Library and Renaissance culture* (Washington, 1993).

Harley, Brian, and Woodward, David (eds.), *The history of cartography*, Vol. I (Chicago and London, 1987).

Harvey, P. D. A., *The history of topographical maps: symbols, pictures and surveys* (London, 1980).

Herodotus, *The history*, trans. David Grene (Chicago and London, 1987).

Hulse, Clark, *The rule of art: literature and painting in the Renaissance* (Chicago and London, 1990).

Karrow, Robert, *Mapmakers of the sixteenth century and their maps* (Chicago, 1993).

Leone, Ambrogio, *De Nola* (1514).

Livy, *The history,* 13 vols (Cambridge, Mass. and London 1919–59).

Lord, Louis, *Aristophanes, his plays and influence* (London, 1925).

Major, John M. *Sir Thomas Elyot and Renaissance humanism* (Lincoln, Nebr., 1964).

Miller, Naomi, 'Mapping the city: Ptolemy's *Geography* in the Renaissance', in David Buisseret (ed.), *Envisioning the city: six studies in urban cartography* (Chicago and London, 1998).

Nicolet, Claude, *Space, geography and politics in the early Roman empire* (Ann Arbor, 1991).

Palladio, Andrea (ed.), *I commentari di C. Giulio Cesare* (Venice 1575).

Pliny, *The natural history*, trans. H. Rackham, 10 vols (Cambridge, Mass. and London, 1938–62).

Ptolemée, *La géographie*, ed. Germaine Aujac (Paris, 1998).

Ptolemy, *Geography*, partial translation and edition by J. Lennart Berggren and Alexander Jones (Princeton and Oxford, 2000).

Ptolemy, *Geography*, edition of 1477 [and many subsequent ones] ed. R. A. Skelton (Amsterdam, 1963).

Ptolomeo, Claudio, *Cosmografia*, ed. Victor Navarro Brotóns *et al.* (Valencia, 1983).

Ptolomeus, Claudius, *Cosmographia*, ed. Lelio Pagani (Wiston, 1990).

Quintilian, *On the early education of the citizen-orator*, ed. James Murphy (Indianapolis, 1965).

Quintilian, *Institutio oratoria*, trans. H. E. Butler, 4 vols (London, 1922).

Strabo, *Geography*, trans. Horace Leonard Jones, 8 vols (Cambridge, Mass. and London, 1917–32).

Taub, Liba, 'The historical function of the *Forma urbis Romæ*', *Imago Mundi*, 45 (1993), 9–19.

Van Dyke, Paul, *Ignatius Loyola, the founder of the Jesuits* (Port Washington, 1968).

Vegetius Renatus, Flavius, *Military institutions*, trans. John Clark (Harrisburg, 1944).

Vitruvius, *On architecture*, ed. Frank Granger (London and New York, 1934).

Vives, Juan Luis, *On education* [the *De tradendis disciplinis*], trans. Foster Watson (Cambridge, 1913).

Weiss, Roberto, *The Renaissance discovery of classical antiquity* (Oxford, 1969).

Whithorne, Peter, *The arte of warre*, translation of Machiavelli's work of 1521 (London, 1573).

Woodward, David *et al.*, *Approaches and challenges in a worldwide history of cartography* (Barcelona, 2001).

Woodward, William Harrison, *Desiderius Erasmus, concerning the aim and method of education* (Cambridge, 1904).

Chapter 2

Alpers, Svetlana, *The art of describing: Dutch art in the seventeenth century* (Chicago, 1983).

Armstrong, Christine Megan, *The moralizing prints of Cornelis Anthonisz* (Princeton, 1990).

Avril, François, *Manuscript painting at the court of France* (New York, 1978).

Baldass, Ludwig, *Jan van Eyck* (New York, 1952).

Belozerskaya, Marina, 'Jean van Eyck's lost *mappamundi*', *Journal of Modern History*, 4/1 (2000), 45–84.

Bertelli, Carlo, *Piero della Francesca* (New Haven, 1992)

Borsi, Franco, *Paolo Uccello* (New York, 1994).

Bosters, Cassandra, *et al.* (eds.), *Kunst in kaart: decoratieve aspecten van de cartografie* (Utrecht, c.1989).

Boutier, Jean, 'Du plan cavalier au plan géomètrique', typescript preserved at the Département des Cartes et Plans, Bibliothèque Nationale de France.

Braider, Christopher, *Refiguring the real: picture and modernity in word and image* (Princeton, 1993).

Brown, Jonathan, *Velásquez: painter and courtier* (New Haven, 1986).

Clark, Kenneth, *Leonardo da Vinci* (Cambridge, 1939).

Clark, Kenneth, *Landscape into art* (New York, 1976).

Cosgrove, Dennis, 'Mapping new worlds: culture and cartography in sixteenth-century Venice', *Imago Mundi* 44 (1992), 65–89.

Cox, Trenchard, *Jean Fouquet* (London, 1931).

Cumming, W. P., Skelton, R. A., and Quinn, D. B. (eds.), *The discovery of North America* (New York, 1972).

Cust, Lionel, *Albert Dürer's engravings* (London, 1894).

Destombes, Marcel, 'A panorama of the Sack of Rome by Pieter Bruegel the Elder', *Imago Mundi*, 14 (1959), 64–73.

Dhanens, Elisabeth, *Hubert und Jan Van Eyck* (Antwerp, 1980).

Dittrich, Christian (ed.), *Jacques Callot (1592–1635)* (Dresden, 1992).

Edgerton, Samuel, *The heritage of Giotto's geometry: art and science on the eve of the scientific revolution* (Ithaca and London, 1991).

Edgerton, Samuel, 'From mental matrix to *mappamundi* to Christian empire', in Woodward (ed.), *Art and cartography*.

Eisler, Colin, *The genius of Jacopo Bellini* (New York, 1998).

Erickson, Carooly, *The medieval vision* (New York, 1976).

Fraprie, Frank R., *The Raphael book* (Boston, 1912).

Friedländer, Max, *From Van Eyck to Bruegel*, 2 vols (London, 1956).

Friedländer, Max, *Landscape, portrait, still-life* (New York, 1963).

Frutaz, Amato Pietro, *Le piante di Roma*, 3 vols (Rome, 1962).

Gadol, Joan, *Leon Battista Alberti: universal man of the early Renaissance* (Chicago, 1969).

Gagel, Ernst, *Pfinzing: der Kartograph der Reichsstadt Nürnberg (1554–1559)* (Hersbruck, 1957).

Gardner, Helen, *Art through the ages* (New York, 1970).

Germanisches Nationalmuseum, *1471 Albrecht Dürer 1971* (Munich, 1971).

Gibson, Walter, *'Mirror of the earth': The world landscape in sixteenth-century Flemish painting* (Princeton, 1989).

Gombrich, E. H., *The image and the eye* (London, 1982).

Gombrich, E. H., *Norm and form: studies in the art of the Renaissance* (London, 1966).

Grossmann, F., *Bruegel, the paintings* (London, 1966).

Hopkins, Jasper, *Nicolas of Cusa's dialectical mysticism* (Minneapolis, 1985).

Huizinga, Johan, *The autumn of the Middle Ages*, new trans. and edn. (Chicago, 1996).

Hulton, Paul (ed.), *The work of Jacques le Moyne de Morgues*, 2 vols (London, 1977).

Huvenne, Paul (ed.), *Pierre Pourbus, peintre brugeois 1524–1584* (Bruges, 1984).

Jardine, Lisa, *Worldly goods: a new history of the Renaissance* (London, 1996).

Karrow, Robert, *Mapmakers of the sixteenth century and their maps* (Chicago, 1993).

Keuning, Johannes, 'Cornelis Anthonisz', *Imago Mundi*, 7 (1950), 51–5.

Kish, Susan, 'Leonardo da Vinci, mapmaker', in *Imago et mensura mundi*, Acts of the IXth International Conference in the History of Cartography, 2 vols (Rome, n.d.), i. 89–98.

Klein, H. Arthur, and Klein, Mina C., *Graphic worlds of Pieter Bruegel the Elder: artist of abundance* (New York, 1968).

Lammertse, Friso, *et al.*, *Het kunstbedrijf van de familie Vingboons* (Amsterdam, 1989).

Lebeer, Louis, *Bruegel, le stampe* (Florence, 1967).

Levey, Michæl, *Dürer* (New York, 1964).

Links, J. G., *Townscape painting and drawing* (London, 1972).

Longnon, Jean (ed.), *Les très riches Heures du Duc de Berry* (London, 1969).

Marshall, Douglas, 'The British military engineers, 1741–1783', Ph.D. thesis (Michigan, 1976).

Meiss, Millard, *The Limbourgs and their contemporaries*, 2 vols (New York, 1974).

Montreal Museum of Fine Arts, *Leonardo da Vinci, engineer and architect* (Montreal, 1987).

Oberhummer, Eugen, 'Leonardo da Vinci and the art of the Renaissance in its relations to geography', *Geographical Journal*, 33 (1909), 540–69.

Panofsky, Erwin, *The life and art of Albrecht Dürer* (Princeton, 1955).

Panofsky, Erwin, *Early Netherlandish painting*, 2 vols (Harvard, 1971).

Paviot, Jacques, 'La mappemonde attribuée à Jan Van Eyck par Facio: une pièce à retirer du catalogue de son œuvre', *Revue des Archéologues et Historiens d'Art de Louvain*, 24 (1991), 57–62.

Peters, Jane, *The illustrated Bartsch 18* (New York, 1982).

Plummer, John, *The last flowering* (New York/London, 1982).

Pons, Nicoletta, *I Pollaiolo* (Florence, 1994).

Popham, A. E., 'Brueghel and Ortelius', *Burlington Magazine*, 59 (1931), 184–8.

Quinn, David, 'Artists and illustrators in the early mapping of America', *Mariner's Mirror*, 72/3 (1986), 244–73.

Rees, Ronald, 'Historical links between cartography and art', *Geographical Review*, 70 (1980), 60–78.

Reti, Ladislao (ed.), *The unknown Leonardo* (New York, 1974).

Rotz, Jean, *see* Wallis.

Rowlands, John, *Holbein: the paintings of Hans Holbein the Younger* (Oxford, 1985).

Shirley, Rodney, *The mapping of the world: early printed world maps 1472–1700* (London, 1983).

Smet, Antoine de, 'A note on the cartographic work of Pierre Pourbus, painter of Bruges', *Imago Mundi*, 4 (1947), 33–6.

Sterling, Charles, 'Jan van Eyck avant 1432', *Revue de l'Art*, 33 (1976), 7–82.

Strong, Roy, *Holbein and Henry VIII* (London, 1967).

Toledo Museum of Art, *El Greco of Toledo* (New York, 1982).

Tolnay, Charles de, *et al.* (eds.), *Michelangelo: artista, pensatore, scrittore*, 2 vols (Novara, 1965).

Turner, A. Richard, *The vision of landscape in Renaissance Italy* (Princeton, 1966).

Wætzoldt, Wilhelm, *Dürer and his times* (London, 1950).

Wallis, Helen (ed.), *The maps and text of the boke of ydrography presented by Jean Rotz to Henry VIII* (Oxford, 1981).

Weiss, Roberto, *The Renaissance rediscovery of classical antiquity* (Oxford, 1969).

Wescher, Paul, *Jean Fouquet and his time* (New York, 1947).

Wieder, Frederik Casper, *Monumenta cartographica*, 5 vols (The Hague, 1925–33).

Wooden, W. W., and Wall, John N., 'Thomas More and the painter's eye', *Journal of Medieval and Renaissance Studies*, 15 (1985), 231–63.

Woodward, David (ed.), *Art and cartography* (Chicago, 1987).

Zurawski, Simone, 'New sources for Jacques Callot's *Map of the siege of Breda*' *The Art Bulletin*, LXX (1988), 621–639.

CHAPTER 3

Akerman, James (ed.), 'Cartography and statecraft', *Cartographica*, monograph 52 (1998).

Armstrong, Edward, *The emperor Charles V*, 2 vols (London, 1902).

Barber, Peter, 'England I: pageantry, defense and government: maps at court' in Buisseret (ed.), *Monarchs, ministers and maps*.

Barber, Peter, 'England II: monarchs, minsters and maps 1550–1625', in Buisseret (ed.), *Monarchs, ministers and maps*.

Barber, Peter, 'Maps and monarchs in Europe 1550–1800', in Oresko, Gibbs, and Scott (eds.), *Royal and republican sovereignty in early modern Europe*.

Biblioteca Apostolica Vaticana, *Quinto Centenario: Catalogo* (Vatican, 1975).

Broc, Numa, *La cartographie de la Renaissance* (Paris, 1980).

Buisseret, David (ed.), *Monarchs, ministers and maps: the emergence of cartography as a tool of government in early modern Europe* (Chicago, 1992).

Cartellieri, Otto, *La cour des ducs de Bourgogne* (Paris, 1946).

Cosgrove, Denis, 'Mapping new worlds: culture and cartography in sixteenth-century Venice', *Imago Mundi*, 41 (1989), 87–97.

Cumming, W. P., Skelton, R. A., and Quinn, D. B., *The discovery of North America* (New York, 1972).

Dainville, R. P. François de, *Le premier atlas de France* (Paris, 1960).

Delano-Smith, Catherine and Kain, Roger, *English maps: a history* (London, 1999).

Delisle, Léopold, *Le Cabinet des Manuscrits de la Bibliothèque Nationale* (Paris, 1884).

Dittrich, Franz (ed.), *Registren und Briefe des Cardinals Gasparo Contarini (1483–1542)* (Braunsberg, 1881).

Doutrepont, Georges, *Inventaire de la 'Librairie' de Philippe le Bon* (Brussels, 1906).

Doutrepont, Georges, *La littérature française à la cour des ducs de Bourgogne* (Paris, 1909).

Dreyer-Eimbcke, Oswald, 'Conrad Celtis: humanist, poet and cosmographer', *The Map Collector*, 74 (1996), 18–21.

Edgerton, Samuel, 'From mental matrix to *mappamundi* to Christian empire: the heritage of Ptolemaic cartography in the Renaissance' in David Woodward (ed.), *Art and cartography* (Chicago, 1987).

Falk, Tilman, and von Bartsch, Adam, *Sixteenth-century German artists* (New York, 1980).

Fryde, E. A., *The private library of Lorenzo de' Medici and his sons, 1419–1510* (London, 1985).

Gallo, R., 'A fifteenth-century map of the Venetian territory of Terra Firma', *Imago Mundi*, 12 (1970), 55–7.

Gambi, Luicio, and Pinelli, Antonio (eds.), *La galleria delle carte geografiche in Vaticano* (Modena, 1994).

Geisberg, Max, *The German single-leaf woodcut, 1500–1550*, 4 vols (New York, 1974).

Harvey, P. D. A., *The history of topographical maps: symbols, pictures and surveys* (London, 1980).

Harvey, P. D. A., *Maps in Tudor England* (Chicago, 1993).

Hervé, Roger, 'L'œuvre cartographique de Nicolas de Nicolay et d'Antoine de Laval', *Bulletin de la section de géographie* (1955), 223–63.

Hoff, Bert van't, *Jacob van Deventer* (The Hague, 1953).

Jardine, Lisa, *Wordly goods: a new history of the Renaissance* (New York and London, 1996).

Kagan, Richard, *Spanish cities of the Golden Age* (Berkeley, 1989).

Kain, Roger, and Baigent, Elizabeth, *The cadastral map in the service of the state* (Chicago, 1992).

Karrow, Robert, *Mapmakers of the sixteenth century and their maps* (Chicago,

1993).

Magini, Giovanni, *Italia* (Bologna, 1620; TOT facsimile, Amsterdam, 1974).

Marín Martínez, Tomás (ed.), *Memoria de las obras y libros de Hernando Colón* (Madrid, 1971).

Marino, John, 'Administrative mapping in the Italian states', in Buisseret (ed.), *Monarchs, ministers and maps*.

Maxwell, William Stirling, *The cloister life of the emperor Charles the fifth* (London, 1853).

Mazzetti, Ernesto (ed.), *Cartografia generale del Mezzogiorno e della Sicilia*, 2 vols (Naples, 1972).

Müntz, Eugène, and Fabre, Paul, *La bibliothèque du Vatican au XVe siècle* (Paris, 1887).

Oresko, Robert, Gibbs, G. C., and Scott, H. M. (eds.), *Royal and republican sovereignty in early modern Europe* (Cambridge, 1998).

Parker, Geoffrey, 'Maps and ministers: the Spanish Habsburgs', in Buisseret (ed.), *Monarchs, ministers and maps*.

Paschang, John Linus, *The popes and the revival of learning* (Washington, 1927).

Pastor, Ludwig von, *The history of the popes*, 40 vols (St Louis, 1923–69).

Quinn, David, 'Artists and illustrators in the early mapping of America', *Mariner's Mirror*, 72/3 (1986), 244–73.

Ravenhill, William, *Christopher Saxton's sixteenth-century maps* (London, 1992).

Roberts, Michael, *Gustavus Adolphus*, 2 vols (London, 1958).

Skelton, R. A. (ed.), *Saxton's survey of England and Wales* (Amsterdam, 1974).

Skelton, R. A., and Summerson, J. N. (eds.), *A description of maps, plans and architectural drawings in the collection made by William Cecil, first Baron Burghley, now at Hatfield House* (London, 1971).

Strauss, G. L., *Sixteenth-century Germany* (Madison, 1959).

Tyacke, Sarah, and Huddy, John, *Christopher Saxton and Tudor mapmaking* (London, 1980).

Ulmann, Heinrich, *Kaiser Maximilian I*, 2 vols (Vienna, 1874/1967).

Valerio, Vladimiro, 'The Neapolitan Saxton and his survey of the kingdom of Naples', *The Map Collector*, 18 (1982), 14–17.

Van Dyke, Paul, 'The literary activity of the emperor Maximilian I', *American Historical Review*, 11 (1905), 16–20.

Vann, James, 'Mapping under the Austrian Habsburgs', in Buisseret (ed.), *Monarchs, ministers and maps*.

CHAPTER 4

Acuña, René, *Relaciones geográficas del siglo XVI*, 10 vols (Mexico City, 1987).

Alvarez Terán, Concepción, *Mapas, planos y dibujos* (Valladolid, 1980).

Angulo Iñiguez, Diego, *Bautista Antonelli* (Madrid, 1942).

Bagrow, Leo, *History of cartography* (several editions since 1951; Chicago, 1985).

Beltrán y Rózpide, Ricardo, *América en el tiempo de Felipe II, segun el cosmógrafo-cronista Juan López de Velasco* (Madrid, 1927).

Berwick and Alba, Duke of, *Mapas españoles de América* (Madrid, 1951).

Black, Jeannette (ed.), *The Blathwayt Atlas* (Providence, 1970).

Brotton, Jeremy, *Trading territories: mapping the early modern world* (Ithaca, 1998).

Buisseret, David, 'Spanish engineers in the New World', in the Garrett Lectures (forthcoming).

Burrus, Ernest, *Kino and the cartography of northeastern New Spain* (Tucson, 1965).

Calderón Quijano, José, *Las fortificaciones españoles en América y Filipinas* (Madrid, 1996).

Campbell, Tony, 'The Drapers' Company and the school of seventeenth-century cartography', in Wallis and Tyacke (eds.), *My head is a map*.

Cardona, Nicolás de, *Geographical and hydrographic descriptions of many northern and southern lands and seas in the Indies*, facsimile and translation (Los Angeles, 1974).

Chueca Goitia, Fernando, and Torres Balbés, Leopoldo, *Planos de ciudades iberoamericanos y filipinos existentes en el Archivo de Indias*, 2 vols (Madrid, 1981).

Cipolla, Carlo, *Guns, sails and empires ... 1400–1700* (New York, 1965).

Comissao nacional para as comemoracœs dos descubrimentos portugueses, *Tesoros da cartografia portuguesa* (Lisbon, 1997).

Cormack, Leslie B., *Charting an empire* (Chicago, 1977).

Coronelli, Vincenzo, *see* Wallis.

Cortesáo, Armando, *The nautical chart of 1424 and the early discovery and cartographical representation of America* (Coimbra, 1954).

Cortesáo, Armando, *History of Portuguese cartography*, 2 vols (Coimbra, 1969–71).

Cortesáo, Armando, and Teixeira da Mota, Avelino, *Portugaliœ monumenta cartographica*, 6 vols (Lisbon, 1960–62).

Cuesta Domingo, Mariano, *Santa Cruz y su obra cartográfica*, 2 vols (Madrid, 1983).

Cuesta Domingo, Mariano (ed.), *Descubrimientos y cartografía en la época de Felipe II* (Valladolid, 1999).

Dahlgren, E. W., *Map of the world, 1542* [Santa Cruz] (Stockholm, 1892).

Du Jourdain, Michel Mollat, and de La Roncière, Monique, *Sea charts of the early explorers* (New York, 1984).

Farrago, Claire (ed.), *Reframing the Renaissance: visual culture in Europe and Latin America 1450–1650* (New Haven, 1995).

Fite, Emerson D., and Freeman, Archibald, *A book of old maps* (Cambridge, 1926; Dover edn. of 1969).

González Rodríguez, Jaime, 'Aprovechamiento informático de las relaciones geográficas de la época de Felipe II', in Cuesta Domingo, *Descubrimientos y cartografía en la época de Felipe II*.

Grafton, Anthony, *New worlds, ancient texts* (Cambridge, 1992).

Guedes, Max, *et al.* (eds.), *Portugal Brazil: the age of Atlantic discoveries* (Lisbon, 1990).

Harley, J. B., *Maps and the Columbian encounter* (Milwaukee, 1990).

Harley, Brian, and Woodward, David (eds.), *The history of cartography*, Vol. I (Chicago and London, 1987).

Hébert, John (ed.), *The 1562 map of America by Diego Gutiérrez* (Washington, 1999).

Heidenreich, Conrad, *Explorations and mapping of Samuel de Champlain, 1503–1632* (Toronto, 1976).

Heidenreich, Conrad E., and Dahl, Edward H., 'The French mapping of north America in the seventeenth century', *The Map Collector*, 13 (1980), 2–11.

Holzheimer, Arthur, and Buisseret, David, *The 'Ramusio' map of 1534* (Chicago, 1992).

Hough, Samuel, *The Italians and the creation of America* (Providence, 1980).

Howse, Derek and Sanderson, Michael, *The sea chart* (New York, 1973).

Lestraingant, Frank, *Mapping the Renaissance world* (Cambridge, 1994).

López de Velasco, *see* Beltrán y Rózpide.

Martin-Merás, Luisa, 'La cartografía de los descubrimientos en la época de Felipe II', in *Carlos V: la naútica y la navegación* (Madrid, 2000).

Moncada Maya, José Omar, *Ingenieros militares en Nueva España* (Mexico City, 1993).

Morison, Samuel Eliot, *Samuel de Champlain: father of New France* (Boston and Toronto, 1972).

Mundy, Barbara, *The mapping of New Spain: indigenous cartography and the maps of the 'relaciones geográficas'* (Chicago, 1996).

Nebenzahl, Kenneth, *The atlas of Columbus and the great discoveries* (Chicago, 1990).

Pastoureau, Mireille, *Les atlas français, XVIe–XVIIe siècles* (Paris, 1984).

Penrose, Boies, *Travel and discovery during the Renaissance* (New York, 1962).

Pinheiro Marques, Alfredo, 'The dating of the oldest Portuguese charts', *Imago Mundi,* 41 (1989): 87–97.

Pinheiro Marques, Alfredo, 'Portuguese cartography in the era of discoveries', in Diogo Homem, *Atlas universal,* facsimile edn. (Madrid, 2002).

Putnam, Robert, *Early sea charts* (New York, 1983).

Randles, W. G. L., 'The alleged nautical school founded in the fifteenth century at Sagres by prince Henry of Portugal', *Imago Mundi,* 45 (1993), 20–8.

Rotz, Jean, *see* Wallis.

Russell, Peter, *Prince Henry 'the navigator': a life* (New Haven, 2000).

Santa Cruz, *see* Cuesta Domingo.

Schilder, Günter, *Australia unveiled: the share of the Dutch navigators in the discovery of Australia* (Amsterdam, 1976).

Schilder, Günter, 'Organization and evolution of the Dutch East India Company's office in the seventeenth century', *Imago Mundi,* 28 (1976): 61–78.

Schmidt, Benjamin, *Innocence abroad: the Dutch imagination and the New World 1570–1670* (Cambridge, 2001).

Seller, John, *The English pilot, see* Verner.

Skelton, R. A., *Explorers' maps* (New York, 1958).

Smith, T. S., 'Manuscript and printed sea charts of seventeenth-century London: the case of the Thames School' in Norman Thrower (ed.), *The Compleat Plattmaker* (Los Angeles, 1978).

Sociedad estatal para la conmemoración de los centenarios de Felipe II y Carlos V, *Carlos V: la naútica y la navegación* (Madrid, 2000).

Teixeira da Mota, A., 'Some notes on the organization of hydrographical services in Portugal before the beginning of the nineteenth century', *Imago Mundi,* 28 (1976), 51–60.

Thrower, J. W. (ed.), *The compleat Plattmaker* (Berkeley, 1978).

Verner, Coolie (ed.), *The English pilot, the fourth book* (London, 1689; facsimile edn., Amsterdam, 1967).

Vindel, Francisco, *Mapas de América en los libros españoles de los siglos XVI al XVIII* (Madrid, 1956).

Vingboons-Atlas, ed. Royal Archives, The Hague (1981).

Waghenær, Lucas Janz, *Spieghel der zeevært* (Leyden, 1584; facsimile edn., Amsterdam, 1954).

Wallis, Helen, 'Edward Wright and the 1599 map', in D. B. Quinn (ed.),

The Hakluyt handbook, 2 vols (London, 1974).

Wallis, Helen, 'Geographie is better than divinitie: maps, globes and geography in the days of Samuel Pepys', in Thrower (ed.), *The Compleat Plattmaker*.

Wallis, Helen (ed.), *The maps and text of the boke of ydrography presented by Jean Rotz to Henry VIII* (Oxford, 1981).

Wallis, Helen (ed.), Vincenzo Coronelli, *Libro dei globi* (Venice, 1693; facsimile edn., Amsterdam, 1969).

Wallis, Helen, and Tyacke, Sarah (eds.), *My head is a map* (London, 1973).

Wawrik, Franz, *et al.*, *Kartographische Zimelien: die 50 schönsten Karten und Globen der Osterreichischen Nationalbibliothek* (Vienna, 1995).

Wolff, Hans (ed.), *America: early maps of the New World* (Munich, 1992).

Wright, John Kirtland (ed.), *The Leardo map of the world* (New York, 1920).

Wroth, Lawrence C., 'The early cartography of the Pacific', *Papers of the Bibliographical Society of America*, 38/2 (1944), 87–268.

Zandvliet, Kees, *Mapping for money: maps, plans and topographic paintings and their role in Dutch overseas expansion* (Amsterdam, 1998).

CHAPTER 5

Allgemeine deutsche Biographie (Berlin, 1967).

Allmand, C. T. (ed.), *War, literature and politics in the late Middle Ages* (Liverpool, 1998).

Anon., *Gedanken über die Wissenschaften eines Ingenieur- und Artillerie-Officiers ...* (Leipzig, 1758) [by an engineer-officer serving the Duke of Braunschweig-Lünenburg].

Atlas des Grossen Kur-Fürsten, facsimile (Stuttgart, 1971).

Ballon, Hilary, *The Paris of Henri IV: architecture and urbanism* (Cambridge and London, 1991).

Biller, Thomas, *Der 'Lynarplan' und die Entstehung der Zitadelle Spandau im 16. Jahrhundert* (Berlin, 1981).

Bonin, Udo von, *Geschichte der Ingenieurkorps und der Pionere in Preussen*, 2 vols (Berlin, 1877–8; reprint Wiesbaden, 1981).

Bourcet, Pierre, *Les principes de la guerre de montagne* (Paris, 1775).

Bousquet-Bressolier, Catherine (ed.), *L'œil du cartographe* (Paris, 1995).

Buisseret, David, 'L'atelier cartographique de Sully à Bontin: l'œuvre de Jacques Fougeu', *XVIIe Siècle*, 174 (1992), 109–16.

Buisseret, David, 'Henri IV et l'art militaire', in *Henri IV et la Reconstruction du Royaume*, Association Henri IV (Pau, 1989).

Buisseret, David, *Ingénieurs et fortifications avant Vauban: l'organisation d'un service royal aux XVIe–XVIIe siècles* (Paris, 2002).

Buisseret, David (ed.), *Monarchs, ministers and maps* (Chicago, 1992).

Buisseret, David, 'Newberry acquisitions' (Waterloo map), *Mapline*, 77 (1995), 11–13.

Buisseret, David, 'Les plans de ville, sources pour l'histoire de l'urbanisation en France', *Urbi* (1989), 85–99.

Buisseret, David, 'Spanish engineers in the New World', forthcoming.

Buisseret, David, and Strove, Wilbert, 'A French engineer's atlas of the River Somme, 1644', *Mapline*, 77 (1995), 1–10.

Carrias, Eugène, *La pensée militaire française* (Paris, n.d.).

Colvin, H. M. (ed.), *The history of the King's works*, 6 vols (London, 1963–82).

Contamine, Philippe (ed.), *Histoire militaire de la France*, vol. I (Paris, 1992).

Dainville, R. P. François de, *Le Dauphiné et ses confins vus par l'ingénieur d'Henri IV, Jean de Beins* (Geneva, 1968).

Dainville, R. P. François de, *Le langage des géographes* (Paris, 1964).

Dainville, R. P. François de, 'Le premier atlas de France: le *Théâtre Français* de M. Bouguereau', in *La cartographie: reflet de l'histoire* (Geneva and Paris, 1986).

Delano-Smith, Catherine, and Kain, Roger, *English maps and society* (London, 1999).

Desbrière, Michel, 'L'œuvre de Jacques Fougeu relative à la Champagne', in Bousquet-Bressolier (ed.), *L'œil du cartographe.*

Deutsche Staats Bibliothek 1661–1961 (Leipzig, 1961).

Doucet, Roger, *Les institutions de la France*, 2 vols (Paris, 1948).

Dubois, N., *Camps topographiques de la campagne de 1757, en Westphalie* (The Hague, 1770).

Duffy, Christopher, *The army of Maria Theresa* (New York, 1977).

Duffy, Christopher, *Siege warfare* (London, 1979).

Duffy, Christopher, *The army of Frederick the Great* (Chicago, 1996).

Fleming, Hans Friedrich von, *Der vollkommene teutsche Soldat* (Leipzig, 1726).

Frederick the Great, *Instructions for his Generals*, (ed.) Thomas R. Phillips (Harrisburg, 1944).

Fronsberger, Leonhard, *Von Kaiserlichen Kriegsrichten* (Frankfurt, 1566).

Gatti, Friedrich, *Geschichte der k.k. Ingenieur- und k.k. Genie-Akademie, 1717–1869*, 2 vols (Vienna, 1901–05).

Geisberg, Max (ed.), *The German single-leaf woodcut*, 4 vols (New York, 1974).

Gorlitz, Walter, *History of the German General Staff, 1657–1945* (Boulder and London, 1985).

Hale, J. R., *Artists and warfare in the Renaissance* (New Haven, 1990).

Hale, J. R., 'A humanistic visual aid: the military diagram in the Renaissance', *Renaissance Studies* (1988), 280–98.

Hale, J. R., 'The military education of the officer class in early modern Europe', in C. H. Clough (ed.), *Cultural Aspects of the Italian Renaissance* (New York, 1976).

Hale, J. R., *Renaissance war studies* (London, 1983).

Harley, J. B., Petchenik, Barbara, and Towner, Lawrence, *Mapping the American Revolutionary War* (Chicago, 1978).

Harvey, P. D. A., *The history of topographical maps* (London, 1980).

Hodson, Yolande, *The Cumberland Collection of military maps at Windsor Castle: an introduction* (London, 1987).

Irvine, Dallas D., 'The origins of Capital Staffs', *Journal of Modern History*, 10 (1938), 161–79.

Jackson, John Brinckerhoff, *Discovering the vernacular landscape* (New Haven, 1984).

Kœman, Cornelis, *Atlantes neerlandici*, 6 vols (Alphen, 1967–85).

Kurth, Willi (ed.), *Complete woodcuts of Albrecht Dürer* (London, 1927).

Lallemand, M., and Boinette, A., *Jean Errard de Bar-le-Duc* (Paris, 1884).

Lanza, Conrad (ed.), *Napoleon and modern war: his military maxims* (Harrisburg, 1943).

Machiavelli, Niccolò, *The Arte of Warre*, trans. by Peter Whithorne (London, 1588).

McNeill, William H., *Keeping together in time: dance and drill in human history* (Cambridge, Mass. and London, 1997).

McNeill, William H., *The pursuit of power* (Chicago, 1982).

Manesson-Mallet, Alain, *Kriegsarbeit oder Neuer-Festungbau* (Amsterdam,

1672).

Maroteaux, Vincent, and d'Orgeix, Emilie (eds.), *Portefeuilles de plans: projets et dessins d'ingénieurs militaires en Europe du XVIe au XIXe siècle* (Bourges, 2001).

Marshall, Douglas, 'The British military engineers, 1741–1783', Ph.D. thesis (Michigan, 1979).

Marshall, Douglas, 'Military maps of the eighteenth century and the Tower of London Drawing School', *Imago Mundi*, 32 (1980), 21–44.

Marshall, Douglas, and Peckham, Howard (eds.), *Campaigns of the American Revolution: an atlas of manuscript maps* (Ann Arbor, 1976).

Merian, Matthæus, *Topographia Electorat. Brandenburgici et Ducatus Pomeraniæ . . .* (Frankfurt am Main, 1652).

Mohrmann, Wolf-Diete, 'Der "Welsche Pawmeister" Chiaramelli in Wolfenbüttel', *Braunschweigisches Jahrbuch*, 57 (1976), 7–22.

Neue Deutsche Biographie, 20 vols (Berlin, 1953–).

Neumann, Hartwig, *Festungsbaukunst und Festungsbautechnik* (Koblenz, 1988).

Nischer-Falkenhof, Ernst von, 'The survey by the Austrian General Staff under the Empress Maria Theresa and the Emperor Joseph II', *Imago Mundi*, 2 (1936), 83–8.

O'Neil, B. H. St J., *Castles and cannon: a study of early artillery fortifications in England* (Oxford, 1960).

Oman, Sir Charles, *A history of the art of war in the sixteenth century* (New York, 1937).

Parker, Geoffrey, *The Military Revolution: military innovation and the rise of the West* (Cambridge, 1988).

Parker, Geoffrey (ed.), *The Thirty Years War* (London, 1984).

Pastoureau, Mireille, *Les atlas français, XVIe–XVIIe siècles* (Paris, 1984).

Pelletier, Monique, *La carte de Cassini* (Paris, 1990).

Pelletier, Monique, and Ozanne, Henriette, *Portraits de la France: les cartes, témoins de l'histoire* (Paris, 1995).

Pepper, Simon, and Adams, Nicholas, *Firearms and fortifications* (Chicago, 1986).

Pirscher, J. D., *Coup d'œil militaire* (Berlin, 1775).

Pollak, Martha, *Military architecture, cartography and the representation of the early modern European city* (Chicago, 1991).

Porter, Whitworth, *History of the Corps of Royal Engineers*, Vol. I (London, 1889).

Rogers, Clifford C. (ed.), *The Military Revolution debate* (Boulder and Oxford, 1995).

Scharfe, Wolfgang, *Berlin und seine Umgebung im Kartenbild* (Berlin, 1987).

Schulz, Günter, *Die ältesten Stadtpläne Berlins* (Weinheim, 1986).

Seymour, W. A. (ed.), *History of the Ordnance Survey* (Folkestone, 1980).

Shelby, W. A., *John Rogers, Tudor military engineer* (Oxford, 1967).

Skelton, R. A., 'The military surveyor's contribution,' *Imago Mundi*, 24 (1970), 77–83.

Strauss, Walter L., *The German single-leaf woodcut 1550–1600* (New York, 1975)

Taylor, F. L., *The art of war in Italy, 1494–1529* (Cambridge, 1921).

Tunstall, Brian, *Naval warfare in the age of sail: the evolution of fighting tactics, 1650–1815* (Annapolis, 1990).

Tyacke, Sarah (ed.), *English mapmaking, 1500–1650* (London, 1983).

Vachée, Colonel, *Napoleon at work* (London, 1914).

Van Belle, Jean-Louis, *Plans inédits de places fortifiées* (Brussels, 1989).

Van Crefeld, Martin, *Technology and warfare from 200 BC to the present* (London and New York, 1989).

Van den Krogt, Peter, *Kœman's Atlantes Neerlandici*, 2 vols to date (Goy-Houten, 1997 and 2000).

Van Eerde, Katherine S., *Wenceslaus Hollar: delineator of his time* (Charlottesville, 1970).

Vauban, Sebastien le Prestre de, *De l'attaque et de la défense des places.* 2 vols (The Hague, 1737 and 1742).

Whithorne, Peter, *Certaine waies for the ordering of souldiers in battelray* (London, 1588).

Zögner, Lothar, and Lindner, Klaus, *Berlin in Kartenbild* (Berlin, 1981).

Zögner, Lothar, and Zögner, Gudrun K., *Preussens amtliche Kartenwerke in 18. und 19. Jahrhundert* (Berlin, 1981).

CHAPTER 6

Andrews, J. H., *Plantation acres: an historical study of the Irish land surveyor and his maps* (Belfast, 1971).

Angelini, Gregorio (ed.), *Il disegno del territorio: istituzioni e cartografia in Basilicata*, 1500–1800, Exhibition-catalogue (Bari, 1988).

Archives de France, *Espace français: vision et aménagement, XVI–XIXe siècles*, Exhibition-catalogue (Paris, 1987).

Barbier, Frédéric (ed.), *La carte manuscrite et imprimée du XVIe au XXe siècle* (New York, London, and Paris, 1983).

Barichi, Walter (ed.), *Le mappe rurali del territorio di Reggio Emilia* (Casalicchio, 1985).

Bendall, Sarah (ed.), *Dictionary of land surveyors and local map-makers of Great Britain and Ireland 1530–1850*, 2 vols (London, 1997).

Bendall, Sarah, 'Enquire "when the same platte was made and by whom and to what intent"', *Imago Mundi*, 47 (1995), 34–48.

Bendall, Sarah, *Maps, land and society* (Cambridge, 1992).

Bloch, Marc, 'Les plans parcellaires', *Annales d'histoire économique et sociale*, i (1929), 60–70 and 390–8.

Braun, Georg, and Hogenberg, Franz, *Civitates orbis terrarum*, 6 vols (Cologne, 1595–1617); facsimile edition (ed.), R. A. Skelton, 3 vols (Cleveland, 1966).

British Library, *The city in maps*, Exhibition-catalogue (London, 1986).

Buisseret, David (ed.), *Envisioning the city: six studies in urban cartography* (Chicago, 1998).

Buisseret, David, 'Perambulating the county of Suffolk with John Norden, 1600', *Mapline*, 63 (1991), 2–9.

Buisseret, David (ed.), *Rural images: the estate map in the Old and New Worlds* (Chicago, 1996).

Cosgrove, Denis, 'Mapping New Worlds: culture and cartography in sixteenth-century Venice', *Imago Mundi*, 44 (1992), 65–89.

Cosgrove, Denis (ed.), *Mappings* (London, 1999).

Cosgrove, Denis, *The Palladian landscape: geographical change and its cultural representations in sixteenth-century Italy* (Leicester, 1993).

Darby, H. C., 'The agrarian contribution to surveying in England', *Geographical Journal*, 82 (1933), 529–35.

Delano-Smith, Catherine, and Kain, Roger, *English maps: a history* (London, 1999).

Desrumeaux, Roger, 'L'arpenteur, témoin du cadre social de son temps', *Actes du Congrès des Sociétés Savantes du Nord* (1985–6), 36–48.

Donkersloot-de Vrij, Marijke, *Topografische kaarten van Niederland vóór*

1750 (Groningen, 1981).

Eden, Peter (ed.), *Dictionary of land surveyors and local cartographers of Great Britain and Ireland, 1550–1850*, 2 vols (Folkestone, 1975 and 1979).

Elliott, James, *The city in maps: urban mapping up to 1900* (London, n.d.).

Faini, Sandra, and Majoli, Luca, *La Romagna nello cartografia a stampa dal cinqueceento all'ottocento* (Rimini, 1992).

Fletcher, David, *The emergence of estate maps: Christ Church, Oxford, 1600 to 1840* (Oxford, 1995).

Fockema, Andreæ, and van t'Hoff, B., *Geschiedenis der Kartografie van Nederland* (The Hague, 1947).

Fowkes, D. V., and Potter, G. R. (eds.), *William Senior's survey* (Chesterfield, 1988).

Frangenberg, Thomas, 'Chorographies of Florence: the use of city views and city plans in the sixteenth century', *Imago Mundi*, 46 (1994), 41–64.

Frutaz, Amato Pietro, *Le piante di Roma*, 3 vols (Rome, 1976).

Gagel, Ernst, *Pfinzing: der Kartograph der Reichsstadt Nürnberg* (Hersbruck, 1957).

Harvey, P. D. A., *The history of topographical maps* (London, 1980).

Harvey, P. D. A., *Maps in Tudor England* (London and Chicago, 1993).

Heslinga, M. W., *et al.*, *Nederland in Kaarten* (Ede, 1985).

Kagan, Richard, *Spanish cities of the Golden Age* (Berkeley, 1989).

Kagan, Richard, '*Urbs* and *civitas* in sixteenth- and seventeenth-century Spain', in David Buisseret (ed.), *Envisioning the city: six studies in urban cartography* (Chicago, 1998).

Kagan, Richard, and Marias, Fernando, (eds.), *Urban images of the Hispanic world* (New Haven and London, 2000).

Kubelik, Martin, *Die villa im Veneto*, 2 vols (Munich, 1977).

Manners, Ian R., 'Constructing the image of a city: the representation of Constantinople in Christopher Buondelmonti's *Liber insularum archipelagi*', *Annals of the Association of American Geographers*, 87/1 (1997), 72–102.

Miller, Naomi, 'Mapping the city: Ptolemy's *Geography* in the Renaissance', in Buisseret (ed.), *Envisioning the city*.

Nuti, Lucia, 'The mapped views by Georg Hœfnagel: the merchant's eye, the humanist's eye', *Word and Image*, 4 (1988), 545–70.

Nuti, Lucia, 'Mapping places: chorography and vision in the Renaissance', in Cosgrove (ed.), *Mappings*.

Pelletier, Monique, 'De nouveaux plans de forêt à la Bibliothèque Nationale', *Revue de la Bibliothèque Nationale*, 29 (1988), 56–62.

Pinto, John, 'Origins and development of the ichnographic city plan', *Journal of the Society of Architectural Historians*, 35 (1976), 35–50.

Puppi, Lionello, *Andrea Palladio* (Venice, n.d)

Schulz, Juergen, 'Jacopo de' Barbari's view of Venice: map making, city views and moralized geography before the year 1500', *Art Bulletin*, 60 (1978), 427–73.

Senior, William, *see* Fowkes and Potter (eds.).

Tooley, R. V., 'Maps in Italian atlases of the sixteenth century', *Imago Mundi*, 3 (1970), 12–47.

Woodward, David, *Five centuries of map printing* (Chicago, 1975).

CONCLUSION

Barber, Peter, 'Maps and monarchs in Europe, 1550–1800' in Robert Oresko (ed.), *Royal and republican sovereignty in early modern Europe*

(Cambridge, 1997).

Buisseret, David, 'The cartographic definition of France's eastern frontier', *Imago Mundi*, 36 (1984), 72–80.

Buisseret, David, 'Jesuit cartography in central and south America', in Joseph Gagliano and Charles Ronan (eds.), *Jesuit encounters in the New World* (Rome, 1997).

Delano-Smith, Catherine, and Ingram, Elizabeth, *Maps in bibles 1500–1600* (Geneva, 1991).

Deuel, Leo, *Flights into fancy* (New York, 1966).

Eisenstein, Elizabeth, *The printing revolution in early modern Europe* (Cambridge, 1983).

Hobhouse, Penelope, *Gardening through the ages* (New York, 1997).

Hough, Graham (ed.), *Sir John Harington's translation of 'Orlando furioso' by Ludovico Ariosto* (Carbondale, 1962).

Konvitz, Josef W., *Cartography in France, 1660–1848* (Chicago, 1987).

Mariage, Thierry, *The world of André Le Nôtre* (Philadelphia, 1998).

Petty, Sir William, *A geographicall description of ye kingdom of Ireland* (London, 1700).

Robinson, Arthur H., *Early thematic mapping in the history of cartography* (Chicago, 1982).

Thrower, Norman J. W., *Maps and civilization* (Chicago, 1998).

Wilford, John Noble, *The mapmakers* (New York, 1981).

Winchester, Simon, *The map that changed the world* (New York, 2002).

Woodward, David, *Five centuries of map printing* (Chicago, 1975).

Woodward, David, *Maps and prints in the Italian Renaissance* (London, 1996).

INDEX